This work is essential reading for students and practitioners who seek an understanding of the theoretical and practical aspects of international crime and law enforcement.

Peter Joyce, Department of Sociology, Manchester Metropolitan University, UK

This book tackles vital issues to do with globalization, crime, terrorism and insecurity. Students will find a wealth of understanding concerning the injustice of global crime control as currently practiced. Wendy Laverick's treatment of these complex issues and themes is clearly formulated and convincing.

James Sheptycki, Professor of Criminology, Faculty of Liberal Arts and Professional Studies, York University, Toronto, Canada

Global Injustice and Crime Control

Global Injustice and Crime Control places cross-border, cross-national and international crime and crime control within its wider context. It examines theory from a range of disciplines and introduces students to the frequently neglected area of the world order and world politics, in an effort to direct attention to the links between events, power, ideas, institutions, policies, actions and counter-actions at the international and domestic level.

In an increasingly interconnected and interdependent world, the various dimensions of globalisation play a pivotal role in issues of crime and criminal justice in the 21st century. This interdisciplinary textbook offers a critical treatment of the development and recent acceleration of national, regional and international efforts at cross-border crime control and law enforcement. The book not only places cross-national and international efforts by police, courts, regional and international agencies within their historical context, but also focuses on elucidating leading theoretical perspectives from within globalisation literature, criminology and international relations to shed light upon both sides of this phenomenon.

Areas covered include:

- cross-border crime and security,
- state crime and corruption,
- international responses to genocide,
- terrorism and counter-terrorism,
- organised crime.

This book will be perfect reading for modules in transnational crime and justice and will be of interest to students in criminology, policing, public policy and international relations.

Wendy Laverick is Senior Lecturer in Criminology at Manchester Metropolitan University, UK.

Global Issues in Crime and Justice

1 Women, Crime and Criminal Justice
A global enquiry
Rosemary Barberet

2 Global Human Trafficking
Critical issues and contexts
Edited by Molly Dragiewicz

3 Critical Issues on Violence against Women
International perspectives and promising strategies
Edited by Holly Johnson, Bonnie S. Fisher and Véronique Jaquier

4 Global Injustice and Crime Control
Wendy Laverick

5 Crimes of the Powerful
An introduction
Dawn L. Rothe and David Kauzlarich

Global Injustice and Crime Control

Wendy Laverick

Routledge
Taylor & Francis Group
LONDON AND NEW YORK

First published 2016
by Routledge
4 Park Square, Milton Park, Abingdon, Oxon OX14 4RN
605 Third Avenue, New York, NY 10017

Routledge is an imprint of the Taylor & Francis Group, an informa business

British Library Cataloguing in Publication Data
A catalogue record for this book is available from the British Library

Library of Congress Cataloging in Publication Data
Laverick, Wendy, author.
Global injustice and crime control / Wendy Laverick.
pages cm. -- (Global issues in crime and justice ; 4)
1. Transnational crime. 2. International crimes. 3. Crime prevention.
4. Law enforcement. 5. International security. 6. Criminal justice,
Administration of. I. Title.
HV6252.L39 2016
364.1'35--dc23
2015030587

ISBN: 978-0-415-69745-3 (hbk)
ISBN: 978-0-415-69746-0 (pbk)
ISBN: 978-1-315-73943-4 (ebk)

Typeset in Times New Roman
by Taylor & Francis Books

For Benjamin, Charlie, Joseph, Emily and Lee

Contents

Part I
Contextualisation

1 Globalisation, cross-border crime and security

> To be sure, dialogue is a difficult art. It means engaging in conversation with the intention of jointly clarifying the issues, rather than having one's own way; of multiplying voices rather than reducing their number; of widening the set of possibilities, rather than aiming at a wholesale consensus (that relic of mono-theistic dreams stripped of politically incorrect coercion); of jointly pursuing understanding, instead of aiming at the other's defeat; and all in all being animated by the wish to keep the conversation going, rather than by a desire to grind it to a halt.
>
> (Bauman, 2011: 172)

At the time of writing, at the end of June 2015, media sources report that the radical Islamist group, Islamic State (IS), continue to capture territory within Syria and Iraq generating fear and outrage across the globe. In the wake of multiple beheadings, mass killings and the kidnap and recruitment of children, IS members are reportedly transcending state boundaries in an effort to create a caliphate (a state ruled by the Islamic State's strict interpretation of Islamic Law), also aspiring to 'free Palestine'. In this endeavour, utilising the internet and social media to communicate their objectives internationally, fighters are being recruited from Western and non-Western states alike.

Regional and international security concerns have also recently been raised regarding ever increasing swathes of migrants reaching the shores of Europe, following the collapse of the Libyan government which has resulted in economic migrants from Libya and other countries, including Mali, Nigeria, Eritrea and Syria seeking to enter Italy, which is viewed as a gateway into Europe. News reports have predicted a figure reaching over 36,000 migrants between January and June 2015, with record numbers also drowning in the Mediterranean at the hands of what are described as 'ruthless trafficking networks and criminal gangs'.

Meanwhile, states remain committed to enacting financial recovery plans instigated by the global economic crisis of 2008–9. Greece in particular has received a great deal of media coverage, gaining notoriety resulting from the unprecedented situation of potentially becoming the first developed nation to default on its international obligations to the IMF and European Central Bank.

Aside from international terrorism, illegal migration and global economic crises, the transmission of new and emerging infectious diseases has also gained significant news coverage within the past year, with aid workers and volunteers grappling with the Ebola crisis in West Africa, a disease which has killed in excess of ten thousand people over the past year, with most deaths located in Guinea, Liberia and Sierra Leone. The pervasiveness of corruption has also featured within the media spotlight, highlighting the increasing resolve of the United States of America in driving forward anti-corruption measures internationally as the FBI investigation expands into the global sporting arena with the Fifa scandal exposing bribery and vote trading affecting the World Cup bid process. In June 2015, the Global Drug Survey revealed that more people started buying drugs online in 2014 than ever before, with other sources focusing upon the Darknet and cybercrime as national, regional and international security threats, implicated as facilitators for organised crime, international terrorism and cyber-espionage.

Each of the examples above has been selected in order to illustrate the near instantaneous nature, and extensive reach of contemporary global communication. Technological advancements have consequently served to heighten public awareness regarding events occurring in geographical locations across the world. The news reports detailed above paint a picture of global instability, internal conflict, ideological challenge, economic crisis, and criminogenic threat, also depicting an international environment conducive to collective problem solving, multi-lateral regional and international cooperation and action to counter current challenges and threats. In an attempt to make sense of the contemporary period, and in order to understand how such a diverse range of social ills have become defined as international and national security threats, theorists have attempted to identify what is novel or unique about the current period, directing attention to the salience of global interconnectivity (culturally, economically and politically) and exploring the relevance of social transformation within these sites for the facilitation of crime and crime control.

These developments have been captured by the use of what has been called a slippery and overused concept (McGrew, 2011: 16), namely ‘globalisation’. Thus, the term ‘globalisation’ has been defined as a process (or set of processes), characterised by an extension of social, political and economic activities across borders, alongside an intensification and speeding up of interconnectiveness, with significant consequences for law enforcement and security, disrupting conventional boundaries between domestic and foreign policy (see Held, McGrew, Goldblatt, and Perraton, 1999). Despite continuing controversy regarding the concept, the term ‘globalisation’ has nevertheless penetrated international, regional and national security and law enforcement discourse. It is increasingly utilised as an ‘influential codeword in political speech’ influencing policy and having real consequences for people’s lives (Sparke, 2013: 1). The concept has been applied within justificatory narratives, aimed towards the organisational expansion of remits and agendas of international and regional law enforcement and security institutions, and has also been implicated as a facilitating factor, influencing the acceleration and intensification of law enforcement cooperation in criminal and judicial matters and the elaboration of global prohibition regimes (Andreas and Nadelmann, 2006; Findlay, 1999, 2008; Bigo, 2013). The dominant political perspective regarding the relationship between aspects of globalisation and crime, conceived as 'the standard view', has, however, recently been rendered problematic and therefore remains contentious.

This chapter has two key objectives: to provide a brief account of the theorisation of globalisation, identifying key perspectives and highlighting significant issues; and to examine the significance of globalisation discourse for our contemporary conceptualisation of security and the emergence of transnational crime, international crimes and terrorism within the security agendas of international society, regional bodies and individual nation-states. Before turning attention towards globalisation however, it is necessary to introduce readers to the objectives of the text and to reflect upon the substantive topics and conceptual difficulties encountered within the subject.

Comparative, international and transnational criminology: conceptual clarification

Within the growing field of comparative, international and transnational criminology, and the expanding literature examining transnational policing and international policing cooperation, there are an increasing number of introductory texts whose titles include terms such as 'transnational', 'international', and 'global'. Significant texts include: Bowling and Sheptycki, 2012, *Global Policing*; Findlay and Henham, 2012, *Transforming Criminal Justice*; Lemieux, 2013, *International Police Cooperation*; Sheptycki and Wardak, 2005, *Transnational and Comparative Criminology*; Shoham, Knepper, and Kett, 2010, *International Handbook of Criminology*; Smith, Zhang, and Barberet, 2011, *Routledge Handbook of International Criminology*; Watts, Bessant, and Hil, 2008, *International Criminology: A Critical Introduction*; Brown, 2008, *Combating International Crime: The Longer Arm of the Law*; Deflem, 2002, *Policing World Society: Historical Foundations of International Police Cooperation*; Sheptycki, 2000, *Issues in Transnational Policing*; Nadelmann, 1993, *Cops Across Borders: The Internationalization of U.S. Criminal Law Enforcement*; Anderson, 1989, *Policing the World*.

The topics covered by such texts often include comparative crime data, discussions regarding issues of governance and accountability, frequently addressing specific 'cross-border' or 'transnational' crime issues. Topics ranging from a variety of transnational organised crimes (e.g. trafficking in persons, drugs, diamonds, antiquities, arms, corruption) to terrorism and a range of transnational white collar crimes may feature, with some texts (predominantly those concerned with adopting a 'critical' stance) expanding to include chapters dedicated to state crimes. This literature is also characterised by discussions of control responses from the position of individual nation-states, regions (such as within the European Union) or internationally (through the work of the United Nations).

Within this literature, it is common for the authors make reference to the conceptual confusion and ambiguity surrounding the use of the concepts 'international crime', 'transnational crime' and 'transnational organised crime'. A number of authors have attempted to clarify the situation. Partin (2003), for example, cited in Reichel (2005: xiv), asserts that the concept of 'international crime includes acts that threaten world order and security (e.g. crimes against humanity, war crimes and genocide), whereas transnational crime affects the interest of more than one state'. While such a definition serves as a useful starting point, the recent expansion of the concept of security to include a range of 'transnational' crimes has rendered this distinction problematic.

Within his very accessible introductory text, *Transnational Organized Crime*, Madsen (2009) employs a pragmatically guided definition. Describing the terminology used by academics and practitioners in this newly emerging field as 'highly unstable' and 'overlapping', Madsen helpfully presents a taxonomy to assist us to make sense of the conceptual difficulties and overlap between the use of the concepts 'transnational crime', 'international crime' and 'organised crime'. Transnational crimes, we are informed, 'are crimes that in one of several ways involve two or more sovereign jurisdictions, but which are codified in the national legislations of these jurisdictions' (Madsen, 2009: 9). Madsen defines 'international crime' as 'criminalised in international criminal law', subject to international conventions. The third group of crimes described by Madsen are presented as transnational (involving two or more sovereign jurisdictions); organised (that is 'groups of two or more … forming some kind of rational, ongoing conspiracy to plan these crimes, with the objective identified as usually profit-making' (Albanese, 2011: 4)); and, violating international law (codified in international criminal law). The fourth and final classification is used to describe crimes which are both transnational and organised but are not violations of international law (they have not been criminalised in international law and are not the subject of international conventions).

Madsen's typology is helpful, directing attention to key factors that have been used to influence the classification of a crime, including whether a crime has been codified within the national legislation of a sovereign jurisdiction, or within international law, in addition to whether organised criminal groups are implicated in the commission of a crime.

When considering the concept of 'international law' employed by Madsen, it is perhaps complicated by the recent development of a new body of law known as 'International Criminal Law' dealing with crimes falling within the jurisdiction of international and hybrid courts (including the International Criminal Tribunal for Former Yugoslavia, International Criminal Tribunal for Rwanda, Special Court for Sierra Leone, Extraordinary Chambers in the Courts of Cambodia, and the International Criminal Court). This body of law deals exclusively with crimes of genocide, crimes against humanity, war crimes and the crime of aggression. Importantly, it does not include piracy, terrorism, slavery, drug trafficking, or other international crimes unless they amount to genocide, crimes against humanity, or war crimes. The acknowledgement of this body of law leans towards Partin's inclusion of crimes against humanity, war crimes and genocide within the 'International Crime' category. These distinctions remind us that despite recent advances, care is still required regarding the terminology used and the application of these terms to particular groups of crimes. Despite the imperfect nature of these definitions, Partin's and Madsen's efforts serve to highlight the complexity and breadth of the subject area under investigation.

Acknowledging contemporary debates and the lack of consensus regarding the classification of crime and harm within this fledgling body of work, the aim of this book is to introduce students to transnational and international crime and terrorism and to provide an overview of international, regional and national efforts towards their control. This text will address each of these substantive areas, 'transnational crime', 'transnational organised crime' and 'international crime'. Within the subsequent pages of this first chapter, the consequences of globalisation processes for cross-border crime and security will be explored. We will examine the expanding concept of security and the destabilisation and blurring of conventional categories between domestic and foreign policy, internal and external security, high and low policing and military and policing action. The consequences of these trends for the development of a global governance complex will be further examined in Chapter 4, which explores regional and international efforts at cooperation to combat transnational crime and terrorism. Key issues identified within the globalisation literature, including the significance and role of the sovereign nation-state as an actor within world politics and the consequences of key aspects of globalisation for criminal opportunities and law enforcement responses, will comprise recurring themes throughout the text. An understanding of globalisation is therefore necessary and it is to this task we now turn.

Theorising globalisation

For the criminologist, the representation of globalisation matters. It influences our interpretation, understanding and actions and may also affect our attitude towards crimes and criminals, law enforcement and criminal justice and the prospects and desirability of social change. Globalisation, understood simply as the 'widening, deepening, and speeding up of worldwide interconnectedness' (McGrew, 2011: 16), or as 'processes of economic, political, and social integration' (Sparke, 2013: 3), remains a highly emotive and contentious concept. While there exists general agreement that 'the world today is unprecedentedly interconnected and interdependent' (Dasgupta, 2004: 15), disagreement remains regarding 'whether globalisation is good, bad or ugly' (Sparke, 2013: xvi) and considerable debate extends to discussing globalisation's constituent aspects, its temporal frame and its purported universality.

Globalisation typologies and ideal types

There have been a number of efforts to separate and categorise the emerging globalisation literature. In 1999, Held and McGrew, for example, identified two main groups of globalisation scholars: 'Globalists' and 'sceptics' (Held, McGrew, Goldblatt, and Perraton, 1999). Globalists present globalisation as 'a real and significant historical development' (Schirato and Webb, 2003: 7), with some globalists going so far as to say that not only is globalisation real, but also that it (universally) brings benefits to all (Busch, 2000: 30–31, cited in Schirato and Webb, 2003: 7–8). In contrast to the positive and optimistic viewpoints contained within the 'globalist' and 'liberal' positions, 'sceptics' question globalisation as a significant historical development, regarding the contemporary period as merely a 'continuation of trends that developed in the period 1870–1914, and were interrupted by the two great wars and the "cold war" of the twentieth century' (Schirato and Webb, 2003: 7). For these theorists, the concept of globalisation is unhelpful, complicating rather than facilitating understanding of contemporary developments. For Busch, the 'sceptic' category directs attention to the negative political and economic outcomes of global tendencies (Busch, 2000: 30–31, cited in Schirato and Webb, 2003: 8) rather than a rejection of the temporal boundaries of the phenomenon of globalisation itself. Thus for Busch, sceptics challenge the assumption of 'universal good', and the notion of trickle-down effect, universally distributing the benefits of globalisation to all.

Holton (2005), cited in Held and McGrew (2007: 5) elaborates further, arguing that scholarship has arisen in 'three overlapping but distinctive waves: the hyper-globalist, the sceptical, and the post-sceptical'. Hyper-globalists (as with Globalists) are described as accepting the 'realness' of the phenomena but also direct attention to the consequences, arguing that globalisation has resulted in the demise of the sovereign nation-state (also known as the 'hollowing-out of the state' thesis). Globalising trends are therefore viewed as rendering governments impotent in their efforts to control their own economies, internal affairs and security challenges including pollution, narcotics trafficking and terrorism (see for example Ohmae, 2004; Strange, 2004; Rodrik, 1997). Viewing the organisation of global politics through a historical lens, Ohmae (2004), for example, presents the nation-state (as the existing structure through which to mediate state-to-state relations and international politics) as a transitional form of organisation for managing economic affairs, which is in the process of being replaced by regional organisation. Similarly, for Strange (2004), evidence of the declining authority of states is reflected in the diffusion of authority to other institutions and associations, local and regional bodies with larger states more able to apply structural power than smaller states, reflecting an enhanced asymmetry between nations. Prompted by technological and financial change and the accelerated integration of national economies into one single global market economy, Strange argues that the authority of governments has been diminished and their incapacity to fulfil their fundamental responsibilities has resulted in a vacuum, with functions no longer adequately discharged by anyone.

Conversely, theorists working within the sceptical frame of reference reject this suggestion, contending instead that states and geopolitics remain resilient and the principal agents and forces shaping world order (McGrew, 2011: 16). Thus Kofi Annan, speaking in his keynote address to a Conference on Globalisation and International Relations in June 2002, asserted that 'in spite or even because of' globalising forces, sovereign states retain their relevance and remain necessary institutions, describing states as 'the very linchpin of human security' (Annan, 2004: 240). Acknowledging the challenges posed by globalisation for states' ability to perform their historic security functions in terms of economic security, physical security and psychological security, Annan promotes state cooperation with the private sector, voluntary agencies, pressure groups, universities, research institutes, think tanks, foundations and individuals in addition to other states. Only by doing so are states able to develop much needed policies, resist aggression, to provide basic services and safety nets and to protect citizens from crime and terrorism. While Annan's position is clearly optimistically progressive, post-sceptical theorists and those adopting 'a transformationalist perspective' (see McGrew, 2011: 16–29) view the proclamations of both the hyper-globalists and sceptical scholars as subject to exaggeration, distortion and simplification. For this third group of scholars, globalisation is less certain and the outcome of globalisation is not determined. Thus, while commentators agree that the nature of national governments is changing, this transformation is not viewed as leading to either the demise or growth of sovereign state influence within global politics.

Held and McGrew's (2007: 5) later schema identifies four successive waves of globalisation scholarship: the theoretical, the historical, the institutional, and the deconstructive. The initial theoretical wave is regarded as generally concerned with debates about the conceptualisation of globalisation, its principle dynamics and its systemic and structural consequences, viewed as a secular process of worldwide social change. Influenced by global development scholarship, the second historical wave is presented as preoccupied with the question as to whether contemporary globalisation is novel and/or unique, in particular, whether globalisation trends mark the emergence of a new epoch or transformation in the organisation of society, or whether they are merely a continuation of earlier trends. The third (institutional) wave is presented by Held and McGrew as a sceptical response to the historical wave's claims regarding historical transformation, with scholars working within the institutional wave concerned to assess claims about global convergence (and divergence). The deconstructive wave is described by Held and McGrew as being influenced by post-structuralist and constructivist thinking, placing emphasis upon the significance of ideas, agency, communication and contingency (a perspective we shall encounter within Chapter 5 in relation to the conceptualisation of state crime). The latter wave therefore examines the existence of what are believed to be 'multiple globalisations' conceived as both historical processes and as hegemonic discourse, creating space for diverging positions, variation in experience and alternative interpretations. Thus, for Sparke (2013), globalisation is the analysis of real global interconnections (the position also taken by Globalists and Hyper-globalists), but also must be understood as an influential key term in political speech. He therefore retains Held and McGrew's theoretical emphasis upon the identification of dynamics and consequences, also highlighting the application of the concept of globalisation as a political buzzword and as a discourse, thereby embracing the focus of the 'deconstructive wave'.

The categorisations of Held and McGrew (2000, 2007), Busch (2000), McGrew (2011) and Sparke (2013) serve as useful heuristic devices, namely tools to facilitate our understanding of a complex, diverse and growing literature. The contributions direct newcomers to think about what globalisation is and to think about its consequences. The typologies also serve to direct one to think about how the concept has been used, and for what purposes.

The application of globalisation discourse within national, regional and international security policy

With regard to the emergence of a global governance complex and global prohibition regimes directed towards crime and security issues, the concept of globalisation is clearly an influential term (Andreas and Nadelmann, 2006). Thus, we can clearly see the 'globalist' position (accepting the reality of global interconnections), articulated within the national and regional security strategies of the United States, United Kingdom and European Union.

The National Security Strategy of the United States of America, published in May 2010, similarly directly implicates globalisation processes in accounting for increasing opportunities linked to peace, democracy and prosperity:

> Time and again in our Nation's history, Americans have risen to meet – and to shape – moments of transition. This must be one of those moments. We live in a time of sweeping change. The success of free nations, open markets, and social progress in recent decades has accelerated globalisation on an unprecedented scale. This has opened the doors of opportunity around the globe, extended democracy to hundreds of millions of people, and made peace possible among the major powers.
>
> (NSS USA, 2010: 3)

However, rather than adopting wholeheartedly the liberal position of Busch (2000), detailed previously, the National Security Strategy of the USA retains a focus on a number of negative consequences linked to processes of globalisation:

> Yet globalisation has also intensified the dangers we face – from international terrorism and the spread of deadly technologies, to economic upheaval and a changing climate.
>
> (NSS USA, 2010: 3)

We see within this strategy, reference being made to a period of change, with freedom, open markets and social progress accelerating globalisation, which, in turn, creates further opportunities alongside the intensification of risks. The direction of change associated with processes of globalisation differs however, according to the policy documentation of decision-makers and takers from a variety of levels of governance. Sometimes globalisation is itself viewed as intensifying as a result of particular trends (as above), yet sometimes particular aspects of globalisation or globalisation as a whole are viewed as acting as the facilitator or driving force behind other social trends. Thus, remaining on a national level, the UK National Security Strategy, 'A Strong Britain in an Age of Uncertainty' also published in October 2010, makes two explicit references to globalisation. The first reference clearly conceives globalisation as a driver of social progress (the liberal perspective) asserting:

> We live in an age of unparalleled opportunity. Globalisation has opened up possibilities which previous generations could not have dreamed of and is lifting billions out of poverty. More open markets mean more open societies, and more open societies mean more people living in freedom. These developments are unambiguously in Britain's national interest and we should seize the opportunities they present, not fear for our future.
>
> (HM Government, 2010: 4)

This reveals a consensus between the UK and the US regarding the relative benefits bestowed by globalisation, including freedom, prosperity and democracy, creating opportunities and peace. There is further agreement in relation to the risks posed by globalisation, as the second reference to globalisation within the UK strategy acknowledges:

> Globalisation in all its forms has made the world more interconnected both through technology, travel and migration and through the global trade in goods, services and capital. This means that it is much harder to isolate the UK from shocks occurring outside our own territory, whether they are economic or geopolitical.
>
> (HM Government, 2010: 16)

On a regional level, the Council of the European Union's 'Internal Security Strategy for the European Union', also published in 2010, highlights the benefits of integration in addition to potential risks. While refraining from utilising the term 'globalisation', the apparent similarities in the discourse utilised and the conclusions reached between the US and UK national perspectives and the United Nations Office on Drugs and Crime international perspective, which follows, are clear to see:

> The European Union (EU) in the twenty-first century consists of 500 million people across the twenty-seven countries which make up the Union. Economic growth, together with the opportunities provided by a free and democratic society based on the rule of law, generate prosperity amongst Europe's citizens – but with such opportunities also come risks, as terrorists and other types of criminals seek to abuse those freedoms in the pursuit of destructive and malicious ends. Furthermore, increased mobility of people in turn increases our common responsibility for protecting the freedoms which all citizens in the Union cherish.
>
> (Council of the European Union, 2010: 11)

The United Nations Office on Drugs and Crime Report, *Promoting Health, Security and Justice*, published in 2010, similarly acknowledges globalisation as a double-edged sword, this time from an international perspective:

> Networks are one of the defining features of the twenty-first century. Globalized systems of trade, transportation and communication enable people and goods, as well as ideas and information, to travel around the world faster than ever before. *For the most part*, these networks contribute to progress, fostering development and increasing prosperity.
>
> But the advances of globalization also make us vulnerable in new ways, and have given rise to other, destructive networks that undermine security and development. Taking advantage of innovations in technology, communication and transportation, loose networks of criminals or insurgents can easily link with each other, and also with organized criminal groups that operate internationally. They smuggle illicit drugs, weapons, natural resources, counterfeit goods and human beings across borders and between continents for the enrichment of criminals, insurgents and crooked officials. In some cases, they generate economic profits that support terrorist groups as well.
>
> (UNODC, 2010: 13)

While there are clear parallels within the national, regional and international security strategies presented above in relation to their use of the term 'globalisation', there is in fact, 'no straightforward or widely accepted definition of the term, either in general use or in academic writing' (Schirato and Webb, 2003: 2). As Panic observes, cited in Madsen (2009: 80) there is 'even less agreement about the processes that bring globalisation about, and no agreement at all about its effects'. Thus while the US and UK present globalisation as within the national interest, and the European Union similarly proclaims the benefits to be within the regional interest of the Union, the UNODC utilises the more cautious phrase *'for the most part'*, which directs attention to contemporary challenges regarding the universal benefits derived from globalisation processes. Indeed, as already mentioned, particularly in relation to the contributions by post-sceptical theorists and those adopting 'a transformationalist perspective', 'globalisation' is viewed by many as an unsatisfactory term inviting overstatement and over-generalisation (Tomlinson, 2007: 148), a view highlighting that 'at present, the benefits of globalisation are far from being equitably shared' (Annan, 2004: 241).

For some, globalisation means the internationalisation of financial markets and of production networks. For example, the security strategies presented already refer to networks, open markets, globalised systems of trade, goods, services and capital. Other theorists understand globalisation as 'the erosion of borders and the end of the nation-state as we know it' (Risse, 2007: 126), facilitated by developments within transportation, communication and technology resulting in mobility and the compression of time and space and having implications for governance, security and world order. Globalisation has been further discussed in relation to the global diffusion of norms and other cultural scripts, drawing upon the circulation of ideas and information highlighted by the UNODC (2010), but moving beyond this to consider ideology and discourse. The UNODC position, captured by the additional inclusion of the phrase *'for the most part'*, is therefore, arguably more closely aligned to Busch's 'moderately optimistic' category rather than Held and McGrew's 'globalist/sceptic' categorisation. Thus, the 'moderately optimistic' position agrees 'that there are globalising tendencies which can be identified and measured, but that they are not as all-encompassing as the literature might imply; and nor are they operating without resistance, and without exceptions' (Busch, 2000: 33, cited in Schirato and Webb, 2003: 8).

The ways in which power-holders and decision-makers utilise the concept of globalisation, and view the processes contained within it, are not inconsequential. Indeed, critical thinkers and revolutionaries alike have questioned the assumptions contained within such policy statements and directed attention to a range of questions which contextualise, historicise and significantly, politicise claims regarding the universal benefits of globalisation. In Chapter 3, we will introduce a range of criminological, sociological and international relations perspectives which have been used to make sense of transnational crime and terrorism and the development and evolution of a criminal justice and security infrastructure tasked with countering the threats posed to national, regional and international peace and security.

While it is evident that a number of these theories adhere to the neo-liberal discourse on globalisation which claims that economic liberalisation and market integration benefit everybody (either explicitly or implicitly), and the related assumption regarding the existence of a so-called global level economic playing field, other theoretical positions question these assumptions, bringing power and geopolitics within their theorising. The stance taken therefore shapes one's perspective regarding the causes of crime, the appropriate subject matter for examination and analysis also influencing views regarding the appropriate criminal justice responses to crime.

The central objective of this text is to place cross-border, cross-national and international crime and crime control within its wider context. The aim then is to examine theory from a range of disciplines and to introduce students to the frequently neglected area of the world order and world politics in an effort to direct attention to the links between events, power, ideas, institutions, policies, actions and counter-actions at the international and domestic level. The motivation for this selection denotes a political choice and a desire to highlight issues relating to inequality, poverty and social exclusion in addition to the more traditional criminological focus upon deterrence, criminal opportunities, crime control methods, risk and securitisation and causal explanations of crime. Engaging with debates both embracing and challenging the notion of 'globalisation' and employing a multidisciplinary approach, this text hopes to provide students with an overview of globalisation theory, in order to set the scene for the chapters that follow, and its contemporary relevance for crime control. Following the worthy scholarly contribution of Andreas and Nadelmann (2006), a further objective is to fundamentally call into question the accelerating trend towards the internationalisation of crime control, exploring measures contained within the existing framework to tackle international piracy, genocide, terrorism, corruption and human trafficking, reflecting upon the implications of these approaches and highlighting possible alternative courses of action which may result in a more just and equitable world order. The aim then, following Bauman's quote at the beginning of this chapter, is to inspire conversation, to encourage the use of an (historically grounded and politically sensitive) interdisciplinary perspective, to awaken critical thinking and to challenge readers to think (and act) towards alternative futures.

The final section of this chapter aims to address how and why globalisation discourse has entered into security and crime discourse, drawing attention to the convergence of crime and security agendas, increased transnational policing and political cooperation in the field of crime and security.

Globalisation and transnational crime

Expanding concepts of security

The intensification and acceleration of worldwide interconnectedness and interdependency which includes processes of economic, political, and social integration, facilitated by advances within information, communication technologies and transportation systems, have collectively been captured by the phrase 'globalisation' (Dasgupta, 2004; Lechner and Boli, 2004; Held and McGrew, 2007; Cohen and Kennedy, 2007; Sparke, 2013). A range of commentators working within a broad array of academic disciplines and sub-fields have implicated these processes and aspects of globalisation as having profoundly impacted upon discourses and conceptions of security. These processes, it has been suggested, have created new challenges and threats, resulting in the emergence of a new security landscape and fundamental shifts within the security agendas of individual states, regions and globally (Aas, 2007; Baylis, 2011; Williams, 2013).

As with the term 'globalisation', scholars broadly accept that the notion of security means different things to different people, with the application of the concept changing over time and used to describe different practices within different disciplines, and within different countries. Yet, despite the contested nature of the concept of security, a consensus has emerged between scholars working within international relations, security studies and world politics that the term implies the alleviation of threats to cherished values (Anderson *et al.*, 1995: 156; Baylis, 2011: 233; Williams, 2013: 1; Bigo, 2013: 125). Scholars point out that while during the Cold War period, security was largely defined in military terms, with the focus of inquiry directed towards 'national security', it has recently been acknowledged that pathologies associated with globalisation have now also directed attention towards regional, international and individual levels of inquiry. This development has resulted in the emergence of an expanded definition of security which now includes political, economic, societal and environmental aspects (Baylis, 2011: 233; Williams, 2013: 1; Buzan, 1983).

As noted earlier within the chapter, it has been argued that networks of global interdependencies and regional integration linked to the development and expansion of global capitalism (now captured by the term 'globalisation') have transcended national borders, generating opportunities for crime and criminals and exposure to the 'cherished values' of others (Naim, 2002). Thus in 2002, the National Security Strategy of the United States of America reiterated the assertion that national security remained the primary obligation of the state, defining the protection of freedom, democracy, human rights and free enterprise as the principal values to be secured. Yet, in the pursuit of this objective, the NSS USA 2002 document clearly articulated the view that the task of national security had changed drastically, with the federal government confronting new circumstances and threats in the twenty-first century:

> Enemies in the past needed great armies and great industrial capabilities to endanger America. Now, shadowy networks of individuals can bring great chaos and suffering to our shores for less than it costs to purchase a single tank. Terrorists are organized to penetrate open societies and to turn the power of modern technologies against us.
>
> (National Security Strategy, USA, 2002: 1)

Similarly, at an international level, in 2004, within the report of the UN High-Level Panel on Threats Challenges and Change entitled 'A more secure world: our shared responsibility' (A/59/565), the traditional preoccupation with state security became further subject to challenge. In an endeavour to forge a new security consensus, the report authors employed a broader conceptualisation defining threats to international security as '[a]ny event or process that leads to large-scale death or lessening of life chances and undermines States as the basic unit of the international system' (UN, 2004: 12). The protection and preservation of the existing society of states framework for organising world politics therefore remains a fundamental aspect of the international definition of security (a point to which we will return throughout the text).

Threats to national security, defined in military terms in relation to states waging aggressive war on other states, while still evidently salient, were no longer regarded as all-encompassing and therefore inadequate in the face of challenges facing the international community in the new millennium, a position also reflected within the NSS, USA 2002. The broader, more comprehensive concept of collective security presented by the Panel extended to poverty, infectious disease and environmental degradation; war and violence within states; the spread and possible use of nuclear, radiological, chemical and biological weapons; terrorism; and transnational organised crime. In addition to the expanded range of threats warranting international action, the sources of threats were also seen to include non-state actors as well as states. Significantly, both documents emphasised the interdependence of the threats listed and the need to adopt a preventative approach, recognising the links between development, weak and failed states, organised crime, corruption and terrorism, inter-state conflict and the need to enhance peace enforcement, peacekeeping and peace building.

> The events of September 11, 2001, taught us that weak states, like Afghanistan, can pose as great a danger to our national interests as strong states. Poverty does not make poor people into terrorists and murderers. Yet poverty, weak institutions, and corruption can make weak states vulnerable to terrorist networks and drug cartels within their borders.
>
> (NSS, USA, 2002)

In 2011 the World Development Report, drawing upon the work of Paul Collier, also openly acknowledged the relationship between the recurrent cycles of weak governance, poverty and violence;

> [T]he problems of fragile states spread easily: They drag down neighbours with violence that overflows borders, because conflicts feed on narcotics, piracy, and gender violence, and leave refugees and broken infrastructure in their wake. Their territories can become breeding grounds for far-reaching networks of violent radicals and organized crime.
>
> (World Bank, 2011: xi)

Thus, following the events of September 11, the National Security Strategy of the United States of America implicated the existence of weak and failed states in the facilitation of global terrorism, thereby fusing internal and external notions of security, foreign policy and national security concerns and serving to destabilise traditional distinctions between crime and war, military, intelligence and police missions. In relation to the blurring of conventional categories, Aas (2007: 105) has recently argued that 'if before it was still possible to distinguish between crime and war, and military and police domains (although the lines have never been clear cut), today this distinction is becoming difficult'. Baylis (2011) similarly points to a profound transformation in the nature of contemporary political conflicts and warfare, emphasising the emergence of a security interdependence between foreign policy and national and local security concerns, and vice versa. For Baylis, foreign policy is no longer properly 'foreign' as external conflicts often have an almost immediate impact on national and local security strategies. While for Bigo (2013: 131), discussing the impact of the discourse of global terrorism upon the conceptualisation of security, policy and institutional mandates 'the terminology of global terrorism has tended to fuse petty criminality, the radicalisation of ideas, and strategic thinking about state enemies coming both from inside and outside'. The traditional preoccupation with national security, defined in military terms as the threat of aggression from one state to another, has therefore become recognised within policy making arenas and academia as increasingly obsolete (although far from irrelevant). These developments have resulted in what has been described as 'criminal justice militarisation' viewed as a convergence of militaristic, police, and penal contexts (Brown, 2005: 985 cited in Aas, 2007: 106), leading to increasing cooperation, overlap and joint missions between the police, intelligence and military actors (Bigo, 2013: 131) within the security field.

While global terrorism has intensified and accelerated national, regional and international cooperation, strengthening the collective resolve to forge a 'new security consensus' and collective security agenda, other authors remind us that the emergence of such developments predates 9/11. Thus, Anderson *et al.* (1995: 156–180) locate the end of the cold war in 1989 as the defining period instigating the redrawing of the relationship between internal and external security. Discussing European security in particular, the authors present the work of Buzan (1991) whose influential work, written from within the International Relations 'realist' position, identified five broad types of security threats (military, political, societal, economic and ecological) within the post-cold war era. Buzan's redefinition of security and his conceptual merger of police organisation and practice, which predates the NSS, USA 2002, 2010, UN 2004, UK NSS 2010, Council for the European Union 2010 security strategies presented already, is viewed as having profound implications for definitions of security, threat analysis, policing methods, organisation and governance arrangements. For Anderson *et al.* (1995) the threat of crime pervades each of Buzan's types of threats. Citing the organised crime examples of drugs and arms trafficking, Anderson *et al.* highlight the link between guerrilla warfare, terrorism, aggressive forms of international economic competition and imperialism, between corruption, fragile states and political threats to states and development, in addition to the interdependencies between illegitimate financial activity and the legitimate activities of manufacture, trade and banking. Consequently, the lines dividing organised crime, corporate crime, international crime, state crime, terrorism and ecological crime are rendered problematic, as are the traditional distinctions between internal and external security threats, military and police actions. Significantly, the collapse of the bi-polar system of international relations is presented as an undercurrent facilitating these trends. While the first and second world war, the cold war and its subsequent demise will be addressed more comprehensively in Chapter 3, it is important to note at this stage the reported significance of the United States' victory over the Soviet Union in facilitating the acceleration and intensification of the processes of globalisation and the redrawing of security agendas and organisational remits and methodologies.

Thus, the collapse of the bi-polar system is widely accepted as instrumental in the emergence of a global economic system, global communications system and redoubled efforts to generate a 'global culture' promoting human rights and fundamental freedoms, alongside American unilateral efforts directed towards democratisation. The consequences of globalisation are however, now widely accepted as uneven, resulting in contradictory trends towards homogenisation and fragmentation, prosperity alongside increased economic inequality, cooperation and consensus contrasted against nationalistic, ethnic and religious rivalries, enhanced peace between nations, coinciding with internal conflicts, civil wars, terrorism and humanitarian crises. The interpretation of these developments will be the focus for Chapter 3.

In the meantime, however, if doubt remains regarding the reality of processes of globalisation, globalists and advocates may well point to the 2008–9 global financial crisis and to the global financial interdependencies, which resulted in most economies around the world experiencing marked declines in growth rates, austerity, losses in income and employment and setbacks in efforts to reduce poverty (World Bank, 2014: 4). The World Development Report 2014 further directs attention to a range of environmental crises rendering national borders obsolete and unilateral responses inadequate. Examples include the 2004 Asian tsunami, the 2010 earthquake in Haiti, and the multiple hazard disaster in north-eastern Japan. Redefined as threats to international security, such crises render the links between development, terrorism, crime, corruption and immigration visible. These events, building upon previous cooperative endeavours, have instigated intensified cooperation and collaborative working relationships between the police, intelligence and military personnel, alongside civil and private sector service providers, generating increasing opportunities to widen institutional mandates, technologies, resources and influence.

As an expanding array of state and non-state actors enter into the changing security arena (see Chapter 4), questions are increasingly directed towards an assessment regarding the impact of globalisation trends upon the role and relevance of states in the post-cold war era. As discussed above, with respect to the hyper-globalist perspective of globalisation, while states have traditionally been regarded as the key actors in the international system (at least since the signing of the Treaties of Westphalia in 1648 which marked the demise of the previous arrangements), scholars have recently directed attention to a series of historical transformations resulting in the internationalisation, erosion and/or transformation of the state as the most important agent and referent of security in international politics (Baylis, 2011: 234; Sheptycki, 1995, 1998). Viewed as a side effect of the bi-polar collapse (Buzan, 1991: 208, cited in Anderson *et al.*, 1995: 160), the emergence of new security communities and the displacement of responsibilities for security from the state to the private sector and the individual citizen have generated questions regarding the governance arrangements within contemporary world politics raising concerns about the adequacy of current accountability and oversight mechanisms, and the implications for the perceived legitimacy of current political and law enforcement and security arrangements. As suggested, the concepts of globalisation and security are far from value neutral. Both terms have been discussed as powerful political tools influencing policy decisions and the agendas of ministers and senior law enforcement and security leaders. Thus, Williams (2013: 2) also drawing upon the work of Buzan (1991) contends that the discourse of security is currently applied as a political endeavour, serving to claim priority in the competition for government attention. Bigo (2013) agrees, similarly arguing that security is the object of competition between actors seeking to control its content. For both authors, politicisation arises from the contested nature of the boundaries of security, with security presented as the product of legitimacy struggles between actors. For Bigo, then, security discourse masks elements of uncertainty, ambiguity and dispute. The successful application of security narratives is therefore regarded as representing relations of power, with victors able 'to claim the monopoly over the certainty of the boundaries of security (for them and for the others), to affirm their capacity to know the future and to have preventative actions, and to eliminate the ambiguity of the practices included in the process' (Bigo, 2013: 125). An awareness regarding the political application of both terms, 'globalisation' and 'security', is therefore important.

For Williams (2013: 2), security discourse reveals 'who gets to decide what security means, what issues make it onto security agendas, how those issues should be dealt with, and crucially, what happens when different visions of security collide'. In Chapter 4 the key institutional framework for the control of transnational crime and terrorism will be identified. It will be demonstrated that the international and regional organisations and agencies reveal remarkable consistency in their mandates and activities. For Bigo, this institutional tendency towards the enumeration of long lists of actions without context, associated with labels such as 'terrorism' and 'serious crime', serves to justify organisational action as responses to such threats. Bigo views such a historical and decontextualised practices as problematic, directing attention away from the processes involved in the decisions to 'normalise, to protect, to care about' particular groups of people while at the same time 'to coerce, to exclude, to filter, to reform, to re-socialise' others (Bigo, 2013: 128–9). Bigo therefore views the categorisation of individuals or groups as a 'danger, risk, threat, or simply unwanted' as the end result of a process informed by political and moral judgements, institutional interests and strategies of justifications. Thus, while a history of informal, then formal political and law enforcement cooperation in criminal matters, may have resulted in the signing of conventions and decisions, in addition to the creation of legal frameworks to deal with a range of criminal matters, Bigo cautions us to remain mindful that the emergence of positive legal systems may give such political processes legality, reflected by the 'force of law', but this does not necessarily legitimise them. For Bigo and Williams, alongside an increasing body of scholars, the emergence of an expanding infrastructure of global crime control should not be viewed as a natural response to an increasing array of threats and challenges prompted by globalisation. Rather, these authors direct attention towards the historical, political and social context in which the emergence of global prohibition regimes and international crime control policies have arisen, raising questions about their implementation and their enforcement.

Working within this vein, Peter Andreas and Ethan Nadelmann's highly influential text, *Policing the Globe* (2006), endeavours to provide a bridge between criminal justice and international relations. Responding to the (partial) portrayal of increased criminal justice harmonisation and policing and judicial cooperation as an inevitable consequence of the dark side of processes of globalisation, Andreas and Nadelmann remind us of the need for historical and political contextualisation. Their account is presented as:

> at once a liberal story about the expansion of international cooperation and institutions built on mutual interest in a context of growing interdependence and transnational flows, a realist story about coercive co-operation and hegemonic leadership, and a constructivist story about transnational moral entrepreneurs and the creation and spread of global norms.
>
> (Andreas and Nadelmann, 2006: viii)

This is an excellent contribution and highlights tensions and contradictions within the contemporary world order where efforts aimed at social cohesion, global security and peace occur simultaneously against a background of power relations, conflict, inequality and insecurity. Controversially, Andreas and Nadelmann contend that international crime control is one of the most important – and one of the most overlooked – dimensions of US hegemony in world politics (Andreas and Nadelmann, 2006: 10). Individual actors and social structures are given intellectual space with which to draw out the complexity of criminalisation and law enforcement, directing attention to continuities and fundamental changes in policy and practice in international crime control efforts, emphasising that there is 'nothing natural, permanent, or inevitable about what states choose to criminalize or decriminalize' (Andreas and Nadelmann, 2006: 13).

Mark Findlay's (2008) *Governing through Globalised Crime* similarly explores the emergence of international criminal justice as a central tool for global governance and draws upon his earlier work (1999) *The Globalisation of Crime: Understanding Transitional Relationships in Context.* Of particular interest is Findlay's recognition of the application of international criminal justice institutions which are regarded as working in the interests of one world order against what is viewed as 'the sometimes legitimate resistance of criminalised communities' (Findlay, 2008: xiv). Findlay explores what he calls 'the new globalisation', which is viewed as an age where (following 9/11) global governance through reaction to terror is employed as a strategy for order maintenance. Within this framework, the risk/security nexus is viewed as comprising a dominant regulatory framework directed towards achieving world order and global governance. Thus for some analysts, 'security' has often been a way of legitimising oppressive structures of surveillance and control. Bigo (2013: 120–133) and Tickner (1992) for example, define security 'as a process of (in) securitisation'. Highlighting the perverse effects of security discourse, Bigo argues that rather than providing reassurance and protection and bestowing certainty about the future, security generates unease, uncertainty, and new struggles (Bigo, 2013: 124–5), a view reiterated in Chapter 7 in relation to existing counter-terrorism strategy and Chapter 8 by feminist scholars in their analysis of the contemporary human trafficking framework. Bigo argues that security claims are utilised to generate acceptance for activities (even if it implies the use of physical and/or symbolic violence), expand organisational remits and justify requests for enhanced resources. Contemporary securitisation processes are consequently regarded as concealing political and moral choices regarding the individuals and groups targeted as the potential source of insecurity, diverting attention from processes of inclusion and exclusion and issues of power and interest. Other authors highlight the costs of such approaches in diverting attention from alternative concepts of security and/or wider economic or structural considerations underpinning the conditions conducive to crime, violence, conflict and exploitation (Aas, 2007; Jacobs, Jacobson and Marchbank, 2000; Tickner, 1992, 2014; True, 2012; Pogge, 2008).

Both Andreas and Nadelmann's (2006) text and Findlay's (1999 and 2008) contributions place criminalisation and global security as defining features of the contemporary era. Furthermore, they also emphasise the significance of political and cultural context and representation of crimes, risks and populations, which are attributed explanatory weight in making sense of security responses and prioritisation of threats. Both texts also acknowledge the links between the current political and economic world order, global inequalities, processes of criminalisation and enforcement. Significantly, while an explicit focus upon power and international history is frequently omitted from criminological texts which are dedicated to discussions of transnational organised crimes and international crimes, the observations of Bigo (2013), Williams

(2013), Aas (2007), Andreas and Nadelmann (2006) and Findlay (1999, 2008) serve to highlight the importance of perspective and interpretation in understanding contemporary social transformations and trends within the field of crime and security. Williams in particular is keen to provide a balanced (less one-sided) portrayal of organised crime. Drawing upon the contributions of Bell (1960), Mittelman (2000), Volkov (2002), and Standing (2003), Williams reminds us that crime can bring benefits as well as inflict harm on societies, enabling social mobility and economic employment for individuals and acting as a safety net and safety valve for states unable to attract foreign direct investment and functioning as an alternative form of governance for socially, politically and economically excluded nations. As we shall see within the following chapters, state use of crime and facilitation of crime control responses are by no means static and are subject to variation over time.

Interpreting the past, understanding the present and influencing the future are, as Williams (2013: 2) correctly states, political endeavours. The intention of this text is therefore to examine the emerging global crime control infrastructure and international security consensus within its historical, political and social context to shed light upon scholarly understandings of how and why we are where we are and where we might be going. The next chapter will therefore explore early efforts at transnational crime control, briefly looking at instances of transnational crime and highlighting significant issues that will be picked up in later chapters, including the role and function of the state; crime, law and security as methods of statecraft and societal control; and the wider theme of continuity and change. Through an examination of slavery and piracy, we will explore how these issues became the focus of prohibition regimes and the relationship of these developments with colonialism, capitalism and the emergence of a dominant world order in which power politics and state interests coincided with moral entrepreneurialism.

The emergence and subsequent development of international society following the first and second world war peace settlements and institution building activities, European imperial collapse and the onset and demise of the Cold War will consequently be explored in order to tease out the significance and continuing relevance of international history for an understanding of global crime control. In particular, the chapter will draw out the links between key transformations in world history and the reported acceleration and facilitation of aspects of globalisation as essential elements in securing global security and world peace. In particular, Chapter 2 will highlight the emergence of a framework which consciously promoted economic, political and socio-cultural integration, a development that had important consequences in relation to the later expansion in the concept of security which moved beyond an original concern with war between states, to a much wider set of concerns, resulting in enhanced law enforcement and judicial cooperation, and a blurring of military, law enforcement and security infrastructures. Chapter 2 will therefore emphasise the relative newness of the existing geopolitical system and territorial boundaries of states. It will further prompt consideration of the continuing legacy of unresolved grievances and tensions underpinning contemporary global governance arrangements. The interpretation of these developments will be addressed in Chapter 3, which will present an overview of key sociological, criminological and international relations perspectives.

While this chapter has served to highlight the contentious nature of globalisation and security, it is evident that we have recently witnessed the political acknowledgement of an association between weak states, international and transnational crimes and terrorism leading towards the development of an international security consensus. Agreement regarding the inclusion of particular crime threats, the signing of legal frameworks and efforts towards harmonisation of criminal justice systems and policing cooperation in criminal matters tell us much about dominant views regarding 'which humans to prioritise' and 'the dominant meaning of security'. While huge inequalities of power and influence remain within international society and also across individuals and groups in contemporary world politics, questions remain regarding alternative visions of what counts as security, about whose security is being focused upon and about the construction processes involved within decision-making arenas and agenda-setting processes. With this in mind, each of the perspectives presented in Chapter 3 contain assumptions regarding the causes of crime and appropriate responses to crime, and make predictions regarding the future. Without wishing to foreclose discussion, the objective of this text remains to prompt readers to think and ask questions, to toy with possible alternative interpretations and to critique, challenge, imagine and act to promote a more just, inclusive and equitable crime control infrastructure (and international society) in years to come.

Bibliography

Aas, K.F. (2007). *Globalisation and Crime.* London: Sage Publications.

Albanese, J. (2011). *Transnational Crime and the 21st Century: Criminal Enterprise, Corruption, and Opportunity.* Oxford: Oxford University Press.

Anderson, M. (1989). *Policing the World.* Oxford: Clarendon Press.

Anderson, M., Den Boer, M., Cullen, P., Gilmore, W., Raab, C., and Walker, N. (1995). *Policing the European Union.* Oxford: Clarendon Press.

Andreas, P. and Nadelmann, E. (2006). *Policing the Globe: Criminalization and Crime Control in International Relations.* Oxford: Oxford University Press.

Annan, K. (2004). 'The Role of the State in the Age of Globalisation', in Lechner, F. and Boli, J. (eds), *The Globalisation Reader.* Oxford: Blackwell Publishing. Pp. 240–243.

Bauman, Z. (2011). *Collateral Damage: Social Inequalities in a Global Age.* Cambridge: Polity Press.

Baylis, J. (2011). 'International and Global Security', in Baylis, J., Smith, S., and Owens, P. (eds), *The Globalisation of World Politics*, 5th edition. Oxford: Oxford University Press. Pp. 232–243.

Bell, D. (1960). *The End of Ideology.* Cambridge, MA: Harvard University Press.

Bigo, D. (2013). 'International Political Sociology', in Williams, P. (ed.), *Security Studies: An Introduction*. London: Routledge. Pp. 120–133.

Bowling, B. and Sheptycki, J.W.E. (2012). *Global Policing*. London: Sage.

Brown, M. (2005). '"Setting the Conditions" for AbuGhraib: The Prison Nation Abroad', *American Quarterly*, Sept.: 973–997.

Brown, S. (2008). *Combating International Crime: The Longer Arm of the Law*. London: Routledge-Cavendish.

Busch, A. (2000). 'Unpacking the Globalization Debate: Approaches Evidence and Data', in Hay, C. and Marsh, D. (eds), *Demystifying Globalization*. Basingstoke: Palgrave Macmillan. Pp. 21–48.

Buzan, B. (1983). *People, States and Fear*. Chapel Hill, NC: University of North Carolina Press.

Buzan, B. (1991). *People, States and Fear. An Agenda for International Security Studies in the Post-Cold War Era*, 2nd edition. New York: Prentice Hall/Harvester Wheatsheaf.

Cohen, R. and Kennedy, P. (2007). *Global Sociology*. Basingstoke: Palgrave Macmillan.

Council of the European Union. (2010). 'Draft Internal Security Strategy for the European Union', 5842/10, 23 February. Available online at: http://register.consilium.europa.eu/doc/srv?l=EN&f=ST%205842%202010%20REV%202.

Council of the European Union. (2010). *Internal Security Strategy for the European Union*. Luxembourg: Publications Office of the European Union.

Dasgupta, S. (2004). *The Changing Face of Globalisation*. London: Sage.

Deflem, M. (2002). *Policing World Society: Historical Foundations of International Police Cooperation*. Oxford: Oxford University Press.

Findlay, M. (1999). *The Globalisation of Crime: Understanding Transitional Relationships in Context*. Cambridge: Cambridge University Press.

Findlay, M. (2008). *Governing through Globalised Crime: Futures for International Criminal Justice*. Cullompton: Willan Publishing.

Findlay, M. and Henham, R. (2012). *Transforming Criminal Justice*. London: Routledge.

Held, D. and McGrew, A. (eds). (2000). *The Global Transformations Reader*. Cambridge: Polity Press.

Held, D. and McGrew, A. (eds). (2007). *Globalisation Theory*. Cambridge: Polity Press.

Held, D., McGrew, A., Goldblatt, D., and Perraton, J. (1999). *Global Transformations: Politics, Economics and Culture*. Cambridge: Polity Press.

HM Government. (2010). UK National Security Strategy, 'A Strong Britain in an Age of Uncertainty', October. London: HMSO. Available online at: www.gov.uk/government/uploads/system/uploads/attachment_data/file/61936/national-security-strategy.pdf.

Holton, R. (2005). *Making Globalisation*. Basingstoke: Palgrave Macmillan.

Lechner, F. and Boli, J. (eds). (2004). *The Globalisation Reader*. Oxford: Blackwell Publishing.

Lemieux, F. (ed.). (2013). *International Police Cooperation*. Abingdon: Routledge.

Madsen, F. (2009). *Transnational Organized Crime*. London: Routledge.

McGrew, A. (2011). 'Globalisation and Global Politics', in Baylis, J., Smith, S., and Owens, P. (eds), *The Globalisation of World Politics*. Oxford: Oxford University Press. Pp. 16–29.

Mittelman, J. (2000). *The Globalization Syndrome*. Princeton, NJ: Princeton University Press.

Nadelmann, E. (1993). *Cops Across Borders: The Internationalization of U.S. Criminal Law Enforcement*. Philadelphia, PA: Pennsylvania State University Press.

Naim, M. (2002). Five Wars of Globalization. The Grotius Lecture Series. Lecture presented at the American Society of International Law's ('ASIL') 96th Annual Meeting on March 13–16. American University Washington College of Law, the ASIL, and the International Legal Studies Program.

Ohmae, K. (2004). 'The End of the Nation State', in Lechner, F. and Boli, J. (eds), *The Globalisation Reader*. Oxford: Blackwell Publishing. Pp. 214–218.

Partin, G. (2003). International Criminal Law. American Society of International Law, October. Available online at: www.asil.org/resource/crim1.htm (accessed December 6, 2003).

Pogge, T. (2008). *World Poverty and Human Rights*, 2nd edition. Cambridge: Polity Press.

Reichel, P. (ed.). (2005). *Handbook of Transnational Crime and Justice*. London: Sage Publications.

Risse, T. (2007). 'Social Constructivism Meets Globalization', in McGrew, A. and Held, D. (eds), *Globalization Theory: Approaches and Controversies*. Cambridge: Polity Press. Pp. 126–147.

Rodrik, D. (1997). *Has Globalization Gone Too Far?* Washington, DC: Institute for International Economics.

Schirato, T. and Webb, J. (2003). *Understanding Globalisation*. London: Sage Publications.

Sheptycki, J.W.E. (1995). 'Transnational Policing and the Makings of a Postmodern State', *British Journal of Criminology*, 35(4): 613–635.

Sheptycki, J.W.E. (1998). 'Policing, Post-modernism and Transnationalisation', *British Journal of Criminology*, 38(3): 485–503.

Sheptycki, J.W.E. (ed.). (2000). *Issues in Transnational Policing*. London: Routledge.

Sheptycki, J.W.E. and Wardak, A. (2005). *Transnational and Comparative Criminology*. London: Glasshouse.

Shoham, S., Knepper, P., and Kett, M. (eds). (2010). *International Handbook of Criminology*. London: Taylor and Francis.

Smith, C., Zhang, S.X., and Barberet, R. (eds). (2011). *Routledge Handbook of International Criminology*. Abingdon: Routledge.

Sparke, M. (2013). *Introducing Globalisation*. Chichester: Wiley-Blackwell.

Standing, A. (2003). *The Social Contradictions of Organized Crime on the Cape Flats*. Johannesburg: Institute for Security Studies Paper 74.

Strange, S. (2004). 'The Declining Authority of States', in Lechner, F. and Boli, J. (eds), *The Globalisation Reader*. Oxford: Blackwell Publishing. Pp. 219–224.

Tickner, A. (1992). *Gender in International Relations: Feminist Perspectives on Achieving Global Security*. Oxford: Columbia University Press.

Tomlinson, J. (2007). 'Globalization and Cultural Analysis', in Held, D. and McGrew, A. (eds), *Globalization Theory: Approaches and Controversies*. Cambridge: Polity Press. Pp. 148–168.

True, J. (2012). *The Political Economy of Violence against Women*. Oxford: Oxford University Press.

United Nations. (2004). 'A More Secure World: Our Shared Responsibility'. Report of the UN High-Level Panel on Threats Challenges and Change (A/59/565). United Nations Department of Public Information.

United Nations Office on Drugs and Crime. (2010). *Promoting Health, Security and Justice*. Vienna: UNODC.

United States (2002). The National Security Strategy of the United States of America September. Available online at: www.state.gov/documents/organization/63562.pdf.

United States (2010). The National Security Strategy of the United States of America May. Available online at: www.whitehouse.gov/sites/default/files/rss_viewer/national_security_strategy.pdf.

Volkov, V. (2002). *Entrepreneurs of Violence: The Use of Force in the Making of Russian Capitalism*. Ithaca, NY: Cornell University Press.

Watts, R., Bessant, J., and Hil, R. (2008). *International Criminology: A Critical Introduction*. Abingdon: Routledge.

Williams, P. (2013). *Security Studies: An Introduction*. Abingdon: Routledge.

World Bank. (2011). *World Development Report: Conflict, Security and Development*. Washington, DC: The International Bank for Reconstruction and Development/The World Bank.

World Bank. (2014). *World Development Report 2014: Risk and Opportunity: Managing Risk for Development*. Washington, DC: The International Bank for Reconstruction and Development/The World Bank.

2 Historical contextualisation

The purpose of this chapter is to examine the historical roots of transnational crime control. Primarily we will be concerned with the issue of slavery and the development and eventual suppression of the African slave trade, followed by an examination of piracy. Both examples serve as case studies, which reveal early efforts towards the internationalisation of criminal law and prohibitions. As within the preceding chapter, which explored processes and discourses of globalisation (viewed as significant in influencing changing conceptualisations of security), this chapter will similarly be concerned with directing attention to shifts in policy priorities, which, it will be suggested, have implications for enforcement activities on behalf of states. Through an examination of the illicit slave trade and attacks of piracy, the intention of this chapter is therefore to direct attention to the various aspects of analysis which have served as the focus for academic study and which have underpinned crime control strategies and policies, nationally and internationally. As will be seen, not only have government positions altered over time in relation to the support for and criminalisation of particular behaviours, but also, the circumstances deemed relevant in the prevention and suppression of criminal activities vary according to the theoretical position adopted, and their respective assumptions regarding human nature and the underlying causes of crime.

> Men make their own history, but they do not make it just as they please; they do not make it under circumstances chosen by themselves, but under circumstances directly encountered, given and transmitted from the past. The tradition of all the dead generations weighs like a nightmare on the brain of the living.
>
> (Marx, 1962: 247, cited in Gray, 2012: 14)

Marx's frequently cited quote directs attention to the need for students and theorists of 'the present' to contextualise phenomena under investigation in relation to the specific political, socio-cultural, economic, technological and historical circumstances (see also Foucault, 1975). National laws, global prohibition regimes, crime and security infrastructures and even aspects of globalisation do not occur by themselves, but rather are social products, embedded within political, social and moral processes. Context is therefore vital to their understanding and provides us with potential navigation aids or heuristic devices to explain and understand their emergence, development and evolution. With this in mind, this chapter will serve as a forerunner to Chapter 3, which will introduce students to a range of (historically contextualised) theoretical perspectives which have been viewed as offering insight into the emergence of cross-border crime, international crime and terrorism, and have also been used to account for the ever-expanding international crime control and security infrastructure.

National, regional and international enforcement efforts directed towards the suppression of the African slave trade, piracy, genocide, drug trafficking, human trafficking, arms trafficking, cyber-crime and terrorism each have their own history. The decision to prioritise each of these areas, to conceptualise such behaviours as significant threats to national, regional and international security and to respond through the negotiation of treaties, legislative frameworks and (informal and formal) international cooperative arrangements and regimes, may be viewed differently according to the theoretical lens through which they are viewed.

Following Andreas and Nadelmann (2006), and in anticipation of the next chapter, it is important to note at this stage that the perceived increasing effectiveness, penetration and consolidation of the transnational crime control infrastructure has, traditionally, been viewed as evidence of progress, namely, as a response to the crime control challenges posed by aspects of globalisation within the latest historical phase, defined by some as late-modernity (Naim, 2002). Viewed in this way, it is possible to analyse particular crime problems, identify their constitutive parts and design more effective interventions aimed towards opportunity reduction and risk enhancement, with a view to deterring such crimes, making them more difficult to complete and enhancing the likelihood of perpetrators being detected and prosecuted. As will be demonstrated in Chapter 3, this approach is associated with the classical school within criminology, and with opportunity theory and rational choice perspectives, which are also aligned with the liberal institutional perspective within international relations. Hence, the focus here is upon the promotion and support of cooperation arrangements and the development of institutions as a means to respond to the various problems generated by the increasing interdependence of states and as a way to manage the processes of globalisation. Enhancing governance arrangements, improving legislative frameworks, police and security cooperation mechanisms, regional and international organisations, bodies and agencies, has therefore been regarded as the appropriate focus for attention in the fight against transnational criminal actors. This view, described by Andreas and Nadelmann as 'the standard view of globalisation', is consistent with the liberal internationalist perspective of Ikenberry (2009), which emphasises cooperative security and collective problem solving, alongside the strengthening of international institutions and the rule of law, as progressive solutions to the security challenges faced by states today.

As will be seen in the chapters that follow, these approaches currently dominate national, regional and international strategies, policies and enforcement efforts directed towards the eradication of transnational and international crimes. However, frequently devoid of contextual reference, critical scholarship spanning a range of academic disciplines has recently called into question this dominant policy response, reconceptualising such approaches as social control mechanisms, directed towards maintaining the status quo in relation to the maintenance of current institutions and regimes underpinning the current international system and world order (Goldsmith and Sheptycki, 2007; Findlay, 2008; Sheptycki, 2000; Andreas and Nadelmann, 2006; Deflem, 2011; Aas, 2007).

Such contributions sensitise readers to the fact that issues of power, inequality between states and the historical legacy of imperialism, colonialism, and capitalism are more often than not absent within these dominant narratives. In contrast, critical approaches aimed at the reform of the current global institutional order, seeking to address global poverty and redressing colonial actions and gendered, race and class hierarchies of the past, interpret current transnational crime control trends in a very different way. The identification, contextualisation and evaluation of these theoretical approaches derived from within sociology, criminology, international relations, international political economy and feminist thought will be the focus for the chapter which follows. First, however, we move towards an examination of slavery and piracy as forerunners to later international crime control efforts.

Colonialisation, slavery and piracy

Slavery

Slavery and the slave trade predate the arrival of Europeans on the west coast of Africa (Agozino, 2005: 121) and have existed since antiquity (Felson and Kalaitzidis, 2005: 7). While until a few centuries ago both practices were 'legal and commonplace features of society and commerce throughout the world' (Andreas and Nadelmann, 2006: 27), academics generally agree that the trade was restricted by geography. According to Felson and Kalaitzidis, having virtually disappeared from the European continent, slavery re-emerged after 1500 initiated by the conquest of the Americas in the sixteenth century. Drawing upon the work of Thomas (1997), Felson and Kalaitzidis note that Spain under King Ferdinand was the first European power to give permission to transfer slaves, shortly followed by the Portuguese, Dutch, French and British, with the latter granting a charter to the Royal African Company to deal in slaves in 1672. Agozino (2005: 121) in contrast argues that it was the Portuguese who were the first to arrive on the coast of Africa in the late fifteenth century. Consequently, while disagreement remains regarding the precise timing and the particular nation initiating the African slave trade it is commonly asserted that at that time barriers remained, constricting the spread of the trade.

The expansion and acceleration of the slave trade has been explained in relation to the development of the plantation economy in the so-called 'New World', which has been viewed as creating a huge market for slaves (Agozino, 2005: 121). Hardt and Negri (2001: 121) suggest that large-scale plantation production with slave labour was initiated in the Caribbean in the mid-seventeenth century by English and French planters who imported African slaves to replace native peoples killed by European weapons and disease. During the seventeenth and eighteenth centuries, the potential areas of supply increased as Europeans established more trading enclaves along the coast (Agozino, 2005: 121) and as European governments acquired a strong interest in developing the transatlantic slave trade, viewing black Africa as a limitless source of labour for the plantations and mines of the Americas (Andreas and Nadelmann, 2006: 27). Andreas and Nadelmann, drawing upon the work of Craton (1974) and Curtin (1969), note that, following the signing of the Peace of Utrecht in 1713, British slavers assumed a dominant role in the highly profitable trade, transporting a substantial portion of the estimated 10 million black Africans ultimately imported into the Americas (Andreas and Nadelmann, 2006: 27). By the end of the eighteenth century, the products of slave labour in the Americas have been estimated to constitute one-third of the value of European commerce (Hardt and Negri, 2001: 121).

The existence of slavery, the slave trade, and its eventual suppression (however incomplete) raise a number of interesting questions for international relations scholars, criminologists, and social and political theorists. Historical accounts detail initial (and sometimes prolonged) governmental support, eventual criminalisation and efforts directed towards enforcement. For example, concerned with the internationalisation of US law enforcement and the emergence of global prohibition regimes, Nadelmann's frequently cited 1993 *Cops Across Borders* and Andreas and Nadelmann's 2006 *Policing the Globe* meticulously chart US efforts to suppress the trade through the introduction of legislation, naval enforcement and efforts to recover fugitive slaves from Florida, Canada and Mexico, through the negotiation of extradition treaties. These scholarly contributions emphasise the difficulties encountered in international law enforcement, highlighting the existence of competing and fluctuating interests both within and between states, the reliance upon military action and the multiplicity of public and private actors involved in law enforcement efforts to suppress illicit slaving and recover fugitive slaves. This work therefore problematises overly deterministic accounts, which view the suppression of slavery as an inevitable consequence of modernity and, also, reveal the inadequacy of state-centric approaches within international relations literature.

Presented as relatively detached from the more intensive international interactions within European states, the lack of US involvement in international policing activities has been accounted for in relation to its geography, transportation and communication systems, which, in the nineteenth century, were not considered sufficiently advanced to bridge the huge distance between America and the world's other continents effectively (Deflem, 2011: 84). For example, in 1890 a conference in Brussels led to the creation of coordination offices in Zanzibar and Brussels to oversee the enforcement of an international agreement outlawing the slave trade and African slavery. Significantly, as argued by Deflem (2011: 85), the United States did not participate in this early international cooperation initiative, content with law enforcement within its own borders and those of its immediate neighbours.

Most historical accounts of African slavery in the criminological literature chart the criminalisation of the slave trade in 1807 following the signing of an 'Act to Prohibit the Importation of Slaves into any Port or Place Within the Jurisdiction of the United States' by President Jefferson (Nadelmann 1993: 31–46; Deflem, 2011: 79). Despite the incremental development of a legislative framework, scholars observe the difficulties and challenges of enforcement recognising that 'enforcement was generally lacking' with the law rejected by Southern politicians and 'repeatedly violated by entrepreneurs all along the eastern and southern seaboard' (Nadelmann, 1993: 31–33). Thus, although British delegates to the Paris Peace Conference of 1814–15, the Congress of Vienna in 1815, and the Congress of Verona in 1822, articulated Britain's desire for multi-lateral condemnation of the slave trade (Andreas and Nadelmann, 2006: 28), authors have noted that the declaration failed to include practical enforcement mechanisms and funding arrangements to bring about the abolition of the slave trade (Bassiouni, 1991, cited in Felson and Kalaitzidis, 2005: 8; Nadelmann 1993: 32). Moreover, while the British Parliament made the slave trade illegal at home, the suppression of slavery within its colonies occurred much later – in the British West Indies in 1838 and British India in 1843 (Bassiouni, 1991, cited in Felson and Kalaitzidis, 2005: 8), highlighting the unevenness of suppression activities. In the United States, although periodic crackdowns on the African slave trade did occur, the prohibition was only minimally and irregularly enforced, certainly, until after the ratification of the Thirteenth Amendment to the US Constitution. Moreover, as noted by Deflem, most cross-border police activity involving Southern slave patrols entailed the pursuit of fugitive slaves who had escaped to free states and foreign jurisdictions where slavery was prohibited (Deflem (2011: 79). Slave patrols were also reportedly tasked with instilling discipline among slaves on plantations and preventing slave insurrections, an observation that reveals that the priorities of enforcement lay with slave owners rather than the enforcement requirements of abolitionists of the slave trade. Prior to the Civil War, international initiatives with the USA entailed unilateral work in the form of US agents working abroad or bilateral forms of cooperation between the United States and its two neighbouring states, Mexico and Canada (Deflem 2011: 85). Enforcement activities were consequently primarily concerned with the recovery of fugitive slaves (as property), rather than with tackling the illicit trade in slaves *per se*.

Moral entrepreneurs, the Enlightenment and modernity

Efforts to explain the existence, development and abolition of slavery have introduced previously neglected actors into the field of inquiry and have resulted in challenges to dominant theories within international relations resulting in a rejection of state-centric approaches that retain the idea that nation-states are always the key actors within international relations. Thus, historians and political scientists have emphasised the role of moral entrepreneurs in driving Britain's reversal on slavery and its subsequent efforts to suppress the slave trade (Andreas and Nadelmann, 2006: 28). Andreas and Nadelmann, for example, highlight the influence of radical Quakers and key individuals including Granville Sharp, William Wilberforce, David Livingstone and Joseph Cooper, in 'applying domestic political pressure on legislators and other government officials and, by influencing the personal moral views of Britain's leaders and high officials', and also in relation to prompting the creation of anti-slavery societies abroad (Andreas and Nadelmann, 2006: 29–30).

Conventional perspectives stress the significance of moral norms presenting the eventual abolition of slavery as evidence of moral progress and modernisation. As noted by Pogge (2008: 2), 'Slavery, autocracy, colonialism, and genocide – practiced openly in the eighteenth and nineteenth centuries and for millennia before – are now outlawed and widely regarded as paradigms of injustice'. Associated with this observation is the view that slavery comprised a form of pre-capitalist production, hence the final banning of the Atlantic slave trade during the first two decades of the nineteenth century is regarded as signalling a new 'progressive' approach to tropical Africa (Agozino, 2005: 121), with the capitalist ideology of freedom viewed as a progressive force of enlightenment leading to the replacement of slavery. However, this perspective has been challenged, with critical scholars calling into question the assumption that slavery comprised a pre-existing form of production and that capitalism was antithetical to slavery. Hardt and Negri (2011: 73) for example, contend that 'Capital's relationship to colonial slavery' is in fact 'much more intimate and complex'. Thus, for Hardt and Negri, the large-scale colonial slave production system, which arose in the Americas between the late seventeenth and mid-nineteenth centuries, should not be viewed as pre-capitalist, but instead, should be understood as part of the complex and contradictory developments of capital. Slave production in the Americas and the African slave trade are therefore reconceptualised as 'a pedestal of super exploitation on which European capitalism stood' (Hardt and Negri, 2001: 122). Citing Marx, Hardt and Negri (2011: 73) emphasise the integral nature of slavery to the development of capitalism and the associated rise of European supremacy conceived as driven in large part by the development and spread of capitalism:

> Without slavery there would be no cotton, without cotton there would be no modern industry. It is slavery which has given value to the colonies, it

> is the colonies which have created world trade, and world trade is the necessary condition of large-scale machine industry.
>
> (Marx, 1982, cited by Hardt and Negri, 2011: 73)

Challenging approaches which view the prohibition against slavery and capitalist production as progressive, Hardt and Negri assert that 'while capitalism's ideology is antithetical to slavery, in practice, capital not only subsumed and reinforced existing slave production systems throughout the world, but also created new systems of slavery on an unprecedented scale' (Hardt and Negri, 2001: 122). In an examination of the legacy of slavery for colonialism and capitalist development, Agozino (2005: 122), similarly, notes the existence of an abolitionist desire for slavery to become gradually replaced by legitimate trade, a position further accepted by Andreas and Nadelmann (2006: 32) who reflect upon the importance of the emergence of other forms of labour for the eradication of slavery, including the employment of former slaves under conditions not much different from their former status, in addition to the importation of wage labourers from abroad, penal servitude, and other types of forced labour. Thus, while for some theorists of slavery the replacement of slavery by other legal and social institutions is regarded as evidence of progress and enlightenment associated with the development of capitalism and modernity, for other critical theorists slave labour enabled capitalism and was in fact an inherent aspect of its development (Andreas and Nadelmann, 2006: 32). Hardt and Negri (2011: 74) conclude that 'without coloniality there is no modernity', viewing modernity, coloniality and racism as a complex, with each serving as a necessary support for the others, each performing constitutive roles within society.

Critical theorists therefore refuse to interpret the eventual suppression of slavery and the African slave trade as the result of successful moral campaigning and enlightenment. As argued by Pogge (2008: 4), 'colonialism, slavery, and the subjection of women, together with the moralities condoning them, endured while they fostered technological growth and were abolished in law when they obstructed newly accessible, more effective ways of combining the factors of production thorough market institutions'. Alternative approaches have consequently moved to examine other factors influencing the enforcement and non-enforcement of the international prohibition against slavery. Thus, while Andreas and Nadelmann (2006: 31) argue it is impossible to explain the abolition of slavery throughout the world without emphasising the powerful role of shared moral notions derived primarily from the religious and secular principles of the Enlightenment, they themselves, alongside a host of other critical theorists, are keen to point out that neither moral arguments at home, nor calculations of profitability abroad could move European capital to dismantle the slave regimes (Hardt and Negri, 2001: 123). Scholars have therefore directed attention to other factors motivating the shift in position by the United Kingdom and other leading slaving nations, such as Britain's increasing commercial and military influence in the eighteenth and nineteenth centuries, in addition to the emergence of new economic ideas and its reduced commercial need for slaves (Felson and Kalaitzidis, 2005: 8).

Historical scholars have also been interested in accounting for the behaviour of states in responding to British demands to eradicate the slave trade globally, pointing to the willingness of the British to use their diplomatic, economic and military resources to suppress slavery, utilising the Royal Navy during the 1840s as an international police force (Nadelmann, 1990 cited in Felson and Kalaitzidis, 2005: 8; Andreas and Nadelmann, 2006: 27). Moral imperatives to acquiesce to Britain's demands were therefore considered to be by no means universal, with other considerations frequently motivating compliance including: monetary and territorial compensation, calculations of trade advantages and/or political advantage, alongside fear of incurring British wrath (Andreas and Nadelmann, 2006: 29). Consequently, while some scholarly research examines motivations and incentives for compliance, other work has explored non-compliance and resistance, identifying the possession of military power, and state interest as explanatory factors in accounting for the defiant actions of the Ottoman Empire, France and the United States, who were viewed as less susceptible to British coercion than Brazilian and black African rulers (Andreas and Nadelmann, 2006: 29).

Issues of power and a focus upon international relations have consequently enabled theorists such as Nadelmann to examine non-cooperation and proactive encouragement of slaves to seek refuge within state territories as potential tools of statecraft, intentionally seeking to weaken competitors economically and to strengthen national efforts towards state-building. Nadelmann examines, for example, the US Congress's refusal to allow British Royal Navy searches of vessels flying the American flag for suspected involvement in the illicit slave trade (Nadelmann, 1993: 31–33), also highlighting Spanish efforts to entice British slaves to Florida and incitement of desertions from plantations as a means to harm their enemy and to strengthen their own colony (Nadelmann, 1993: 34–36). These examples, together with Mexican and Canadian examples of resistance, including efforts to lure slaves across the border and refusals to return fugitive slaves, are further presented as evidence of the prohibition of slavery being used as a weapon for checking the growing influence of North Americans. Thus, while humanitarian imperatives, domestic and international moral condemnation and isolation may certainly be seen to have played a part in the strengthened efforts directed towards the suppression of slavery and the African slave trade, research has also served to highlight the significance of power, state interest and the dynamics of the international political system within the eighteenth, nineteenth and early twentieth centuries. Authors working within this area have consequently directed attention to the role of resistance and revolution on the part of slaves themselves, in instigating the direction of change. Citing the examples of the Civil War in the United States, and the Haitian revolution, Andreas and Nadelmann (2006: 31) and Hardt and Negri (2001: 123) present these events as watershed moments within the history of slave revolt, making slavery untenable and unprofitable as a form of production and opening the way for the development of alternative forms of domination and exploitation to emerge (Hardt and Negri, 2011: 76).

The issue of slavery and the slave trade has also raised questions regarding the mechanisms and rhetorical devices, which enabled such abhorrent practices to take place. Cohen's (2001) *States of Denial* and Sykes and Matza's (1957) 'Techniques of Neutralization', while not focusing specifically upon slavery, are useful criminological studies in this regard, directing attention to the existence of a range of techniques of neutralisation which are critical in lessening the effectiveness of social controls, rendering social deviances possible and shielding individuals from internalised values. This work has been supplemented more recently by Ruggiero's (2013) *The Crimes of the Economy*, which examines the justificatory narratives of colonisers arguing that classical economic thought rationalises and neutralises the social harm it causes. Critiquing economic accounts that present social harm as intrinsic and necessary to economic initiative and prosperity and in particular, the harms associated with the slave trade as a necessary precursor to capitalist development and European domination, Ruggiero suggests that classical economic thought, devoid of ethical constraint, has served to rationalise, neutralise and cover up victimisation and marginalisation of entire populations. This body of work alongside literature within critical race theory, post-structural feminism and post-colonial scholarship have sought to highlight the legacy of colonial actions, shedding light upon injustices faced by excluded groups and bringing into focus relations of gender, race, culture, inequality, exploitation and colonialisation. Contributing to the theorisation of the present, scholars working within this expanding field present the current era as post-colonial (building upon the current 'globalisation' literature), emphasising the persistence of colonial patterns of trade, governance and social relations in contemporary society (Sylvester, 2014: 184–197).

Examining the relationship between the slave trade, colonialisation, capitalism and the European rise to power, Agozino (2005) describes the transformation which occurred following British enforcement of the global prohibition against the slave trade, detailing how coastal chiefs were persuaded to accept 'protection' and, in some cases, financial compensation in return for abandoning the slave trade and turning over small trading enclaves to one or another of the European powers (Agozino, 2005: 121). The 'Scramble to Africa' and the later process of decolonialisation and independence are therefore regarded as significant for understanding present day relations. Similarly, for Pogge (2008: 6), while (for the most part) the affluent Western states are no longer practising slavery, colonialism, or genocide, the present circumstances of the global poor are considered to have been significantly shaped by the historical processes of conquest and colonialisation – a process which is viewed as destroying the native institutions and cultures of four continents. Pogge consequently calls into question what he describes as 'two common prejudices', namely '(1) that the persistence of severe poverty abroad does not require our moral attention, and (2) that there is nothing seriously wrong with our conduct, our policies, and the global economic institutions we forge and uphold' (Pogge, 2008: 7). In a world in which Western states retain economic, political and military dominance over less developed states, Pogge challenges the moral disconnection and narratives of denial of his Western readership, powerfully arguing that such a 'morally deeply tarnished history should not be allowed to result in radical inequality' (Pogge, 2008: 209). While Western states now pay native rulers and 'elites' for imports, including the reliance upon natural resources and energy supplies, many people remain desperately poor and oppressed. Pogge consequently advocates global institutional reform challenging the citizens of the more powerful countries to bear the collective responsibility for their governments' role in designing and imposing an unjust global order and for their governments' failure to reform it towards greater human rights fulfilment (Pogge, 2008: 179). Viewed in this way, the evolving transnational criminal justice and security infrastructure, which has been tasked with the suppression of transnational and international crime, may in fact be seen as part of the problem. Such institutions are consequently viewed as reflecting dominant state interests serving to perpetuate inequalities and global injustices, raising questions regarding those who have the power to set national, regional and global crime control and security agendas, and imposing upon those who are the focus for enforcement efforts. This work therefore directs attention towards the particular social, political, economic and historical circumstances in which criminalisation processes, and criminal justice and security regimes occur, challenging liberal economic assumptions regarding the inevitability of social progress and economic prosperity linked to modernity.

Seeking redress for social injustices, Hudson's (2006) article entitled 'Beyond White Man's Justice: Race, Gender and Justice in Late Modernity' advocated the development of a 'reflective justice' approach to justice, challenging contemporary criminal justice practices which abstract circumstances from wider social structures and social inequalities. For Hudson, reflective justice entails situating particular circumstances in their wider social context rather than only considering the restricted range of legal categories of crimes, aggravations and mitigations, which are viewed as functioning to abstract individuals from wider inequalities and oppressions. Without wishing to dilute or deflect acknowledgement regarding the wrongness of an act, Hudson advocates a form of justice which allows for an openness of discourse and the admission of all relevant considerations and circumstances, reflecting post-colonial and post-structural feminist efforts to grant a voice to colonialised and exploited peoples, identifying and challenging mechanisms of colonial control and the perpetuation of relations of power and domination.

One final strand of literature takes forward this theme of continuity and change, further emphasising the links between slavery, colonialism, capitalism and modernity, paying particular attention to continuity within penal systems over time. Here, scholars such as Sellin (1976) have emphasised similarities in patterns of control and exploitation between the slave trade and convict trade, critically examining practices of slavery, transportation, convict leasing, chain gangs and prison farms. This work examines the continued resemblance of modern penal systems to slavery, emphasising how colonial conditions of the past have continued to influence contemporary penal practice, challenging the interpretation of penal developments as evidence of progress and modernity with perspectives that identify changing manifestations of racism, colonial exploitation and social control within the penal practices of today (see also Foucault, 1975). Wacquant (2000), for example, examines continuity within an institutional complex comprising several 'peculiar institutions' which have operated to 'define, confine, and control' African-Americans in the history of the United States, including chattel slavery from the colonial era to the Civil War; the Jim Crow system in the agrarian South from Reconstruction to the Civil Rights revolution; the ghetto in the northern industrial metropolis; and, in the post-Keynesian age of desocialised wage labour and welfare retrenchment. These works therefore highlight and theorise the legacy of colonialism for penology, transnational policing and the policing of ethnic minorities within economically advanced and economically disadvantaged nations.

To summarise, this section has briefly introduced a selection of slavery scholarship emerging from within criminological and international relations literature. Commencing with a discussion regarding the emergence and expansion of the African slave trade and the subsequent creation of a global prohibition regime and legislative framework directed at the suppression of slavery and the trade in slaves, we moved to discuss challenges in enforcement and US engagement, both in relation to the eradication of the slave trade and efforts directed towards the recovery of fugitive slaves. Andreas and Nadelmann's (2006) inclusion of moral entrepreneurs as non-governmental actors who are significant in influencing world politics, and their sensitivity to the role played by particular individuals and groups in the development of global prohibition regimes, call into question state-centric approaches to the study of slavery. Such work also highlights the contingent, fragile and constructed nature of law enforcement infrastructures and also serves to raise questions regarding the significance of interest and power in agenda setting and enforcement processes.

While academics have tended to present the eventual suppression of slavery and the advent of capitalism as evidence of progress and enlightenment, it is clear to see that a new stream of analysis has emerged that examines the interpenetration of slavery and colonialisation with capitalism and the continuing legacy of colonial relations upon the present world order. Conceived as an era of globalisation, and more recently as a period of post-colonialism, the contemporary era is evidently regarded as signifying lingering hierarchies and relations which may be observed within colonial discourses and representations, penal complexes and architectures of justice. Later critical race theorists, post-colonial theorists, post-structural feminist theorists and critical criminologists, have therefore questioned the notion that slavery is pre-capitalist and its suppression evidence of moral progress. As a forerunner and model for the development of subsequent global prohibition regimes, discussions of slavery have charted the emergence of diplomatic devices signalling the more effective application of global justice, including the imposition of economic sanctions in peace time, both as an individual deterrent (punishing those countries that refused to abolish the slave trade), and as a general deterrent (signalling to other states what may happen to them if they followed suit), alongside the creation of a multinational oversight committee to monitor compliance with international agreements (Nicolson, 1946, cited in Andreas and Nadelmann, 2006: 28). Influenced by classical criminological assumptions regarding the rational actor, scholars continue to identify the rewards and motivations of slavers and the cost–benefit calculations of actors in their decisions to criminalise and suppress the global trade in slaves or as perpetrators of the illicit slave trade. Attention is therefore directed towards effective deterrents, in relation to the prevention of slaves from attempting escape, and against those involved in the perpetration of illicit slave trading, through controls, formal and informal procedures directed towards the recovery and punishment of slaves, including the negotiation of extradition agreements, domestic legislation and bilateral arrangements between states and/or officials.

While useful, such approaches, which, emphasise opportunity reduction and risk enhancement, frequently fail to contextualise criminal and deviant acts within their wider social, political and historical context. The more recent critical scholarship therefore provides a useful addition to this traditional focus, placing emphasis upon wider social structures, social inequalities and the continuities of colonial actions in the Third World with the present. This emphasis upon social and economic development and the significance of international relations within the current world political order, may similarly be seen to add new and previously neglected dimensions to the study of piracy, which like the initial regime to ban the slave trade, became institutionalised through the signing of international conventions, similarly reflecting changing state positions and allegiances, moral entrepreneurial actions and criminalisation.

Piracy

Like slavery, piracy has existed since ancient times. Felson and Kalaitzidis (2005: 9), for example, drawing upon the work of De Souza (1999), note that piracy was the subject of Homeric poems dating around the seventh or eighth centuries BC and has also been implicated in the creation of the Delian League in 478 BC which comprised an alliance of coastal and Aegean city-states directed against Persia. This association, we are informed, was originally motivated by a collective concern over piracy, eventually developing into the Athenian Empire that challenged Sparta in the Peloponnesian War, thereby representing early efforts towards city-state cooperation against commonly defined security threats.

As with slavery and the slave trade, it is evident that academic commentators have viewed piracy as intimately associated with the formation, preservation, undermining and strengthening of state power and empire building. Piracy has therefore been conceptualised as both an internal and external security issue, entailing both a challenge to states (and the safety of their citizens), and also, historically being used as a tool of statecraft directed against their enemies. Indeed, as argued by Andreas and Nadelmann (2006: 22), piracy was 'widely sanctioned in much of the world with kings, princes, sultans, and assorted other political magnates viewing piracy as a source of wealth and political power' (see also Vagg, 1995). As a tool of statecraft, piracy was utilised to accumulate wealth, and also, as a means of undermining the strength of competitors. Thus for the Spartans, piracy formed an instrument of state policy explicitly seeking to weaken its Athenian opponent (Felson and Kalaitzidis, 2005: 9).

The common practice of privateering involved the employment of private sea vessels to assist in attacks against opponents, with states receiving a share of the proceeds from such activities. This officially sanctioned version of piracy was applied towards state enemies and anyone engaging in trading with its enemies (Andreas and Nadelmann, 2006: 22). From the ninth century, a Muslim Mediterranean state, the Emirate of Crete (which existed from the late 820s to 961), gave safe haven to the Mediterranean corsair fleets who were known for ravaging the Byzantine-controlled shores of the Aegean Sea. Later examples include the English support for privateering against the French during the 1200s, and against Spain after 1500 (Felson and Kalaitzidis, 2005: 9).

Piracy has therefore been linked to state competition for the amassing of wealth, territorial expansion and access and control over trade routes. Piracy followed the trading patterns set by Spain, Britain, and the other colonial powers, and was concentrated around the Caribbean, the Atlantic seaboard of America, the English Channel, and later the coast of West Africa (Vagg, 1995), with (as will be seen shortly) the safety of commercial maritime routes remaining prioritised today in anti-piracy control efforts. According to Andreas and Nadelmann (2006: 22), the expansion of European maritime commerce in the sixteenth century increased the rewards and the incidence of piracy dramatically, with much of it officially or unofficially sponsored by European governments with colonial governors, directed not to interfere with pirates by the French, British and United States governments, offering safe harbour in return for a share of their goods (Andreas and Nadelmann, 2006: 22).

Associated with the expansion of the Ottoman Empire, from the sixteenth century, Barbary pirates operating in the western Mediterranean seized ships and engaged in raids against English and other European shipping along the north coast of Africa (Felson and Kalaitzidis, 2005). In the seventeenth century, Turkish corsairs expanded their piratical activities from the Mediterranean to the Atlantic prompting the French, Spanish, Dutch and English to send fleets against the pirate bases in North Africa between 1609 and 1620. Consequently, according to Andreas and Nadelmann (2006: 23), 'In a Europe strongly divided by political and religious difference, the one objective on which all Christian nations were agreed was the desirability of crushing the Turkish pirates', thereby 'transcending their own powerful disputes to unite against a more feared common enemy'.

Trends in piracy were also associated with conflict resolution. Thus, Gosse (1946) and Rule (1977), cited in Vagg (1995), suggested that the numbers of pirates in the western world tended to increase following the discharge of superfluous sailors from navies after the resolution of disputes. Able to supply goods at reduced prices, piracy flourished, these authors suggest, receiving widespread support from local magistrates, other officials and local inhabitants who were frequently involved in piracy and wrecking between the sixteenth and eighteenth centuries.

Consequently, while colonial governors and local officials actively supported or turned a blind eye to piratical activities, often lacking the capacity to affect the practice in any significant way, by the end of the seventeenth century the perceived benefits of piracy were called into question as trade and diplomacy increased, and as governments sought to establish stable commercial relations (Felson and Kalaitzidis, 2005: 10). If prior to the seventeenth century, 'international norms proscribing banditry on the high seas remained limited' (Andreas and Nadelmann, 2006: 23–24), the seventeenth century witnessed increased internal and external state control, strengthened navies and targeted British, American and Dutch action directed towards the eradication of piracy, resulting in a reconceptualisation of such activities as an 'international threat', subject to widespread criminalisation (Felson and Kalaitzidis, 2005: 10). As argued by Vagg (1995: 65), citing the work of Gosse (1946) and Mitchell (1976), with the exception of states controlled by warlords (e.g. North Africa during the 1500s, Malaysia and China until the nineteenth century), 'the history of piracy suggests that it can only flourish when and where the authorities allow it, either in the furtherance of national interests or because local or provincial officials are corrupt'. The British Royal Navy was therefore considered pivotal in driving efforts towards the eradication of piracy, seeking to protect their growing empire and introducing norms in both the domestic and international spheres (Williams, 1961, cited in Felson and Kalaitzidis, 2005: 10), resulting in a virtual ban by the mid-eighteenth century. Furthermore, in accounting for the marked reduction in piracy by the middle of the nineteenth century, in addition to the significance of state control of sea-lanes and officials, Vagg (1995: 67) directs attention to the importance of state infrastructure, particularly highlighting improvements made to roads, which, were recognised as 'decisively' changing 'the transport patterns on which piracy depended', with consequences for the introduction of effective policing.

While efforts directed towards the abolition of privateering commenced during the nineteenth century, Andreas and Nadelmann note that the delegitimisation of government sanctioned piracy took much longer to achieve with the USA refusing to sign the Declaration of Paris due to its reliance upon privateers to support its diminutive navy. Consequently, it was only following the growth of the US Navy at the end of the century that the US government finally legislated against the practice (2006: 24–25). It is significant therefore, that having benefited from acts of piracy, key proponents were pivotal in redefining it, generating moral condemnation and eventually pursuing the development of a legal framework against the practice. By the end of the nineteenth century, as noted by Andreas and Nadelmann (2006: 25), 'a once customary form of waging war had been all but eliminated from the face of the earth'. Piracy in European and North Atlantic waters was virtually extinguished coinciding with the advent of the modern nation-state, and attempts to end practices which came to be regarded as official corruption (Vagg, 1995: 65).

As with the previous consideration of slavery, the decision to engage with or to ignore the rich historical contextualisation of piracy will have implications for the way in which we perceive and respond to the practice, to our theoretical preferences and our object of study. In the following chapter a range of sociological, criminological and international relations perspectives will be introduced, some of which engage with historical lessons; the dynamics of the international political system; issues of power and inequality, and some of which do not, preferring to focus upon immediate preventative measures, risk reduction and deterrence. In anticipation of these approaches and their utility for understanding, explaining and responding to piratical activities, we shall now move to address contemporary forms of piracy and efforts to contain it. In doing so, several themes which will be recurrent throughout the text will be introduced, including the link between national and international security; the relationship between crime types and broader categories of harm; assumptions underpinning the selection of crime prevention methods; the key actors involved in crime control responses; and the effectiveness or adequacy (and omissions) of current law enforcement and security approaches.

Contemporary piracy

While most academic commentators agree that the nineteenth century observed a marked reduction in piratical activities, there were of course exceptions, and significantly, a number of scholars have argued that more recently we have witnessed a resurgence, with implications for international peace and stability in different regions of the world. Andreas and Nadelmann (2006: 26), for example, suggest that the increasing prominence of piracy as an international law enforcement concern reflects 'growing worries over the potent nexus between piracy and terrorism', with others directing attention towards the association of piracy with other forms of maritime crime, transnational organised crime, including illicit weapons and drug trafficking, corruption and illegal immigration (UN Resolution 2039, 2012; UN Resolution 2020, 2011; Twyman-Ghoshal and Pierce, 2014; Abhyankar, 2005; Vagg, 1995). More recently, concerns have been raised in relation to the association of piracy with the sexual exploitation of women and girls and the recruitment of children in piracy and related activities (UN Resolution

2184, 2014), thereby emphasising the inter-related nature of international security threats.

As highlighted above, historically, piracy was employed by both nation-states and private actors for economic gain and has also been criminalised under international and domestic laws (Felson and Kalaitzidis, 2005: 9). Commercial interests were pivotal in providing the motivation for unilateral state action and multi-lateral criminalisation. Within this process, discourses of globalisation and altered conceptions of national, regional and international security have provided an added incentive for international and regional intervention within this area. For example, as a specialised agency of the United Nations, the International Maritime Organization (IMO), which has responsibility for the safety and security of shipping and the prevention of marine pollution by ships, describes today's interconnected and globalised world as characterised by freer movement of people, goods, services and information (IMO, 2014 A 28/Res.1060: 3). This position therefore reflects Andreas and Nadelmann's (2006) 'standard view' discourse, which implicates processes of globalisation in creating opportunities for crime and as a driving force for international crime control responses. Thus, the IMO describes maritime transport as fundamental to world trade and access to global markets, providing considerable economic opportunities to states while at the same time presenting criminal groups with illicit opportunities, reflecting the sentiments regarding globalisation expressed within the US, UK, Council of the European Union and UN security strategies presented in the previous chapter.

With the cost of piracy estimated to have reached between \$7 and \$12 billion per year, including supply side costs to both industry and government (Bowden, 2010, cited in Twyman-Ghoshal and Pierce, 2014: 664), it is therefore perhaps unsurprising that individual nation-states, regional bodies and the international community have stepped up efforts to eradicate piracy, armed robbery at sea and maritime criminality more generally. Employing the 'standard view' position, globalisation processes are consequently viewed as generating illicit opportunities, social control weaknesses and motivations to engage in piracy (Passas and Twyman-Ghoshal, 2012: 62), a position which requires immediate action to close legislative loopholes, build criminal justice infrastructure and strengthen moral consensus and multi-lateral action to eradicate collective security threats.

Definitions of piracy come from several sources. Thus, piracy is defined in Article 101 of the 1982 United Nations Convention on the Law of the Sea (UNCLOS), as:

a any illegal acts of violence or detention, or any act of depredation, committed for private ends by the crew or passengers of a private ship or a private aircraft, and directed:

   i on the high seas, against another ship or aircraft, or against persons or property on board such ship or aircraft;

  ii against a ship, aircraft, persons or property in a place outside the jurisdiction of any State.

b any act of voluntary participation in the operation of a ship or of an aircraft with knowledge of facts making it a pirate ship or aircraft;

c any act of inciting or of intentionally facilitating an act described in subparagraph (a) or (b).

Both the Convention on the Law of the Sea (1982) and the earlier United Nations Convention on the High Seas (1958) define piracy as an attack mounted for private ends on a ship, involving violence, illegal detention of persons or property, or the theft or destruction of goods. However, scholars have pointed to the limitations of such definitions suggesting that the 'private ends' element of the definition excludes from international jurisdiction acts of piracy that are condoned or organised by nation-states, as well as those directed at a state (Halberstam, 1988, cited in Twyman-Ghoshal and Pierce, 2014: 653). Such definitions therefore ignore observations regarding the historical utilisation of piracy as a tool of statecraft and as a means of undermining state power and commercial interests, by both state and non-state actors.

The UNCLOS definition has also been subject to criticism for applying only to the high seas, namely waters outside the territorial limits of any nation, thereby excluding the majority of contemporary piracy incidents that occur in territorial waters of nation-states, also challenging the inclusion of a two ship requirement which excludes attacks that occur while a ship is in dock (Vagg, 1995; Twyman-Ghoshal and Pierce, 2014). In attempting to circumvent the jurisdictional issues identified above, the ICC International Maritime Bureau, which is a specialised division of the International Chamber of Commerce with consultative status to the United Nations (UN), employs a much broader notion of piracy to include: 'any act of boarding any vessel with the intent to commit theft or other crime and with the capability to use force in furtherance of the act' (International Maritime Bureau 1992: 2, cited in Vagg, 1995: 64). Recent research, alongside a range of stakeholders, has subsequently argued that a more adequate approach to piracy would need to be capable of accounting for 'theft and robbery from ships either at sea or at anchor, whether force is used or not', also accounting for 'the kidnapping of persons aboard boats and ships, the taking of whole ships and cargoes', and for the involvement of 'organised crime syndicates, and the seizure of ships and passengers as hostages in terrorist operations' (Vagg, 1995: 64). Others emphasise the additional need to extend the definition to include incidents arising from civil war conflicts (Twyman-Ghoshal and Pierce, 2014: 654). It is evident then that the UNCLOS definition is subject to limitation and has been castigated for effectively excluding many incidents and restricting the development of a full understanding of the subject. This discussion sensitises readers to the blurring of conceptual boundaries and traditional categories, further highlighting the complexity of the topic under investigation. As detailed in

Chapter 1, the recent location of international piracy as an international security threat directs attention to the relationship between recurrent cycles of weak governance, poverty and violence (serving to destabilise the conventional divide between domestic and foreign policy, military and law enforcement action), the relationship between licit and illicit behaviours and between varieties of criminal actions and terrorism.

In endeavouring to clarify the different types of contemporary piracy, Abhyankar (2005) classifies piracy as a particular form of maritime crime and fraud, defined as a 'combination of various acts where one or more parties end up losing money, goods or even the vessel' (Abhyankar, 2005: 158). Within his typology, Abhyankar identifies seven types of maritime crime and fraud, namely: documentary; charter party; insurance; container crime; deviation frauds (involving the theft or misappropriation of cargo by the shipowner); phantom ship frauds; and piracy. Piracy is further sub-divided into: Asian piracy; West African and South American piracy; heinous piracy (involving robbery, murder and rape); hijacking; political piracy and state piracy. While the types themselves contain geographical reference, and allowance is made for the utilisation of state piracy, the categorisations also emphasise the degree (and methods) of violence utilised by the perpetrators, the location of incidents and the target and objective of the offence. Thus, Asian piracy, which is described by Abhyankar as relatively non-violent, involving an intent to take cash from the ship's safe and occurring within the territorial waters of one or the other of two countries (therefore not within international waters), is contrasted against West African and South American piracy. This second type is presented as 'violent', occurring mainly at anchor, targeting cash, cargo, personal effects and ships' equipment. The third type, 'heinous piracy', is used to describe particularly brutal and callous attacks upon refugees such as the Vietnamese boat people, highlighting a disregard for human life and the suffering of victims, while 'political piracy' has been applied to account for piracy occurring in the waters around Somalia.

As previously noted, historical analysis of early manifestations of piratical activities alludes to the political and economic nature of the phenomenon itself and also to the emergence of counter-activities. Somali piracy, as a manifestation of contemporary piracy, has it seems also become recently identified as having political and economic foundations. However, as will be seen, international efforts to prevent piracy through initiatives to tackle socio-structural (economic and political) root causes remain inconsistent and subject to contention, revealing a preference on the part of individual nation-states and of regional and international bodies to employ ahistorical and depoliticised crime prevention strategies, a framework that is repeated in efforts to tackle genocide, human trafficking, terrorism and a range of other transnational and international crimes.

Challenging the traditional 'unitary focus upon clan rivalry as the destructive force fuelling genocidal conflict, state disintegration', and violence (including piracy) in Somalia, Besteman (1999) examines the legacy of slavery, colonialism, imperialism and cold war power politics in shaping the events leading to the collapse of Somali society, and to its contemporary status as a failed state and threat to international security. In an aptly titled book *Unraveling Somalia: Race, Class and the Legacy of Slavery*, Besteman argues that the dissolution of the Somali nation-state can be understood only by analysing Somalia's turbulent history, a history marred by exploitation, resistance, occupation, US and Soviet influence, militarisation and foreign aid. It is a history frequently omitted by international and regional security policy and by mainstream criminological theory.

The International Maritime Bureau (IMB) presents Somali piracy as a recently reduced but continuing threat. With eighteen actual or attempted attacks occurring off the coast of Somalia in 2010, eighty-five in 2011 and twenty-eight in 2012, incidents have markedly declined to a figure of three in 2013, two in 2014, with no further incidents reported within the first quarter of 2015 (ICC-IMB, 2015: 16). Attacks attributed to Somali pirates in the Arabian Sea, Red Sea and Gulf of Aden have also reduced considerably within the same time frame, an achievement attributed to the presence of international navies in containing the threat of Somali piracy within the region, alongside 'increased hardening of vessels and Industry Best Management Practices (BMP4) compliance', and 'the employment of privately contracted armed security personnel'.

International efforts involving collaboration between naval and military forces, international shipping organisations, insurance companies and private vessel tracking companies have consequently tended to concentrate upon what has been termed 'primary crime prevention' within criminological circles, focusing upon the physical environment within which a crime occurs, otherwise known as 'situational methods of crime prevention' (Joyce, 2012: 52–58). Intended to reduce the opportunity for piracy, the BMP4 advice proposes that vessels should enhance watch keeping by providing additional lookouts, shorter rotations of the watch period and placing dummies at strategic locations to give an impression of a higher number of crew onboard. Other precautions include the fortification of the bridge using razor wire; locking all access to doors and hatch; the use of water spray; sounding alarms; using evasive manoeuvring; switching on deck and navigation lights; designating mustering points and citadels and installing closed circuit television (BMP4, 2011, cited in Twyman-Ghoshal and Pierce, 2014: 665).

Anti-piracy measures therefore comprise a form of target hardening or target insulation designed to make it more difficult for perpetrators to successfully conduct attacks against vessels, also seeking to deter individuals from such attempts by introducing initiatives that increase the likelihood of detection and therefore prosecution. Based upon the assumption that pirates are rational actors who consciously weigh up the costs and benefits of their actions, these initiatives seek to enhance the risks (and costs) involved for individuals and groups who may engage in piracy.

Despite the reduction in successful attacks, against the introduction of such measures, research has suggested that piracy continues to adapt with attacks carried out further at sea, targeting moving vessels, increasingly armed, with incidents now as likely to be carried out during the day as at night (Twyman-Ghoshal and Pierce, 2014: 666). Observing notable variation between Indonesian, Bangladeshi, Nigerian and Somali piracy, in terms of readiness to utilise violence and the type of arms employed, with Nigerian and Somali piracy revealing higher levels of threatening behaviour and violence, being armed with automatic weapons and explosives (Twyman-Ghoshal and Pierce, 2014: 661), it also seems that motivations and targets alter over time. Thus, the ICC-IMB Piracy and Armed Robbery Against Ships Report (First Quarter 2014) notes that Somali pirates now sometimes use skiffs launched from mother vessels (often hijacked fishing vessels or dhows) to conduct attacks far from the Somali coast, with the more recent 2015 First Quarter report cautioning against complacency, noting: '[t]he IMB PRC believes that a single successful hijacking of a merchant vessel, will rekindle the Somali pirates' passion to resume its piracy efforts' and reminding vessel owners that as of 31 March 2015, Somali pirates continue to hold twenty-nine crew members for ransom (ICC-IMB, 2015: 16).

If we return to Abhyankar's (2005) typology of maritime crime, we can also see how hijacking may be used to facilitate other forms of crime. Thus, having been hijacked, vessels may subsequently be given a new identity and turned into a phantom ship with a phantom identity, used to commit container crime (comprising the theft of containers, their contents, or part of their contents); charter party frauds (where charters abscond with the entire freight at some point from the loading port to the agreed destination); deviation fraud (which again involves departure from the contract route and the illegal sale of the cargo, sometimes involving insurance fraud by sinking or 'scuttling' vessels to make false insurance claims).

The potential for piracy to morph into further variations of maritime crime and the reliance of false registrations upon documentary fraud and corruption also highlights the potential link between legitimate business practices, maritime crime, official corruption, state complicity, local support and other forms of transnational crime, again emphasising a blurring of contemporary international and regional security threats. Such complexity has led to recent criticism regarding multilateral and international efforts to address piracy, suggesting that such measures have a tendency to focus upon 'short-term solutions' without addressing significant contextual and historical issues. While situational crime prevention approaches are viewed as important and useful, Twyman-Ghoshal and Pierce (2014: 666–669) advocate a broader social approach to crime prevention which seeks to eliminate piracy by tackling its underlying social, political and economic causes. It is significant therefore that the ICC-IMB 2015 First Quarter report also directs attention to the stabilising influence of the government in Somalia.

With this in mind, UN Security Council resolution 2184 (2014) underlined the primary responsibility of the Somali authorities in the fight against piracy and armed robbery at sea off the coast of Somalia, further crediting the Permanent Representative of Somalia, for their willingness to collaborate with other states and regional organisations, and for their participation with regional partners in the 17th plenary session of the Contact Group on Piracy off the Coast of Somalia (CGPCS), in October 2014. Key methods of prevention undertaken by the CGPCS (as cited within the UN resolution) include judicial, penal, and maritime capacity-building efforts, facilitating the prosecution of suspected pirates and disruption activities, directed towards pirate networks ashore and illicit financial flows linked to piracy, in addition to the establishment of a Law Enforcement Task Force, described as an on-going network and mechanism for sharing information and evidence between investigators and prosecutors (UN, 2184, 2014).

In relation to the Somalian example, while Twyman-Ghoshal and Pierce agree that international naval intervention has been extremely important in reducing incidents, these authors also direct attention to what are described as 'equally important governance developments in Somalia', aspects which are often overlooked. Vagg (1995) agrees, emphasising the importance of accounting for the historical linkage between piracy and official corruption, with other critical piracy literature recently shifting analytical focus to address those individuals and groups deemed at risk of offending alongside those who have already offended. Such work consequently examines the 'range of reasons which together must have made piracy an available, feasible, attractive, and rational choice for at least some young males with seafaring experience' (Vagg, 1995: 76); measures conceived as 'secondary' and 'tertiary' crime prevention, respectively (see Joyce, 2012: 52). Vagg's approach therefore simultaneously addresses social crime prevention including addressing the economic context in which piracy occurs. Thus, for Vagg (1995), contemporary piracy occurs mainly in areas that are undergoing rapid economic development, and as such, may be seen as one type of violent crime brought about by the economic and social dislocation attending development, a point similarly made by Passas and Twyman-Ghoshal (2012), who further direct attention to the availability of illicit opportunity structures, motivations and social control weaknesses, alongside geographical suitability (reflecting the modernisation perspective detailed in the next chapter). This position therefore advocates the need to recover a broader social, economic and political view of crime problems and policies, with Vagg highlighting the need for theorists to examine linkages between economic and geographic opportunity, legal provisions, law enforcement, and alternatives to crime, thereby fusing situational crime prevention and social crime prevention measures. This position, however, falls short of the historical analysis of Besteman, with the legacy of slavery, colonialism, imperialism, capitalism and world politics remaining well beyond the remit of investigation.

Somalian piracy: the international response

Since 2008, the United Nations has adopted thirteen resolutions addressing maritime piracy, focusing specifically upon attacks taking place off the coast of Somalia. UN action has been primarily concerned to protect the World Food Programme (WFP) maritime convoys, delivering humanitarian aid to Somalia. Within this context, piracy is regarded as a threat 'to the safety of commercial maritime routes and to international navigation'. Later Resolutions extend the list of threats to include 'other vulnerable ships' (Resolution 1846, 2008), other seafarers and commercial maritime routes (Resolution 2184, 2014), lengthening the range of the piracy threat to include the western Indian Ocean, thereby acknowledging changing targets, location and methods by Somali pirates during the period (Resolution 1897, 2009). By 2011, piracy and armed robbery were explicitly conceived as threats to the security and economic development of states in the region (Resolution 2018, 2011), warranting collective international and regional action.

Reflecting the centrality of situational crime prevention approaches within the international approach to piracy, UN Resolution 1816 (2008) called for increased international cooperation, information sharing and technical assistance to address the issue, including United Nations efforts targeting security, capacity building and joint operations. International and regional efforts have therefore directed attention towards creating a legal framework implementing the UN Convention on the Law of the Sea and the SUA Convention, the United Nations Convention against Transnational Organized Crime and other relevant instruments in order to effectively investigate and prosecute piracy and armed robbery at sea offences. The international response therefore employs a liberal framework, placing faith in the strengthening of international institutions, the rule of law, and cooperative security arrangements as effective means of collective problem solving (Ikenberry, 2009).

However, later UN resolutions supplemented the early focus upon 'strengthening State institutional development', with UN Resolution 1846 (2008), including a focus upon 'peace and stability', 'economic and social development' and 'respect for human rights' and 'the rule of law', factors viewed as necessary precursors serving to create the conditions for 'a full eradication of piracy and armed robbery at sea off the coast of Somalia' (UN Resolution 1846, 2008). In this regard, the incidents of piracy and armed robbery against vessels in the territorial waters of Somalia and the high seas off the coast of Somalia were interpreted by the international community as exacerbating the situation in Somalia, reflecting the enlarged conceptualisation of security discussed within Chapter 1.

Following a ministerial meeting of the Security Council in December 2008 to examine ways to improve international coordination in the fight against piracy and armed robbery off the coast of Somalia, also seeking to ensure that the international community has the proper authorities and tools at its disposal to assist it in these efforts (Resolution 1846, 2008), later resolutions stressed the need for a comprehensive response by the international community to tackle piracy and its underlying causes (Resolution 1950, 2010). This shift reflected the emergence of a more social approach to crime prevention underpinning international responses to Somali piratical activities.

Addressing the political and social context in which Somali piracy has occurred, Twyman-Ghoshal (2014), for example, views Somali piracy as a political act (at least within its infancy). With the first recorded piracy incident off the coast of Somalia occurring in 1991, Twyman-Ghoshal explains the advent of Somali piracy as coinciding with political instability. This situation, it is suggested, resulted from the ousting of President Barre from government, civil war and the subsequent inability to control and regulate foreign marine encroachment of foreign fishing vessels and toxic dumping. Twyman-Ghoshal suggests that this situation led to the growth of a local vigilante response, as unemployed fishermen sought to protect their waters and livelihoods in an act of resistance, defiance and economic necessity.

Reflecting the observations by Twyman-Ghoshal and Pierce (2014) and Vagg (1995), regarding the need to address the social and political roots of crime, and adopting a more social approach to crime prevention, UN Resolution 1838 (2008) and UN Resolution 1976 (2011) also directed attention towards Somalia's rights with respect to offshore natural resources, including fisheries, emphasising the need to investigate allegations of illegal fishing and illegal dumping of toxic substances, both of which had been cited as key motivations by individuals involved in Somali piracy, threatening the livelihood of those involved in the local fishing industry. The resolution also stressed the need to build Somalia's potential for sustainable economic growth as a means to tackle the underlying causes of piracy, including poverty. Facilitating peace and stability, alongside economic and social development within Somalia, consequently became key objectives in UN Resolution 2020 (2011), the solution to which, again, involved the application of a liberal framework, seeking to encourage the strengthening of state institutions, respect for human rights and the rule of law as means to create a durable solution.

With respect to international efforts to eradicate piracy, we can see how links between development and political stability are associated with state vulnerability and susceptibility towards crime, corruption and terrorism, reflecting the broadened conception of security presented within the previous chapter. Thus in May 2014, talking at a conference organised under the auspices of the Critical Maritime Routes programme and funded by the European Union, Marcus Cornaro, Deputy Director-General of the European Commission's EuropeAid, reiterated the need to assist partner countries in addressing the systemic economic and social factors that cause maritime crime, not only in the Horn of Africa, but also in other regions at risk such as the Gulf of Guinea and in South-East Asia (Interpol, 2014).

Global politics and the structure of the global world economy are consequently increasingly acknowledged and emphasised as relevant considerations for anti-piracy efforts, with UN Resolution 2020 (2011) extending the search for social causes of piracy to include the lack of enforcement of the arms embargo established by Resolution 733 (1992), as fuelling the growth of piracy off the coast of Somalia. However, while the earlier UN resolutions advocated investigation into illegal fishing and toxic dumping, representing the emergence of social crime prevention approaches within international responses to piracy, Resolution 2077 (2012), which referred to the report of the Secretary-General (S/2012/783), noted difficulties involved in providing such information in the absence of adequate monitoring or reporting systems. The resolution further stated that the United Nations had to date received little evidence to justify claims that illegal fishing and dumping are factors responsible for forcing Somali youths to resort to piracy, and that there is currently no evidence of toxic waste dumping on land or at sea. The resolution consequently concluded by stating that the concerns previously raised about the protection of the marine environment, in addition to the resourcing constraints mentioned previously, 'should not be allowed to mask the true nature of piracy off the coast of Somalia', thereby rejecting the political nature of Somali piracy.

The most recent UN resolutions in relation to piracy therefore reject the historical, social and political factors evident in the work of Twyman-Ghoshal and Pierce (2014) and Vagg (1995), and continue to neglect the uncomfortable international history of slavery, and of imperial and colonial expansion dating from the sixteenth century onwards, or indeed the consequences of cold war power politics and international intervention, including militarisation and the location of security bases within Somali territory, issues identified by Besteman as integral to an understanding of the current levels of violence within Somali society. The arguments presented within the ICC-IBM reports and UN Security Council resolutions, while raising issues of development and of poverty, eliminate the possibility of serious consideration of the economic structures in which the phenomenon of piracy and associated 'crimes' occur. Indeed, the liberal international economic vision is accepted without question, issues which will be picked up in later chapters. Satisfied with conceptualising Somali piracy as a 'transnational criminal enterprise driven primarily by the opportunity for financial gain' (Resolution 2077, 2012), and influenced by both the discourse of modernisation and the 'standard view' of globalisation, this framework therefore shifts the crime prevention focus once more to situational factors, promoting the implementation of anti-money-laundering laws, the establishment of Financial Investigation Units and strengthening forensic capacities, as tools against international criminal networks involved in piracy. The current approach therefore stresses the need to support the investigation and prosecution of those who illicitly finance, plan, organise, or unlawfully profit from pirate attacks off the coast of Somalia (Resolution 1976, 2011). Within this discourse, social crime prevention concern with social and economic development, critical race theory and post-colonialist attention to the legacy of exploitation and colonialisation for the present are side-lined, while political considerations are defined narrowly in terms of the election of the President and the subsequent appointment of a Prime Minister and Cabinet, developments which are presented as completing the transition in Somalia to a more stable and accountable system of governance. The solution therefore is to embrace the Western liberal vision of democracy, rule of law, human rights and free enterprise as the solution to global peace and prosperity.

Conclusion

Here we have demonstrated how the practices, conceptualisations and responses to slavery and piracy have altered over time with both practices and the enforcement (and non-enforcement) of prohibition regimes conceived as legitimate tools of statecraft, used to strengthen state capacity and undermine the interests of competitor and enemy nations. Both examples serve to highlight the utility of international relations concerns within world politics, emphasising the significance of relations of power between states in the current world order and raising questions regarding the key role played by non-state actors in shaping world affairs within the contemporary era, a period defined by some as an era of globalisation, late-modernity, post-colonialism and post-modernism. Highlighting the significance of interest, and reiterating Andreas and Nadelmann's concern with the importance of moral entrepreneurs affecting the direction and agenda of crime control responses, this chapter has also served to emphasise the emergence of new players in the arena of international crime control, including private corporate players. Within the newly emerging regulatory system, state actors retain their significance, however, now increasingly interacting with intergovernmental organisations, as well as non-state actors such as industry and special interest groups and agencies.

Historical attention to the criminalisation of the slave trade and piracy, to the emergence of global prohibition regimes, to enforcement patterns and sanctions, sheds light upon the many challenges posed by transnational crime control, highlighting areas of continuity between difficulties faced by law enforcement bodies in the past as well as in the present. Issues include scholarly attention to the challenges generated by the application of the notion of sovereignty as the most extensive form of jurisdiction under international law denoting full and unchallengeable power over territory. Crime control efforts have also been concerned with the negotiation and implementation of international conventions and treaties and the creation and enforcement of domestic legislation and extradition arrangements, marking a trend towards homogenisation of criminal laws and the regularisation of law enforcement. Criminological and international relations scholars direct attention to the perfection of situational crime prevention initiatives and the strengthening of cooperative regimes and institutional arrangements. While such an orientation dominates crime and security policy and practice, nationally, regionally and internationally, wider concerns addressing the underlying causes of the slave trade and piracy have come to the fore, advocating the need to contextualise such issues within their wider social structures, social inequalities and oppressions, further directing theoretical attention to the continuing legacy of imperialism, colonialism and capitalism for the conceptualisation of security threats, criminalisation and criminal justice responses to globalisation challenges in the twenty-first century.

The chapter which follows will summarise a selection of key theoretical views which have dominated criminological thought and world politics. The intention will be to give readers a flavour of their key themes and assumptions, identifying areas of similarity and compatibility to enable students to apply these approaches to specific examples of transnational and international crimes and to assess their relative value in helping students to understand and explain contemporary developments within the cross-border crime and security arena.

References

Aas, K.F. (2007). *Globalisation and Crime*. London: Sage Publications.

Abhyankar, J. (2005). 'Maritime Fraud and Piracy', in Williams, P. and Vlassis, D. (eds), *Combating Transnational Crime: Concepts, Activities and Responses*. London: International Scientific and Professional Advisory Council of the United Nations Crime Prevention and Criminal Justice Programme. Pp. 157–194.

Agozino, B. (2005). 'Crime, Criminology and Post-Colonial Theory: Criminologial Reflections on West Africa', in Sheptycki, J.W.E. and Wardak, A. (eds), *Transnational and Comparative Criminology*. Abingdon: GlassHouse Press. Pp. 117–134.

Andreas, P. and Nadelmann, E. (2006). *Policing the Globe: Criminalization and Crime Control in International Relations*. Oxford: Oxford University Press.

Bassiouni, M.C. (1991). 'Enslavement as an International Crime', *International Law and Politics*, 23: 445–517.

Besteman, C. (1999). *Unraveling Somalia: Race, Class, and the Legacy of Slavery*. Philadelphia, PA: University of Pennsylvania Press.

Bowden, A. (2010). *The Economic Cost of Maritime Piracy. One Earth Future*. Available online at: http://oneearthfuture.org/images/imagefiles/The%20Economic%20Cost%20of%20Piracy%20Full%20Report.pdf.

Cohen, S. (2001). *States of Denial: Knowing about Atrocities and Suffering*. Cambridge: Polity Press.

Craton, M. (1974). *Sinews of Empire: A Short History of British Slavery*. Garden City, NY: Anchor Books.

Curtin, P. (1969). *The Atlantic Slave Trade*. Madison, WI: University of Wisconsin Press.

Deflem, M. (2011). *Policing World Society: Historical Foundations of International Police Cooperation*. Oxford: Oxford University Press.

De Souza, P. (1999). *Piracy in the Greco-Roman World*. Cambridge: Cambridge University Press.

Felson, D. and Kalaitzidis, A. (2005). 'A Historical Overview of Transnational Crime', in Reichel, P. (ed.), *Handbook of Transnational Crime and Justice*. London: Sage Publications. Pp. 3–19.

Findlay, M. (2008). *Governing through Globalised Crime*. Cullompton: Willan Publishing.

Foucault, M. (1975). *Discipline and Punish: The Birth of the Prison*. New York: Vintage.

Goldsmith, A. and Sheptycki, J.W.E. (2007). *Crafting Transnational Policing: Police Capacity-Building and Global Policing Reform*. Oxford: Hart Publishing.

Gosse, P. (1946). *The History of Piracy*. New York: Tudor.

Gray, C. (2012). *War, Peace and International Relations*. London: Routledge.

Halberstam, M. (1988). 'Terrorism on the High Seas: The Achille Lauro, Piracy and the IMO Convention on Maritime Safety', *The American Journal of International Law*, 82: 269–310.

Hardt, M. and Negri, A. (2001). *Empire*. London: Harvard University Press.

Hardt, M. and Negri, A. (2011). *Commonwealth*. London: Harvard University Press.

Hudson, B. (2006). 'Beyond White Man's Justice: Race, Gender and Justice in Late Modernity', *Theoretical Criminology*, 10(1): 29–47.

ICC-IMB. (2014). *Piracy and Armed Robbery Against Ships Report – First Quarter 2014*. London: ICC International Maritime Bureau.

ICC-IMB. (2015). *Piracy and Armed Robbery Against Ships Report – First Quarter 2015*. London: ICC International Maritime Bureau.

Ikenberry, G.J. (2009). 'Liberal Internationalism 3.0: America and the Dilemmas of Liberal World Order', *Perspectives on Politics*, 7(1): 71–87.

International Maritime Bureau. (1992). *Special Report: Piracy*. London: International Maritime Bureau.

International Maritime Organization, IMO resolution 1060. (2014). [Strategic Plan for the Organization], 27 January, A 28/Res.1060.

Interpol. (2014). 'EU and Interpol: combating transnational organized crime at sea', 21 May. Available online at: www.interpol.int/en/News-and-media/News/2014/N2014-087/ 21 May 2014 EU and INTERPOL: combating transnational organized crime at sea.

Joyce, P. (2012). *Criminology: A Complete Introduction*. London: Hodder and Stoughton Ltd.

Marx, K. (1962). 'The Eighteenth Brumaire of Louis Napoleon', in Marx, K. and Engels, F. (eds), *Selected Works in Two Volumes*, Vol. 1. Moscow: Foreign Languages Publishing House.

Marx, K. (1982). 'Marx to Pavel Vasilyevich Annenkov, 28 December 1846', in Marx, K. and Engels, F., *Collected Works*, Vol. 38. New York: International Publishers.

Mitchell, D.J. (1976). *Pirates*. London: Thames and Hudson.

Nadelmann, E.A. (1990). 'Global Prohibition Regimes: The Evolution of Norms in International Society', *International Organization*, 44: 479–526.

Nadelmann, E. (1993). *Cops Across Borders: The Internationalization of U.S. Criminal Law Enforcement*. University Park, PA: Pennsylvania State University Press.

Naim, M. (2002). *Five Wars of Globalization. The Grotius Lecture Series*. Lecture presented at the American Society of International Law's ('ASIL') 96th Annual Meeting on March 13–16. American University Washington College of Law, the ASIL, and the International Legal Studies Program.

Nicolson, H. (1946). *The Congress of Vienna: A Study in Allied Unity 1812–1822*. New York: Harcourt, Brace.

Passas, N. and Twyman-Ghoshal, A. (2012). 'Controlling Piracy in Southeast Asia – Thinking Outside the Box', in Beckman, R.C. and Roach, J.A. (eds), *Piracy and International Maritime Crimes in ASEAN: Prospects for Cooperation*. Cheltenham: Edward Elgar.

Pogge, T. (2008). *World Poverty and Human Rights.* Cambridge: Polity Press.
Ruggiero, V. (2013). *The Crimes of the Economy: A Criminological Analysis of Economic Thought.* London: Routledge.
Rule, J. (1977). 'Wrecking and Coastal Plunder', in Hay, D., Linebaugh, P., Rule, J., Thompson, E.P., and Winslow, C., *Albion's Fatal Tree: Crime and Society in Eighteenth-Century England.* Harmondsworth: Penguin.
Sellin, T. (1976). *Slavery and the Penal System.* Oxford: Elsevier Scientific Publishing Co. Inc.
Sheptycki, J.W.E. (ed.). (2000). *Issues in Transnational Policing.* London: Routledge.
Sykes, G. and Matza, D. (1957). 'Techniques of Neutralization: A Theory of Delinquency', *American Sociological Review,* 22(6): 664–670.
Sylvester, C. (2014). 'Post-colonialism', in Baylis, J., Smith, S., and Owens, P. (eds), *The Globalization of World Politics: An Introduction to International Relations.* Oxford: Oxford University Press. Pp. 184–197.
Thomas, H. (1997). *The Slave Trade: The Story of the Atlantic Slave Trade, 1440–1870.* New York: Simon and Schuster.
Twyman-Ghoshal, A. and Pierce, G. (2014). 'The Changing Nature of Contemporary Maritime Piracy', *British Journal of Criminology,* 54: 652–672.
UN Security Council, Security Council resolution 733. (1992). [On the Situation of Somalia], 23 January, S/RES/733.
UN Security Council, Security Council resolution 1816. (2008). [On Piracy Off the Coast of Somalia] , 2 June, S/RES/1816.
UN Security Council, Security Council resolution 1838. (2008). [On Piracy Off the Coast of Somalia], 7 October, S/RES/1838.
UN Security Council, Security Council resolution 1846. (2008). [On Piracy Off the Coast of Somalia], 2 December, S/RES/1846.
UN Security Council, Security Council resolution 1897. (2009). [On Piracy Off the Coast of Somalia], 30 November 2009, S/RES/1897.
UN Security Council, Security Council resolution 1950. (2010). [On Piracy Off the Coast of Somalia], 23 November 2010, S/RES/1950.
UN Security Council, Security Council resolution 1976. (2011). [On Piracy Off the Coast of Somalia], 11 April, S/RES/1976.
UN Security Council, Security Council resolution 2018. (2011). [On Piracy in the Gulf of Guinea], 31 October, S/RES/2018.
UN Security Council, Security Council resolution 2020. (2011). [On Piracy Off the Coast of Somalia], 22 November, S/RES/2020.
UN Security Council, Security Council resolution 2039. (2012). [On Piracy in the Gulf of Guinea], 29 February, S/RES/2039.
UN Security Council, Security Council resolution 2077. (2012). [On Piracy Off the Coast of Somalia], 21 November, S/RES/2077.
UN Security Council, Security Council resolution 2184. (2014). [On Piracy in the Gulf of Guinea], 11 November, S/RES/2184.
Vagg, J. (1995). 'Rough Seas? Contemporary Piracy in South East Asia', *British Journal of Criminology,* 35(1): 63–80.
Wacquant, L. (2000). 'The New "Peculiar Institution": On the Prison as Surrogate Ghetto', *Theoretical Criminology,* 4(3): 377–389.

Part II

Theorising crime and its control in a global and transnational context

3 From Enlightenment to post-liberal internationalism

Chapter 1 has been concerned to identify the emergence of globalisation discourse within international, regional and national security strategy, emphasising recent changes to the conceptualisation of security, also seeking to draw out the implications of these developments for law enforcement and governance arrangements in the twenty-first century. A key premise of this text is that while the liberal institutional framework (which emphasises normative consensus, law and order, collective security and the utility of international and regional institutions to tackle collective security problems) has been taken as 'given' by international, regional and national authorities, alongside generations of criminologists and social theorists, this framework is a relatively new development, subject to historical contextualisation. Chapter 2 consequently reflected upon early international crime control efforts to counter slavery and piracy, drawing upon scholarship that has highlighted the utilisation of what we now view as crimes, and emergent crime control regimes, as historical tools of statecraft, subject to change over time. Addressing the issue of contemporary piracy, Chapter 2 further raised questions regarding the prevalence of the liberal framework and situational crime prevention methods within recent crime control strategy, advocating the necessity of including historical and political dimensions as necessary correctives, thereby enabling a fuller understanding of the crime issues under investigation, and as a means of developing more adequate crime control strategies in the future. This book therefore engages with, and builds upon, the contributions of a group of scholars who have been concerned to transcend the narrowness of debate on transnational crime and crime control within the disciplines of both international relations and criminology, employing a more nuanced and historically grounded narrative (Andreas and Nadelmann, 2006; Bowling and Sheptycki, 2012; Deflem, 2002; Findlay, 2008; Goldsmith and Sheptycki, 2010; Nadelmann, 1993).

The aim of this chapter is therefore to bridge the gap between criminological, sociological and international relations theory, placing in context the emergence of the liberal framework and the 'standard view' of globalisation, which has come to dominate contemporary crime control discourse and policy. The objective is to introduce students to a selection of theories and ideas that have been used to make sense of transnational organised crime, international crime and terrorism, and to identify the theoretical approaches underpinning crime control strategies and counter-terrorism policies at national, regional and international levels. This chapter therefore serves as a forerunner to the subsequent chapters which will endeavour to encourage students to examine critically the unfolding international and regional, collective security and multilateral problem-solving efforts and associated strategic approaches to genocide, terrorism and human trafficking. Students are invited to consider the heuristic value of the perspectives outlined within this chapter, and to reflect upon the significance of issues of power, inequality and justice in relation to the causes of crime and the acceleration of international crime control efforts.

Identifying the strengths in such an approach, here it is argued that studying the historical roots of the contemporary world order and reflecting upon the legacy of imperialism, colonialism and capitalist development for contemporary territorial boundaries, in addition to the distribution of power and resources across the globe, and the supply and demand dynamics of criminal markets, may prove fruitful for criminological investigation, rendering partial, contemporary crime prevention strategies directed towards countering transnational crime, international crime and terrorism. The present chapter is divided into four sections. Initially, Andreas and Nadelmann's theoretical challenge to the 'standard view' of globalisation will be provided to sensitise readers to the utility of undertaking interdisciplinary analysis, placing historical and political issues within the realm of theorising. The second section will comprise a discussion of proto-globalisation, the Enlightenment and modernisation as precursors to the contemporary period of globalisation. In this endeavour, students will be introduced to imperialist developments, colonial expansion and early efforts directed towards the facilitation of free trade. Against this historical background, the influence of Enlightenment thought upon international relations scholarship will be examined. Here, assumptions regarding human nature, the behaviour of states within the international system and the emergence of defining principles within the international society of states, including 'the principle of state sovereignty', 'law as reciprocal accord', 'non-intervention', and 'the state as the legitimate authority to undertake international action' will be presented.

Having examined the impact of Enlightenment ideas upon international relations scholarship, the chapter will next move to consider the influence of Enlightenment thought upon classical criminology, particularly, the promotion of the liberal belief in the utility of law and punishment, as institutions capable of preventing crime. This will be followed by a brief examination of the conservative sociological response to Enlightenment thought and processes of modernity, a position which promotes normative consensus and institutional reform as potential solutions to modernist pathologies within industrial society. There follows a brief examination of one further strand of liberal thought, namely, economic liberalism. As will be seen, this position rejects government interference in the economy and promotes free trade, global integration and economic interdependence as tools to secure international peace and global prosperity, an assumption integral to the globalist position in relation to globalisation as identified in Chapter 1.

Having examined the gradual development of liberal thought, the third section details the embedding of liberal ideas within an emerging international society, describing periods of optimism and then pessimism which correspond with institutional construction, failure and descent into warfare. Here the development of the League of Nations (following the First World War) and its successor organisation, the United Nations (following the Second World War), is outlined in addition to the Cold War dispute between the United States and the Soviet Union.

To end, the fourth and final section reflects briefly upon Marxist thought and the World Systems Analysis of Wallerstein, examining recent projections regarding the demise of the current liberal world order, and considering alternative futures. While necessarily incomplete, the purpose of the chapter is therefore to sensitise students to the relative newness of the current liberal international world order, characterised by an international society of states, global capitalist world economy and accompanying institutional framework. In anticipation of the chapters which follow, this chapter therefore assists students to contextualise normative assumptions underpinning contemporary crime control strategy, directing attention to the legacy of key historical events upon patterns of inequality, criminal victimisation and perpetration, criminalisation and enforcement, justice and injustice.

Challenging the 'standard view' of globalisation

In Chapter 1, we briefly engaged with the concept of globalisation. Viewed as a heuristic device capturing significant worldwide changes and the dramatic shift in the organisation of human affairs, the concept of globalisation has also been used by academic commentators to depict a series of objective, external elements serving to profoundly change the world in which we live. Within this expanding literature, globalisation has been associated with a reported growth in the intensity of worldwide interconnectedness, with academic commentators describing a process whereby the world has been transformed from discrete but independent nation-states to a shared social space, or single arena impacting upon every sphere of social organisation, from commerce and trade, to ideas, law enforcement and security (Baylis, Smith and Owens, 2014; Cohen and Kennedy, 2007). While disagreement exists regarding the utility of the construct, with arguments continuing regarding the newness of such developments and the temporal frame denoted by the concept, consensus emerges regarding the unprecedented interconnection and interdependence of the world today. While some commentators suggest that globalisation developed from immanent forces like modernity and capitalist industrialisation, with specific features of world society having their roots in earlier periods (Sparke, 2013), other authors argue that globalisation depicts a historical structure of material power and a transformation in the economy, remaining integral to, and inseparable from, capitalist development. The latter position notes the mutually constituting nature of states and markets, emphasising the pivotal role of state-sanctioned violence to facilitate capitalism, colonisation and imperialism (Schwartz, 2006) and patriarchy, alongside other stratificatory markers (Jacobs, Jacobson, Marchbank, 2000; Tickner, 1992, 2014). Scholars therefore point to continuity in addition to uniqueness within their narratives of globalisation.

Framed historically, such trends have raised questions regarding the consequences of such developments. Thus, while the concept of globalisation within the early literature denotes universalisation and processes of homogeneity, transforming diversity or difference into sameness, local systems into global systems, and tradition into modernity, highlighting benefits including poverty reduction and material well-being (Dasgupta, 2004), later commentators have been seen to challenge such positive assumptions and connotations, with scholars further recognising the word 'globalisation' as a weapon of political combat and as an influential term in political speech masking a more sinister and coercive tendency towards Westernisation and/or American imperialism (Sparke, 2013).

As suggested in Chapters 1 and 2, within criminology and social policy arenas, globalisation trends have been implicated as causal factors generating opportunities for crime (alongside other security threats), and providing a rationale for the pursuit of international, multilateral crime control strategies, legislative and normative frameworks, alongside enhanced law enforcement and judicial cooperation and in some instances, harmonisation. Responding to this position, which interprets the growth of international criminal law enforcement as explainable by the growth of transnational crime in an era of globalisation, Andreas and Nadelmann (2006) present what they call an 'analytically eclectic approach'. The former perspective described as the 'standard view', as evident within the official discourse of policy-makers and crime control strategies, is regarded by Andreas and Nadelmann as a partial approach devoid of historical contextualisation, and lacking in its failure to engage with power politics within international relations. Consequently, in their revised approach, the liberal perspective is supplemented with realist and constructionist insights. Andreas and Nadelmann employ a perspective which consists of three international relations approaches, which are applied to account for the growth of international police cooperation and the proliferation of global prohibition regimes, criminalisation and enforcement. In doing so they highlight the enduring importance of power politics and conflict within the field of global criminal justice and law enforcement, factors which are used to account for the influence of dominant states in shaping the agenda and prioritisation of international crime control, impacting upon the reach and intensity of specific regimes and initiatives. Taken together, the theoretical strands of international relations including the liberal, realist and constructivist perspectives are conceived as capturing an essential part of the internationalisation of crime control, serving to shed light upon the interaction among power and norms. The discipline of international relations is therefore advocated as theoretically valuable for the discipline of criminology, potentially offering a more complete lens through which to examine transnational crime and crime control.

While theories have a tendency to simplify, distort and omit certain factors, they are also useful, indeed, essential in allowing us to make sense of events and the world around us. Theories, maps or paradigms therefore serve as intellectual constructs enabling simplification of complex reality to enable us to see where we have been, where we are and perhaps, where we might be going. As guides to action, the significance of perspectives, theories and paradigms should not be underestimated, generating emotive responses at individual and state levels. Agreeing with Andreas and Nadelmann regarding the utility of international relations theory for the study of crime and crime control, and employing an interdisciplinary approach, it is the central premise of this text that in order to assess the adequacy of crime control responses and of theoretical interpretations of the emergence of the contemporary architecture devoted to the suppression and eradication of transnational and international crime and terrorism, it is necessary for students to have a basic appreciation of international history. Such an appreciation enables us to contextualise the emergence of the liberal world order of international society, and the theoretical and normative assumptions informing contemporary crime control strategies. The purpose of this chapter is therefore to provide a brief historical sketch directing attention to key events, which served to shape the emergence of the 'standard view' within official discourses of crime. While necessarily selective, the ensuing history endeavours to locate the emergence of significant ideas and theoretical positions within an historical and social framework, directing attention to the significance of key historical events which have influenced the current structure of our international society of states, identifying links between sociological, criminological and international relations perspectives. In doing so, it is intended that this chapter will provide a context against which to frame the subsequent chapters of this text, which ultimately intends to assist students to assess the adequacy of the contemporary liberal framework of crime control and specific national, regional and international crime control strategies to counter transnational crime, international crime and terrorism.

Here, we examine the emergence of the liberal perspective within international relations theory and the modernisation approach within sociology. It will be suggested that these perspectives share an optimism for the future and while variation is evident among the range of contributors within them, both perspectives share a modernist belief in progress and the assumption that enhanced cooperation and harmonisation will lead to a significant reduction in conflict in global politics, also comprising a means of tackling global social ills. Liberalism and modernisation perspectives both embrace the notion of a progressive evolution towards ideological consensus, presenting the universalisation of Western liberal democracy as the final form of human government.

Proto-globalisation, the Enlightenment and modernity

Utilising the term 'proto-globalisation', historians have examined the pre-modern world, exploring continuity and early aspirations to universalism, which, for one reason or another, failed to achieve global interconnectivity. As noted by Cohen and Kennedy (2007: 67–69), ancient civilisations of the Middle East, China, Greece and Rome achieved a degree of unification over large geographical areas with Christianity binding an array of separate kingdoms and aristocratic fiefdoms within Europe from the ninth to the thirteenth century. In the seventh century, Islamic states similarly extended their reach to North Africa and Southern Europe. Historians therefore emphasise a degree of continuity over time in relation to the existence of globalising tendencies, providing evidence to suggest that the transmission of ideas, culture, technology and the trade in goods predate the sixteenth century, a point in time which has been recognised as the beginning of capitalist modernity. For Cohen and Kennedy, despite the significant influence of early civilisations and ancient empires, and despite the aspirations of monolithic religions to extend their reach to all people, this goal was never achieved. Thus, while interconnectivity and the transmission of goods, ideas, people and culture predate the period defined as the beginning of modernity, denoting continuity with the past, a significant difference between such forms of proto-globalisation and the contemporary period of globalisation has been observed. Globalisation and its precursor, known as a period of modernisation, are consequently regarded as unique and identifiable phenomena in their own right, warranting separate analysis despite an acknowledgement of continuity with the past.

Modernisation has been described as involving a range of processes occurring simultaneously, including industrialisation, urbanisation, capitalisation, secularisation, democratisation, and has also been associated with increasing levels of literacy, education, wealth and social mobilisation, alongside more complex and diversified occupational structures and a more empirical and analytical approach to knowledge (Huntington, 1997: 68; Morrison, 1997: 28). Processes of modernisation are broadly depicted as commencing in the eighteenth century. Approximated to have begun three centuries ago during the 'Enlightenment', it is presented as a period in which philosophers depict a transformation from religion, illusion and superstition toward scientific reason, knowledge, progress and rationalisation (Morrison, 1997: 28), bringing with it the prospect of control, social enhancement and individual freedom. During this period, the emergence of the nation-state, the rise of the Enlightenment and the development of science were mutually reinforcing (Cohen and Kennedy, 2007: 69), with other commentators pointing to the significance of this period in the consolidation of other hierarchical dichotomies. Tickner, for example, draws attention to the interrelationship between the development of the capitalist world economy, the birth of the modern state, modern science, and the exploitative attitude towards nature, the delegitimisation of the feminine in public life, and hierarchies of race (Tickner, 1992: 135) – issues frequently ignored, until recently within both criminological and international relations literature.

Imperialism and colonial expansion

The fifteenth and sixteenth centuries witnessed colonial expansion and navigational exploration leading to European trading domination over much of the non-Western world, a process made possible because of the economic, military and intellectual advantages transmitted from other civilisations within the pre-modern period (Cohen and Kennedy, 2007). The period known as the Enlightenment accordingly occurs simultaneously with the extension of colonial expansion, the slave trade and piracy as detailed previously in Chapter 2. Colonial expansion and colonial rule extended into the late nineteenth century, culminating in the Berlin Conference of 1884–1885, which formalised European colonisation of Africa, demarcating European claims to territory and an agreement to facilitate free trade in addition to the creation of a framework for future negotiations. As noted by Cohen and Kennedy, Enlightenment thinkers conceived humanity as a single species on a gradual path to 'civilisation', with European states serving as the model for emulation, described as 'the white man's burden' to civilise the rest of the earth. By the 1870s however, European nations such as Belgium, France, Germany and Great Britain reoriented their focus upon the extraction of natural resources and the identification of markets. By the twentieth century, 90 per cent of African territory had reportedly been claimed by European states. The legacies of imperialism and colonialism are profound, with recent scholarship emphasising the consequences of these developments for the emergence of unequal social structures and access to economic, social and political resources for those located within affected states. However, both criminology and international relations scholars overlooked the ethnocentric orientation of Enlightenment philosophers and theorists of modernity, a point to which we shall return shortly.

The classical frame of reference

Within the discipline of criminology, the Enlightenment is commonly cited as a period where spiritualist explanations of crime became challenged by a naturalist scientific approach, associated with the writing of Hobbes, Spinoza, Descartes and Leibniz in the sixteenth and seventeenth centuries. Underpinned by the view of human nature as inherently rational and hedonistic, with actions subject to 'free will' as opposed to otherworldly influences, the classical frame of reference within criminology was also reflected within other emerging disciplines such as philosophy, political science and economics (Vold, Bernard and Snipes, 1998: 6). Indeed, both international relations scholarship and criminological theory drew heavily upon classical insights, guiding leaders as to how to conduct themselves both within states, and also, in their relations with other states within the realm of international politics.

Classical realism

In 1513, Machiavelli wrote *The Prince*, a handbook on ruling and the exercise of power. In this work he described men as 'ungrateful and fickle, dissemblers, avoiders of danger, and greedy of gain' (Machiavelli, 1997: 65). This view of human nature is also evident in the work of Thomas Hobbes (1588–1678) who argued that people naturally pursue their own interests without consideration of others. Self-preservation is man's primary interest, resulting in a 'war of each against all' resulting in distrust and fear for one's own safety (Vold, Bernard and Snipes, 1998: 15). Viewed as rational beings, and faced with such hostile conditions, men, it is suggested, turn to the state to find security collectively (Waltz, 1959). The civil state is therefore the solution for Hobbes as men sacrifice some liberties by entering into a social contract, defined as a guiding idea, which serves to legitimise the state to use force to enforce the contract. Hobbes' ideas provided the basis of right, the basis of law and state legitimacy and power. Prior to the nineteenth century, monarchies appealed to the doctrine of divine right in order to justify their power, the notion that monarchs were ordained with authority directly from God (Bodin, 1967: 40, cited in Reus-Smit, 2011: 282). Hobbes' views effectively dismissed God's will as the foundation of modern law, placing in its stead the will and desire of man and rational endeavours to organise collectively to generate social stability in the face of the human condition. Morrison (1997: 72) articulates the implication of this position well, noting 'if the will of the law was not God's, then whose?' Two contrasting positions are offered: the will of one of us (the strongest, the position taken by realist scholars) or the will of all of us (the position taken by liberal scholars). These diverging positions, evident within the realist drive to power maximisation and the liberal promotion of republican constitutionalism and the creation of a federal contract, mark a fundamental distinction between the two dominant international relations perspectives, with implications for the organisation of state to state behaviour, the legacy of which remains important today.

As observed by Tickner, while Hobbes did not particularly engage with international politics, his ideas have been applied by realist international relations scholars to account for the behaviour of states in the international system:

> Driven by competition for scarce resources and mistrust of others' motives in a system that lacks any legitimate authority, states, like men, must rely on their own resources for self-preservation.
>
> (Tickner, 1992: 45)

Through a rejection of religious authority, early classical realist theorists therefore argued that international politics occurred within an arena with no overarching central authority, a condition described as 'anarchy'. The history of international relations consequently reflects the application of theory to explain contemporary world politics, prompted by the vacuum left by the classical, modernist rejection of the moral authority of religion.

The Peace of Westphalia and the foundation of modern international politics

In the absence of God, and within an international order characterised by a situation of anarchy and the absence of political authority, both men and states were consequently regarded as both fearful and self-interested. It is useful to place this view in context. Hobbes lived during a period of conflict known as the Thirty Years War, which began in 1618 and became known as one of the most devastating conflicts in the history of Europe. Initiated by the Austrian Habsburgs in their efforts to impose Roman Catholicism on their Protestant subjects, the war ended with the signing of the Peace of Westphalia in 1648. The peace negotiations concluded between 1644 and 1648 produced the treaty of Osnabruck and two further treaties at Munster (known collectively as the Peace of Westphalia). The concept of sovereignty emerged at this time and has been regarded as a method for consolidating and conceptualising claims to land, provinces, cities, towns, enclaves and castles emanating from various authorities during and long before the Thirty Years War, with some wishing to restore the status quo and others wishing to create a new regime (Williams, Hadfield and Rofe, 2012: 104). The Peace of Westphalia has been regarded as responsible for delimiting the political rights and authority of European monarchs, establishing the sovereign state as the singular mode of constitutional authority, thereby also 'signalling the defeat of religion as a scheme for organising international authority' (Tickner, 2014: 153–154). The treaties therefore initiated the emergence of a system of sovereign states, 'denying the right of authorities to enforce religious practices outside their territory' (Tickner, 2014: 154), ending intervention on religious issues or pretexts and serving largely to stamp out religious wars in Western Europe (Williams, Hadfield and Rofe, 2012: 104). It is within this context that the new conceptualisation of law as a reciprocal accord was embedded within major European states with contractual international law evolving to become a foundation of modern international politics. International law is therefore regarded as the product of negotiations between sovereign states (now viewed as the legitimate actors within interstate relations), who enter into binding agreements reflecting the mutual will of the nations concerned, rather than ordained by God, or within the body of the ruler (Reus-Smit, 2011: 282).

The treaties consequently consolidated a number of organising principles governing international relations with continuing resonance today including: non-interference in the sovereign affairs of others; legal equality of sovereign states; and, the right to make and enter into treaties. Secularisation prohibited religious and imperial interference, providing a legislative framework for a new international order and a method for securing peace between equal and sovereign states within an anarchic and hostile international environment. The Peace of Westphalia therefore marked the second position identified by

Morrison above, reflecting the 'will of all' to organise collectively to generate social stability within a condition of anarchy, a position similarly adopted to regulate behaviour internally, within states.

Classical criminology and liberal thought

While international relations scholars were influenced by the barbarity of war between states, focusing internally, classical criminology, following Hobbes and other social contract philosophers, represented an endeavour to counter the arbitrary administration of justice and abuses of power and cruel punishments from within the nation-state. Classical criminologists are therefore social reformers protesting against inconsistency in the application of justice, advocating the creation of a coherent and rational criminal justice framework. Law was accordingly deemed legitimate to the extent that it was authored by those subject to the law (the will of all of us) or their representatives, rather than a command of God. As above, classical criminologists rejected the religious basis of state legitimacy and legislative authority. In *On Crimes and Punishment* (1764), Beccaria (1738–1794) considered crime as an injury to society (as opposed to God or the monarch), depicting law as a kind of contract which would guide and bind society, laying out clear, rational rules and punishment as a rational tool of government:

> In order for punishment not to be, in every instance, an act of violence of one or of many against a private citizen, it must be essentially public, prompt, necessary, the least possible in the given circumstances, proportionate to the crimes, dictated by the laws.
>
> (Morrison, 1997: 72)

According to Vold, Bernard and Snipes (1998: 20–21), while Beccaria's text was (perhaps predictably) condemned by the Catholic Church, his principles were subsequently embedded within the French Code of 1791, forming the basis for new criminal justice systems, following the American Revolution of 1776 and French Revolution of 1789, spreading throughout the industrialised world. His work consequently directed attention to the consequences of criminal justice policy for criminal behaviour with later social reformers such as Jeremy Bentham (1748–1832) working to perfect a calculation of pain compared to pleasure as an efficient means of preventing or deterring crime (Morrison, 1997: 74). Interestingly, while identified as a father of modern criminal justice systems, and placed within the classical school of criminology in criminological texts, Bentham's ideas and those of Immanuel Kant are similarly located as leading liberal thinkers within the discipline of international relations. Used domestically, Bentham's ideas promoted the use of law and punishment as a method to prevent crime. Applied externally, his work has been used to examine the utility of law as a method of preventing war and managing state-to-state relations. Revulsion towards 'the lawless state of savagery' resulted in

Bentham, Kant and later Durkheim, forging plans to facilitate social cohesion, recognising the threat that the modern scientific view of the world, captured by the term 'Enlightenment', posed to both morality and religion.

Presenting human reliance upon religion and other forms of 'alien guidance' as immaturity, Immanuel Kant (1724–1804) conceived freedom as autonomy or self-regulation, suggesting that human dignity requires humans to make the laws that they themselves must obey, rather than unthinkingly depending upon the moral guidance or prescriptions of others (Kant, 2001: 51). In 'Perpetual Peace: A Philosophical Sketch', Kant details a treaty for a permanent peace containing core liberal ideas. While Bentham proposed a common court of judicature to adjudicate differences between states, Kant was convinced that giving a direct voice to those who suffer most in war would drastically reduce its incidence, advocating republican constitutionalism and the development of a federal contract between states to abolish war, also retaining the belief that liberal states are pacific in their international relations with other states (Dunne, 2011: 104–105). For Waltz (1959: 101–103) (a key realist scholar), the liberal perspective is utopian, based upon an assumption of harmony and of the infinite perfectibility of states. For its proponents however, liberal theory contained the promise that reason, applied both domestically and internationally would lead to a situation where war would become increasingly unlikely. Liberalism consequently held the key to both domestic and international peace and security.

In detailing the influence of classical thought upon classical realism and classical criminology, it is evident that early influences within both the disciplines of international relations and criminology emerged from common foundations, resulting in common assumptions regarding human (and state) nature and common assertions regarding the utility of institutions such as law, to regulate state-to-state, and sovereign-to-citizen relations. Liberal thought is also associated with the utility of normative consensus as a socialising force, a mechanism which became increasingly important for conservative theorists reacting to the consequences of Enlightenment thought for traditional religious moral and ethical frameworks.

Conservative sociological reaction to modernity

Emile Durkheim (1858–1917), a politically liberal theorist associated with the emerging discipline of sociology, wrote during the end of the nineteenth century in reaction to the classical assumptions that humans were free and rational in a contractual society (Vold, Bernard and Snipes, 1998: 122). Retaining the emphasis on science, and within the context of the French Revolution (which fundamentally altered how people conceived political change and views of sovereignty), social sciences were born 'to understand what it was that explained the nature and pace of change, and how the "people" arrived at, could arrive at, the decisions they were said to be making' (Wallerstein, 2005: 4). As existing faculties divided into multiple disciplines, Durkheim was concerned to identify a disciplinary home for the emerging subject of sociology, separate from the existing disciplines of philosophy and psychology. Committed to the empirical study of the social world and concerned by the turmoil generated by the French Revolution and by the rapid industrialisation of France, Durkheim conceived the Enlightenment as a negative and destabilising influence. Most of his work was consequently dedicated to the study of social order and the search for general laws governing social behaviour. According to Vold, Bernard and Snipes (1998: 124), sociologists were concerned with the regeneration of society and the reestablishment of social solidarity, providing 'rational, scientific analysis of monumental social changes that were occurring'. In *The Division of Labour in Society*, Durkheim (1965) undertook a comparative analysis of what held society together in primitive 'mechanical' forms of society and within more advanced modern 'organic' forms of society. Significantly, Durkheim presented all societies as being at some stage of progression between these two ideal types of society. Like the earlier liberal thinkers mentioned previously, Durkheim was a social reformer who believed that the problems generated by processes of modernisation including industrialisation and urbanisation were temporary aberrations, pathologies which could be resolved by the social physician through structural reform. According to Ritzer (1996: 85), Durkheim argued that increasing numbers of people within a society and increasing interaction among them (dynamic density) results in a transformation from mechanical to organic solidarity as individuals struggle for survival within a climate of scarce resources. While the rise of the division of labour reduces the strength of the common morality in the modern world, and as individuals become isolated by specialised activities, this results in a pathological loosening of social bonds. However, the division of labour within society is also presented by Durkheim as a source of cohesion, potentially facilitating coexistence through interdependency and making for greater efficiency. Indeed, according to Ritzer, Durkheim recognised occupational organisations as potential solutions to the problem of modern society, promising to restore collective morality and enabling people to recognise common interests. This belief led Durkheim to conclude that what is needed is to create an integrative moral system with associated rules and laws to bind and guide people together. Durkheim's liberal framework therefore advocated consensus building and institutional reform, underpinned by unstated assumptions regarding human nature. Like Hobbes, Durkheim considered that 'people are endowed with a variety of egoistic drives that, if unbridled, constitute a threat to themselves as well as to society' (Ritzer, 1996: 99). Thus, the creation of common morality (collective conscience) within modern society served not only to bind people together in a period of flux where norms, values and expectations varied, but also to free the individual from their passions. Ritzer suggests that the ethic of individualism served this function, grounded in human freedom and common solidarity giving recognition to the inherent dignity, rights and freedom of individuals.

Durkheim's ideas were influential upon later modernisation theorists who argued that processes of rapid social change such as industrialisation and urbanisation were associated with patterns of crime and victimisation (Shelley, 1981). Drawing upon the work of Neapolitan (1997) and Shelley (1981), Barak (2001) notes that modernisation theorists retain Durkheim's emphasis upon pathologies associated with the loosening of collective conscience resulting from clashing norms and values as societies transform from agricultural to industrial and service-oriented economies. This outcome of modernisation is however regarded as temporary, with all nations viewed as undergoing the same patterns in crime and crime control as they adapt to similar levels of rapid development. Within this perspective, crime is affected by the loosening of legalistic and customary social controls upon the individual, as old beliefs and values are replaced by new ones, generating social disorganisation and anomie. The liberal emphasis upon the creation of collective belief and the utility of institutional reform are therefore evident within modernisation approaches, posed as appropriate solutions to problems of modernity.

Morrison describes the discipline of criminology as a synthesis of social science comprising 'the discourse concerning crime and the methods by which society deals with crime' (Morrison, 1997: 5). Criminology has however been predominantly focused upon crimes occurring within state boundaries and, with a few exceptions, it is only within the past few decades that criminologists have engaged with the issue of cross-border crime, transnational, international and state crimes (see Chapter 5). Similarly, international relations scholarship has traditionally been concerned with understanding the causes of war between nation-states. Crime has therefore not been a central focus and only entered into international relations discourse following the reconceptualisation of security, detailed in Chapter 1. However, as noted above, similarities are clearly evident. Thus, both disciplines are concerned to understand the modern world, reflecting disagreement regarding the subject-matter under investigation and the methodology to be utilised to examine it. Both disciplines also reflect the work of scholars who embrace an optimistic belief in the modernist rational programme of improvement, production of knowledge, progress and efforts to build the good society (nationally and internationally). More recently, both disciplines have also revealed an acknowledgement regarding the limits of such a project, increasingly expressing complexity, ambiguity and self-doubt in relation to the reality of social progress from the mid-1970s, resulting in a debate about whether modernity, or modern society, has become radically transformed to something new. Hence, both criminology and international relations scholarship have grappled with the terms post-modernity or late-modernity accompanied by the increasing salience of discourses of globalisation. Thus, as detailed in Chapter 1, for many commentators we are currently in the early stage of a whole new structure and are experiencing a transformation out of modernity, with globalising processes impacting upon the traditional conceptualisation of security, governance arrangements and the roles and remits of law enforcement, security, intelligence and border control agencies and institutions. This debate, it seems, is ongoing with the outcome of such developments subject to contention within both disciplines.

Each of the contributions discussed thus far reflect a fundamental belief in social change. Clark (1989: 49–66), cited in Dunne (2014: 114), presents the belief in the possibility of progress as a key identifier of the liberal approach to politics, supplemented by an assumption of judicial equality, human rights, and the location of legislative authority as based within the people (as opposed to God or those ordained by God). Other aspects characterising the liberal approach draw attention to what has become known as 'economic liberalism', a position that conceives market-driven economic exchange as an effective system. Thus Adam Smith (1776), in *An Inquiry into the Nature and Causes of the Wealth of Nations*, writing some time before Durkheim, identified that higher levels of specialisation within the division of labour in industry could increase productivity, increasing the surpluses a society could produce resulting in greater economic efficiency and increased wealth and prosperity for all. Reflecting the earlier assumption regarding human nature espoused by Hobbes, Smith asserted that 'as individuals pursue their own best interests motivated by greed, they unwittingly realise an important public good – a more productive society with a broader division of labour and more for all' (Kratke and Underhill, 2006: 27). Reacting to the perceived abuses of the rich and powerful, Smith recognised the need to ensure that restrictive practices and self-interested behaviour of the commercial classes were curbed and regulated to ensure market-based outcomes and benefits (Kratke and Underhill, 2006: 28). Smith therefore rejected government interference in the economy, advocating the separation of politics and economics. David Ricardo (1772–1823) extended Smith's observations to the international sphere, promoting specialisation and free trade as the route to global wealth and human welfare, suggesting that global economic integration and interdependence contain the additional benefits of facilitating peace between nations (Tickner, 1992: 71). Richard Cobden (1804–1865) similarly advocated free trade (anti-protection) as essential for improved international relations between states and as a means of generating a peaceful world order. However, with the onset of the First World War (1914–1918), assumptions regarding the inherent pacific nature of liberal states were called into question raising the possibility of liberal engineering to secure the objective of international peace and global prosperity.

The emergence of international society

The First World War, the League of Nations and the creation of a liberal international order

In many respects, the League of Nations, an international organisation created in the wake of the First World War, pulls together the various strands of liberal thought identified above. Based upon the ideas of Woodrow Wilson, the League represented the development of a unified international legal order organised around a collective security body, which sought to transform the old system based on the balance of power, spheres of influence and military rivalry, advocating open trade, national self-determination and a belief in progressive global transformation (Ikenberry, 2009). Retaining a focus upon the rule of law and the sovereignty of nation-states as *the* legitimate actors within international relations, the Hobbesian preference for a social contract is reflected in the signing of the Treaty of Versailles, and through the provision the Covenant of the League of Nations (which placed an obligation upon Members to respect and preserve the territorial integrity and existing political independence of all Members against external aggression). Beccaria's and Bentham's emphasis upon the utility of law and punishment as deterrence is also evident with the charter, which subjected disputes to arbitration or judicial settlement, with violation initiating punitive sanctions in the form of an agreed cessation of financial, commercial or personal intercourse between the nationals of the covenant-breaking state and the nationals of any other state. However, as noted by Ikenberry, Wilson regarded international law with respect to its socialising dynamic, thereby gradually influencing states into compliance rather than as a formal, legally binding entity enforced by international or supranational authorities. In the event however, Wilson's vision of law as organic was perhaps naïve as the threat of economic sanction with the absence of enforcement mechanisms was insufficient in preventing further aggression, particularly in the absence of US and Soviet Union membership and support. Dunne (2011: 106) describes the experience of the League of Nations as a 'disaster', 'dealing a fatal blow to [liberal] idealism'. Despite the apparent failure of this liberal experiment, Dunne nevertheless reminds us that liberal ideas remain, with the USA subsequently embedding liberal principles within the replacement international organisation, the United Nations, and its associated institutions and regulatory rules (Dunne, 2011: 108).

The interwar period and the realist critique of liberal idealism

According to Dunne and Schmidt (2011), the interwar period (1919–39) marked the emergence of a new generation of realist writers including E.H. Carr, Hans J. Morgenthau, R. Niebuhr and others, who provided a critique of liberal interwar scholarship in the aftermath of the First World War. In particular, these realist international scholars directed attention to the continuing salience of power, politics and state self-interest (Morrison's 'will of one of us') in directing state behaviour within a hostile and threatening environment. Liberal idealism was accordingly challenged for overstating the rational nature of human beings; for the overly optimistic position adopted; and for its mistaken faith in moral and ethical consensus building and the capacity of universal institutions to secure peace and to overcome the problems of contemporary society.

Built upon the classical realist perception of human nature (as detailed earlier, when referring to the contribution of Machiavelli and Hobbes, which conceived self-interest as rooted within the biological drives of human beings), realist international relations scholars initially conceptualised the behaviour of states as a reflection of fundamental aspects of human nature (Dunne and Schmidt, 2011: 89), later locating the characteristics of insecurity, anxiety, competition and egoism within the structural conditions of international society. Significantly, despite the lack of consensus regarding the aetiology of such characteristics, agreement exists between both liberal and realist scholars regarding the hostile environment in which states are currently placed, with the former advocating institutional and normative reform as a means to militate against such conditions and with the latter remaining sceptical regarding the prospects of such an approach to fulfil the goal of global peace, security, prosperity and collective problem solving. The outbreak of the Second World War in 1939 confirmed the utility of realist theory for understanding international relations, emphasising the need for prudent state leaders to pursue power (and later security) maximisation strategies and self-help in order to ensure the survival of the state ('the will of one of us').

The Second World War and the United Nations

Described by Underhill (2006) as 'one of the most important punctuation marks in human history', the Second World War is viewed as fundamentally impacting upon economic and security matters, altering the balance of power and distribution of wealth among territories of the globe and serving to undermine European dominance. Underhill (2006: 103) argues 'it is difficult to understand the contemporary period without at least some reference to the new beginning that war constituted', a new beginning which underpinned the emergence of the global state-market system of today, and which, despite its purported importance, remains frequently absent from mainstream criminological theorising.

Underhill's helpful introduction questions the role of America within this process and in doing so is keen to challenge what are described as three important and interrelated myths. Critiquing narratives which present: (1) the USA as a consistent sponsor of liberalisation; (2) the centrality of the US 'state-as-actor'; and (3) the USA as a moral and 'enlightened' sponsor of liberalisation, Underhill argues that progress toward liberalisation occurred during a period of US decline, that the USA behaved inconsistently and ambivalently regarding its implementation, acting out of self-interest and indeed deviating from liberal multilateralism as and when it suited, also emphasising the significant role played by non-state actors in driving forward these trends. For Underhill, while US leadership is important, other variables such as the underlying social and economic interest base behind state policies are more important factors influencing liberalisation, the consequences of which are to have 'intensified competition among producers and enhanced political and economic instability' linked with market-led adjustments.

Whether the US state acted alone and with imperial ambition or as part of a more complex interactive body of actors is therefore currently disputed. The outcome generally is not. Economic liberal ideas were embedded within this system following the creation of the International Monetary Fund, and World Bank (initially known as the International Bank for Reconstruction) in 1946, and through the signing of the General Agreement on Tariffs and Trade (GATT) in 1947. These public multilateral institutions are known collectively as the Bretton Woods system. The IMF sought to stabilise the exchange rate regime and provide emergency assistance to countries facing a temporary crisis in their balance of payments. It had been argued that volatile short-term capital flows had contributed to the interwar period of economic disaster and therefore these multilateral bodies were designed to provide a cushion to assist states to adjust to balance-of-payments and economic development problems over the short and longer term (Underhill, 2006: 105; Woods, 2014: 244). This system, it was suggested, could avoid excessive intervention, protectionist policies and economic nationalism which characterised the pre-war market system, facilitating the Second World War. The International Bank for Reconstruction and Development was therefore created to facilitate private investment and reconstruction in Europe. The latter became a forum for negotiations on trade liberalisation. However, as noted by both Woods (2014) and Underhill (2006) plans faltered, reflecting US ambivalence to fund the IMF and World Bank, together with the onset of the Cold War, which affected US prioritisation preferences.

In addition to the Bretton Woods institutions, which sought to create a new economic world order, a new global institution was designed to replace the failed League of Nations collective security body. Established in 1945, the United Nations was designed to overcome a number of the difficulties experienced by its predecessor. With the explicit objective of protecting mankind from the scourge of war and again employing a contract based, rule of law framework, the UN Charter sets out the basic principles of international relations, promoting self-determination, equal rights, collective security, and international cooperation in solving international problems of an economic, social, cultural, or humanitarian character (Charter of the United Nations). While self-interest and power politics penetrated the functioning of the economic order detailed above, the tension between a tradition of universalism ('the will of all of us', stressing the equality of states) and that of great power consensus ('the will of one of us', recognising the existence of power politics within international affairs) is similarly evident within the structure of the United Nations organisation. Thus, in order to facilitate the coordination of military or economic sanctions against offending states, and as a means of incentivising powerful nations to join the organisation, the UN Security Council was created. This body was granted overall responsibility for maintaining peace and security, with the power to make binding resolutions with five (the major powers at the time the UN was founded) of the 15 permanent members also possessing veto power over all Security Council decisions. These structural reforms and privileges were conceived as explicitly recognising power within the international order, thereby addressing fundamental weaknesses within the earlier League's structure (Taylor and Curtis, 2008: 314–315).

As with the economic institutions detailed previously, the performance of the United Nations was fundamentally influenced by international political circumstances, with the Cold War effectively stalling decisions since the veto was used whenever the major interests of the USA or Soviet Union were threatened. As noted by Taylor and Curtis, 'From 1945 to 1990, 193 substantive vetoes were invoked in the Security Council, compared to only 23 substantive vetoes from 1990 to 2010' (Taylor and Curtis, 2011: 316). The transition from the League of Nations to the United Nations therefore represents a shift, moving away from classical liberalism which promoted the 'will of all' towards a more hierarchical society of states in which the United States retained additional responsibilities accompanied by privileges and power (Ikenberry, 2009; Goldsmith and Sheptycki, 2010: 1). While in practice it was never fully implemented, this manoeuvre away from the classical ideological basis of liberalism has been regarded as generating tension and resistance. Thus, as will be seen shortly, the emerging liberal basis of international society became subject to challenge, resulting in far reaching consequences for global prosperity, security, militarisation, crime and crime control.

The Cold War

The Cold War has been regarded as of paramount importance in international politics, crucially affecting the dynamics of world affairs – directly or indirectly – for every part of the globe (Scott, 2008: 60). Williams, Hadfield and Rofe (2012: 56) describe the Cold War as an 'embedded nest of incidents, crises and full-on wars', prompted by the failure to implement post-war principles agreed during war time conferences which took place in Yalta and Potsdam, resulting in dispute between both superpowers regarding the division of Germany and parts of Central and Eastern Europe, with Scott (2008: 61) also implicating the ideological threat posed by each side to the other. As noted by Underhill (2006: 103), until the collapse of the Soviet bloc in 1989 there were in fact two world orders, organised around two distinct forms of political economy, the 'Western' market economy order and the centrally planned economies of the Soviet bloc.

Following a brief period of cooperation between the United States and the Soviet Union during the Second World War, and occurring within a context of decolonisation, initiated by the belief in national self-determinism (resulting in the withdrawal of empire by Britain, Holland, France, Belgium and Portugal), Cold War competition between the East and West became manifested through the Warsaw Pact and the North Atlantic Treaty Organisation (NATO). These developments are described by Dunne and Schmidt (2011: 88) as prominent examples of formal alliance building, resulting in the rise of Soviet hegemony in Eastern Europe and American hegemony in Central America.

Fearing the rise of communism in war-ravaged Europe, in 1947 the US Truman administration declared support for those threatened by Soviet subversion or expansion, a doctrine associated with the policy of containment which underpinned the 1947 Marshall Plan, which permitted financial aid to Europe to facilitate economic recovery (Scott, 2008: 61; Woods, 2014: 245). These developments were also accompanied by the shift from the UN Security Council global security system to an alliance-based security created around democratic solidarity through the North Atlantic Treaty Organisation (NATO) and other US alliances (Ikenberry, 2009), reflecting a commitment of the USA to defend Western Europe to deter Soviet 'aggression'. However, as noted by Scott (2008: 61), the resulting 'political encirclement ... entailed a growing military, and specifically nuclear, threat'.

In possession of nuclear capabilities, hostilities between the USA and Soviet Union were not direct, resulting in a series of proxy wars fought in Korea, Vietnam, Afghanistan, Mozambique, Angola, Namibia and Eritrea-Ethiopia. The association between industrialisation, total war, the end of empire, the Cold War and more recent internal conflict within states, patterns of atrocity crime, terrorism and organised crime, along with other international 'security threats' is therefore complex and difficult to appreciate without a basic grasp of the significance of international history and international politics. Scott argues that the ideological battle reflected within the Cold War between these two superpowers facilitated change, providing inspiration for liberation within many 'Third World' nations, with direct involvement further serving to prolong and escalate conflicts elsewhere. For Goldsmith and Sheptycki (2010: 9), the sudden break-up of the USSR and its satellite system was seismic, generating global policing concerns at 'the coming anarchy' and a perceived urgency to find ways to stabilise the 'fragile', 'failing', and 'collapsed' states of sub-Saharan Africa, Central America, Eastern Europe and elsewhere. This development is also credited with initiating new agendas and technologies for engagement in crafting transnational policing across the globe. These events marked fundamental changes towards the decline in inter-state conflict and the increasing significance of asymmetrical warfare and internal conflict, serving to blur the boundaries between 'police' and 'military' missions, 'internal' and 'foreign' affairs, and the relationship between international crime, transnational crime and terrorism. These events also raised questions regarding the role of non-state actors in international politics, fundamentally altering (and broadening) conceptions of security (as detailed in Chapter 1), and impacting upon the role, remit, methods and objectives of law enforcement, security and intelligence agencies.

Having sketched, albeit incompletely, the march towards enlightenment and the gradual embedding of liberal ideas and principles associated with modernity, viewed as the precursor to the modern period of globalisation, it is useful to examine the development of Marxist thought as an alternative and competing ideology, whose demise prior to the end of the Cold War was by no means certain. Within the final section of this chapter, Marxist concepts will briefly be detailed before presenting the World Systems Analysis of Wallerstein and the realist perspective within international relations who call into question the assumptions underpinning the liberal internationalist framework of the contemporary world order.

Beyond the contemporary liberal framework

Marx and World Systems Theory

As detailed above, early sociologists and liberal theorists reacted fearfully and conservatively to the disruption caused by modernisation and industrialisation, endeavouring to create moral consensus and institutions to reintegrate individuals within communities and to facilitate the conditions necessary for social solidarity. However, while liberal economists such as Adam Smith and David Ricardo acknowledged the detrimental consequences of capitalism, conceiving such evils as inevitable, Karl Marx (1818–1883) rejected this position, refuting the acceptance of capitalism and castigating economic theorists for their failure to recognise the inherent tension between capitalists and labourers. His writing identified the oppressiveness of capitalism and subsequently sought to formulate a plan of action to overthrow the system. While the classical philosophers detailed previously were influenced by a conceptualisation of human nature that depicted man as inherently selfish and hedonistic, Marx's image of human nature was based on an assumption of human beings as inherently productive and social. Capitalism, for Marx, effectively alienated people from the product of their labour, resulting in production for a small group of capitalists rather than naturally producing for themselves. Agreeing that labour is the source of wealth, Marx identified that the profit of the capitalist is derived from the exploitation of the labourer, effectively paying the individual less than the value of what they produced. The profit, or surplus value, was subsequently retained and reinvested, expanding the system resulting in further exploitation of larger numbers of workers, generating further patterns of resistance, oppression, exploitation and the distortion of humanity. While Marx recognised the contradictions and tensions within the capitalist system, his work sought to bring about its demise, offering a political programme to initiate the creation of an alternative 'more humane' socialist society, in which people would be able to express their humanity. Marx's writing therefore comprises a critical analysis of capitalist society, exploring the relationship between people and large-scale structures that cause alienation (Ritzer, 1996). As noted by Sheptycki (2010: 305), drawing upon the work of Reiner, Marxian analysis views liberal policing as a means to control the 'dangerous classes', contain the poor and disadvantaged and maintain class privileges, maintaining the circumstances that give rise to social disparity and social conflict.

According to Swingewood (1991: 60), the term 'socialism' was employed for the first time by Pierre Leroux in 1832. As a political theory, socialism required the abolition of private property rights, the elimination of poverty, the assertion of equality and the organisation of production through the agency of the state. Swingewood argues that the period between 1789 and

1830 was crucial to the development of both sociology and socialism, which both responded to rapid political and economic changes associated with industrialisation and urbanisation, creating opposition to the dominant ideas of political liberalism, individualism and the market economy. The appeal and proliferation of Marxism has consequently been described, as organically bound up with a burgeoning labour movement associated with the growth of industry and new social relations of capitalist production, with socialism promoted as a means of resolving internal conflicts produced by capitalist production (Swingewood, 1991: 60–61). However, the influence and acceptance of Marxist ideas has been subject to variation and contention. As noted by Ritzer (1996), while Marxist theory was very influential within Eastern Europe and variable within Western Europe, within the United States, Marxist insights were virtually ignored.

While Marx did not particularly incorporate the international dimension within his writing, concerned more with analysing nineteenth-century British capitalism, he was keen to examine the social world as a whole, emphasising the insatiable appetite of capitalism with regard to the accumulation of capital and the search for new markets. His work has been utilised by a range of scholars, examining the transnational functioning of capitalism within the contemporary period. World Systems Theory is identified with the work of Immanuel Wallerstein, who, like Marx, espoused the need for historical and interdisciplinary analysis of social structures. In analysing the transition from feudalism to capitalism, and through a discussion of the structures of knowledge and mechanisms of the modern world system, Wallerstein questions the assumption underpinning modernisation theory that all states follow the same developmental pattern as they progressively move from primitive to modern societies, also questioning the belief that liberalism is universally beneficial. For Wallerstein the modern capitalist economic world system contains many institutions, consisting of states, an interstate system, productive firms, households, classes and identity groups, which together form a matrix. As a social construction, with a beginning, middle and inevitably an end, the current world system is depicted by Wallerstein as subject to internal contradictions associated with the ceaseless quest for accumulation and the tension between efforts to reduce remuneration (worker wages), transaction, input and infrastructural costs, and longer-term structural trends which have reduced the global rural population and increased the costs of production. These trends, and the recurrent difficulties generated, are no longer able to be resolved without transcending the existing world system, marking a period of transition, initiated by the 1968 World Revolution and continuing into the present day. The outcome of the current period of systemic crisis is by no means regarded as certain, and while Wallerstein identifies instability, anxiety, violence and social conflict as symptoms, progressive social change (through intellectual, moral and political action) remains a distinct possibility. Described as a protest against the deep inequalities which remain intrinsic within the current world system, and against conventional knowledge systems which influence our perception about how to think about the world, World Systems Analysis is presented as both a method and as a point of view offering a new perspective on social reality.

The liberal framework of the current international society of states, with its globalisation rhetoric and modernist assumptions are consequently called into question. In an aptly named introductory chapter entitled 'Understanding the World in Which We Live', Wallerstein rejects the view that presents globalisation and terrorism as fundamentally new and distinct phenomena, castigating the analytical tendency towards separation and specialism evident with the contemporary structures of knowledge, which has resulted in the emergence of distinct academic disciplines, which are viewed as an obstacle to understanding. He further suggests that such an approach obfuscates the historical appreciation of continuity and fails to recognise that such phenomena are actually closely intermeshed and tied to the history and fate of the modern world system. With its origins in the sixteenth century, the modern capitalist world system is regarded by Wallerstein as intrinsically tied to the imposition of colonial rule and Western structures of knowledge. Originally located within Europe and America, over time the capitalist system expanded to encompass the whole world, marking a divergence from proto-globalisation, referred to earlier. Drawing upon the work of dependency theorists, World Systems Theory rejects the notion of underdevelopment as an original evolutionary stage of development, arguing instead that it is a direct consequence of historical capitalism, based upon unequal exchange and exploitative relations between core, semi-periphery and periphery countries, denoted by the degree to which production processes were relatively monopolised or relatively free market. Given that monopolised processes generate greater profits, it is understood that countries with more core-like processes tend to be wealthier. Wallerstein's analysis examines states within the framework of the interstate system, identifying that states are differentially positioned with regard to their relative power, wealth and resources with consequences for the degree to which they can exercise authority both internally and externally.

As detailed above, the post-Second World War political settlement emerged within the context of US dominance, the Cold War and decolonisation. Within this climate, US commitment to free trade required negotiation with European powers, particularly given the necessity to contain the ideological threat posed by the Soviet Union. As detailed by Kiely (2004), these developments enabled advanced capitalist powers and newly decolonised nations to develop their national economies, with the former nations negotiating favourable concessions facilitated by labour organisations, committing to full employment, welfare rights, and improved living standards. Nations within the developing world did not however obtain these concessions, which were more frequently substituted for national development. By the 1960s and 1970s, as profit rates declined, the United States abandoned the fixed exchange rate system agreed at Bretton Woods, facilitating a system of floating exchange rates and the initiation of deregulation of international finance. Difficulties were compounded by an increase in oil prices in 1973–74 which led to many Third World states borrowing money in an effort to maintain growth levels, particularly (although not exclusively) among oil importing nations, culminating in the debt crisis of the 1980s. Kiely (2004: 266–267) notes that 'when faced with increasing rates of interest payments on debts, several Third World countries threatened to default'.

Wallerstein's World Systems Analysis details the historical contours of the modern capitalist world-economy, arguing that strong states retain the capacity to pressure weak states to keep their frontiers open 'to those flows of factors of production that are useful and profitable to firms located in the strong states, while resisting any demands for reciprocity in this regard' (Wallerstein, 2005: 55). For Wallerstein, the economic difficulties faced particularly by governments in the South and in the former communist zone from the 1970s onwards made it very difficult for such states to resist pressure for structural adjustment and the opening of frontiers to the free flow of goods and capital. Imbalance is also evident through the capacity of strong states to install and keep in power political leaders whom they find acceptable and through the capacity to coerce weaker states to adhere to the policy needs and political agendas of the strong states. With their roots within the economic expansion of the world system, colonies are defined as the weakest states within the modern world system, with stronger states exploiting such states to control the production processes and to prevent competitors from gaining access to their resources or markets. Semi-peripheral states remain in competition with each other and endeavour to enhance their status as a producer and relative power and military strength. As the hegemonic power from the mid-twentieth century, the United States has, according to Wallerstein therefore been able to 'establish the rules of the game in the interstate system, dominating the world-economy (in production, commerce, and finance)' (Wallerstein, 2005: 58), getting their own way politically and also formulating the cultural language, thereby dominating the knowledge structures and presentation of reality within the contemporary era.

In the previous chapter, a cursory examination of piracy and slavery revealed initial explicit state support and engagement with practices now viewed as abhorrent and inhumane. The narrative of criminalisation as evidence of progress was cast into doubt, with authors such as Andreas and Nadelmann (2006), Nadelmann (1993), Vagg (1993, 1995) and Felson and Kalaitzidis (2005) presenting slavery, piracy, war and law as tools of statecraft, representing overt military power and more subtle forms of domination respectively as applied on the world stage. Alternative interpretation therefore offers a different perspective on contemporary global politics of which law enforcement and criminal justice remain a key aspect.

In attempting to draw out the characteristics of the contemporary period, Mittelman (2006) identifies three current patterns of globalisation: multilateral (consent based 'will of all'), militarised (coercion based 'will of one') and democratic, which are viewed as intersecting and competing thereby shaping the future contours of the coming world order. In particular, Mittelman argues that in the post-9/11 era, we have witnessed a shift from 'consent-based' globalisation towards US reliance upon 'coercion-based' globalisation utilising military power and covert agencies. Mittelman's patterns align crudely to dominant approaches within international relations and have implications for how we view tendencies towards law enforcement harmonisation, enhanced policing and security cooperation, policy transfer and mutual recognition.

Placed within a temporal framework, Wallerstein argues that the current world system has reached systematic crisis, with US use of military force (coercion-based globalisation), conceived as indicative of the first sign of weakness. Predicted to last anywhere between twenty-five and fifty years, the present period of transition is described as characterised by instability and violence as people endeavour to maintain the status quo and retain their acquired privileges and hierarchical rank. Wallerstein concludes by projecting future possibilities as responses to the ensuing crisis, suggesting that while middle-run adjustments to the system remains highly likely as individuals adhere to customary patterns of behaviour, such solutions will have little effect over the longer term. Alternatively, the construction of a successor system (or systems) is postulated, the formulation of which will either lean towards a hierarchical system, 'bestowing or permitting privileges according to rank in the system', or conversely towards 'a relatively democratic, relatively egalitarian system'. The end result is left open, raising questions regarding the structure of international relations and the organisation of the society of states in the coming years. For Ikenberry (2009), the decline in the relative power of the US and EU, and changing circumstances of world politics have indeed created a crisis 'of authority, rule of law and governance'. Ikenberry argues that as we move from a hierarchical liberal framework towards 'post-hegemonic liberal internationalism', we are witnessing increasing pressure and incentives for reform and reorganisation of the existing liberal political and economic institutional framework. A reformed liberal international order will need to become more universal and less hierarchical, a position which would require the United States to cede authority and control to a wider set of states and to relinquish some of its hegemonic rights and privileges. As liberal internationalist ideas including democratisation, free markets and US military power continue to be called into question, Ikenberry's (2011) more recent work explores the possibility that the current world order based upon openness and rule-based relations enshrined in institutions such as the United Nations and norms such as multilateralism could be replaced by a more contested and fragmented system of blocs, spheres of influence, mercantilist networks and regional rivalries. Described as the autocratic-capitalism thesis, Ikenberry regards such a possibility as unlikely given the economic and security incentives to preserve the existing order.

For Wallerstein however, such revisionist liberal solutions remain tied within the existing world economic system and therefore are unlikely to resolve the inherent contradictions within the capitalist system, merely replacing one hegemonic power with another, within a repeated and cyclical pattern.

He argues: 'The capitalist world-economy needs states, needs the interstate system, and needs the periodic appearance of hegemonic powers' (Wallerstein, 2005: 59). Thus, for Wallerstein, without dealing with the capitalist prioritisation of the endless accumulation of capital, 'political struggle, rivalry, exploitation and unequal exchange' will remain.

An awareness regarding the development of the institutional and moral framework underpinning the contemporary international society of states, while frequently absent from standard criminology text books, is of crucial importance for theorists endeavouring to assess the adequacy of crime control responses at national, regional and international levels. The First and Second World Wars situated within the context of modernisation, industrialisation, urbanisation, imperial expansion, nationalism and subsequent decolonisation remain key transformations within world history, the legacies of which are evident today. Ahistorical and frequently depoliticised, vary rarely do 'standard view' criminologists, employing globalisation narratives and liberal institutional reformism, examine the assumptions underpinning contemporary crime prevention strategies or question modernist assumptions of progress, the functioning of liberal economic ideas or the discrepancy between liberal rhetoric and lived realities (both within, and between nations).

Tickner (2014: 120), drawing upon the work of Halperin, cautions against uncritical acceptance of such historical accounts, warning that the early liberal and modernisation narrative incorrectly locates 'Europe at the centre of modernity and transforms Europe's imperial expansion into a story of enlightenment and progress'. Tickner consequently questions the dominant practice of locating the Treaty of Westphalia in 1648 as the foundation of modern international politics, a discourse which renders invisible European colonialism and imperialism, which we are told 'has shaped the present and future of more than two thirds of the world's population' (Tickner, 2014: 121). Drawing upon the contribution of ecofeminists, Tickner, suggests that the consolidation of gender hierarchies and the domination of nature are interrelated, emerging during the seventeenth century as a product of Enlightenment thinking, which subsequently encouraged human mastery over nature with detrimental consequences for native populations and women alike. According to Tickner, these developments occurred 'coincidentally' at the same time as the modern state system 'signalling the defeat of religion as a scheme for organising international authority' and 'denying the right of authorities to enforce religious practices outside their territory' (Tickner, 2014: 154). As will be seen in following chapters, Tickner's observations and these developments are not inconsequential.

Chapter 5 retains the Marxist emphasis upon the notion of ideas, knowledge systems and normative frameworks as mechanisms of power through which inequalities are maintained and reproduced. Through an engagement with critical scholarship from within criminology and within international relations scholarship, legalistic and state-centric approaches are critiqued, addressing the significance of symbolic interactionist and constructivist thought for the interpretation of crime control regimes and the current structure of international politics.

Chapter 6 examines the emergence of the modern humanitarian system and the recent development of the international norm of humanitarian intervention known as 'The Responsibility to Protect' (R2P). Modernisation theory, World Systems Analysis, realist and liberal institutionalist insights are applied in order to shed light upon the utility of a range of theoretical perspectives to assess the adequacy of the contemporary international framework to prevent genocide and other atrocity crimes. As will be seen, the existing liberal solution reveals a continuing tension between universalism (Morrison's 'will of all of us' perspective) and power politics (the geo-political realisation of 'the will of one'). Framed historically, and in the light of significant revisions made to the original formulation of the R2P concept (following the World Summit in 2006), the future and effectiveness of the current institutional and normative framework is far from certain, with the principles of 'non-intervention' and 'sovereignty', discussed earlier in this chapter, remaining key barriers affecting the international responses to atrocity crime. While liberal institutionalists optimistically advocated institutional reform to address the limitations within the existing framework, other commentators direct attention to the legacy of colonialism, imperialism and neo-liberal economic policy attached to the spread of the global capitalist world system and the liberal normative programme, advocating transformative change to tackle deep-seated inequalities and injustices rooted within the existing order.

Chapter 7 examines counter-terrorist strategy, identifying the penetration of globalisation rhetoric and modernisation assumptions alongside a preference for situational crime prevention methods and a liberal institutional framework for action. The chapter then applies World Systems Analysis and liberal institutional insights in order to address the adequacy of current measures to deal with the conditions conducive to the spread of terrorism, particularly the legacy of historically inherited vulnerabilities and grievances. Returning to the historical contextualisation of modern world politics, Chapter 7 therefore engages with the legacy of this development for terrorism. In doing so, attention is directed to the salience of Tickner's observation, that Al-Qaeda and its affiliates are currently articulating a desire to restore the Islamic form of government known as the Caliphate, which, for Tickner, constitutes a fundamental challenge to the Westphalian secular interstate political order:

> The ultimate goal of radical revivalists is the Islamization of the international political order – replacing the secular state system and Western-led international institutions with an Islamic system under God's rule.
>
> (Tickner, 2014: 154)

Having touched upon the utility of current strategic responses to international crime and terrorism, Chapter 8 moves to address the issue of human trafficking as a manifestation of transnational organised crime. Structured in two parts, the first section of the chapter examines international (UN), regional (EU and CoU) and national (UK) counter trafficking responses, engaging with feminist scholarship within international relations, criminology, and international political economy. Drawing together many of the debates and insights from earlier sections of the text, Chapter 8 reminds us of the relevance of ideas, discourse, knowledge systems and power in relation to both the categorisation of behaviour as criminal and in relation to responses. This work again emphasises the need to transcend both legalistic and state-centric formulations of crime and again sensitises readers to the significance of wider structural economic and social conditions associated with trade liberalisation and the contemporary structure of the international society of states which both prescribe and limit appropriate courses of action on the trade and exploitation of human beings.

The next chapter will provide an overview of key international and regional organisations and agencies tasked with combating crime and terrorism. By introducing students to the remit, structure and activities of such institutions, it is anticipated that an awareness regarding the strategic priorities, methods and working practices may be developed. In doing so, the chapter returns to key debates regarding the consequences of globalising trends upon governance, accountability and crime and security arenas, and as such it is a necessary precursor to Chapters 5 to 8, which follow.

References

Andreas, P. and Nadelmann, E. (2006). *Policing the Globe: Criminalization and Crime Control in International Relations*. Oxford: Oxford University Press.

Baylis, J., Smith, S., and Owens, P. (2014). *The Globalisation of World Politics*, sixth edition. Oxford: Oxford University Press.

Barak, G. (2001). 'Crime and Crime Control in an Age of Globalization: A Theoretical Dissection', *Critical Criminology*, 10: 57–72.

Bodin, J. (1967). *Six Books of the Commonwealth*. Oxford: Basil Blackwell.

Bowling, B. and Sheptycki, J.W.E. (2012). *Global Policing*. London: Sage.

Charter of the United Nations. Available online at: www.un.org/en/documents/charter/ (accessed June 13, 2015).

Clark, I. (1989). *The Hierarchy of States: Reform and Resistance in the International Order*. Cambridge: Cambridge University Press.

Cohen, R. and Kennedy, P. (2007). *Global Sociology*. Basingstoke: Palgrave Macmillan.

Dasgupta, S. (2004). *The Changing Face of Globalisation*. London: Sage Publications.

Deflem, M. (2002). *Policing World Society: Historical Foundations of International Police Cooperation*. Oxford: Oxford University Press.

Dunne, T. (2011). 'Liberalism', in *The Globalisation of World Politics*, fifth edition. Oxford: Oxford University Press.

Dunne, T. (2014). 'Liberalism', in Baylis, J., Smith, S., and Owens, P. (eds), *The Globalization of World Politics*. Oxford: Oxford University Press. Pp. 113–125.

Dunne, T. and Schmidt, B. (2011). 'Realism', in *The Globalisation of World Politics*, fifth edition. Oxford: Oxford University Press.

Durkheim, E. (1965). *The Division of Labor in Society*, translated by George Simpson. New York: The Free Press.

Felson, D. and Kalaitzidis, A. (2005). 'A Historical Overview of Transnational Crime', in Reichel, P. (ed.), *Handbook of Transnational Crime and Justice*. London: Sage. Pp. 3–19.

Findlay, M. (2008). *Governing Through Globalised Crime*. Cullompton: Willan Publishing.

Goldsmith, A. and Sheptycki, J.W.E. (2010). *Crafting Transnational Policing: Police Capacity-Building and Global Policing Reform*. Oxford: Hart Publishing.

Huntington, S. (1997). *The Clash of Civilizations and the Remaking of World Order*. London: Simon and Schuster.

Ikenberry, G.J. (2009). 'Liberal Internationalism 3.0: America and the Dilemmas of Liberal World Order', *Perspectives on Politics*, 7(1): 71–87.

Ikenberry, G.J. (2011). 'The Future of the Liberal World Order: Internationalism After America', *Foreign Affairs*, 90(3): 56–62.

Jacobs, S., Jacobson, R., and Marchbank, J. (2000). *States of Conflict: Gender, Violence and Resistance*. London: Zed Books.

Kant, I. (2001). 'An Answer to the Question: What is Enlightenment?', in Cahoone, L. (ed.), *From Modernism to Postmodernism: An Anthology*. Oxford: Blackwell Publishers Ltd.

Kiely, R. (2004). 'Neo-Liberal Globalization Meets Global Resistance: The Significance of "Anti-Globalization" Protest', in Dasgupta, S. (ed.), *The Changing Face of Globalisation*. London: Sage.

Kratke, M. and Underhill, G. (2006). 'Political Economy: The Revival of an Interdiscipline', in Stubbs, R. and Underhill, G. (eds), *Political Economy and the Changing Global Order*. Oxford: Oxford University Press.

Machiavelli, N. (1997). *The Prince*. Ware: Wordsworth Editions Limited.

Mittelman, J. (2006). 'Globalization and Its Critics', in Stubbs, R. and Underhill, G. (eds), *Political Economy and the Changing Global Order*. Oxford: Oxford University Press.

Morrison, W. (1997). *Theoretical Criminology: From Modernity to Post-Modernity*. London: Cavendish Publishing.

Nadelmann, E. (1993). *Cops Across Borders: The Internationalization of U.S. Criminal Law Enforcement*. University Park, PA: Pennsylvania State University Press.

Neapolitan, J.L. (1997). *Cross-National Crime: A Research Review and Sourcebook*. Westport, CT: Greenwood Press.

Reus-Smit, C. (2011). 'International Law', in *The Globalisation of World Politics*, fifth edition. Oxford: Oxford University Press.

Ritzer, G. (1996). *Sociological Theory*, fourth edition. Singapore: McGraw-Hill International Editions.

Schwartz, H. (2006). 'Globalization: The Long View', in Stubbs, R. and Underhill, G. (eds), *Political Economy and the Changing Global Order*. Oxford: Oxford University Press.

Scott, L. (2008). 'International History 1900–1990', in Baylis, J., Smith, S., and Owens, P. (eds), *Globalization of World Politics*, fourth edition. Oxford: Oxford University Press.

Shelley, L.I. (1981). *Crime and Modernization: The Impact of Industrialization and Urbanization on Crime*. Carbondale: Southern Illinois University Press.

Sheptycki, J.W.E. (2010) 'The Constabulary Ethic Reconsidered', in Lemieux, F. (ed.), *International Police Cooperation*. Abingdon: Routledge.

Sparke, M. (2013). *Introducing Globalisation*. Chichester: Wiley-Blackwell.

Swingewood, A. (1991). *A Short History of Sociological Thought*, second edition. London: Macmillan.

Taylor, P. and Curtis, D. (2008). 'The United Nations', in Baylis, J., Smith, S., and Owens, P. (eds), *Globalization of World Politics*, fourth edition. Oxford: Oxford University Press.

Taylor, P. and Curtis, D. (2011). 'The United Nations', in Baylis, J., Smith, S., and Owens, P. (eds), *Globalization of World Politics*, fifth edition. Oxford: Oxford University Press.

Tickner, A. (1992). *Gender in International Relations: Feminist Perspectives on Achieving Global Security.* Oxford: Columbia University Press.

Tickner, A. (2014). *A Feminist Voyage Through International Relations.* Oxford: Oxford University Press.

Underhill, G. (2006). 'Introduction: Conceptualizing the Changing Global Order', in Stubbs, R. and Underhill, G. (eds), *Political Economy and the Changing Global Order.* Oxford: Oxford University Press.

Vagg, J. (1993). 'Context and Linkage: Reflections on Comparative Research and "Internationalism" in Criminology', *British Journal of Criminology.* 33(4): 541–554.

Vagg, J. (1995). 'Rough Seas? Contemporary Piracy in South East Asia', *British Journal of Criminology*, 35(1): 63–80.

Vold, G., Bernard, T., and Snipes, J. (1998). *Theoretical Criminology*, fourth edition. Oxford: Oxford University Press.

Wallerstein, I. (2005). *World-Systems Analysis: An Introduction.* London: Duke University Press.

Waltz, K. (1959). *Man, the State and War: A Theoretical Analysis.* New York: Columbia University Press.

Williams, A., Hadfield, A., and Rofe, S. (2012). *International History and International Relations.* London: Routledge.

Woods, N. (2014). 'International Political Economy in an Age of Globalization', in Baylis, J., Smith, S., and Owens, P. (eds), *Globalization of World Politics*, sixth edition. Oxford: Oxford University Press.

4 Regional and international crime control

In Chapter 1 it was argued that a range of significant developments, collectively understood under the banner of 'globalisation', have cumulatively entered into policy-maker, practitioner and popular discourse, influencing conceptions of security and impacting upon structures of governance. While generally recognising the positive consequences of these developments, for example, through the generation of economic opportunities and prosperity, a consensus has emerged regarding the potential dark side of these trends, including a range of threats to national security and challenges to law enforcement and crime control agencies within sovereign states. These developments include urbanisation, the development of rapid transportation and postal systems, improvements in information and communication technology, mobilisation of people, increases in financial and commercial transactions and the development of international markets which have resulted in the increasing acknowledgement that the territories of states are susceptible to external influences rendering governments reliant upon close international, regional and bilateral cooperation to perform their functions adequately (Anderson, 1989).

In Chapter 2, the emerging structure of world politics was presented against the backdrop of key historical events including the First and Second World Wars, European imperial collapse, in addition to the Cold War and its demise. It was argued that an appreciation of these social, political and economic developments and an awareness of the emerging system of governance within global politics are essential for anyone wishing to understand the emergence of informal and formal mechanisms of police and intergovernmental cooperation to combat transnational crime and terrorism. The chapters which follow will demonstrate that such an awareness is also vital in order to appreciate the varied political, legal and pragmatic barriers to cooperation and to assess the utility of criminological, sociological and international relations perspectives applied within this complex and challenging arena.

The purpose of the present chapter is to provide an overview of key international and regional organisations, agencies and programmes directed towards international police and intergovernmental cooperation. However, before doing so, a word of caution is necessary in order to avoid confusion. In the contemporary world order, characterised by an absence of overall world authority (a situation described within international relations literature as 'anarchy'), we are unable to speak of a truly 'international police force' or 'international police community'. We also currently lack a coherent global police infrastructure. Indeed, the notion of the existence of a global police force has been described as a 'chimera' by Bowling and Sheptycki (2012: 3), and as 'aspirational' by Loader and Walker (2007: 113), this despite the existence of policing organisations such as INTERPOL and UN Police. Deflem (2002: 217) for example forcefully asserts: '[a]vailable historical evidence indicates that no international police force in modern society has ever been modelled as a supranational force', pointing to the 'fierce opposition' received following suggestions to create such a system. On a (European) regional level, as pointed out by Brown (2008: 59) there are no EU criminal offences to investigate and no EU criminal court in which offenders could be prosecuted. Thus, literature on the subjects of 'transnational policing', 'international police cooperation' and 'international law enforcement', 'international crime' and 'cross-border crime' emphasises the resilience of sovereign nation-states and national state interests within multilateral and bi-lateral efforts towards police cooperation, acknowledging that 'the criminalization of certain behaviour is still predominantly a matter of national criminal laws' (Anderson *et al.*, 1995: 3–4), while police systems across the world display variation in structure and activities according to national traditions and cultures (Deflem, 2002).

Despite the absence of a world police force, global policing is however a reality. The term 'transnational policing' has been used to describe a diverse set of formal and informal practices including order maintenance and law enforcement activities, joint operations, peacekeeping and capacity-building programmes, crime investigation, intelligence sharing and surveillance, personnel exchanges, training programmes and technical assistance programmes, alongside the functions undertaken within liaison networks and alternative aspects of police work that extend beyond national boundaries, generated by increased connectivity. Mutual assistance can include the taking of evidence, statements of persons, search and seizure, the provision of documents or evidentiary items, the service of documents, and the temporary transfer of persons to assist an investigation or appear as a witness. Mutual assistance is also used in order to obtain the restraint and confiscation of proceeds and instruments of crime (Prost in Brown, 2008: 143).

Associated with aspects of globalisation, theorists of transnational policing draw upon the notion of a shrinking world, directing attention to processes of contact and enhanced communication facilitated by technological developments, tendencies towards homogenisation (and/or Americanisation/Westernisation) and convergence in legislation, agenda setting, practices and processes. However, as indicated in Chapter 3, the theoretical lens through which we look influences our opinion regarding the desirability of such developments. Modernisation theorists, neo-liberalists and classical school inspired criminologists (for example, routine activity theorists and opportunity theorists), viewing such trends pragmatically, in terms of necessary resolutions to crime demands and risks generated by the time lag between increased opportunities for crime to occur and the impotency of geographically located national criminal justice systems to adapt to such challenges generated by the latest phase of modernity or globalisation. Conversely, Marxist inspired theorists and realists are more likely to question the assumptions of progress and adaptation underpinning such work, highlighting instead the significance of power relations, global capitalism, world politics and state interest in accounting for the direction of change and the emergence of global prohibition regimes. Viewed in this light, transnational policing may be observed with suspicion and scepticism, denoting connotations of contagion and even as a new form of American imperialism and/or Westernisation.

Regardless of the theoretical position adopted, such activities may be undertaken multilaterally (extending between several countries) or bi-laterally (from one country to another) (Goldsmith and Sheptycki, 2007: 11; Bowling and Sheptycki, 2012) and may occur at global, regional and local levels (Anderson, 1989: 1). The role of the state is significant in this regard, setting the parameters for study and the material viewed by researchers as appropriate for inclusion and analysis. Many texts on the subject of transnational policing, particularly legalistic works and those undertaken by law enforcement practitioners, tend to remain confined to examination of legal frameworks and the workings of key institutions and agencies. Other researchers have opted to expand the field of their enquiries beyond sovereign states to include a range of other key actors and to examine in greater detail the historical, political and economic contexts in which specific agencies and institutions were created. This work is particularly significant in the light of the 'hollowing out of the state' thesis which directs attention to the salience and potency of state actors in international relations and the function of state actors in agenda setting and decision-making. Bowling and Sheptycki (2012: 3) for example, remaining sensitive to this distinction, contrast the use of the term 'international' (denoting interactions between states) with the term 'transnational' (denoting phenomena that transgress national boundaries). Other authors, such as Anderson (1989) and Lemieux (2010), prefer to utilise the concept of 'police co-operation' to avoid overly restrictive categorisation, enabling attention to be directed towards a range of private and public policing within a variety of forms and guises.

With this thesis in mind, several commentators have argued that recent developments have fundamentally altered state institutions and governance arrangements marking a new era or phase of social organisation (defined as 'late-modernity' or 'post-modernity'), thereby challenging the salience of international relations theories which place a premium upon the nation-state as the key actor within international relations. Against this work, recent contributions have highlighted both the legal and illegal, intentional and unintentional, formal and informal nature of such transnational policing activities and exchanges, and also, the plurality of organisations, agencies and actors undertaking such functions. Within such perspectives, we observe how the state monopoly over policing functions has been passed upwards, emphasising the emerging international legal framework and supranational groups such as UN peacekeeping forces and regional bodies such as Europol alongside other state and non-state significant actors within law enforcement arenas including international donors, national governments, police and law enforcement agencies, military organisations, security services and private security corporations, in addition to activities undertaken between police personnel (Manning in Sheptycki, 2000: 181; Goldsmith and Sheptycki, 2007). Policing decisions and activities, contacts and exchanges are also therefore passed downwards to 'non-state', or quasi-state actors, emphasising the importance of discretion and individual interest in establishing priorities for action, shaping institution creation and the setting of agendas, objectives and institutional remits (Andreas and Nadelmann, 2006). Such contributions, while acknowledging the importance of economic and political factors, endeavour to move beyond deterministic accounts remaining sensitive to the role of agency, choice and serendipity in the transnational crafting of policing.

While necessarily brief, this introduction to transnational policing has pointed to a range of 'hot topics' currently being played out within academic and practitioner literature within the field. Controversy remains regarding the direction and interpretation of these developments, and the importance and role attributed to sovereign state governments alongside other non-state actors. Whether referred to as 'transnational policing', 'international police cooperation', 'cross-border law enforcement' or as 'global policing', a consensus is apparent regarding the relative newness of the subject as a focus for systematic study, and also regarding the complex and mystifying nature of the international and regional criminal justice infrastructure, which has resulted in common misunderstandings regarding the operational jurisdiction and powers of those involved (Anderson, 1989: 8; Brown, 2008; Den Boer in Lemieux, 2010: 61; Bowling and Sheptycki, 2012).

Within the next section of this chapter, forms of intergovernmental and law enforcement cooperation will be presented with a view to providing students with a brief introduction to the key organisations, agencies and programmes which have emerged internationally and transnationally to address cross-border crime and terrorism. The remit, structure and activities of a selection of international organisations will be outlined, including: Interpol, NATO, the World Customs Organisation, the Financial Action Task Force on Money Laundering and the United Nations (including the UN Police and IMF). Focusing upon Europe, regional bodies, including: the Council of Europe, the European Union, particularly the Area of Freedom, Security and Justice, Frontex, Europol and Eurojust; in addition specialised bodies such as the European Agency for Fundamental Rights, European Asylum Support Office, European Monitoring Centre for Drugs and Drug Addiction, European Commission Anti-Fraud Office, Southeast European Law Enforcement Center and the European Police College will also be introduced. This chapter will highlight the evolving nature of the current intergovernmental and transnational policing infrastructure, directing attention to key issues and contemporary challenges faced by law enforcement agencies in their efforts to detect, investigate, prosecute and punish transnational offenders. Acknowledging the selective and necessarily brief treatment of these mechanisms, the intention is to provide an overview of the role and functions of these bodies, key cross-border crime related activities and to direct attention to useful websites and wider literature. The final section of the chapter will return to address emerging issues for intergovernmental and transnational police cooperation, emphasising barriers which have placed limitations upon current efforts and pointing to concerns raised with respect to contemporary accountability mechanisms, human rights issues and the implications of existing governance arrangements.

Key organisations and agencies

There are several useful contributions, which have endeavoured to provide clarity in relation to the global policing architecture for the student of policing cooperation. In particular, Bowling and Sheptycki's (2012) *Global Policing* and Reichel's (2005) *Handbook of Transnational Crime and Justice* provide valuable overviews of selected global and regional police agencies. These works may be supplemented by practical contributions written from the perspective of practitioners, including Brown's (ed.) (2008) *Combating International Crime* and Lemieux (ed.) (2010) *International Police Cooperation*, which both offer useful insight into the realities of international law enforcement and describe the role and remit of a selection of international organisations. Viewed as ground breaking, Deflem's (2002) *Policing World Society* is also particularly useful in providing detail regarding the historical foundations of international police cooperation, focusing specifically upon Germany and the United States. Anderson's (1989) *Policing the World* provides an excellent historical account of the evolution of Interpol as a global policing organisation, while other useful works include the frequently cited Nadelmann (1993) *Cops Across Borders* which examines the internationalisation of US criminal law enforcement. At a regional level (while now rather dated) Anderson, den Boer, Cullen, Gilmore, Raab and Walker's (1995) *Policing the European Union* and Sheptycki's (1995) 'Transnational Policing and the Makings of a Postmodern State' trace the development of a police facility across the European Union and therefore remain helpful in presenting the early foundations of policing cooperation within that organisation. Significantly, Sheptycki's (1998) 'Policing, Postmodernism and Transnationalisation' and (2000) 'Issues in Transnational Policing' and Goldsmith and Sheptycki's (2007) *Crafting Transnational Policing* serve as useful reminders regarding the plurality of transnational policing networks and the morphology of governance within the contemporary period.

This body of literature, while not exhaustive, will provide those with an interest in understanding transnational policing with an excellent foundation upon which to build. Below, the key institutional framework (as evident within this literature and beyond) will be presented. A brief history for each body will be followed by a description of its remit, principle tasks and structure. Significant developments in relation to cross-border crime and terrorism will also be indicated, directing the reader to organisational websites and useful literature.

International organisations

International Criminal Police Organization (INTERPOL)

Established in 1923 as the International Criminal Police Commission (ICPC) and subsequently renamed in 1956 as the International Criminal Police Organization-Interpol, Interpol is an intergovernmental organisation widely acknowledged as the world's largest international policing organisation. The organisational aims, as set out in Article 2 of its Constitution, are to ensure and promote the widest possible mutual assistance between all criminal police authorities and to establish and develop all institutions likely to contribute effectively to the prevention and suppression of ordinary law crimes.

Interpol currently provides support and assistance to 190 Member States, facilitating operational police cooperation, including Interpol-coordinated operations, also supporting security in fragile settings and strengthening law enforcement partnerships. Interpol's policing cooperation extends to include information exchange and database searches.[1] Interpol retains records on wanted persons, known criminals and missing persons, enabling police officers to search for stolen and lost travel documents and stolen motor vehicles and also to compare and identify fingerprints and DNA profiles.[2] Interpol notices are used to alert police worldwide to fugitives, suspected terrorists, dangerous criminals, missing persons and potential threats.[3] The organisation hosts an annual meeting and regional conferences providing training and workshops and has recently launched the 'Interpol Global Learning Centre' which provides online learning materials for the global police community in addition to the 'Interpol Global Complex for Innovation' (IGCI), which, is described as a cutting-edge research and development facility built to focus on cybercrime, capacity building and training, also providing operational support.

Interpol also has seven regional offices across the world and in 2004, it inaugurated an 'Interpol liaison office' and Special Representative within the United Nations, followed in 2009 with the opening of the Office of the Special Representative to the European Union. Additional partners include NATO, the East African Community, the International Multilateral Partnership Against Cyber Threats (IMPACT), the Small Arms Survey (SAS), and Mercosur among others.

Interpol describes its role as enabling police around the world to work together to make the world a safer place. Interpol's structure is defined in its constitution originally adopted by the General Assembly in 1956 and subsequently amended with the most recent version adopted in 2008 (I/CONS/GA/1956(2008)). The General Assembly is Interpol's supreme governing body, meeting annually and responsible for policy decisions, budget, activities and programmes, working methods and resources.

Each member country maintains a National Central Bureau (NCB) staffed by its own law enforcement officials forming the link between the Member State and Interpol's global network. The Command and Coordination Centre forms the connection between the General Secretariat and NCBs, serving as a contact point for any member country faced with a crisis, coordinating the exchange of information, handling crisis management during serious incidents, undertaking checks utilising the range of Interpol databases, supporting operations and monitoring open and closed sources for potential threats. The Centre also provides for the deployment of Incident Response Teams (IRTs) and Major Events Support Teams to deliver emergency assistance following a disaster or crime, or assist with security implementation at international events.

Interpol's priorities include the provision of a Secure Global Communications Network; 24/7 providing support to policing and law enforcement agencies across the world; capacity building; the identification of crimes and criminals. Key activities include: cooperation between Interpol and NATO to counter maritime piracy; efforts to counter ivory trafficking and the trade in protected species and wildlife crime;[4] detection and investigation of trafficking in illicit goods and counterfeiting; continuing efforts to tackle trafficking in drugs, weapons and human beings; the recovery of stolen artwork, jewellery theft and robbery; pharmaceutical crime; radiological and nuclear investigation and nuclear terrorism; border security; and the use of fake documents (travel document initiative), integrity in sports, in addition to training and capacity-building programmes in post-conflict environments.[5] Genocide, war crimes prevention and gender-based violence and terrorism also feature strongly within Interpol's recent activities.[6]

See www.Interpol.int/.

North Atlantic Treaty Organization (NATO)

Founded in 1949, the North Atlantic Treaty Organization is an alliance between Europe and North America, which seeks to safeguard the freedom and security of its members by political and military means. It consists of a transatlantic forum for consultations on all matters that affect the territorial integrity, political independence and security of its members.

Member states are represented within the North Atlantic Council by an Ambassador or Permanent Representative, assisted by advisors and officials who attend a range of NATO committees. Meetings of the Council are also organised at various levels including Heads of State or Government, Ministers of Foreign Affairs and Ministers of Defence. Partner states attend NATO committee meetings and also attend meetings of the Euro-Atlantic Partnership Council (EAPC), NATO-Russia Permanent Joint Council or NATO-Ukraine Commission.

With regard to structure, NATO is divided into a Civilian structure, a Military structure and NATO Organisations and Agencies. The NATO Secretary General is the head of the Organisation's International Staff and is responsible for decision-making and directing the consultation processes. The International Staff (comprising the Office of the Secretary General, six Divisions, Office of Resources and Office of Security) support the work undertaken by the North Atlantic Council and its committees.

The Military structure consists of the Military Committee, supported by an integrated International Military Staff composed of seconded military personnel and civilian staff from national military establishments. The Military Representatives constitute the Military Committee in Permanent Session. NATO Strategic Commands are responsible for the development of defence plans and for the forces under their command control.

NATO's Civilian and Military structures are supported by a range of programmes, working groups, agencies and committees, which comprise the Organisations and Agencies structure. This includes a number of NATO accredited Centres of Excellence, offering expertise and training in a range of thematic areas including cyber defence and terrorism.

The Strategic Concept for the Defence and Security of Members of the North Atlantic Treaty Organization (NATO) adopted by Heads of State and Government in November 2010 details the core tasks and principles of the organisation. The organisation remains committed to the Charter of the United Nations affirming the primary responsibility of the Security Council for the maintenance of international peace and security, signing a UN-NATO Declaration in 2008 to deepen political dialogue and practical cooperation. As mentioned in the previous chapter, while the alliance was originally directed towards deterring Soviet expansionism during the Cold War, preventing the revival of nationalist militarism in Europe through a strong North American presence on the continent, and encouraging European political integration, NATO currently focuses upon the effective fulfilment of three key tasks, namely: collective defence, crisis management and cooperative security. In particular, in accordance with Article 5 of the Washington Treaty, NATO members are committed to deterring and defending against any threat of aggression, and against emerging security challenges where they threaten the security of individual Allies or the Alliance as a whole. With respect to crisis management, NATO retains political and military tools to assist in the management of developing crises, to stop ongoing conflicts and consolidate security in post-conflict situations. NATO engages in partnerships with non-member states and international organisations including the United Nations, the European Union and the Organization for Security and Co-operation in Europe.

In addition to conventional military threats, including the proliferation of nuclear weapons and other weapons of mass destruction between nations, the concept of security has been extended to include terrorism, extremism and transnational illegal activities including trafficking in arms, narcotics and people, cybercrime, piracy, energy, resource and environmental security and technology-related developments including laser weapons, electronic warfare and technologies that impede access to space.

See www.nato.int/.

The United Nations

As discussed in Chapter 3, created in 1945 following the Second World War, the United Nations is an international organisation tasked with the maintenance of international peace and security. As detailed within Article 1 of the Organisation's Constitution, in achieving this objective, Member States have agreed: to take effective collective measures for the prevention and removal of threats to peace; for the suppression of acts of aggression or other breaches of the peace; and, to bring about by peaceful means settlement of international disputes or situations which might lead to a breach of the peace. Based upon the principle of equal rights and the self-determination of peoples, the United Nations also seeks to develop friendly relations among nations, facilitating international cooperation and the harmonisation of actions in solving international problems of an economic, social, cultural, or humanitarian character, and in promoting and encouraging respect for human rights and for fundamental freedoms.

With respect to the structure and governance of the United Nations, the General Assembly (consisting of representatives from 193 Member States) comprises the main deliberative body of the UN with each Member State having one vote ('the rule of all of us'). There are numerous subsidiary organs of the General Assembly, including Committees (e.g. Ad Hoc Committee on the Administration of Justice at the United Nations and Ad Hoc Committee on the Elaboration of a Convention Against Corruption), Commissions (e.g. the Disarmament Commission; International Law Commission; UN Commission on International Trade Law and UN Peacebuilding Commission), Boards (e.g. Advisory Board on Disarmament Matters and the Executive Boards of the Children's Fund and Development Programmes), Councils, Panels and Working Groups (for example, including those addressing disarmament and development issues), Programmes and Funds (e.g. United Nations Office on Drugs and Crime), in addition to Research and Training Institutions (e.g. United Nations Interregional Crime and Justice Research Institute).

A second body, the Security Council, is responsible for the maintenance of peace and security and contains representation from five permanent members (France, the United States, the United Kingdom, the Russian Federation and China – 'the rule of one of us' or at least, the five most powerful!), and ten non-permanent members, elected for two year terms by the General Assembly. Importantly, the five permanent members maintain veto rights over all Security Council decisions, reflecting tension between the universalism represented within the General Assembly and the power politics evident within the Security Council. As detailed within the previous chapter, while this development has its roots in efforts to avoid the institutional failure of its predecessor international organisation (the League of Nations), this situation has led to numerous (unsuccessful) calls for the reform of the Security Council and has also been identified as a key factor influencing inconsistency and selectivity in the application of Security Council authorisation of humanitarian intervention (see Chapter 6).

A number of subsidiary bodies report directly to the Security Council including the Counter-Terrorism Committee, the International Criminal Tribunals for former Yugoslavia and Rwanda, the Working Group on Children and Armed Conflict, in addition to 'Peacekeeping Operations and Missions' (which oversees the work of the UN Police Division, which will be discussed shortly).

The Secretariat undertakes the day-to-day administration of the organisation. The Secretary-General is the head of the Secretariat and is appointed by the General Assembly on the recommendation of the Security Council for a five-year renewable term. The Economic and Social Council (ECOSOC) coordinates the economic, social and related work of the UN and oversees the activities of the many specialised agencies and institutions, also comprising a forum for debate, making policy recommendations. A number of bodies report directly to ECOSOC, including: Functional Commissions (e.g. Commission on Crime Prevention and Criminal Justice, the Commission on Narcotic Drugs, the Commission for Social Development and the Commission on the Status of Women); Regional Commissions; Standing Committees; Ad Hoc bodies; and Expert bodies and other related bodies (e.g. International Narcotics Control Board).

The International Court of Justice (ICJ) serves to settle legal disputes between Member States and to offer advisory opinions on legal questions to UN bodies and specialised agencies.

With regard to cross-border crime, the prevention of crime and terrorism and the treatment of offenders have featured within the remit and agenda of the UN since its inception in 1945 (including the Single Convention on Narcotic Drugs of 1961, amended by the 1972 Protocol, and the Convention on Psychotropic Substances of 1971). Other significant early developments include the elaboration of legal instruments to prevent terrorism and their subsequent amendments. From 1955, the United Nations Congresses on Crime Prevention and Criminal Justice have been held every five years, bringing together practitioners, academics, parliamentarians and experts in the field, contributing to both policy and practice at national, regional and international level. However, as detailed by Gregory in Sheptycki (2000: 116), crime issues were merely given cursory attention within the Economic and Social Council until 1983. The UN Congress on the Prevention of Crime and the Treatment of Offenders (UNCPCTO) reportedly addressed crime more systematically from 1975 onwards, addressing issues such as corporate practices, organised crime and corruption. Gregory identifies the 7th Congress of the UNCPCTO in 1985 as the forum during which a broad international crime agenda became transmitted, eventually manifesting in the Milan Action Plan, resulting in the raised profile of crime issues within the UN's overall agenda and expanded conceptions of national security. The Congress directed attention to the existence and activities of transnational organised crime groups and the need for collective action to counter the threats posed by this group of transnational actors.

The 1988 United Nations Convention against Illicit Traffic in Narcotic Drugs and Psychotropic Substances (1988 Drug Convention) is widely viewed as one of the most significant multilateral instruments influencing the development of subsequent conventions. In particular, the Convention enhanced extradition, mutual assistance and asset confiscation also serving to facilitate cooperation in relation to drug trafficking and the proceeds of drug trafficking offences. Later UN action included a recommendation to create a global crime prevention and criminal justice network, and the creation of a World Ministerial Conference on Organised Transnational Crime in 1994 (leading to the production of the Naples Political Declaration and Global Action Plan Against Organised International Crime) (see Gregory in Sheptycki, 2000).

In 1992 (following resolution 1992/1 and on the request of the General Assembly), the Commission on Crime Prevention and Criminal Justice (CCPCJ) was established by the Economic and Social Council (ECOSOC) as one of its functional commissions. This body acts as the principal policymaking body of the United Nations in the field of crime prevention and criminal justice. It also offers Member States a forum for exchanging expertise, experience and information in order to develop national and international strategies, and to identify priorities for combating crime. Another significant body, the United Nations Office on Drugs and Crime (UNODC), was established five years later, through the merger of the UN Drugs Control Programme and the Centre for International Crime Prevention. The UNODC provides legal and technical assistance, working with Member States to enhance their responses to the interconnected problems of drug use, illicit drug trafficking, trafficking in human beings and firearms, transnational crime, corruption and terrorism. Its mission, articulated within the '2012–15 UNODC Strategy' (E/RES/2012/12), is 'To promote effective responses to transnational organized crime, illicit trafficking and illicit drug trafficking by facilitating the implementation at the normative and operational levels of the relevant United Nations conventions'.

With a mandate to facilitate the ratification and implementation of relevant international conventions on crime, drugs and terrorism, the UNODC employs an integrated approach directed towards the eradication or alleviation of conditions that encourage criminal activities. The organisation also facilitates the implementation of existing international legal instruments and their transformation into global norms and international legal instruments, undertaking research and analysis and offering technical assistance to Member States.

Guided by international mandates, the work of the UNODC is organised thematically (addressing transnational organised crime, illicit trafficking and illicit drug trafficking; countering corruption; preventing terrorism; strengthening the rule of law through criminal justice and crime prevention; drug abuse prevention through prevention, reintegration and alternative development; research, trend analysis and forensics; and policy support). The UNODC works directly with governments, international organisations, other United Nations entities, the private sector and civil society groups. Its work is supported by country and regional programmes through the development of localised hubs of action and expertise. The UNODC offers advice and assistance, awareness raising, best practice dissemination, evidence-based research, legislative and legal support and technical assistance. Ultimately, the UNODC is tasked with enhancing the capacity of governments to build and sustain safe and stable societies, countering security threats, informing policy and operational decision-making and strengthening criminal justice institutions (UN, 2012).

The UNODC relies on voluntary contributions (mainly from governments), which cover more than 90 per cent of their budget. The CCPCJ functions as a governing body of the UNODC and also acts as the preparatory body of the United Nations Congresses on Crime Prevention and Criminal Justice.

In December 1998, the UN General Assembly adopted resolution 53/111 establishing an open-ended intergovernmental ad hoc committee for the purpose of elaborating a comprehensive international convention against transnational organised crime. The committee's work was carried out at the UNODC headquarters in Vienna and continued following resolution 54/126 of 17 December 1999. This work led to the signing in December 2000 of the United Nations Convention against Transnational Organized Crime (TOC Convention), known as the Palermo Convention, which entered into force on 29 September 2003. It is supplemented by three additional protocols that target trafficking in persons, especially women and children; the smuggling of migrants; and the illicit manufacturing and trafficking of firearms (United Nations Protocol to Prevent, Suppress and Punish Trafficking in Persons). The Trafficking Protocol came into force on 25 December 2003, the Smuggling Protocol on 28 January 2004 and the Firearms Protocol on 3 July 2005. More recently, the United Nations Convention against Corruption (Corruption Convention) came into force on 14 December 2005, with Member States currently negotiating a draft comprehensive convention on international terrorism to complement the existing framework (see un.org).

The UN General Assembly's proposed strategic framework for 2016–17, divided into nine sub-programmes, includes efforts to promote and support effective responses to TOC, illicit trafficking and illicit drug trafficking. The framework promotes the ratification of existing conventions, also advocating the development of regional initiatives and cooperation agreements; cooperation, coordination and capacity building; technical assistance and training on anti-money laundering and countering the financing of terrorism; the promotion of drug use prevention interventions; the implementation of drug treatment rehabilitation and social reintegration, reducing vulnerability to HIV/AIDs; the development of illicit crop control strategies; measures to counter corruption and terrorism; and the promotion of effective, fair, humane and accountable criminal justice systems. The Strategic Framework also remains committed to undertaking research and trend analysis of drugs and crime and criminal justice issues, taking steps to enhance the organisation's forensic and scientific capacity.

The UNODC's strategy and priorities contribute to, and flow from, wider UN policy goals including those outlined within the Millennium Declaration; the twentieth special session of the General Assembly on countering the world drug problem; the 2005 World Summit Outcome; Economic and Social Council resolutions 2007/12 and 2007/19; and the Political Declaration and Plan of Action on International Cooperation towards an Integrated and Balanced Strategy to Counter the World Drug Problem.

See www.unodc.org/.

The UN Police Division

The United Nations does not have its own military force or police force. It depends instead upon contributions from Member States. United Nations Peacekeepers assist countries torn by conflict to create the conditions for sustainable peace, assisting with political processes; reforming judicial systems; training law enforcement and police forces; disarming and reintegrating former combatants; and supporting the return of internally displaced persons and refugees.

United Nations police officers were originally deployed alongside military personnel in 1960 to serve in the UN Peacekeeping Operation in the Congo (ONUC). This activity was undertaken under the limited mandate to 'monitor, observe and report'. Four years later, the first 'component' of police was deployed to the United Nations Peacekeeping Force in Cyprus (UNFICYP), with the number of deployments increasing during the 1990s to include El Salvador (ONUSAL), Mozambique (ONUMOZ) and Cambodia (UNTAC). Since 1993, a Civilian Police Unit (CIVPOL) became embedded within the Department of Peacekeeping Operations (DPKO), with officers playing a significant role within UN Operations in the former Yugoslavia (UNPROFOR), Eastern Slavonia, Barania and Western Sirmium (UNTAES), Bosnia and Herzegovina (UNMIBH), Croatia (UNCRO) and Kosovo (UNMIK). Formed Police Units are regarded as an efficient and cost-effective method of bridging the gap between the military component of UN Missions and the capacity of national police forces within post-conflict situations.

Following the publication of the 'Brahimi Report', the Police Division was established in 2000. Originally known as Civilian Police or CIVPOL, in 2005 the organisation changed its name to United Nations Police and in 2007 it became part of the 'DPKO Office of Rule of Law and Security Institutions', which reports directly to the UN Security Council as a subsidiary body. UN police officers support host-state police and law enforcement agencies in the execution of their functions. However, they are not law enforcement officers under the legislation of the host country and therefore their role, duties and powers are limited to those specified within the mandate of the mission and the specific directives issued by the Department of Peacekeeping Operations (DPKO). Currently, over 13,000 police officers from more than 82 countries are deployed in 19 field missions across four continents.

UN Police are deployed in most UN peacekeeping operations, also functioning as advisors in UN special political missions. While the mandate and activities of UN Police Officers vary from mission to mission, it is evident that since 2000 the traditional mandate to monitor and observe has been expanded, with the force playing a more direct, hands-on role, evolving to include institutional capacity building for local forces. Approved in 2006 by UN Member States, the United Nations Standing Police Capacity (comprising police officers from around the world who are deployed for short periods to UN missions) became operational in 2007, first deployed in missions in Chad (MINURCAT) and Timor-Leste (UNMIT).

The varied roles of UN Police Officers include taking responsibility as an interim law enforcement agency; assisting security sector reforms to protect civilians; the facilitation of humanitarian assistance; rebuilding and supporting the reform and restructuring of domestic police and other law enforcement agencies and security through training, mentoring, advising and capacity building in the areas of policing and law enforcement. UN Police Officers provide support to enhance crowd control capacity and provide security for elections. Other functions have included patrolling and the establishment of community policing; helping to ensure compliance with human rights standards and democratic policing; public order and administration. UN Police also assist in a wide range of other areas including: direct assistance, such as the provision of trust funds to refurbish facilities (for example crime labs and forensic capability, communication equipment and other law enforcement material); the procurement of vehicles and the implementation of traffic systems. Increasingly, the UN Police are mandated to take on specific crime-fighting roles, thereby directly or indirectly involved in investigations and providing for the safety and security of residents (as in the case of Kosovo). UN Police also play a key role in the protection of United Nations personnel and facilities. Today, UN Police Officers create policy and guidance, engage in strategic planning activities, engage in selection and recruitment processes, provide operational support through the Standing Police Capacity, assist host states in their response to sexual and gender-based violence, also facilitating wider partnerships and regional cooperation (a remit recently subject to question, as detailed in Chapter 8 in relation to human trafficking).

On 21 January 2013, Security Council resolution 2086 was adopted, emphasising the multidimensional nature of peacekeeping. During the same year, a new vision for the UN Police was unveiled during the 8th Annual Heads of Police Components Conference. The vision of the UN Police, in cooperation with Member States and other relevant stakeholders, is to work in tandem with host-state authorities to translate day-to-day public safety into long-term peace and security – supporting effective and efficient policing and providing strategic advice and guidance (UN Police Magazine, 2014). UN Police have recently published their Strategic Guidance Framework for UN policing, setting out the core functions of a generic UN Police peacekeeping operation. It lays down approaches to capacity building and identifies core principles upon which the UN Police operate. Following recent examples of criminal misconduct (including corruption and sexual predation) by UN police officers (see Chapter 8), efforts have been undertaken to promote transnational standards, democratic norms and procedures (see Hills, 2009: 310). A commitment has subsequently been made to share good practice to ensure consistency of approach across UN missions, placing human rights and accountability as central within the strategy on UN Policing. Developments in this regard have included: (operational and tactical) mission specific training materials on the protection of civilians; the creation of a standard training manual for FPUs; a uniform code of conduct including guidance upon how to prevent sexual exploitation and abuse; and the introduction of Women Protection Advisors, preventing and investigating sexual and gender-based violence and pre-deployment training on child protection. Moreover, a dedicated international training centre was created in 2013 under the auspices of the G-8 to provide technical and financial assistance in order to increase global capacity for sustaining peace support operations.

In order to make this vision of 'sustainable peace' a reality, key UN police mandates include reform through capacity and institution building, operational support to host-state police and other law enforcement services, interim policing and the protection of civilians. Police related mandates are furthermore tasked with the promotion of the rule of law and democratic policing, respect for human rights standards, and more recently, efforts directed towards 'guarding against peace spoilers' (for example, transnational organised crime and corruption).

Consequently, police related activities are described as integral to the mandate of the Security Council in relation to its objective to create stable and secure environments. The Department of Peacekeeping Operations has recognised and acknowledged links between organised crime, terrorism, armed groups, arms traffickers and corruption and their role as 'spoilers' undermining weakened states and impacting upon development efforts. Actions are therefore currently directed towards the prevention, disruption and dismantling of organised crime in post-conflict situations. Working in partnership, the UN Police Division cooperates closely with the United Nations Office on Drugs and Crime, the United Nations Development Programme, Interpol and also with regional groups including the Economic Community of West African States, the African Union, the European Union and individual Member States. Cooperation is directed towards drug production and trafficking, human trafficking, the exploitation of natural resources and weapons trafficking.[7]

See www.un.org/en/peacekeeping/sites/police/division.shtml.

International Monetary Fund (IMF)

Created in 1944 alongside the International Bank for Reconstruction and Development (IBRD) (now known as the World Bank), the IMF is a specialised agency of the United Nations established by the International Monetary and Financial Conference (in Bretton Woods, USA). While the IBRD was originally designed to provide underdeveloped nations with needed capital, the IMF was designed to monitor exchange rates and lend reserve currencies to nations with trade deficits. While the role of each institution has evolved over time, the IMF continues to work with the objective of fostering global growth and economic stability. It provides policy advice, financial and technical assistance to members and also works with developing nations to help them achieve macroeconomic stability and reduce poverty. The IMF's main objective is to ensure the stability of the international monetary system. However, in 2012 the Fund's mandate was updated to include all macroeconomic and financial sector issues that bear on global stability.

Surveillance comprises a key activity of the IMF, which includes reviewing member state policies, assessing regional and global financial developments, financial markets and global prospects, also providing economic outlooks.

The decision-making body of the IMF is the board of governors, comprising one governor and one alternate governor from each Member State (usually the minister of finance or head of the central bank). The International Monetary and Financial Committee (IMFC) and the Development Committee advise the IMF Board of Governors, providing guidance for the IMF's work programme. The Executive Board undertakes the day-to-day business of the IMF.

In 2000, the IMF expanded its work in the area of anti-money laundering (AML), extending its remit further in 2001 to include combating the financing of terrorism (CFT). In 2004, the Executive Board (IMF, 2015) agreed to make AML/CFT assessments and capacity development activities a regular part of IMF work.

The IMF's AML/CFT programme was originally concerned with anti-money laundering and combating the financing of terrorism, which were undertaken as part of the Reports on the Observance of Standards and Codes (ROSC) programme and of the Financial Sector Assessment Program (FSAP), and capacity development activities. Over time, the IMF's AML/CFT issues have entered other areas of IMF work, particularly its surveillance and Fund-supported programmes.[8]

In its efforts to address money laundering and the financing of terrorism, the IMF cooperates with a number of bodies including the World Bank, the Financial Action Task Force (FATF) and FATF-Style Regional Bodies (FSRBs). The IMF also contributes to various working groups and international initiatives directed towards anti-corruption including Extractive Industries Transparency Initiative, the G20 Anti-Corruption Working Group, the OECD Working Group on Bribery in International Business Transactions, and the Stolen Assets Recovery (StAR) initiative.[9]

Work to counter corruption, money laundering and the financing of terrorism therefore feature as essential aspects of the IMF's renewed remit, viewing such activities as having the potential to threaten market integrity, distort competition, and endanger economic development and stability.

See www.imf.org/.

International Maritime Organisation (IMO)

In 1948, an international conference in Geneva adopted a convention formally establishing the IMO (the original name was the Inter-Governmental Maritime Consultative Organisation, or IMCO, but the name was changed in 1982 to IMO). The IMO Convention entered into force in 1958 and the new Organisation met for the first time the following year. As a United Nations specialised agency, the mission of the International Maritime Organisation (IMO) is to promote safe, secure, environmentally sound, efficient and sustainable shipping through cooperation. IMO Member States and intergovernmental and non-governmental organisations have collectively introduced measures in the maritime transport sector designed to enhance maritime and port security, prevent and suppress unlawful acts against the safety of maritime navigation and protect against disruptions to global trade. As detailed in Chapter 2, piracy and armed robbery against ships are currently viewed by the IMO as 'a real and ever-present danger to those who use the seas for peaceful purposes'. Consequently, the United Nations, regional bodies, governments (acting collectively or individually), military forces, shipping companies, ship operators and ships' crew currently work together in order to counter the threat posed by piracy. IMO has continued to develop guidance to Member States and the shipping industry on measures to deter or prevent piracy attacks from being successful, and to investigate offences. Recognising that, although piracy manifests itself at sea, the roots of the problem are to be found ashore, IMO has also promoted the development of regional initiatives to develop states' capacity to address piracy collectively.

See www.imo.org/.

World Customs Organisation (WCO)

Established in 1952 as the Customs Co-operation Council (CCC), the World Customs Organisation (WCO) comprises an independent intergovernmental body, which acts as a forum for dialogue and exchange between national Customs delegates, with competence in Customs matters. Representing 179 Customs administrations, and claiming to be 'the global centre of Customs expertise', the organisation's mission is presented as enhancing the effectiveness and efficiency of Customs administrations, contributing to the economic and social well-being of Members, enhancing the protection of society and national territory and aiming to secure and facilitate international trade.

With regard to the structure of the WCO, the governing body known as 'the Council' draws upon the competence and skills of a Secretariat in addition to a range of technical and advisory committees. Employing a range of Conventions, technical assistance, training services, research and analysis, the WCO aims to promote harmonised Customs procedures and standards, facilitating international cooperation and information exchange, alongside knowledge and capacity-building activities. The WCO also functions to stimulate the growth of legitimate international trade, and to combat fraudulent activities.

With respect to cross-border threats, WCO's strategic goals include: activities to combat illicit trade to protect public health and safety, society and economic prosperity; and also work to promote integrity and good governance. In particular, the Enforcement Committee contributes to work on anti-smuggling, compliance and intelligence in areas including security, commercial fraud, illicit drug trafficking and money laundering, facilitating cooperation between Customs administrations, the business/private sector and government and non-governmental organisations.

The WCO Annual Report 2012–13 details a number of activities within this area including a joint operation, 'Meerkat', undertaken in July 2012 (initiated between WCO, Interpol and customs and police administrations), which sought to tackle the illicit trafficking of cigarettes, tobacco and alcohol in East and Southern Africa. Other initiatives have included the Customs enforcement operation, 'Operation VICE GRIPS 2' undertaken in July 2012 and 'Operation Pangea V' undertaken between September and October 2012 (coordinated between WCO, Interpol, Europol, the Permanent Forum of International Pharmaceutical Crime, the Heads of Medicines Agencies Working Group of Enforcement Officers and the Pharmaceutical Security Institute). Both operations were directed towards the seizure of illicit medicines (including anti-malarial and anti-parasitic drugs, antibiotics, cough syrups, contraceptive pills and infertility treatments), estimated to be worth over US$40 million. Further operations undertaken in 2012 have been targeted towards seizures of drugs or precursor chemicals within postal or express mail channels (Operation SKY-NET), seizures of endangered flora and fauna and their derivatives (prohibited or regulated by the Convention on International Trade in Endangered Species of Wild Fauna and Flora) (e.g. Project GAPIN II).

See wcoomd.org.

The Financial Action Task Force on Money Laundering (FATF)

Created in 1989 by the G-7 nations, the Financial Action Task Force (FATF) is an intergovernmental policy-making body tasked with setting standards and promoting the effective implementation of legal, regulatory and operational measures for combating money laundering. Its mandate was expanded in 2001 to include terrorist financing and other related threats to the integrity of the international financial system with recent activities extending, following a request made by the G-20, into efforts to counter corruption.

In 1990, FATF issued a number of Recommendations (known as the International Standards on Combating Money Laundering and the Financing of Terrorism & Proliferation), subsequently revised in 1996, 2001, 2003 and 2012, which have become widely recognised as the international standard for combating money laundering, the financing of terrorism and the proliferation of weapons of mass destruction. The FATF Recommendations are used by a global network of 188 countries.

FATF was not created as a permanent body and operates under a fixed life-span requiring renewal via a specific decision by its Ministers to continue. The 2012–2020 Financial Action Task Force mandate was adopted in April 2012, setting out the objectives, functions and tasks of the organisation.

In addition to the implementation of the legal, regulatory and operational measures mentioned previously, FATF also works to identify national-level vulnerabilities with the purpose of protecting the international financial system from misuse. Key tasks include threat and trend analysis, the development of international standards, assessment and monitoring of Members to determine levels of compliance and system effectiveness, engagement with deficient, high risk and vulnerable jurisdictions and states coordinating action to strengthen national regimes. FATF promotes the full and effective implementation of its recommendations through a global network of FATF-style regional bodies and international organisations including the UN Security Council and G-20 (consulting with the World Bank and International Monetary Fund), also engaging with the private sector and civil society through a consultative forum. Eurojust, Europol, Interpol, the United Nations Office on Drugs and Crime, the Organisation for Security and Co-operation in Europe (OSCE) and the World Customs Organisation are among the bodies listed with Observer Status to FATF.

The structure of the organisation comprises the Plenary, a decision-making body, meeting three times a year, consisting of member jurisdictions and organisations, responsible for approving the work programme and budget of FATF and for appointing the President, Vice-President and Steering group. The President, appointed for a term of one year, convenes and chairs the meetings of the Plenary and of the Steering Group, also overseeing the FATF Secretariat, assisted by a Vice-President. The Steering Group is an advisory body tasked with monitoring and guiding the progress of the FATF's ongoing work; facilitating coordination across the working groups; disseminating information to all Members and taking forward any other work necessary for FATF to fulfil its mandate. The Secretariat is composed of the Executive Secretary and Secretariat staff, provided by the OECD, and located at the OECD Headquarters in Paris. The Secretariat is responsible for supporting the activities of the FATF, undertaking administrative functions and the day-to-day management of the organisation. Its membership extends to 36 member jurisdictions and organisations including the European Commission and Gulf Co-operation Council.

The FATF Annual report 2012–13 details recent activities undertaken by the organisation in areas such as: confiscation and asset recovery; vulnerabilities of new payment products and services susceptible to money laundering; guidance related to politically exposed persons and legal professionals and their potential vulnerability to bribery and corruption; guidance relating to the prevention, suppression and disruption of proliferation of weapons of mass destructions (WMD) and its financing (including the issuing of a 'best practice paper' addressing the abuse of non-profit organisations, predominantly the use of charitable organisations for the purpose of financing terrorism); and initiatives addressing counterfeiting of currency.

See www.fatf-gafi.org.

Regional programmes

Organisation for Security and Co-operation in Europe (OSCE)

The Organisation for Security and Co-operation in Europe (OSCE) is the world's largest regional security organisation and provides a forum for high-level political dialogue on a range of security issues. The organisation's forerunner, 'the Conference on Security and Co-operation in Europe' (CSCE) was originally created during the 1970s as a forum for dialogue and negotiation between East and West. Following the signing of the Helsinki Final Act in 1975, a number of key commitments and fundamental principles were established guiding the behaviour of states to one another and towards their citizens. In 1990 the CSCE's remit was expanded to respond to challenges posed by the post-Cold War environment (including the fall of the Berlin wall in 1989, the end of the Cold War, the breakup of former Yugoslavia and Balkan conflicts), resulting in the acquisition of permanent institutions and operational capabilities. During this time the CSCE engaged in crisis management and post-conflict rehabilitation efforts. In 1994 CSCE changed its name to the Organisation for Security and Co-operation in Europe (OSCE).

Security considerations and the activities of the organisation have consequently altered over time, and now include arms control, terrorism, good governance, energy security, human trafficking, democratisation, media freedom and minority rights. With currently 57 participating states, the OSCE claims to work to ensure peace, democracy and stability within Europe. With respect to the structure of the organisation, overall political responsibility lies with the Chairperson-in-Office (the foreign minister of the country holding the OSCE Chairmanship), which rotates annually. Member States' foreign ministers meet annually to review the organisation's activities and programmes and to provide overall direction to the Organisation. Each member is viewed equally. Employing a three-pronged approach to security addressing politico-military, economic and environmental dimensions, the OSCE's practical work is presented as effectively addressing cross-dimensional security challenges including terrorism, organised crime, cyber-crime, and trafficking in drugs, arms and human beings.

See www.osce.org.

Council of Europe

Founded in 1949, and viewed as a leading body contributing to enhanced cooperation in criminal matters (Anderson *et al.*, 1995), the Council of Europe comprises a human rights organisation, and pan-European platform for cooperation and dialogue, representing 47 Member States (28 of which are also members of the European Union). New Member States are required to commit themselves to signing the European Convention of Human Rights upon becoming members and to ratifying it within one year. Thus, the Convention has been incorporated into the domestic legal orders of all 47 Member States. Organisational efforts are directed towards three operational pillars: human rights, democracy and the rule of law.

In terms of the organisational structure, the head of the Organisation, responsible for strategic planning and the direction of the Council's work programme and budget is the Secretary General, elected by Parliamentary Assembly. The Committee of Ministers, comprising ministers of foreign affairs from Member States decides Council of Europe policy and approves its budget and programme of activities. The Parliamentary Assembly comprises Member State members of parliament and serves the function of a democratic forum for monitoring and debate. Additional voices are heard within the Congress of Local and Regional Authorities, the Conference of INGOs and through the Commissioner for Human Rights and the European Court of Human Rights.

Significantly, adopting a partnership approach, the Council of Europe cooperates closely with the UN, OSCE, the European Union, Regional Intelligence Liaison Office (RILO), the Financial Action Task Force (FATF), the International Monetary Fund (IMF), the World Bank and civil society. Within the 'Council of Europe Programme and Budget for 2014–15', with respect to cross-border threats and challenges, four focal areas are identified as priorities, alongside on-going actions. These include action against corruption and the misuse of power; work against intolerance, hate speech, extremism and violence; the protection of minorities and vulnerable groups; and the consolidation of the Council of Europe legal space. Particularly significant in relation to transnational policing efforts and the development of instruments of cooperation are the European Convention on Mutual Assistance in Criminal Matters, which was developed by the Council of Europe in 1959, entering into force in June 1962. Also relevant is the work undertaken by the Pompidou Group (established in 1971 and integrated in the Council of Europe in 1980) to combat drug abuse and illicit trafficking in drugs.

Further activities include efforts to counter human trafficking, including the Europe Convention on preventing and combating violence against women and domestic violence, which is expected to enter into force during the biennium and will give rise to a new monitoring mechanism (GREVIO). The Council of Europe has also developed a strategy on the Rights of the Child (2012–2015), principally addressing sexual violence through the 'Convention on the Protection of Children against Sexual Exploitation and Sexual Abuse' (Lanzarote Convention). Two further programmes are worthy of mention here: the first aimed towards the development and implementation of common standards and policies, and the second addressing threats to the rule of law. The former programme promotes cooperation between ministries of justice in Member States, common standards, practical guidelines and the strengthening of the rule of law (viewed as essential in guaranteeing the effective enjoyment of human rights). Work is undertaken to tackle organised crime, corruption and money laundering, terrorism, as well as cyber-crime and counterfeiting of medical products, with sport and integrity recently added to the agenda. Experts are brought together in a range of committees including: Group of States against Corruption (GRECO); Committee of Experts on the Evaluation of Anti-Money Laundering Measures and the Financing of Terrorism (MONEYVAL); the Council of Europe Committee of Experts on Terrorism (CODEXTER); Group of Experts on Action against Trafficking in Human Beings (GRETA), with the Council of Europe's significant work in the area of data protection also worthy of mention.

See www.hub.coe.int.

The European Union

Created in the aftermath of the Second World War (during the early 1950s), six founding Member States (Germany, France, Italy, the Netherlands, Belgium and Luxembourg) sought deeper cooperation within Europe. Based on the Schuman Plan (after the French Foreign Minister), the 'European Coal and Steel Community' endeavoured to integrate European countries economically and politically to secure a lasting peace through interdependence. The Coal and Steel Treaty was followed by the Treaty of Rome, which created the European Economic Community (EEC) (or Common Market) allowing the removal of customs duties on goods imported from each other, thereby allowing free cross-border trade from 1968 onwards and generating the world's biggest trading group. In 1973 Denmark, Ireland and the United Kingdom formally entered the EU, with Greece, Spain and Portugal entering during the 1980s and Austria, Finland and Sweden joining during the 1990s.

In 1975, the TREVI forum was established comprising an intergovernmental framework created by the European Council of Ministers for policing terrorism. Under the auspices of European Political Cooperation, TREVI existed outside the EC framework, with ministerial meetings occurring biannually with law enforcement practitioners meeting more regularly. Objectives included cooperation in countering terrorism in addition to information exchange in areas such as police tactics, training and equipment. The remit of the TREVI Working Groups expanded during the 1980s and early 1990s to include: drugs; bank robberies; arms trafficking; the cross-border movement of stolen goods; fraud; money laundering; and international organised crime (specifically the Mafia and Eastern European Organised Crime). TREVI Working

Group activity also anticipated the potential consequences of the abolition of internal border controls in preparation for the signing of the Maastricht Treaty (for a discussion, see Bigo, 2000; Gregory in Sheptycki, 2000; Anderson *et al.*, 1995).

The 'Treaty on the European Union' was signed in Maastricht in February 1992 marking a name change from the 'European Community' to the 'European Union' and also establishing clear rules for the future of the single currency (enabling the free movement of goods, services, people and money) and for foreign and security policy, alongside closer cooperation in justice and home affairs. This development marked the emergence of a more public crime control agenda within the EU, particularly given the 'closed nature' of the TREVI forum discussed previously. Significantly, matters relating to justice and home affairs came to be dealt with under Title VI of the Treaty on European Union (the 'third pillar'). The Maastricht Treaty is also important in relation to its recommendation to create Europol and for absorbing the work of TREVI into the pillar of Justice and Home Affairs (the 'third pillar').

The Schengen Agreement (originally signed in 1985) and the Schengen Convention (originally signed in 1990) both entered into force in 1995. The intention was to create genuine freedom of movement for persons, enabling travellers of any nationality to travel between Belgium, Germany, Spain, France, Luxembourg, the Netherlands and Portugal without passport control at the frontiers, while adopting accompanying measures in relation to the controls at the external borders, visa policy and judicial and police cooperation in criminal matters. The Agreement and the Convention in addition to the associated agreements and rules form the 'Schengen Acquis', comprising part of the institutional and legal framework of the EU by virtue of a protocol to the Treaties. The Convention effectively abolished checks at the internal borders and created a single external border, standardising procedures for external border checks and homogenising the rules governing visas and the right to asylum.

In 1997, the signing of the Treaty of Amsterdam built on the achievements of the Treaty on the European Union and amended the Maastricht Treaty on the European Union. The Treaty sought to maintain and develop the Union as an area of freedom, security and justice, enabling the free movement of people alongside the development of measures in relation to external border controls, immigration, asylum and the prevention and combating of crime, introducing the possibility of judicial cooperation in civil matters. These policy areas were therefore effectively 'communitised' and relocated from the 'third pillar' to the 'first pillar' (under Title IV of the Treaty establishing the European Community). The EU's 'third pillar' (Justice and Home Affairs) was effectively cropped to focus upon police and judicial cooperation in criminal matters.

The Treaty of Amsterdam also incorporated the intergovernmental Schengen Acquis into the legal and institutional framework of the European Union. This development allowed for operational cross-border police activities to take place within the Schengen area including: hot pursuit; information exchange; cross-border surveillance; and controlled delivery, in combination with standardised measures for the execution of border controls. Police cooperation therefore was an essential element of the Schengen Acquis, and this became subject to further expansion through the signing of the Prum Treaty in 2005, by a selection of Schengen countries which placed requirements upon partners to create national DNA databases, allowing for the collection of fingerprints, biometric data and vehicle registration and expanding the remit of Schengen to include terrorism (see den Boer, in Lemieux, 2010: 56).

In 2003, replacing NATO units with EU-led forces, the EU engaged in peacekeeping operations in the Balkans (Former Yugoslav Republic of Macedonia and Bosnia and Herzegovina). Internally, the EU agreed to create an area of freedom, security and justice for all citizens by 2010. In 2004, following Enlargement (enabled by the Treaty of Nice in 1997) ten new Member States were added (Czech Republic, Cyprus, Estonia, Latvia, Lithuania, Hungary, Malta, Poland, Slovenia and Slovakia), with Bulgaria and Romania joining in 2007. Within the same year, the 27 Member States signed the Treaty of Lisbon. The Lisbon Treaty effectively abolished the pillar structure and regrouped matters relating to justice and home affairs in 'the Treaty on the Function of the European Union'. Under this revised structure, the Justice and Home Affairs Council (consisting of the justice and home affairs ministers of Member States) is required to meet biannually to discuss the development and implementation of cooperation and common policies. The Council retains responsibility for adopting directives and regulations acting as the co-legislator of the EU, supported by a number of working groups and committees including: CATS (police and judicial cooperation); the Strategic Committee on Immigration, Frontiers and Asylum; COSI (Committee on Internal Security); and the Working Party on Civil Law Matters.

In July 2013, Croatia became the 28th EU member, whilst the Former Yugoslav Republic of Macedonia (FYROM), Montenegro and Serbia were officially accepted as candidates for EU membership. Albania and Bosnia and Herzegovina have also applied. In terms of structure, the ultimate decision-making body in the European Union is the European Council, bringing together heads of state and government from the 28 member countries. The Council meets four times a year to define the principles and general guidelines of policy.

With regard to cross-border crime, the 'Area of Freedom, Security and Justice' is covered by Title V of 'the Treaty on the Functioning of the European Union'. It includes policies on border checks, asylum and immigration, with judicial cooperation in civil and criminal matters, and with police cooperation. As with the Schengen Agreement mentioned previously, opt-out arrangements exist with Denmark (who have opted out fully) and the United Kingdom and Ireland (who have retained the right to opt out although in practice they appear to have opted in on most initiatives). Following the Lisbon Treaty, decisions in these fields are mostly taken by qualified majority voting. The

European Parliament has co-decision powers with the Council in the majority policy areas (ordinary legislative procedure).

The Stockholm Programme (adopted by the European Council in December 2009) set out the priorities for developing the European area of freedom, security and justice for a five-year period. It aims to bring about 'a determined and adequate European response to European and global challenges' (EC/COM/2010:0171:FIN) and also, enabled by the Lisbon Treaty, the EU Internal Security Strategy, 'Towards a European Security Model' (ISS), endeavoured to make further progress in this area. The ISS presented the key challenges, principles and guidelines for dealing with security issues within the EU remaining committed to the values and principles set out in the Charter of Fundamental Rights. The key threats facing Europe were identified as including: terrorism, serious and organised crime, drug trafficking, cyber-crime, trafficking in human beings, sexual exploitation of minors and child pornography, economic crime and corruption, in addition to the trafficking in arms.

The ISS was followed in 2010 by the Commission's adoption of the Communication 'EU Internal Security Strategy in Action' to implement the strategy (European Commission, 2010). The ISS advocated increased law-enforcement and judicial cooperation, including: coordination between law enforcement and border-management authorities, measures viewed as essential tools in adapting to the challenges of an enlarged European Union, overseen by the recently created Standing Committee on Operational Cooperation on Internal Security (COSI) and tasked with the effective functioning of agencies such as Europol, Eurojust, Frontex, Cepol, Sitcen (which will be dealt with separately below). Effective tools for mutual recognition including the European Arrest Warrant, provision for the freezing of assets, Joint Investigation Teams and information sharing databases are also emphasised as essential instruments in countering organised crime and terrorism. The European Parliament, national Parliaments, the European Court of Justice and the European Convention on Human Rights are attributed a role in relation to the democratic and judicial supervision of security activities.

Acknowledging the recently altered notion of security discussed earlier in Chapter 1, the Internal Security Strategy argues that internal security increasingly depends upon external security, thereby emphasising the interdependence between internal and external security policy and action. With regard to the latter, the European Security Strategy (ESS), adopted by the European Council on 12–13 December 2003, provides the conceptual framework for the Common Foreign and Security Policy (CFSP), including what would later become the Common Security and Defence Policy (CSDP). The document, entitled 'A Secure Europe in a Better World', identifies five key threats including terrorism, the proliferation of weapons of mass destruction, regional conflicts and state failure alongside organised crime. Thus an association is made within the external security strategy between weak and failed states, terrorism and trafficking in people, drugs and arms, immigration and piracy with implications for the internal security of Europe and internationally (see also 2008 Report on the Implementation of the European Security Strategy – Providing Security in a Changing World).

The 2009 Lisbon Treaty further strengthened the EU's common foreign and security policy, creating the post of EU High Representative for Foreign Affairs and Security Policy alongside a European Diplomatic Service (the European External Action Service, which supports the work of the High Representative in defining and implementing an effective and coherent foreign policy of the European Union). Endeavouring to preserve peace and strengthen international security, to promote international cooperation and to develop and consolidate democracy, the rule of law and respect for human rights and fundamental freedoms, the Union utilises its status as the largest donor of development aid internationally, alongside trade, security and defence, to resolve conflicts and achieve international understanding. Significant work includes the 2004 Hague Programme, the Strategy for the External Dimension of Justice and Home Affairs 2005, the EU Counter Terrorism Strategy 2005, the EU Strategy for a Secure Information Society 2006, EU Strategy to combat illicit accumulation and trafficking of small arms and light weapons (SALW) and their ammunition.

See http://europa.eu/.

The EU Intelligence Analysis Centre (EU INTCEN)

The EU Intelligence Analysis Centre (EU INTCEN) provides intelligence analysis to the High Representative for Foreign Affairs and Security Policy, as well as to the various decision-making bodies of the European Union in the fields of Common Foreign and Security Policy, Common Security and Defence Policy, Counter-Terrorism and Member States. As detailed within the EU INTCEN Factsheet, the EU Intelligence Analysis Centre's mission is to provide intelligence analyses, early warning and situational awareness to the High Representative and to the European External Action Service. 'Timely intelligence' is viewed as essential to inform 'wise policy decisions' in order to maintain 'a secure Europe in a better world' (Council of the European Union, 2010).

INTCEN became part of the European External Action Service (EEAS) in 2010 and is therefore not, strictly speaking, a police cooperation body. Nevertheless, the European Parliament credits INTCEN's contribution to police cooperation, directing attention to its role in producing threat assessments based on information provided by intelligence services, the military, diplomats and police services. INTCEN is also viewed as operationally useful in the provision of information on the destinations, motives and movements of terrorists, in order to raise awareness in all Member States and to help them each to take appropriate measures. In addition to terrorism, INTCEN also monitors and assesses other international events, particularly concentrating upon sensitive geographical areas, the proliferation of weapons of mass destruction and other global threats.

(CSFP/CSDP and CT), as well as to the Member States. The agency is also tasked with acting as a single entry point in the EU for classified information coming from Member States' civilian intelligence and security services and in providing support and assistance to the Presidents of the European Council and Commission in the exercise of their respective functions in the area of external relations.

The Joint Situation Centre (SitCen) was the forerunner to EU INTCEN, described as an EU intelligence-sharing bureau. In 2002, EU SitCen was established as a directorate of the Council General Secretariat, directly attached to the office of the High Representative and comprising seconded intelligence personnel from Member States. From 2007, EU SitCen expanded to include EU Military Staff (EUMS) Intelligence Directorate, generating joint products prepared under the 'Single Intelligence Analysis Capacity' (SIAC). While endorsed by the Council, SitCen lacked a legal basis and no legal act was adopted to formalise SitCen as an EU agency. Following the entry into force of the Lisbon Treaty in 2009, EU SitCen came under the authority of the High Representative, eventually transferring to the European External Action Service (EEAS) in 2011. In 2012 SitCen was restructured and renamed INTCEN, however, questions regarding the lack of formal legal framework, democratic accountability, oversight and transparency remain, with Statewatch directing attention to the agency's expanded remit, activities and intelligence sources in recent years.

See www.statewatch.org/analyses/no-223-eu-intcen.pdf;
www.statewatch.org/news/2009/aug/SitCen2009.pdf;
www.asktheeu.org/en/request/637/response/2416/attach/5/EU%20INTCEN%20Factsheet%20PUBLIC%20120618%201.pdf;
www.europarl.europa.eu/ftu/pdf/en/FTU_5.12.7.pdf;
http://eeas.europa.eu/factsheets/docs/20150206_factsheet_eu_intcen_en.pdf (accessed June 15, 2015).

The EU institutions are backed up by a number of specialised bodies, these are discussed below.

Europol

Europol is described as the European Union's law enforcement agency and as an EU centre of expertise, whose main goal is to help achieve a safer Europe for the benefit of all EU citizens. Following requests made from within the TREVI forum and externally to formalise police cooperation within the EC during the 1970s and 1980s, the German chancellor proposed the creation of a European Police agency to be established emulating the FBI model in America. As mentioned earlier within the chapter, the 1992 Maastricht Treaty on the European Union established Justice and Home Affairs as one of the three pillars of the new EU structure. More specifically, Article K1 (9) of the Treaty made explicit reference to a European Police Office (Europol), allowing for police cooperation between Member States to counter terrorism, drug trafficking and other international crime. In 1993, the European Council created the Europol Drugs Unit (EDU) which formalised European police cooperation. The mandate of the unit was to assist national forces in criminal investigations through exchange and analysis of criminal intelligence. Significantly, the EDU had no powers of arrest.

In 1995, the Convention establishing Europol under Article K3 of the Maastricht Treaty was agreed and following ratification came into force in 1998. Under the Convention, requirements were placed upon Member States to designate a national unit to liaise between its own competent authorities and Europol, with national units seconding liaison officers to the Europol headquarters to represent the interests of their national authorities and to enhance information exchange. Europol's mandate was further expanded following three amendments which entered into force in 2007. The protocols, signed in 2000, 2002 and 2003, created a more efficient network for detecting and seizing assets and interrupting criminal networks, enabled Europol's participation in joint investigation teams and allowed for third states with a Europol operational cooperation agreement to become associated to Analysis Work Files (AWFs).

In 2007, the Justice and Home Affairs Council agreed Europol should be aligned with other agencies within the Justice and Home Affairs pillar of the EU. It was decided that the Europol Convention should be replaced by a Council Decision thereby altering financing arrangements (from direct contributions from Member States to financing from the Community budget) (Council Decision 2009/371/JHA). These amendments also meant the Europol would become subject to the EC Financial and Staff Regulations, further extending the mandate and tasks of the agency and purportedly resulting in improvements to data processing and protection in addition to enhanced operational and administrative capabilities. The new legal framework came into force in 2010, at which time Europol became officially known as an EU Agency. According to Article 3 of the Council Decision, the objective of Europol shall be to support and strengthen action by the competent authorities of the Member States and their mutual cooperation in preventing and combating organised crime, terrorism and other forms of serious crime affecting two or more Member States. The main tasks of Europol are set out in Article 5 of the Council Decision. Activities include: the collection, storage, processing, analysis and exchange of information and intelligence; notification of Member States' national units regarding information concerning them and any connections identified with criminal offences; to aid investigations (particularly through the forwarding of relevant information to competent authorities); requesting Member States to initiate, conduct or coordinate investigations; the provision of intelligence and/or analytical support to Member States in relation to major international events; and the preparation of threat assessments, strategic analysis and general situation reports (for example, the European Organised Crime Threat Assessment (OCTA) and the EU Terrorism Situation and Trend Report (TE-SAT)).

Europol is held accountable at EU level by the Council of Ministers for Justice and Home Affairs (consisting of Justice and Home Affairs ministers from all EU Member States). The Council is also responsible for the main control and guidance of the agency, approving Europol's budget, together with the European Parliament. The Europol Management Board is Europol's governing body, providing the agency with strategic direction overseeing the implementation of its tasks and reviewing current activities and future developments. On a recommendation by the Management Board, the Council sets out the priorities for Europol, taking particular account of strategic analyses and threat assessments prepared by Europol. The Management Board is also responsible for submitting a general report to the Council on annual activities for endorsement, which is then submitted to the European Parliament for information. At the time of writing, Europol's mission is described as supporting Member States in preventing and combating all forms of serious international crime and terrorism. With respect to the agency goals and vision, Europol sets out to deliver a unique set of operational services within the EU. In particular, Europol aims to function as the principal EU Support Centre for law enforcement operations; to become the criminal information hub of the EU; and to develop further as an EU centre for law enforcement expertise. Europol's Strategy 2010–2014 currently identifies terrorism, international drug trafficking and money laundering, organised fraud, counterfeiting of the euro currency, and people smuggling as the biggest security threats facing the EU. However, further issues have become a focus for Europol activities including cyber-crime and the trafficking of human beings (with the European Cybercrime Centre known as EC3 based within Europol becoming active in January 2013).

See www.europol.europa.eu/.

Eurojust

Eurojust is the European Union's judicial cooperation unit, bringing together law enforcement and judicial authorities from Member States and third states. Eurojust facilitates cooperation in strategic and operational actions and works to resolve procedural and practical difficulties encountered in investigations and prosecutions in the fight against serious cross-border crime affecting the European Union.

In October 1999 during a European Council Meeting in Tampere, Finland, attended by heads of state and government, the proposal to create a judicial cooperation unit was discussed. In particular, it was agreed that a unit comprising national prosecutors, magistrates, or police officers of equivalent competence, should be created. In 2000 Pro-Eurojust was created (operational from 1 March 2001), comprising a provisional judicial cooperation unit based within the Council building in Brussels. The legal basis of the unit became formalised through Council Decision 2002/187/JHA, which created 'Eurojust' as a judicial cooperation unit, financed from the general budget of the European Union. The Decision placed a requirement upon each Member State (in accordance with its legal system) to second one national member (a prosecutor, judge, or police officer of equivalent competence).

Article 3 sets out the objectives for Eurojust. In addition to the provision of support to Member States, goals include the stimulation and improvement of coordination between the competent authorities of Member States in the context of investigations and prosecutions. These usually concern two or more Member States in relation to serious crime. However, Eurojust may also assist in cases concerning only one Member State and a third state or one Member State and the European Union. Further objectives include improving cooperation between competent authorities through the facilitation of the execution of mutual legal assistance and the execution of extradition requests (more recently through the application of mutual recognition instruments such as the European Arrest Warrant).

In particular, as set out in Article 6 of the Decision, Eurojust (acting through its national members) may request competent authorities of the Member States to consider undertaking an investigation or prosecution of specific acts; coordinate between competent authorities; set up a joint investigation team; provide information to competent authorities and notify and assist Member States. Eurojust may also provide logistical support in cases, which includes assistance for translation, interpretation and the organisation of coordination meetings. Eurojust is also tasked with cooperating, consulting and assisting partner bodies such as the European Judicial Network, Europol and the European Anti-Fraud Office (OLAF), with Memorandums of Understanding recently signed to facilitate cooperation with Interpol, Frontex, CEPOL, United Nations Office on Drugs and Crime and IberRed. Furthermore, in non-operational strategic matters, Eurojust works closely with EU and Member State institutions including the European Parliament, national parliaments, the Council and the Commission.

The legal framework of Eurojust was revised by Council Decision 2009/426/JHA, which strengthened the status and powers of National Members and the operational capacities of National Desks and strengthened relationships with third states and partner agencies. With 28 National Members, Eurojust's mission is to support and strengthen coordination and cooperation between national authorities; it includes the sharing of best practice and knowledge, promoting the implementation and correct application of legal instruments for judicial cooperation. The National Members form the College of Eurojust, which is responsible for Eurojust's organisation and operation. Eurojust is supported by an administration headed by an Administration Director, and hosts the Secretariat of the European Judicial Network (EJN), the JITs Network and the Genocide Network. The president of Europol is required to submit an annual report to the European Parliament and the Council on the activities and management (including budgetary management) of Eurojust. The annual report highlights any criminal policy problems within the Union raised as a result of Eurojust's activities and may also make proposals for the improvement of judicial cooperation in criminal matters.

Eurojust's competences include the priority areas of drug trafficking, trafficking in human beings, illegal immigration, fraud and corruption and cybercrime (including child sexual abuse images), money laundering, criminal offences affecting the EU's financial interests, terrorism, and mobile organised-crime groups (MOCGs) in addition to other key areas such as counterfeiting, crime against property or public goods, maritime piracy and environmental crime. However, at the request of a national authority Eurojust may assist in investigations and prosecutions regarding any other type of offence. The Eurojust Annual report for 2013 identifies Eurojust's key coordination tools as comprising coordination meetings, coordination centres and joint investigation teams, with the JITs Network Secretariat at Eurojust celebrated as a centre of expertise and information hub in JIT-related matters. Alongside casework, policy work and administrative work, other key Eurojust tasks include awareness-raising activities, recently within the area of freezing orders and confiscation of criminal assets.

With regard to future developments, the Lisbon Treaty provided a legal basis for the creation of a European Public Prosecutor's Office (EPPO) from Eurojust (Article 86 of the Treaty on the Functioning of the European Union) and also initiated a Task Force on the Future of Eurojust to consider reforms to Eurojust's mission and framework. The EPPO would become responsible for investigating, prosecuting and bringing to judgement (in liaison with Europol) the perpetrators of, and accomplices in, offences against the Union's financial interests (Eurojust News, Issue 8, May 2013). A conference on the EPPO took place in September 2013. Progress in this area is therefore fully expected to take the form of a regulation which will be binding in its provisions and directly applicable to Member States (Eurojust Annual Report 2013).

See http://eurojust.europa.eu/.

European Judicial Network

The European Judicial Network (EJN) is a network of more than 300 national contact points for the facilitation of judicial cooperation in criminal matters, particularly in actions to combat forms of serious crime. It was created in 1998 (by Joint Action 98/428/JHA of 29 June 1998), to fight serious crime in a decentralised, flexible and horizontal way. The Joint Action was later replaced by Council Decision 2008/976/JHA which provides its legal basis.

The Council Decision requires one or more contact points to be established within each of the 27 Member States and the appointment of a National Correspondent for the EJN. The EJN is therefore composed of Contact Points comprising a community of judges, prosecutors and representatives of Ministries of Justice, who act as intermediaries to facilitate judicial cooperation. Member States are also required to appoint a tool correspondent tasked to deal with the matters related to the electronic tools of the EJN.

The functions of these Contact Points include the provision of practical and legal information to enable local judicial authorities to prepare an effective request for judicial cooperation or to improve judicial cooperation in general (for example, European Arrest Warrants and Mutual Legal Assistance). In particular, Contact Points are responsible for coordinating requests for information and replies by Member States, providing secure telecommunication connection, mediating to resolve difficulties or delays, which may arise in the implementation of requests for judicial cooperation and also providing advice in relation to particular complex cases. The Contact Points are also involved in and promote the organisation of training on judicial cooperation. In addition to the Contact Points of the Member States, the EJN is comprised of the European Commission and of a Secretariat based in The Hague.

Eurojust hosts the EJN Secretariat facilitating interaction between Eurojust National Desks and the National Correspondent. Currently, an EJN-Eurojust Taskforce is undertaking work to clarify the services provided by Eurojust and the EJN to enable practitioners to select between these bodies in individual cases. The Secretariat is the EJN's managerial body with responsibility for the functioning and continuity of the EJN. The Secretariat supports the Contact Points in the fulfilment of their tasks, maintains the EJN website and e-tools, in addition to disseminating information on EJN activities and judicial cooperation and establishing relations with other judicial networks within and beyond the EU.

Current European Judicial Network partners include: Eurojust; Joint Investigation Teams Network; European Judicial Training Network (EJTN); the Academy of European Law (ERA); the European Anti-Fraud Office (OLAF); the Network of Judicial International Cooperation of the Portuguese speaking countries (Rede judiciaria da CPLP); the Commonwealth Network of Contact Persons (CNPC); Platform 'Justice' of the Indian Ocean Commission Member States (COI); the United Nations Office on Drugs and Crime (UNODC); Council of Europe; Euro-Mediterranean area of cooperation in the field of justice (Euromed); Network of contact points in respect of persons responsible for genocide and crimes against humanity (Genocide); EJN Civil Commercial; E-Justice; Europol; the Iberoamerican Network for International Legal Cooperation (IberRed); the Southeast European Prosecutors Advisory Group (SEEPAG); the Moroccan Judicial Network for International Cooperation (RMCJI); Platform of Judicial Cooperation from the Sahel Countries (SAHE); the EU-Philippines Justice Support Programme (EPJUST); European Criminal Law Academy Network (ECLAN).

The EJN's main responsibilities include the EJN plenary and regional meetings, which provide a platform for EJN Contact Points to share experiences and identify problems in the field of judicial cooperation in criminal matters. The E-Justice Portal is intended to integrate the EJN website to provide a useful tool for practitioners (conceived as a future electronic one-stop-shop in the area of justice, providing information on justice systems and improving access to justice throughout the EU in 23 languages). With respect to contemporary issues, the agenda of the 42nd Plenary Meeting of the EJN, 23–24 June 2014 in Athens, sought to achieve a better understanding of national laws focusing on the practical implementation of the European Arrest Warrant (EAW), examining specifically the challenges faced by members in relation to the different wording of offences under the laws of Member States; practical issues arising from the execution of the EAW due to different national laws of EU Member States; the competencies and actions of the EJN and Eurojust; in addition to the EJN role in assisting on the EAW. Additional sessions included an EJN Task Force presentation in relation to judicial cooperation in criminal matters, a session entitled the 'European Public Prosecutor's Office' and a session entitled 'Protection of the financial interests of the European Union' highlighting areas of contemporary concern to the Network.

See www.ejn-crimjust.europa.eu/ejn/.

Frontex

Frontex is a European Agency with a mandate to support, coordinate and develop border management between border authorities within the EU. Building upon the work undertaken by the 'External Border Practitioners Common Unit', in the area of migration, asylum and security, under the European Council on Justice and Home Affairs in the late 1990s (particularly the projects and operations overseen by the six Ad-Hoc Centres on Border Control), Council Regulation (EC) No 2007/2004 of 26 October 2004 established a 'European Agency for the Management of Operational Cooperation at the External Borders of the Member States of the European Union'. Frontex (as it became known) was consequently tasked with improving the integrated management of the external borders (land and sea borders) of Member States of the European Union, in line with the Charter of Fundamental Rights of the EU.

The main tasks of the Agency, as set out within Article 2 of the Council Regulation included: the coordination of operational cooperation between Member States in the field of management of external borders; assisting Member States in relation to the training of national border guards and the establishment of common training standards; assisting Member States in the provision of technical and operational assistance and support in organising joint return operations (which relates to the return of foreign nationals staying illegally, who have failed to leave voluntarily) in addition to the performance of risk analysis and research activities with respect to control and surveillance at external borders. The Frontex Regulation and subsequent amendment (Regulation (EU) No 1168/2011) also provides for the agency to plan, coordinate, implement and evaluate joint operations at the external borders in addition to providing a rapid response capability in the event of a 'crisis situation' at the external border through the recent creation of European Border Guard Teams. Council Decision 2005/267/EC set out the commitment to establish a secure web-based Information and Coordination Network for Member States' Migration Management Services, which would allow the exchange of operational information on irregular migration, illegal entry and immigration and the return of illegal residents. Viewed as a state-of-the-art information-exchange platform, the European Border Surveillance System (Eurosur) became active with the entry into force of the Eurosur Regulation on 2 December 2013, establishing a pan-European framework for information sharing, enhancing situational awareness and reaction capabilities, via the National Coordination Centres of Member States.

Liaising with a range of partners including: Europol, Eurojust, EASO, FRA and CEPOL, Frontex also works closely with the border-control authorities of non-EU/Schengen countries, particularly those countries which have been identified as a source or transit route of irregular migration. Frontex's Mission Statement, as articulated within the 2013 Annual Report, identifies migration flows, serious organised crime and terrorism as key challenges facing the agency in the coming year. Furthermore, following the disaster off the Island of Lampedusa in which 364 migrants drowned attempting to reach the EU, the Task Force Mediterranean was established to develop and pose solutions in this highly emotive area. In December 2013, a European Commission Communication was published identifying five main areas of action including actions in cooperation with third countries; regional protection, resettlement and reinforced legal avenues to Europe; reinforcement of the fight against human trafficking, smuggling and organised crime; reinforced border surveillance contributing to an enhanced maritime situational picture and to the protection and saving of lives in the Mediterranean, and finally, assistance to and solidarity with Member States dealing with high migratory pressure (Frontex Annual Report, 2013). The Executive Summary of the 2015 Frontex Annual Risk Analysis, particularly recognised 'the conflict in Syria and the continued volatility in North African countries, notably Libya' in addition to the ongoing crisis in Ukraine, as geopolitical factors influencing population movement. Thus, in 2014, detections of illegal border-crossing were reported as reaching a new record, resulting in what the report refers to as 'the worst refugee crisis since the Second World War'.

See http://frontex.europa.eu/.

Cepol

The European Police College (CEPOL) is a European Union (EU) Agency with a mandate for Law Enforcement Learning and Training. It was created in 2005 following Council Decision 2005/681/JHA. The purpose of the agency, as set out in Article 5 of the Council Decision, is to help train the senior police officers of Member States and the development of a European approach to the main problems facing Member States in relation to the cross-border dimensions of crime, crime prevention, the maintenance of law and order and public security.

Cepol's objectives include the facilitation of cross-border police cooperation within the European Union, strengthening of knowledge in relation to national police systems, structures and international and Union instruments, including knowledge of EU institutions (including Europol and Eurojust), legal instruments and decision-making mechanisms. Key tasks for the agency, as provided for in Article 7 include: the provision of training sessions, based on common standards, for senior police officers; harmonised programmes, advanced training programmes and training for trainers; specialist training for officers playing a key role in countering cross-border crime; the dissemination of best practice and research findings; non-military crisis management training; training for police authorities from candidate countries; the facilitation of exchange programmes and secondments. Additional tasks include the development of an electronic network to support the work of Cepol (e-net) and the acquisition of language skills for senior police officers.

The CEPOL Governing Board, responsible for CEPOL's Strategy, Work Programme, draft Budget, and other decision making comprises representatives from the EU Member States (typically the Directors of the National Police Training Colleges). The Chair of the Governing Board is a representative of the Member State holding the Presidency of the European Union, while the Secretariat carries out the day-to-day work in support of the network. CEPOL's Work Programme explicitly contributes to the achievement of the goals of the EU internal security strategy (and its Action Plan), the Stockholm Programme (e.g. cyber-crime and civilian crisis management), and EU policy cycle 2014–2017 (for organised and serious international crime). Functioning as a network, the Work Programme is implemented within the National Police Training Colleges of Member States. National Contact Points provide the link between Member States and CEPOL, with each Member State also appointing a National Training Coordinator; a National e-Net Manager; a Research and Science Correspondent and National Exchange Coordinator to disseminate information, coordinate training and to provide administrative and logistical support for the activities and programmes undertaken by the European Police College. CEPOL contributes to the Justice and Home Affairs Agencies Coordination Mechanism (Contact Group), cooperating with Frontex, Eurojust, Europol, ENISA, EU-LISA, EASO, OLAF, EMCDDA and FRA in the identification of strategic topics and priorities for action.

Courses and seminars include training for senior police officers in policing cooperation and policing within Europe (linked to the Stockholm Programme and Internal Security Strategy), courses on fundamental rights and police ethics in addition to bespoke training designed to enhance legal and practical competencies of specific roles and in relation to particular crime issues. In 2014, the course programme included: training of SIRENE officers; courses targeting the manufacturing and distribution of counterfeit commodities; child abuse in cyberspace; the trafficking in stolen artworks and theft of cultural heritage; synthetic drug production and the dismantling of illicit laboratories; trafficking in human beings, road traffic control and road safety; the freezing and confiscation of assets; cocaine smuggling; counter-terrorism; firearms trafficking; container shipment trafficking; forensic investigation; joint investigation teams; crisis management, emergency planning and public order.

See www.cepol.europa.eu.

European Agency for Fundamental Rights (FRA)

Established in 2007 by Council Regulation (EC) 168/2007, the European Union Agency for Fundamental Rights (FRA) provides independent, evidence-based advice to the institutions of the EU and the Member States with the purpose of protecting the fundamental rights of people living in the EU. FRA is the successor organisation to the former European Monitoring Centre on Racism and Xenophobia (EUMC), which was established in 1997 and ceased in 2007. FRA consists of legal experts, statisticians, political and social scientists in addition to communication and networking experts. As an EU Agency, FRA works in partnership with the EU institutions, maintaining close links with the European Commission, the European Parliament and the Council of the European Union, its Member States and other international organisations including the Council of Europe, the United Nations (UN) and the Organisation for Security and Co-operation in Europe (OSCE). FRA also maintains links with civil society organisations, academic institutions, equality bodies and National Human Rights Institutions.

The agency is governed by the FRA Management Board, which retains responsibility for establishing work priorities, approving its budget and overseeing the agency's activities. The board consists of two European Commission representatives, one independent expert appointed by each Member State and one independent expert appointed by the Council of Europe. Key tasks for the agency, as set out in Article 4 of the Council Regulation, include: the collection, recording, analysis and dissemination of information and data; to develop methods and standards to improve the comparability, objectivity and reliability of data at European level; to undertake and encourage research compatible with agency priorities and its annual work programme; to publish thematic reports and disseminate conclusions and options on specific thematic topics; and to publish an annual report on fundamental-rights issues.

The thematic areas, as established within the 2013–2017 Multi-annual Framework agreed by the Justice and Home Affairs Council of the EU in March 2013, include: access to justice; victims of crime; information society (particularly, respect for private life and protection of personal data); Roma integration; judicial cooperation (except in criminal matters); rights of the child; discrimination; immigration and integration of migrants, visa and border control and asylum; racism, xenophobia and related intolerance. The agency's work programme was proposed by the European Commission and subject to consultation with the European Parliament. With respect to cross-border crime, the work undertaken by the FRA contributes to the achievement of EU policy including, for example, within the area of labour exploitation (EU Strategy towards the Eradication of Trafficking in Human Beings 2012–2016 and 2009–2012 Work Programmes). Projects completed by the FRA between 2009 and 2013 have examined the situation of irregular immigrants in the EU, the examination of return procedures, the treatment of third-country nationals at the EU's external borders, with projects undertaken in cooperation with Frontex and the European Asylum Support office (EASO). Recent activities in the area of data protection include cooperation with eu-LISA (EU Agency for large-scale IT systems Biometric data in large IT borders, immigration and asylum databases), focusing particularly upon the collection and storing of biometric data within EU Member States.

See http://fra.europa.eu/en.

The European Asylum Support Office (EASO)

Established in 2010 following Regulation (EU) 439/2010, the European Asylum Support Office is a regulatory EU decentralised agency tasked with improving the implementation of the Common European Asylum System (the CEAS), and providing practical cooperation (including the exchange of information, identification and pooling of good practice on asylum matters) among Member States, and support in relation to asylum and reception systems. EASO provides Member States with operational support, scientific and technical assistance in regard to policy and legislation of the Union in all areas having direct or indirect impact on asylum, serving as a reference point for Member States and working closely with Member States' asylum authorities, national immigration and asylum services, other national services and the Commission.

EASO's main tasks as set out within the 2014–2016 multi-annual work programme include: permanent support (through the provision of common training, common asylum training material, common quality and common country of origin (of asylum seekers) information); special support (in the form of tailor-made assistance, capacity building, relocation, specific support and special quality-control processes); emergency support for Member States facing particular pressures upon their asylum and reception systems (through the provision of temporary support and assistance to repair or rebuild asylum and reception systems); information and analysis support (specifically the sharing and merging of information and data), analyses and assessments at EU level (including common trend analyses and common assessments); and finally, third-country (i.e. non-member country) support (in the form of capacity building and regional protection programmes, coordinating Member States' actions on resettlement).

EASO is governed by a Management Board and an Executive Director responsible for the adoption of work programmes, the production of annual reports and the budget. The board comprises one representative from each

Member State (with the exception of Denmark), two members of the European Commission and one non-voting member of the United Nations High Commissioner for Refugees (UNHCR). EASO works in partnership with international and intergovernmental organisations (for example, UNHCR, International Organisation for Migration, the Council of Europe, the General Directors of Immigration Services Conference, and the Intergovernmental Consultations on Migration, Asylum and Refugees). As a member of the Justice and Home Affairs (JHA) interagency cooperation, EASO also works with EU bodies and agencies (including Frontex, FRA, Europol, Cepol, Eurojust, the European Monitoring Centre for Drugs and Drug Addiction, the European Institute for Gender Equality, the European Anti-Fraud Office and eu-LISA). Further partners include academics, European and national courts and tribunals (for example, through the International Association of Refugee Law Judges and the Association of European Administrative Judges) and civil society organisations.

With reference to cross-border crime, as detailed in the EASO Work Programme 2014, there are activities undertaken in the field of early warning and preparedness systems, and in the field of illegal immigration, trafficking in human beings and unaccompanied minors, alongside training focusing upon the use of false or forged documents in asylum claims, facilitated by organised crime groups, in partnership with Europol, Cepol and Frontex. Significantly, EASO was appointed the chair of JHA's agencies network in 2014 facilitating cooperation between EU agencies, sharing best practice and participating in a range of consultative forums related to JHA-specific topics and coordinating actions in the context of the JHA multiannual programmes.

See http://easo.europa.eu/.

The European Monitoring Centre for Drugs and Drug Addiction (EMCDDA)

Established in 1993 by Council Regulation (EEC) No 302/93 of 8 February 1993, the European Monitoring Centre for Drugs and Drug Addiction (EMCDDA) is described as a European hub for drugs information, providing the EU and its Member States with an evidence-based overview of European drug problems, informing legislation and drugs policy. As an EU decentralised agency, Article 1 of Regulation (EC) No 1920/2006 describes the Centre's objective as the provision of factual, objective, reliable and comparative information regarding drugs, drug addiction and their consequences to EU Member States and the Community.

The Centre's tasks include: the collection, registering and analysis of information; research; organising meetings of experts and setting up ad hoc working parties; facilitating the exchange of information; establishing indicators and common criteria to enhance data-comparison between Member States; developing tools and instruments to assist Member States to monitor and evaluate their national policies; and the dissemination of data (including the publication of an annual European Drugs Report, the successor to the annual report on the state of the drugs problem in Europe).

The national focal points of the European Information Network on Drugs and Drug Addiction (Reitox) comprise the link between EMCDDA and Member States, acting as the focal point for the collection and analysis of data at the national level. EMCDDA is governed by a Management Board, which remains the main deliberative body (comprising a representative from each Member State, two representatives from the European Commission and two representatives designated by the European Parliament). The Board is responsible for adopting a three-year Work Programme, an annual Work Programme for each coming year, the budget, and also for the production of an annual general report of activities. The Centre's Scientific Committee also advises and assists the Management Board and the Director, comprising a maximum of fifteen well-known scientists appointed by the Management Board, reviewing the EMCDDA Work Programme and publications and supporting the different working areas of the Centre.

EASO works in partnership with international organisations including: UNODC, WHO, UNAIDS, the Pompidou Group, CICAD, WCO and Interpol, and also maintains close cooperation and collaboration with EU institutions and agencies, the European Parliament, the Council of the EU and the European Commission, Europol, EMA, ECDC, Eurojust and CEPOL, providing information within a variety of drug policy forums and contributing within institutional meetings (for example, Horizontal Drugs Group, the EU policy dialogues, the National Drug Coordinators and the Standing Committee on Internal Security of the European Union).

EMCDDA contributes to the achievement of the goals of the EU drugs strategy for 2013–20 providing the information necessary for its effective implementation. The EMCDDA strategy and work programme for 2013–15 sets out the agency's core tasks. These are structured around five thematic areas: (a) monitoring the state of the drugs problem, in particular using epidemiological indicators, and monitoring emerging trends; (b) monitoring the solutions applied to drug-related problems; (c) providing information on best practices in the Member States and facilitating information exchange among them; (d) assessing the risks of new psychoactive substances and maintaining a rapid information system; (e) developing tools and instruments to help Member States to monitor and evaluate their national policies, and the Commission to monitor and evaluate European Union (EU) policies.

In relation to cross-border crime, it is significant that drugs remain a key issue on the European security agenda. The EMCDDA, for example, has recently been tasked, jointly with Europol, to implement activities under the operational action plan (OAP) for 2012–13 of the new policy cycle within the Council on Internal Security (COSI) of the European Union. In addition to contributing to this internal security priority-setting process, the EU drugs strategy for 2013–20 also highlights network building and cooperation with the law enforcement and forensic science communities (including Eurojust and CEPOL) remains high on the agenda, facilitating enhanced data collection and analysis and training collaboration on drug issues for law enforcement personnel. Further work, building upon an initial mapping exercise undertaken in 2012, includes a review of the tools, tactics and practices of specialised drug law enforcement units in Europe ('drug squads').

See www.emcdda.europa.eu/.

European Commission Anti-Fraud Office (OLAF)

Established in 1999 following Commission Decision 1999/252, the European Anti-Fraud Office's (OLAF) mission is threefold. OLAF works to protect the financial interests of the European Union, by investigating fraud, corruption and any other illegal activities; it detects and investigates serious matters relating to the discharge of professional duties by members and staff of the EU institutions and bodies that could result in disciplinary proceedings; and it supports the EU institutions in the development and implementation of anti-fraud legislation and policies (OLAF Report 2013).

All allegations received by OLAF are subject to initial assessment to determine whether the allegation falls within the remit of the Office and meets the criteria for opening an investigation. Cases are classified as internal investigations, external investigations, coordination cases or criminal assistance cases. Internal investigations refer to administrative investigations within the European Union institutions and bodies for the purpose of detecting fraud, corruption, and any other illegal activity affecting the financial interests of the European Communities (including serious matters relating to the discharge of professional duties). External investigations entail administrative investigations outside the European Union institutions and bodies for the purpose of detecting fraud or other irregular conduct by natural or legal persons. Coordination cases involve OLAF cooperation with national authorities or other Community department investigations, facilitating the gathering and exchange of information and contacts. Finally, criminal assistance cases are cases in which the competent authorities of a Member State or third country carry out a criminal investigation with assistance from OLAF.

Article 2 of the Decision provided for OLAF to support Member States in the fight against fraud including the preparation of legislative and regulatory initiatives; developing a fraud prevention infrastructure; collecting and analysing information and providing technical support including training to institutions, bodies and competent national authorities. OLAF replaced its predecessor, 'the Task Force for Coordination of Fraud Prevention', which was created in 1988 to provide coordination and assistance to tackle transnational organised fraud. The legal basis for EU action against fraud is Article 325 of the Lisbon Treaty. The general rules for OLAF investigations had previously been set out in Regulation 1073/1999 which was later repealed and replaced with Regulation

(EU, EURATOM) No 883/2013 of 13 September 2013 which defined OLAF's main role and remit for carrying out its administrative investigations.

The Supervisory Committee is OLAF's governance structure, mandated to monitor OLAF's investigative function in order to reinforce its independence (as set out in Article 15 of Regulation (EU, EURATOM) No 883/2013). The Committee is composed of five members, appointed following agreement between the European Parliament, the Council and the Commission. OLAF works closely on a daily basis with prosecutors' offices, investigating judges, police and customs bodies both in the Member States and in non-EU countries and has formal cooperation agreements with Interpol, Europol and Eurojust and is a full member of the European Judicial Network. According to Vlogaert and Pesta (2008: 86), what is less widely known is that OLAF has also maintained close cooperation between the investigative services of the UN (the Office of Internal Oversight Services), the World Bank (Department of Institutional Integrity), the European Investment Bank, and the regional development banks. Described as 'international investigators', this group reportedly meets on a regular basis both to improve the sharing of information and with regard to the creation of Joint (Administrative) Investigation Teams, maintaining a facility for exchanging staff between OLAF, the UN and the World Bank and organising an annual conference.

With respect to cross-border crime, the 2013 OLAF Report details emphasis on strengthening cooperation between OLAF, Europol and Eurojust in the fight against fraud, corruption and other illegal activities affecting the financial interests of the Union including action against trade customs fraud and especially the illicit trade in tobacco products. Thus, OLAF-coordinated joint customs operations have targeted the smuggling of excise goods including alcohol, in addition to work conducted under the auspices of the Hercule (I, II and II) and the Pericles Programmes (dedicated to countering fraud, corruption and other illegal activities such as cigarette smuggling and Euro counterfeiting).

See http://ec.europa.eu/anti_fraud/index_en.htm.

Southeast European Law Enforcement Centre (SELEC)

Established in 2011 following the entry into force of the SELEC Convention, SELEC comprises a regional law enforcement organisation, providing support for Member States and enhancing cooperation to prevent and combat crime involving trans-border activity. Developing the operational and strategic capabilities of its predecessor organisation (the SECI Centre), SELEC provides a setting for the Member States to cooperate through the exchange of law enforcement related information and criminal intelligence and offers operational assistance, coordinating multinational investigations and operations in the Southeast European region. The Convention further provides for SELEC to collect, collate, analyse, process and disseminate information and criminal intelligence, providing strategic analysis and threat assessments. Comprising twelve Member States (Republic of Albania, Bosnia and Herzegovina, Republic of Bulgaria, Republic of Croatia, the Former Yugoslav Republic of Macedonia, Hellenic Republic, Hungary, Republic of Moldova, Montenegro, Romania, Republic of Serbia and Republic of Turkey), SELEC cooperates with a range of international organisations including: the United Nations Office on Drugs and Crime (UNODC) and World Customs Organisation (WCO), formally establishing and negotiating cooperation agreements with many European and non-European countries and international organisations to create Observer and Operational Partner status in the facilitation of information exchange and regional assistance in relation to the Centre's investigative activities.

Liaison Officers made up of Police and Customs authorities are appointed by Member States, serving together at the SELEC Headquarters in Bucharest. National Focal Points within each Member State comprise the link between Member States and SELEC, receiving and responding to requests for regional assistance and exchanging information.

Operational activities are structured within the frames of eight Task Forces (TF) addressing issues of trafficking of drugs and human beings, stolen vehicles, smuggling and customs fraud, financial and computer crime, terrorism, container security and environmental and nature related crimes. In addition to operational activities (including joint investigations), SELEC activities also include the hosting of conferences and meetings, disseminating good practices in law enforcement and offering specialised training and workshops. The Centre also provides strategic analysis covering the most sensitive trans-border criminal fields in the South Eastern European region.

See www.secicenter.org/.

Contemporary issues and challenges

Previously regarded as a neglected and 'low-level technical-administrative exercise' (Anderson, 1989: 12; Deflem, 2002), it is evident that police and law enforcement cooperation has resulted in a proliferation of interest, activity, instruments and initiatives over the past four decades (den Boer in Lemieux, 2010).

The preceding sections of this chapter highlight the complexity and evolution of the transnational and (European) regional political and law enforcement infrastructure tasked with countering cross-border crime and terrorism. The selective description of key international and regional organisations and agencies serves to reveal the remarkable homogenisation and cross-fertilisation of issues now defined as significant security threats and challenges facing international society, regional trading blocs and individual nation-states. The overview provided also enables us to return to the key questions raised at the beginning of the chapter relating to the role and significance of the nation-state and the relative importance of non-state actors within the governance structure of the contemporary world order.

Describing the contemporary transnational state system as: 'precarious, fragile and insecure', Sheptycki (1998) details a recent transformation in the governance structure and forms of policing within post-modernity. Johnston similarly argues that we are witnessing a changing 'morphology of governance in which partly fragmented states interact with commercial, civil and voluntary bodies, both within and across national jurisdictional boundaries' (Johnston, 2000: 38).

The organisations and bodies listed here challenge the one-dimensionality of orthodox accounts, which privilege the centrality of states in our contemporary understanding of global politics. However, as is also immediately obvious, neither has the state lost significance. It is clear that in the field of transnational crime and terrorism, a global governance complex has evolved. Described as: a 'security field' (Bigo, 2000; Johnston, 2000); a 'patchwork quilt of agencies' (Sheptycki, 1995); a 'multi-level, multi-centred security governance' (Loader and Walker, 2007); or a 'fragmented regulatory regime' (den Boer in Lemieux, 2010: 61), it is evident that this complex comprises a diverse range of informal clubs and international institutions, attended by Heads of State or government, foreign ministers, ministers of defence and other state representatives and officials (including senior police representatives).

These international actors are joined by an array of transnational actors including regional organisations, agencies and networks, commercial security and information communication services, non-governmental organisations and civil society. Sheptycki (2000) contends that, rather than reflecting a 'hollowing out of the state' (referring to the trend towards internationalisation and the erosion of the state), the emerging governance framework represents contradiction, fragmentation and the 'diffusion, multiplication and intensification of governmental practice', both outwards and downwards. Thus, where the state was previously conceived as the virtual monopoly-provider of security and social control, transnational policing within the post-modern era is presented as a situation where state provision is less and less predominant, subject to remote forms of governance, plurality and flux (Sheptycki, 1998). Den Boer (in Lemieux, 2010: 45) similarly stresses that the exercise of governance within the 'newly emerging security paradigm' is currently undertaken 'under plural auspices', including the private sector.

These observations caution us against overly deterministic and state-centric accounts of recent developments. Anderson's (1989) early examination of the emergence and development of Interpol for example, remained acutely aware of the fact that, while police organisations are powerful institutions of the state, many policing organisations have acquired a degree of autonomy and independence from governmental control, with informal practice often occurring outside the existence of formal legal frameworks, with the potential for individual actors to influence agenda setting, policy and practice on a global, regional and local level. Deflem's (2002) history of international policing similarly challenges the notion that police cooperation across borders was based on formal intergovernmental accords, suggesting that certain socio-economic conditions determine the likelihood of police institutions engaging in international policing, including the achievement of bureaucratic autonomy from government and the alignment of common interests between nations. Micro-political factors associated with the individual, and organisational dynamics of decision making are therefore viewed as a necessary complement to economic and macro-political factors to understand the dimensions and aspects of law enforcement cooperation (see also Anderson *et al.*, 1995). Further, Sheptycki's post-modern account describes transnational order maintenance efforts as subject to 'contingency, the chaos of ruthless fate and fumbling chance' (Sheptycki, 1995: 619), thereby challenging determinism and redirecting attention to the significance of agency and serendipity in accounting for the evolution of transnational policing, a point to which we shall return in the next chapter. Drawing upon the work of Nadelmann (1993), Sheptycki also directs attention to the significance of justificatory myths and the identification of folk devils in facilitating this process, a focus also evident in the work of Bigo (2000), who describes actors within the European Security Field as professionals of threat management, deriving their power from their capacity to define the sources of our insecurity and to produce techniques to manage them.

Agencies derived from military, intelligence and security services, national police services, border police, and immigration, customs and financial services increasingly share information and intelligence, mounting joint operations and engaging in operational law enforcement activities. Partnership working, collaboration and cooperative agreements with state representatives, agencies and organisations, individual member (and non-member) states, civil society and the private sector characterise the methodologies and working practices of many of these bodies, particularly in the light of increasing budgetary and resourcing restraints and demands for financial accountability in the recent era of austerity.

Transnational policing and political cooperation has consequently resulted in an alignment of the organisational agendas, concerns and remits of a vast array of law enforcement and security bodies. Many of these bodies have observed an expansion of their role and activities, blurring the boundaries between domestic and foreign policy, internal and external security, 'high and low' policing, policing and military action. Within the newly established common agenda, the achievement of stability, the protection of human rights and democratisation have become central alongside more traditional efforts directed towards transnational organised crime and terrorism, now reconceptualised as 'spoilers' of international, regional and national 'peace' and 'security'.

The shift from government to governance towards a 'polycentricity of power' (see Stenson in Sheptycki, 2000) has resulted in uncertainty and criticism regarding the transparency, external democratic control and accountability of the emerging infrastructure (Anderson *et al.*, 1995; Sheptycki, 1995; Brodeur, 2000; Goldsmith and Sheptycki, 2007; Lemieux, 2010; Bowling and Sheptycki, 2012). As has been observed in the recent activities of the bodies discussed above, we have consequently witnessed efforts to establish and/or strengthen the legal framework, governance and accountability structures, with the TEU viewed as an important catalyst moving European police cooperation towards a system of accountability and parliamentary control (Anderson *et al.*, 1995: 84). However, in 2000, Sheptycki concluded that 'mechanisms for ensuring the democratic accountability of transnational policing practices are not being laid in the emerging transnational state system' (Sheptycki, 2000: 168). More recently, within the European Security Field, following the signing (in 2007) and the entry into force of the Lisbon Treaty in 2009 (which aimed to make the EU more democratic and efficient), contentious bodies, such as EU SitCen and OLAF, have been integrated within the EU Framework. Furthermore, agencies such as Europol, Eurojust, Frontex, Cepol, and FRA have witnessed an improved legal status and are also now formally established as EU agencies, with other agencies such as EASO and EMCDDA having achieved decentralised EU agency status and Justice and Home Affairs interagency cooperation membership. These bodies have therefore recently enhanced the role of the European Parliament and Council over the agencies' respective programmes of activities and management. However, considerable dispute and criticism remains regarding the adequacy of the new mechanisms of democratic accountability, oversight and transparency, within the evolving supranational and intergovernmental frameworks with several bodies (e.g. EU Chief of Police Task Force) continuing to exist without the establishment of formal legal frameworks. Concern therefore remains regarding the powers and expanding remits of several agencies, task forces and organisations, particularly in relation to due process considerations and human and fundamental rights protection.

The alignment of organisational agendas and the emergence of a common security agenda have also resulted in what Sheptycki (1995: 618), drawing upon the work of Egger (1990), describes as 'linkage blindness', namely, jurisdictional conflict, interagency competition and rivalry between departments, and an overlapping and duplication of functions and expertise. More recently, Lemieux (2010: 2) has emphasised the tension arising from limited resources and the tendency towards nationalistic/discretionary information-sharing, observations which are shared in practitioner focused studies which highlight the realities of bilateral and multilateral policing cooperation. Guille (2010: 27), for example, points to the importance of personal and informal contacts and the presence of good will as facilitators of efficient cooperation amongst practitioners. Trust and the timeliness of responses to requests for assistance, the utilisation of a common language and continuity in contacts in addition to the existence of knowledge regarding the national legislation and policing structures of other countries are also highlighted as significant factors in conjunction with legal frameworks, hierarchy dynamics and structures of accountability and transparency. Practitioner studies have also directed attention to the existence of a continuing preference for bilateral and informal methods of policing cooperation as opposed to formal multilateral mechanisms, highlighting incongruity between the rhetoric and practices of political law enforcement cooperation and law enforcement 'on the ground' within the lower echelons of rank and file officers and law enforcement agents. Viewed as essential tools for cooperation at a European level, Europol and Eurojust have been challenged for failing to work as they should, with writers such as Guille (2010: 35) viewing their conventions as 'too broad', the volume of bureaucracy involved as 'too great' and the general awareness of their operation as 'insufficient'. Both agencies are consequently described as suffering from a lack of information sharing stemming from an absence of trust on the part of law enforcement practitioners.

Much writing in the area of transnational policing and international cooperation in criminal matters has therefore directed attention to practical difficulties faced by law enforcement practitioners identifying barriers to effective international cooperation. The early work of Anderson (1989: 30), for example, directed attention to difficulties surrounding extradition and national variation with respect to rules of evidence, data protection and differences in police powers in addition to communication difficulties. Anderson (1989: 12–13) also highlights the significance of power politics and state and commercial interest, noting national variance in levels of economic and social development, ideological and foreign-policy conflicts which are viewed as inhibiting 'the effective suppression of drug trafficking and other types of serious crime'. Focusing specifically upon the EU, Anderson *et al.* (1995: 279) further identify the necessity for a favourable political context and the commitment of political elites as pre-requisites for progress towards operational police powers, with commentators also pointing to variation in criminal laws, penalties and incompatibilities within policing organisational structures, systems, cultures, information and communication technologies, procedures, policies and politics as inhibiting factors creating barriers to international cooperation in criminal matters (Lemieux, 2010: 4). Thus, differences remain resulting in significant challenges for practitioners and academics alike. Den Boer in Lemieux (2010: 43) for example, has recently concluded that European Police Cooperation as it is currently shaped within the European Union is regarded as bureaucratic, difficult to understand, barely workable and utopian, resulting in confusion regarding accountability and responsibility for the implementation of various instruments in the field of European Police Cooperation (den Boer in Lemieux, 2010: 43–44).

Thus, while the overview of significant national and regional organisations, agencies and networks provided within this chapter suggests a broad tendency towards homogenisation and alignment in agendas, methods of law enforcement, and the gradual emergence of a global constabulary community (facilitated by a wide range of cooperative measures, tools and practices), recognising common security problems and solutions, it is perhaps prudent not to overstate the degree of convergence and to remain mindful of national variation despite the development of cooperative mechanisms and aptitudes of policy-makers and law enforcement leaders. While evidence suggests that we have witnessed an acceleration and intensification in bilateral and multilateral law enforcement and political cooperation to counter transnational crime and terrorism, this process is, to date, imperfect, incomplete, continuously evolving and influenced by a range of micro and macro factors, which evade generalisation.

Regardless of our preference of terminology to describe the emerging infrastructure, it is hoped that the preceding pages have revealed the remarkable convergence of security and law enforcement priorities within and between the international and regional institutions, organisations, agencies and bodies detailed above. Advocating multilateral action, collaboration, and information sharing, and through a focus upon legislative, criminal and judicial capacity building and assistance, it is clear to see that the contemporary framework is decidedly liberal in nature. Returning to the previous chapter, it is evident that the United Nations and European Union (along with their associated agencies and bodies) embrace the 'standard view' of globalisation emphasised in the work of Andreas and Nadelmann, employing an expanded conceptualisation of security. In doing so, they articulate a discourse aligned with an updated version of the modernisation perspective. This picture, which presents contemporary global society as subject to a period of rapid social change, influenced by globalising tendencies which generate a range of security threats and opportunities for crime and terrorism, is viewed as malleable, and open to collective problem-solving efforts. Prioritising law and order responses, institution creation and reform and embracing normative consensus (including the liberal values of democracy, human rights, freedom and free trade), the existing framework remains committed to the preservation of the current world order, a structure which embraces neo-liberal economic globalisation as the route to global peace, security and prosperity. As detailed in the previous chapter however, the current framework is historically and temporally bounded. In the chapters that follow, the adequacy of current liberal approaches to the issues of international crime, transnational organised crime and terrorism will be examined, drawing upon the insights of the theoretical perspectives introduced in Chapter 3. Students are invited to contemplate the relevance of historical and political analysis to the issues at hand, and to evaluate the prospects of success for the expanding global policing and security governance complex.

Notes

1 For example, Interpol provides a number of secure communication channels including 'I-24/7 Global Communications system', which enables investigators to search and cross-check data, and the 'I-Link electronic system', for exchanging information.

2 Interpol databases include the 'Stolen and Lost Travel Documents' (SLTD) database, created in 2002; the 'I-Checkit' (which utilises unique security features to assess product legitimacy); the 'Fast and Efficient International Disaster Victim Identification database' (which is used to identify and link missing persons and unidentified bodies); the 'Interpol International Child Sexual Exploitation' database;

'Interpol Illicit Firearms Records and Tracing Management System'; 'Interpol Ballistic Information Network'; and the 'CBRNE Intelligence Report' (directed towards countering the illicit trafficking of nuclear and radiological materials). 'Interpol Secure Cloud' has also been recently introduced to save, use and share information securely through the channels of Interpol.

3 'Red notices' for instance alert police to wanted persons; 'Blue notices' to individuals of interest in relation to a crime; 'Green notices' issuing warnings and intelligence about serious criminals; 'Yellow notices' regarding missing persons; 'Black notices' for unidentified bodies; 'Orange notices' in relation to dangerous materials, criminal acts or events that pose a potential threat to public safety; 'Purple notices' alerting officers to objects, devices or concealment methods used by criminals; and more recently, from 2005, 'Interpol-United Nations Security Council Special Notices' issued for individuals or entities associated with Al-Qaeda and the Taliban.

4 For example, Interpol's Project Combat Wildlife Crime and the deployment of IRTs in Togo, Uganda and Sri Lanka to assist with wildlife crime investigations.

5 Including Project RELINC tasked with rebuilding Libya's Investigative Capacity.

6 The Interpol Sixth International Expert Conference on Genocide, War Crimes and Crimes against Humanity which took place on 14 April 2014 in Rwanda, highlighted Interpol's efforts within this area including the issuing of over 200 Red Notices, the creation of the Fugitive Investigative Support unit and law enforcement tools and the creation in 2004 of the Rwandan Fugitives Project tasked with arresting genocide fugitives and bringing them to justice, the result of a partnership between Interpol, the Rwanda National Police, the Prosecution Authority and the International Criminal Tribunal for Rwanda (ICTR).

7 A memorandum of understanding was signed between DPKO and Interpol in 2002, further strengthened by an additional agreement signed between the United Nations and Interpol in 2009, addressing action targeted towards the investigation of transnational crime. Recent examples include the West African Coast Initiative (WACI) comprising a joint partnership with Interpol and the UN Office on Drugs and Crime (UNODC) on transnational organised crime.

8 In April 2009, the IMF launched a donor-supported trust fund to finance capacity development in AML/CFT. In 2014, a new five-year phase of the trust fund commenced. Further IMF activities within these areas include: the publication of a guidance note in 2012 on the inclusion of AML/CFT in surveillance and financial stability assessments (FSAs); a 2014 Board review of the Fund's AML/CFT strategy which endorsed a revised FATF AML/CFT standard and assessment methodology and encouraged the integration of financial integrity issues into its surveillance and Fund-supported programmes.

9 Good governance linked with the IMF's surveillance lending and technical assistance functions have also led to the publication of a Guidance Note entitled 'The Role of the IMF in Governance Issues' in 1997, followed more recently by a 'Transparency Policy', a 'Standards and Codes Initiative', a 'Code of Good Practices on Fiscal Transparency' and a 'Guide on Resource Revenue Transparency'.

References

Anderson, M. (1989). *Policing the World.* Oxford: Clarendon Press.

Anderson, M., DenBoer, M., Cullen, P., Gilmore, W., Raab, C., and Walker, N. (1995). *Policing the European Union*. Oxford: Clarendon Press.

Andreas, P. and Nadelmann, E. (2006). *Policing the Globe: Criminalization and Crime Control in International Relations.* Oxford: Oxford University Press.

Bigo, D. (2000). 'Liaison Officers in Europe: New Officers in the European Security Field', in Sheptycki, J.W.E. (ed.), *Issues in Transnational Policing*. London: Routledge.

Bowling, B. and Sheptycki, J.W.E. (2012). *Global Policing*. London: Sage.

Brodeur, J. (2000). 'Transnational Policing and Human Rights: A Case Study', in Sheptycki, J.W.E. (ed.), *Issues in Transnational Policing*. London: Routledge.

Brown, S. (2008). 'The EU Solution Europol and Eurojust', in Brown, S. (ed.), *Combating International Crime: The Longer Arm of the Law*. Abingdon: Routledge Cavendish.

Council of the European Union. (23 February 2010). 'Draft Internal Security Strategy for the European Union', 5842/10. Available online at: http://register.consilium.europa.eu/doc/srv?l=EN&f=ST%205842%202010%20REV%202.

Deflem, M. (2002). *Policing World Society: Historical Foundations of International Police Cooperation*. Oxford: Oxford University Press.

Den Boer, M. (2010). 'Towards a Governance Model of Police Cooperation in Europe: The Twist Between Networks and Bureaucracies', in Lemieux, F. (ed.), *International Police Cooperation*. Cullompton: Willan Publishing.

Egger, S. (1990). *Serial Murder: An Illusive Phenomenon*. New York: Praeger.

European Commission. (2010). *Communication from the Commission to the European Parliament, the Council, the European Economic and Social Committee and the Committee of the Regions: Delivering an Area of Freedom, Security and Justice for Europe's Citizens*. Action Plan Implementing the Stockholm Programme. [COM (2010)171 final].

Eurojust News. (2013). Issue 8. *Eurojust*. May. Available online at: www.eurojust.europa.eu/doclibrary/corporate/newsletter/eurojust%20news%20issue%208%20(may%202013)%20on%20the%20creation%20of%20a%20european%20public%20prosecutor%20office/eurojustnews_issue8_2013–2005-en.pdf (accessed June 15, 2015).

Frontex. (2015). *Annual Risk Analysis 2015*. Warsaw: European Agency for the Management of Operational Cooperation at the External Borders of the Member States of the European Union. Risk Analysis Unit.

Goldsmith, A. and Sheptycki, J.W.E. (2007). *Crafting Transnational Policing: Police Capacity-Building and Global Policing Reform*. Oxford: Hart Publishing.

Gregory, F. (2000). 'Private Criminality as a Matter of International Concern', in Sheptycki, J. (ed.), *Issues in Transnational Policing*. London: Routledge.

Guille, L. (2010). 'Police and Judicial Cooperation in Europe: Bilateral Versus Multilateral Cooperation', in Lemieux, F. (ed.), *International Police Cooperation*. Cullompton: Willan Publishing.

Hills, A. (2009). 'The Possibility of Transnational Policing', *Policing and Society*, 19(3): 300–317.

IMF (2015). 'The IMF and the Fight Against Money Laundering and the Financing of Terrorism'. Available online at: www.imf.org/external/np/exr/facts/pdf/aml.pdf (accessed August 28, 2015).

Johnston, L. (2000). 'Transnational Private Policing: The Impact of Global Commercial Security', in Sheptycki, J.W.E. (ed.), *Issues in Transnational Policing*. London: Routledge.

Lemieux, F. (ed.). (2010). *International Police Cooperation*. Abingdon: Routledge.

Loader, I. and Walker, N. (2007). 'Locating the Public Interest in Transnational Policing', in Goldsmith, A. and Sheptycki, J.W.E, (eds), *Crafting Transnational Policing: Police Capacity-Building and Global Policing Reform*. Oxford: Hart Publishing.

Manning, P. (2000). 'Policing New Social Spaces', in Sheptycki, J.W.E. (ed.), *Issues in Transnational Policing*. London: Routledge.

Nadelmann, E. (1993). *Cops Across Borders: The Internationalization of U.S. Criminal Law Enforcement*. University Park, PA: Pennsylvania State University Press.

Prost, K. (2008). 'No Hiding Place: How Justice Need Not be Blinded by Borders', in Brown, S. (ed.), *Combating International Crime*. Abingdon: Routledge.

Reichel, P. (ed.). (2005). *Handbook of Transnational Crime and Justice*. London: Sage.

Sheptycki, J.W.E. (1995). 'Transnational Policing and the Makings of a Postmodern State', *British Journal of Criminology*, 35(4): 613–635.

Sheptycki, J.W.E. (1998). 'Policing, Post-modernism and Transnationalisation', *British Journal of Criminology*, 38(3): 485–503.

Sheptycki, J.W.E. (ed.). (2000). *Issues in Transnational Policing*. London: Routledge.

UN. (2012). Economic and Social Council Resolution 2012/12 [Strategy for the period 2012–2015 for the United Nations Office on Drugs and Crime], 10 August, E/RES/2012/12

UN Police Magazine. (2014). 12th Edition. United Nations Department of Peacekeeping Operations, January. Available online at: www.un.org/en/peacekeeping/publications/unpolmag/unpol-mag-2014.pdf (accessed June 15, 2015).

Vlogaert, J. and Pesta, M. (2008). 'OLAF: Fighting Fraud in the EU and Beyond', in Brown, S. (ed.), *Combating International Crime: The Longer Arm of the Law*. Abingdon: Routledge.

5 International crime, state crime and corruption

According to Chambliss, Michalowski and Kramer (2010: 1), 'criminology has always had a difficult time in addressing harmful actions that fall outside the narrow range of wrongdoings selected by states' condemnation', particularly when committed by states themselves. Indeed, as noted by Aas (2007: 183), traditional criminology has tended to neglect a variety of actors, activities and human rights violations, with the prevailing methodological nationalism of Western criminology creating a 'blind spot' for violations committed by states themselves and state-supported agencies. Distinguishing between crimes 'against the state' and those 'by the state', Chambliss, Michalowski and Kramer (2010: 1) identify acts of torture, aggressive war and political repression as instances of the latter, noting that these actions are rarely criminalised by offending states nor are they frequently investigated and/or prosecuted. When such instances are investigated, they suggest, this is often undertaken some time after the acts occurred, 'only after they have served their purpose or failed to advance state interest'. This argument is evident within Chapter 2, which examined historically, state promotion and utilisation of slavery and piracy, in addition to subsequent efforts directed towards the criminalisation and enforcement of such acts. Chapter 2 consequently engaged with critical scholarship which has conceptualised the law and criminal justice as instruments of geo-political strategy or state-building (Goldsmith and Sheptycki, 2007), and as a tool of global governance (Findlay, 1999, 2008), integral to the maintenance of social order, alongside other hard and soft manifestations of power and statecraft. This return in attention to the political function of law enforcement, described by Sheptycki (2000) as 'high policing', serves to remind us of the need to remain cautious regarding our interpretation of the present. Andreas and Nadelmann (2006: 253), for instance, direct readers to be 'wary of overstating how new and different the contemporary era is from past historical experience'. They note that policing has been preoccupied with counter-terrorism since its inception, with securitisation and militarisation featuring strongly within past methodology, alongside privatisation and the internationalisation of the policing function more generally (see also, Sheptycki, 2000; Deflem, 2002), aspects recently identified as new, and markers of the contemporary phase of globalisation. Thus, while the 'high policing', involving a 'political' or 'normative' dimension of policing, is not conceived as a recent invention, it seems that the degree of covertness regarding such an objective may well be, directing attention to the need to historically contextualise criminalisation processes and to attend to geo-political considerations and issues of power.

More recently, further examples of state crimes have been provided by other commentators. The list has consequently extended to include corruption, corporate crime, natural disaster, police crime, organised crime, state terror, war crimes and genocide (Green and Ward, 2004). These crimes, however, have generally been excluded from 'mainstream' or 'administrative' criminological discourse, which has tended to retain its focus upon national criminal justice processes and the positivist 'natural' definition of crime which assumes that there are essential differences between criminal behaviour and legal behaviour (Vold, Bernard and Snipes, 1998: 9). Thus, as noted by Aas (2007: 184), '[t]here are no official statistics on political violence [and] [w]hile international organisations collect statistics from governments on health, education, environment etc., there are no official data on human rights abuses, political and state violence'.

Within the field of international policing cooperation and international criminology, other authors have similarly identified limitations resulting from a state-centric and legalistic conceptualisation of crime. Thus, for Bowling and Sheptycki (2012) the dominant discourse of law enforcement and national security leaves several omissions within global policing practice. For Aas (2007), Bowling and Sheptycki (2012), Andreas and Nadelmann (2006) and an increasing number of scholars working within the area of international crime, transnational crime, international criminology, and global policing, it has therefore become imperative to transcend the 'nation-state' frame of reference, in order to direct attention to a much broader range of harms and social ills, which fall short of criminal categorisation.

Smith, Zhang and Barberet (2011: 2), for example, seeking to transcend the prescriptive focus of international criminology upon international crime and transnational crime, have recently defined international criminology as 'a culturally sensitive and globally mindful approach to crime and social control problems where they happen'. In expanding the focus from 'crime' to 'social control', these authors permit the inclusion of the normative and political aspects of criminalisation processes and enforcement, explicitly seeking to 'embrace cultural and political diversity', and encouraging a more nuanced appreciation of different interpretations and applications of phenomena. In focusing upon these issues, there is an acknowledgement within this emerging scholarship that the ontology of crime has been disrupted. This development is associated with a critical turn within criminology which reconceptualised the focus of study, accepting that 'crime is a social product of political choice and not an immutable fact' (Chambliss, Michalowski and Kramer, 2010: 5). This shift in attention by a new branch of critical and globally oriented criminologists consequently drew attention to the application of power in the criminalisation of prohibited acts, enforcement practices and the emergence of, and priorities within, crime control agendas and regimes (Andreas and Nadelmann, 2006). Critical scholarship also raised questions about the utility of mainstream or traditional perspectives on crime and introduced an alternative viewpoint, which examined criminalisation as a form of social control and/or hegemonic power. This new perspective consequently challenged both classical theory (identified in Chapter 3), which conceived crime as the commission of prohibited acts defined by law (by rational free-thinking individuals), and the later positivist approach which sought to identify the biological, psychological and/or social causes of crime (Vold, Bernard and Snipes, 1998).

Having briefly directed attention to the emergence of a critical turn within criminology, this chapter aims to return to the sociological roots of this paradigm shift, introducing the symbolic interactionist approach of George Herbert Mead, with a view to highlighting its influence upon criminological and international relations thinkers. As detailed within the previous chapters, in presenting what they called 'an analytically eclectic approach', Andreas and Nadelmann endeavoured to weave together three theoretical perspectives which they believed offered a more nuanced and historically grounded approach to the study of international criminal law enforcement. Thus, the liberal perspective emphasising collective problem solving, cooperation and mutual interest, became supplemented within their work with the realist focus upon power, geo-politics and enduring conflicts. The third and final theoretical strand within their analysis is described by Andreas and Nadelmann as 'Constructivism'. This approach is regarded as a necessary corrective 'to the common tendency to bracket and take for granted the prior process of delegitimising and criminalising particular transnational activities' (Andreas and Nadelmann, 2006: 13). Thus, 'constructivism' within international relations, and 'symbolic interactionism' within sociology and criminology, both focus on how the criminal law is written and enforced, directing attention to the question of why some individuals are officially defined as criminals while others who act in essentially similar ways are not (Vold, Bernard and Snipes, 1998: 9–10).

These questions also remain central within the emerging critical 'state crime' literature. The final component of the chapter will therefore be dedicated to an examination of Green and Ward and Michalowski's categorisation of variants of state crime, examining criminological engagement with acts perpetrated, initiated or overtly or covertly supported by the state. With Chapters 6 and 7 dedicated to an analysis of what has been described as particularly 'heinous' variants of state crime, namely strategic responses to the perpetration of genocide and to acts of terror, the chapter will end with a brief discussion of genocide, terrorism and corruption as depicted through the alternative lens of critical state crime scholarship.

Continuing with the theme of crime and criminalisation as tools of statecraft, the academic contributions detailed within this chapter once again sensitise the reader to the importance of perspective, of power, and international politics in shaping the expanding global policing and security governance complex. This work again serves to highlight the contemporary destabilisation of conceptual distinctions between legitimate and illicit action, war and crime, police and military action, domestic and foreign policy, national and international security, organised crime, corporate crime, international crime, state crime, terrorism, in addition to regular state and corporate practice. By adding a further layer of complexity, this chapter comprises a necessary precursor for the final part of the text, completing the framework, which will be utilised in Chapters 6 to 8, to enable readers to address the adequacy of contemporary regional and international strategy to counter genocide, terrorism and human trafficking.

Symbolic interactionism

As noted by Ritzer (1996), the term 'symbolic interactionism' was coined by Herbert Blumer in 1937. This perspective is associated with the ideas of George Herbert Mead, Charles Horton Cooley, W.I. Thomas, Herbert Blumer and Erving Goffman and was influenced by the philosophical position of pragmatism and psychological behaviourism. This work directs attention to the centrality of the actor who is defined as creative and dynamic, and also to the importance of meaning, and particularly, the process by which actors construct meaning. This approach therefore rejects the deterministic accounts detailed in Chapter 3, which explain behaviour on the basis of (social structural and socio-cultural) external forces such as 'social systems', 'social structure', 'institutions', 'norms' and 'values'. The state-centric and institutional focus of the realist and liberal institutionalist perspectives within international relations, and the structural focus upon economic world systems and attention to material and non-material social facts, evident within the work of Wallerstein and Durkheim are consequently challenged for their failure to address 'the social construction of reality'. In particular, the structural approaches discussed thus far are critiqued for their failure to attribute significance to the interaction between society and the actor in the construction of meaning, in addition to the dialectical processes informing social action.

Drawing upon the work of Blumer (1969), Manis and Meltzer (1978) and Rose (1962), Ritzer (1996: 347–348) presents the key principles underpinning symbolic interactionism. These include the belief that human beings are endowed with the capacity for thought; that this capacity is shaped by social interaction; that it is in social interaction that individuals learn the meaning and symbols that allow them to exercise their capacity for thought; that meaning and symbols allow people to act and interact; that people are able to modify or alter the meanings and symbols that they use in action and interaction, on the basis of their interpretation of the situation; that such modifications and alterations are made possible due to the ability of individuals to interact with themselves, allowing them to examine possible courses of action, assess relative advantages and disadvantages and to select between alternatives; and, finally, that intertwined patterns of action and interaction make up groups and societies.

Within this perspective then, rational thought, reflexivity, socialisation, meaning, interpretation and social context are vital aspects of a dynamic process of action and interaction. Society and culture are consequently interpreted as sites of political struggle, a position that raises interesting questions about the production of cultural meaning and the association of power dynamics within such processes. The symbolic interactionist frame of reference subsequently enabled scholars to deconstruct grand narratives, hegemonic discourses and normative frameworks, directing attention to the existence of rival interpretations regarding the meaning of concepts, examining who has the power to define, their motivations and their interests, and the consequences for those involved.

Within international relations scholarship, constructivism, associated with the work of Onuf (1989) and Katzenstein (1996), has been applied to shed light upon the making and re-making of world politics, exploring the convergence by states around similar ways of organising domestic and international life and how norms have become internationalised and institutionalised over time (Barnett, 2014: 156). Thus, for constructivists, the structures of international politics, alongside international norms such as 'human rights', 'humanitarian intervention and the responsibility to protect', are regarded as socially constructed phenomena and, as such, may be deconstructed by changing the way scholars and decision-makers think about international relations and by challenging dominant ideas and discourses. This position therefore suggests that international relations are affected by ideas, and that by transcending state-centric analysis, the focus upon norms and values may help to explain the behaviour of state and non-state actors within world affairs. As noted by Williams (2013: 6–7), states can be both providers of security and also providers of insecurity, a point similarly made by feminist theorists and post-colonial scholarship (see Tickner, 1992). Thus, for Williams, ideas, discourse and the 'logic of interpretation' are essential for understanding international politics and security. As noted by Tickner (2014: 157), linguistic constructivists such as Kubalkova conceive the world as created through human action, and also through the meaning that humans give to their actions. This perspective therefore enables such scholars to challenge contemporary knowledge production processes, raising questions regarding the adequacy of the epistemological foundations of Western modern secular knowledge, providing space for the inclusion of previously neglected religious and cultural traditions. For constructivists then, realism as a dominant discourse of power politics within international relations has actively encouraged security competition between states, fostering a lack of trust, insecurity and anxiety with consequences for strategies of power and security maximisation. As such, the realist position is regarded as part of the problem requiring deconstruction and replacement with alternative interpretations of security (and insecurity), with the purpose of social theorising directed towards the deconstruction and dismantling of global structures of domination and hierarchical relations. Thus, employing a feminist international relations position, Tickner (2014) joins a growing number of scholars who reflect upon the relationship between hegemonic knowledge structures and power, observing how knowledge has been constructed in the interests of the powerful, and has also been complicit in legitimising hierarchical structures and relations, resulting in marginalisation, insecurity and oppression.

In addition to the focus upon the need to deconstruct knowledge structures, the symbolic interactionist position of Mead, Blumer and Goffman further explicitly recognised that people symbolically communicate meanings to others, with such others interpreting those symbols and orienting their responding action on the basis of their interpretation (Ritzer, 1996: 351). Agency, perception and legitimacy therefore remain important – with one's view of one's own behaviour and that of others, alongside one's perception of the others' perception of one's behaviour, remaining significant factors within decision-making processes (both for individuals within criminology, and for states and non-state actors within international relations theorising). This assumption is similarly evident within the constructivist position within international relations scholarship, which retains space for human consciousness and agency 'recognising that agents have some autonomy and their interactions help to construct, reproduce and transform' structures within global politics (Barnett, 2014: 158). This position therefore emphasises the socially constructed nature of actors, identities, knowledge systems, normative systems and regulatory systems. For Barnett, the social construction of reality directs attention to the normative function of social constructs, asking analysts to question, historically contextualise and deconstruct previously taken for granted concepts such as 'refugees', 'weapons of mass destruction', to which we may add 'terrorists', 'human trafficking victims', 'humanitarian intervention' and 'security'. For Barnett (2014: 167) constructivism offers alternative ways of thinking about a range of concepts and challenges received wisdoms, opening up new lines of enquiry.

Towards a criminology of state crime

The symbolic interactionist and constructivist concern with meaning and social construction is retained within recent scholarship drawing from a range of disciplines, including criminology, law, political science and international relations, which have been concerned with exploring the causes and consequences of social harms resulting from the use and abuse of state power. Keen to demarcate a distinctive criminology of state crime, Chambliss, Michalowski and Kramer (2010) and Green and Ward (2004) are among a growing number of scholars who are employing an interdisciplinary approach, transcending nation-state definitions of crime and deviance, to include the wide spectrum of acts and harms which have tended to be neglected within mainstream criminology. This work acknowledges the traditional relationship between criminological knowledge and the state, directing attention to the primacy of Western, particularly Anglo-American scholarship and knowledge structures in explaining crime. Endeavouring to frame state crime within the context of increasing global integration (thereby engaging with the globalisation discourse discussed in Chapter 1), this work directs attention to the consequences of neo-liberal globalisation, examining human rights violations committed by states themselves, in addition to a wider range of injustices and inequalities derived from state action, which, as noted by Aas (2007: 183–4), 'tends to be neglected and uncensored by that nation state penal system'. This scholarship consequently adopts a sceptical perspective regarding globalising trends, also raising questions regarding the administrative focus of mainstream criminology, criminalisation and international crime control, which it is suggested serves to obfuscate insight, preventing alternative framing and solutions, diverting attention away from more fundamental political, social and economic reforms to achieve transformative change (Andreas and Nadelmann, 2006: 251).

For Chambliss, Michalowski and Kramer (2010: 7), four external forces have fuelled this recent growth in interest in state crime. This includes:

> the collapse of the Soviet block of nations and the emergence of the United States as the dominant force in a "new world order"; a growth in the political significance of the international human rights regime first envisioned by the UN Charter and the Universal Declaration of Human Rights; the spread of neo-liberal globalisation; and, the seeming return of empire as a key element of international politics as symbolised most prominently by the US-UK invasion and occupation of Iraq.

Consequently, for these authors, attention resulted from changes within the international order of states and in response to the emergence of a global neo-liberal internationalist order. An Atlantic alliance was therefore regarded as engaging in an aggressive form of consensus building and collective problem solving, embracing liberal economic policies, democratic principles and human rights, with a view to imposing 'their will on the collapsed economies and governments of the former bloc of both socialist and non-aligned nations' (Chambliss, Michalowski and Kramer, 2010: 7). Scholars therefore began to address the consequences of these developments, challenging the globalist position outlined in Chapter 1, which espoused the universal benefits of globalising tendencies, particularly the proliferation of liberal values and free enterprise as a means of securing global peace, security and prosperity. Scholarship consequently pointed to a period of increased exploitation, commercialisation and increasing evidence of US imperialism, following the collapse of the Soviet Union and end of the Cold War.

As mentioned previously, Ikenberry (2009) has termed this transformation from a bipolar to a unipolar international order, following the end of the Cold War, 'hierarchical liberalism'. This new order, it is argued, became characterised by the United States achieving a super-ordinate position within the world order, a position reflected in the shift of security cooperation from collective security under the UN Security Council to an 'alliance security' built around democratic solidarity in the Atlantic region via NATO and other

US-led alliances. Hence, as US roles, responsibilities, authority and privileges increased within the liberal international order, and as neo-liberal economic policies were driven forward, often, as sceptical globalisation theorists note, to the detriment of socialist and non-aligned nations (as detailed in Chapter 3), questions were raised regarding the consequences of state power, economic exploitation and corporate crime. These political and economic global transformations also served to blur previously drawn boundaries surrounding legitimate and illegitimate behaviour, crime and harm, and links between corporate, state and organised crime (Chambliss, Michalowski and Kramer, 2010: 7).

Critical criminologists were therefore required to engage with the subject matter in an interdisciplinary way, incorporating scholarship from within international relations, international political economy and within globalisation literature alongside contributions from a range of other disciplines. Such an approach required an historical, political, economic as well as a social contextualisation of the phenomena under investigation. Domestic and international law, the state, human rights, the international political and economic order, their institutions and their behaviour could all be located historically and temporally and analysed to examine the impact of such socially constructed phenomena upon gendered, class, race hierarchies and other social cleavages (Jacobs, Jacobson and Marchbank, 2000).

According to Vold, Bernard and Snipes (1998: 218), within the discipline of criminology, criminologists in the symbolic interactionist tradition make theoretical arguments in four general areas related to criminology: (1) the effect that defining an individual as criminal has on that individual's behaviour; (2) the meaning of crime to criminals; (3) the processes by which general categories of behaviour are defined as crimes in the criminal law and specific people and events are defined as criminal by criminal justice agencies; and (4) the meaning of crime in the context of state power. As will be seen shortly, state crime scholarship retain a focus upon each of these areas directing attention to the process of defining and suppressing action through the passing and enforcing of laws, to the function of labelling and criminalisation, and to the consequences and meaning for those involved.

State crime scholarship consequently draws parallels between licit state activity and illicit criminal activity asking interesting questions regarding how similar acts result in dissimilar societal responses. Thus, drawing upon the work of Tilly, and observing a parallel between the state behaviour and that of racketeers, Green and Ward observe that all states, whether autocratic or liberal, share one characteristic, namely 'they claim an entitlement to do things which if anyone else did them would constitute violence and extortion – Weber's monopoly of the legitimate use of force' (Green and Ward, 2004: 2–3). States, it seems, generate a great deal of harm and bestow a great deal of violence, yet state crime has traditionally remained outside of the subject matter of criminology despite the scale and extent of the harms inflicted. Why is this so? For Green and Ward (2004: 1), the key issue at hand is that states retain the power to define what is criminal and therefore it 'can only be criminal on those rare occasions when it denounces itself for breaking its own laws'. This has meant that scholars interested in such harm have needed to transcend state-centric and strictly legalistic definitions of crime, generating a more inclusive language and remaining sensitive to the symbolic interactionist and constructivist concern with knowledge structures and relations of power.

In defining the parameters of their criminology of state crime, Green and Ward define state crime as 'state organisational deviance involving the violation of human rights' (Green and Ward, 2004: 2). The term 'state' is applied in relation to the activities of 'material adjuncts, prisons, institutions of coercion', 'agencies which levy taxes', political entities 'which deploy organised violence, control substantial territories and levy formal or informal taxes', but which 'are not accepted as members of the international society of states' (Green and Ward, 2004: 3). These bodies are described as manifestations of 'public power' which are contrasted against civil society, referring to pressure groups, voluntary associations, religious bodies, the mass media and academic institutions, which are described as playing a crucial role in legitimising the state and also calling state actions into question – identifying state deviance when moral or legal rules are violated.

Green and Ward describe state crime as one manifestation of organisational deviance, defining an act as deviant 'where there is a social audience that: (1) accepts a certain rule as a standard of behaviour, (2) interprets the act (or similar acts of which the state is aware) as violating the rule, and (3) is disposed to apply significant sanctions ... to such violations' (Green and Ward, 2004: 4). The symbolic interactionist concern with the importance of context, meaning, interpretation and their dialectical relationship for action and reaction is therefore retained, in addition to the constructivist focus upon the relationship of ideas and discourse to (individual and state) behaviour.

Human rights are the normative standard applied in their analysis of state organisational deviance. However, while human rights and liberal ideas have tended to be treated ahistorically and depoliticised within much criminological work, Green and Ward make explicit their rationale regarding the selection of human rights as the normative marker against which state behaviour will be judged. They argue in particular, that such international norms are 'almost universally accepted', contextualising the formalisation of human rights within the existing framework of international society following the Second World War, within the United Nations' founding Charter, and the adoption of the 1948 Universal Declaration of Human Rights, which placed human rights within international law. Acknowledging that not all human rights receive equal treatment by domestic and international society, Green and Ward are keen to discover why, in the face of pressure to conform to particular norms, states nevertheless violate them.

More recently, Michalowski (2010) has engaged with the debate regarding which deviant acts to include as the appropriate focus for state crime study, presenting alternative preferences which extend beyond legalistic conceptions of crime and the violation of human rights standards as detailed by Green and Ward above. Three categorisations are identified. Thus, Michalowski observes that for some theorists, state crime entails an examination of Partin's (2003) concept of 'international crimes' (detailed with Chapter 1), namely, acts that threaten world order and security including: crimes against humanity; war crimes; genocide; and terrorism. A second categorisation entails the inclusion of the prosecution or transgression of acts which violate national or international laws which comprise the criteria for inclusion. One further category of scholars identified by Michalowski are those who focus instead upon harm and social injuries resulting from state deviance, acts which may not necessarily have become subject to criminalisation or the focus of prohibition regimes, thereby transcending the conceptual limits of officially designated 'crimes' and 'human rights violations'. Green and Ward, and Michalowski therefore remind us of the considerable diversity within this fledgling area of criminology, with both contributions offering alternative frameworks with which to approach the subject area, one which remains seemingly incongruent with contemporary international, regional and frequently, national strategies dedicated to countering crime and terrorism.

Despite wide variation, Michalowski (2010: 13) argues that 'most analysts of state crimes tend to focus on the wrongful acts committed to serve the organisational interests' rather than 'acts designed to serve the personal interests of the offender', although it is accepted that on occasion personal motivations and organisational goals may intersect. Taking exception to the narrow conceptualisation of the state (often depicted as the governmental and administrative agencies and institutions of a society), Michalowski further problematises the treatment of government as organisationally separate from economic institutions, suggesting such action may inhibit a comprehensive understanding of the interrelated 'political, economic and cultural practices that can be deeply injurious to human life and planetary survival' (Michalowski, 2010: 14). The same objection is applied to strictly legal definitions of acts as crimes, since, it is argued, uncriminalised state wrongs often victimise the greatest number of people and can be particularly injurious and therefore should remain the focus of attention, a position which directs attention to broad structural arrangements which have consequences for the achievement of human rights.

As detailed in Chapter 3, Marxist inspired World Systems Analysts such as Wallerstein have offered alternative perspectives through which to view the social ills facing society today. For Wallerstein, an interdisciplinary and historically grounded analysis must address the shortcomings of the modern global capitalist world system, which is regarded as currently entering a period of systemic crisis due to the inherent contradictions resulting from the endless pursuit to accumulate capital. Pogge (2008) similarly, (working within the arena of international affairs), argues that the existing global institutional order has been shaped and upheld by powerful governments and by other actors they control (such as the EU, NATO, UN, WTO, OECD, World Bank and IMF), and by privileged and influential citizens of the more powerful countries. This order, Pogge suggests, in its present design is manifestly unjust, effectively sustaining and perpetuating the social factors which underpin poverty, corruption and violence within less developed countries. Moreover, it is argued that the present circumstances of the global poor are significantly shaped by the earlier period of conquest and colonisation (detailed within Chapters 2 and 3), during which oppression, enslavement and genocide destroyed native institutions and cultures across four continents. For Pogge, the present radical inequality witnessed across the globe is the cumulative product of this tarnished history and decades and centuries in which the more affluent societies and groups used their advantages in capital and knowledge to expand these advantages even further. Thus, the contemporary international focus upon bad governments and upon corruption within weak and failed states in which poverty, atrocity crimes, organised crime and terrorism emerge, conceals, for Pogge, the significance of the existing global order in influencing local factors and their effects:

> Yes, a culture of corruption pervades the political system and the economy of many developing countries. But, is this culture unrelated to the fact that most affluent countries have, until quite recently, allowed their firms to bribe foreign officials and even made such bribes tax-deductible? … Yes, developing countries have shown themselves prone to oppressive government and to horrific wars and civil wars. But, is the frequency of such brutality unrelated to the international arms trade, and unrelated to international rules that entitle anyone holding effective power in such a country to borrow in its name and sell ownership rights in its natural resources?
>
> (Pogge, 2008: 206)

Pogge's contribution consequently places collective responsibility upon citizens of wealthier nations to rectify past wrongs. However, while Wallerstein advocates the replacement of the existing world system with a less hierarchical and more egalitarian world system, Pogge, along with Ikenberry, remains content with global institutional reform, advocating the dismantling of existing protectionist barriers and international privileges which, it is argued, currently perpetuate extreme inequalities and injustices throughout the world. Thus, for Pogge, it is the current global institutional order which creates the greatest harm, with each participant viewed as culpable 'in the largest human rights violation in human history' (Pogge, 2008: 264).

Other commentators working within the realm of political economy similarly direct attention to the need to address social, political and economic inequalities that shape vulnerability to violence within different settings, examining structural political-economic causes of violence attached to material processes linked to neo-liberal economic globalisation. Employing a feminist political economy approach to the study of violence against women, True (2012), for example, examines gender identity construction, differential access to economic and political opportunity, labour exploitation and gendered inequalities and the impact of financial liberalisation and deregulation, addressing peacetime, conflict and post-conflict contexts, making explicit linkages between the economic, the social and the political. Within the contemporary global macroeconomic environment, capitalist competition and deregulation have, True suggests, served to destabilise local economies, changing labour markets, leading to economic migration, poor regulation, low pay, diminished public services and social provision, resulting in the feminisation of poverty, marginalisation and disempowerment. Criminalisation and international crime control are consequently regarded as diverting attention from the need to make more fundamental structural reforms to the existing world order, a point which has led Andreas and Nadelmann (2006: 251) to argue: 'punitive policing increasingly overshadows and substitutes for a retreating welfare state, even as the social dislocations that result fuel further calls for more policing'. Sheptycki (2010: 306) similarly directs attention to the paradox of coercion implicit within contemporary transnational policing practice, emphasising the consequences of an American imposition of 'international policing power', entailing 'dictating democracy'; 'enforcing freedom'; and 'extorting emancipation' – practices which are cumulatively described as comprising a 'transnational organized crime racket', involving an intensified militarisation of policing and a growing surveillant assemblage, which facilitates social exclusion and fuels resentment, with implications for transnational crime, international crime and terrorism. Madsen (2009: 130) also reflects upon the hypocrisy of the current world order, considering the consequences of the global economic crisis and the behaviour of corporate and political actors, noting that it is 'a propitious moment in which to reflect on the differences between the underworld and the upper-world, if any'.

War, crime, terrorism, poverty and violence are therefore placed within a much wider lens within this work, which places economic and political factors to the foreground. Thus, even when harmful acts are perpetrated by non-state actors, the actions of states retain relevance in setting the conditions in which localised events may occur, implicating wider structural causes for crime and societal harm. Returning to the critical state crime scholarship, for Michalowski (2010) and Green and Ward (2004), the organisational deviance perspective to the study of state crime offers the most promise, permitting an analysis of harms that have not risen to the level of law violations, in addition to those which have.

Three interconnected levels of analysis are provided by Michalowski (2010: 23), arguing that it is essential to employ a critical approach to the study of state crime, remaining vigilant to 'the layered dynamics that often lie behind or well underneath the more obvious crime'. In doing so, the typology remains sensitive to the interconnections between economic, political and social factors noted by Pogge and True above. The first category, termed 'High Profile' acts, includes genocide, war crimes and terrorism. The second category, entitled 'Semi-tolerated violence', includes war-related death, injury and illness of combatants and civilians; torture; human consequences of embargos; juridogenic crimes and brutal punishments. The final category, 'Structural Violence', affecting the largest number of people and embedded within the deep fibre of the neo-liberal state includes: injury, illness or death due to preventable, state-facilitated forms of poverty and inequality; workplace hazards; consumer risks; environmental pollution; sexism, racism and ethnic 'othering'. Significantly, for Michalowski (2010: 23), structural violence also includes loss of life, health, economic resources and autonomy due to neo-colonialism, neo-imperialism and neo-liberal globalisation, thereby remaining consistent with the Marxist inspired World Systems theory of Wallerstein and with feminist international political economy and international relations scholars like True (2012) and Tickner (1992, 2014).

The extent to which these insights have entered into law enforcement and security policy, and strategic responses to international crime, transnational organised crimes and terrorism will be assessed within the remaining chapters. By taking a cursory look at genocide, terrorism and corruption as illustrations of state crimes, it is evident that the scope of causal factors and of preventative action remains constrained by the ahistorical and depoliticised liberal framework described in Chapters 3 and 4, and also, through the dominant discourses of modernisation and globalisation, detailed in Chapter 1. Institutional reform, the strengthening of societal controls and normative consensus, the creation of legislative frameworks, and the facilitation of judicial and policing cooperation and harmonisation (as the prescribed solution to crime and terrorism), are consequently called into question by the burgeoning scholarship from within this alternative perspective. In particular, it is suggested that the existing normative strategic response to crime and terrorism diverts attention away from wider political and economic structural root causes, also neglecting the legacy of historical events and relations of power implicit within the processes of criminalisation and enforcement. Reconceptualised as manifestations of state crime, patterns of genocide, terrorism and corruption, along with counter efforts, remind us of the importance of perspective in addressing such phenomena, sensitising us to neglected issues, which will become significant in assessing the adequacy of contemporary approaches to counter international crime, transnational crime and terrorism. Viewed from the position of critical state crime theory, which remains consistent with the symbolic interactionist and constructivist traditions within sociology and international relations scholarship, it is evident that both crime and crime control may be reinterpreted as strategically advantageous, for both state and non-state actors, with attitudes and practices (including the willingness to cooperate with others and to pursue multilateral action), subject to alteration over time, associated with power and geo-politics within the international system.

Reinterpreting genocide, terrorism and corruption

Chapter 6 will introduce the emotive issue of genocide and invite readers to consider the adequacy of the emerging international norm known as 'the Responsibility to Protect' to prevent instances of mass murder and systematic rape committed with intent to destroy, in whole or in part, a national, ethnic, racial or religious group. Before doing so however, it is useful to apply Green and Ward's insights to the phenomenon of genocide and to return to relevance of historical and political contextualisation for a comprehensive analysis of international crime.

Examining what they describe as 'the three greatest post-war genocides', those in Cambodia, Rwanda and Sudan, Green and Ward endeavour to identify common features of genocidal societies also emphasising similarities in their respective historical conjunctures. Viewed as very different kinds of crime-prone state, these examples are presented as having had marked peculiarities which underpinned the genocidal manifestation of state violence. The analysis consequently directs attention to continuities between corporate organisational goals and other manifestations of exploitation, in addition to revisionist aspirations, paying attention to the existence of a history of grievances, alongside the detrimental impact of economic crisis, structural adjustment and aid programmes within affected nations. These concerns, which comprise economic and political, in addition to specific cultural factors and historical circumstances, are regarded by the authors as crucial in understanding why genocide occurs. To explain 'how' genocide occurs, Green and Ward retain the classical and modernisation focus upon the prevalence of criminogenic opportunities and the absence of societal controls (capable guardians to act as a deterrent against the commission of crime/harm). However, this is further supplemented by consideration of what is termed 'the application of the logic of exclusion' and efforts to reinforce solidarity which are regarded as deliberate and systematic policies by states facing a crisis of legitimacy, in addition to processes of dehumanisation serving to remove the perpetrators' sense of obligation to the victim. In doing so, this work retains the symbolic interactionist emphasis upon an examination of the meaning, function and consequences of labelling for individuals (and states) and upon individual and state efforts to retain legitimacy and to preserve 'face' in the light of perceived condemnation, vilification and/or criticism.

This work therefore draws upon criminological insights relating to the use of 'psychic defences' and 'techniques of neutralisation' to protect the individual from self-blame and the blame of others after the commission of a deviant act (Sykes and Matza, 1957: 666; Cohen, 2001). This work also engages with social control literature which directs attention to the particular groups who retain the power to define others as deviant, in addition to the processes of defining and suppressing deviance, emphasising the significance of power, interest, and the use of language, discourse, ideas and structures of knowledge to maintain legitimacy and to conceal coercive motives (Foucault,

1969; Garland, 2002; Cohen, 1985). This work therefore examines the function of law and law enforcement to maintain social order, reminding readers of the historical legacy of politicalisation and militarisation attached to criminalisation, interpreting criminal justice agencies as part of a much broader range of social control mechanisms including welfare, mental health, education, the mass media and the military used by states for the purpose of controlling 'problem' populations (Vold, Bernard and Snipes, 1998). With the advent of international law and the emergence of international norms, states embedded within the international society of states liberal framework are subject to legal and moral constraints and expectations resulting in a relatively new requirement to employ more subtle forms of manipulation and social control activities to maintain legitimacy and face. Within the current climate however, as noted by Green and Ward, the legacy of industrialisation, economic crisis and structural adjustment have generated memories of defeat, revolutionary zeal and geo-political revisionist aspirations, resulting in crises which are described as generating 'deep-rooted crisis of state legitimacy' alongside 'a pool of ready recruits for violent solution to the crisis' (Green and Ward, 2004: 169).

Green and Ward conclude their discussion of genocide by identifying five key features or common patterns found within their analysis:

> (1) the propagation by the ruling elite of an ideology excluding the victim group from the perpetrators' universe of obligation; (2) the elite's perception of the victim group as a threat or obstacle in the context of economic and political crisis, generally against a background of war; (3) a competing ideology, rooted in national and/or international culture, that does recognise the victims as worthy of moral concern; (4) the use of psychological mechanisms of denial and neutralisation to overcome the inhibitions created by the more inclusive ideology, and (5) the perpetration of excesses that reaffirm the banishing of those inhibitions.
>
> (Green and Ward, 2004: 184)

Thus, as noted by Alvarez (2010), drawing upon the examples of Nazi Germany and Rwanda and influenced by the sentiments of Gourevitch, Macdonald, Turk and Goffman, both law and ideology are implicated as powerful tools authenticating and lending credibility to certain groups, actions and behaviours, while also delegitimising, stigmatising and marginalising others. As noted in Chapter 2, the normative functions of legislative and ideological frameworks remain powerful coercive tools of statecraft with consequences for both state and non-state actors. Drawing upon the work of Douglas, Alvarez also directs attention to the function of scapegoating, targeting specially selected groups of people as convenient explanations for the emergence of difficult problems and as a means of deflecting blame and criticism away from economic forces, bad government, political miscalculation, catastrophe or natural disaster. Other facilitating factors examined by Alvarez include the role of revolutionary movements and their utilisation of both violence and terror as tools to rapidly transform society and instil their particular philosophy and ideology, and the association of war with totalitarianism. However, while democratic regimes engage in less killing than other forms of government, examples of direct and indirect support for genocide, alongside support for economic policies that serve to foster the conditions conducive to genocidal action, are evidently not in short supply.

Alvarez (2010: 42–43) and Chomsky (2012: 30–31) are among several authors who redirect attention towards wider contextual issues, such as democratic state support for genocidal regimes involved in systematic human rights abuses, particularly during the Cold War in order to maintain power and to support anti-communist policies, including within Argentina, Chile, El Salvador, Guatemala and Uruguay. Motivation for genocide is also located by Alvarez as a particularly effective method of accessing and exploiting the natural resources of an area. Drawing upon the contribution of Fein, this example is defined as 'Developmental Genocide', associated with genocidal action as colonial powers have sought to take over, occupy, exploit and develop the land of indigenous peoples, including within Central and South America. Further categories of motivation include 'Despotic Genocide', where totalitarian states seek to remove threats to the political power structure, 'Ideological Genocide' motivated by a system of belief, which encourages or demands the elimination of a population and 'Retributive Genocides', described by Alvarez as genocides committed against a group in order to protect a privileged position within society (Alvarez, 2010: 46–48).

Rejecting the notion that genocide results solely from spontaneous eruption of ethnic conflict and hatred, Alvarez (2010: 28–29) argues that the best way to understand genocide is as a form of state criminality, suggesting 'in almost every case of genocide, the responsibility lies with the state', effectively 'subverting notions of community, belonging, and legality in order to pursue destructive policies' (Alvarez, 2010: 48). In applying the state crime lens to the study of genocide and particularly in relation to the question of why and how such horrors emerge, Green and Ward (2004: 165) argue that it is necessary to analyse 'complex issues of political economy, history and culture'. Drawing attention to the conceptual difficulties arising from the lack of consensus regarding the definition of genocide, and highlighting the significance of politicide against politically active communal groups (a significant form of genocide which remains absent from the 1948 Convention on the Prevention and Punishment of the Crime of Genocide), Green and Ward adopt a relatively narrow definition of genocide based on those provided by Chalk and Jonassohn (1990) and Levene (1994):

> Genocide is the systematic, one-sided mass killing of persons selected on the basis of their perceived membership of an ethnic or communal group, with the aim either of eliminating the group in its entirety, or of eliminating whatever threat it is perceived to pose.
>
> (Green and Ward, 2004: 166)

Thus, for Green and Ward, both genocide and politicide have the potential to be contained within this definition, prompting consideration of action perpetrated by constitutionally responsible rulers, public officials or private individuals (as in the Convention on the Prevention and Punishment of the Crime of Genocide, 1948). The definition provided by Green and Ward consequently permits analysis of mass killings undertaken by both state and non-state actors, thereby provoking reflection regarding the recent activities of Islamic State Jihadists including: targeted mass killings; rapes; abductions; and the forced separation of families from the minority Yazidi community in Iraq (BBC News, March 2015). Such actions have served to raise questions regarding the distinction between atrocity crimes, including genocide and terrorism, with Bellamy (2015) recently reminding us that both examples utilise violence intentionally targeting civilians, with both offences also comprising crimes against humanity, thereby amounting to international crime. For Bellamy therefore, the emerging norm of humanitarian intervention, known as 'the Responsibility to Protect' (R2P), and counter-terrorism responses (the subject matter of Chapters 6 and 7), 'are simply different ways of talking about the same problem: violent attacks on civilian populations' (Bellamy, 2015). Bellamy further argues that describing such crises in terms of counterterrorism or as an emerging R2P situation ought not to be conceived as mutually exclusive, suggesting that the failure to explicitly articulate the responsibilities of non-state armed groups, alongside the responsibilities of states themselves to protect populations from genocide, war crimes, crimes against humanity, ethnic cleansing, and their incitement, comprises an unfortunate oversight, subject to correction through the provision of a clear statement by the UN Security Council, articulating the applicability of the R2P obligations for non-state armed groups. For Bellamy, then, more work needs to be undertaken to understand the relationship between the R2P and counter-terrorism. His work also serves as a timely reminder regarding the temporally and culturally constructed nature of 'genocide' and 'terrorism', 'the R2P' and 'counterterrorism strategy', and the normative aspect of both the commission of crime and societal reactions from within individual nation-states and collectively, directed to the preservation of the current world order and of cultures and societies resistant to it.

For Green and Ward (2004: 106), terror is 'an increasingly prevalent means of warfare', and also 'a mode of governance used by many modern states'. However, as a form of deviant behaviour, modern state terror entails the veneer of concealment or denial, thereby remaining distinct from the experience of totalitarian regimes who are regarded as often openly employing such means. Within their text, Green and Ward identify a variety of forms of terror, including extra-judicial executions, massacres, disappearances and torture engaged in or instigated by states, including the commission of terrorist acts by state personnel, and/or the instigation or condoning of actions by non-state agencies, direct state sponsorship of terrorist acts against sections of their own populations, or against those of other states. Other manifestations of state terror are the utilisation of law courts (with minimal regard to due process); the destruction of homes; the provision of aid and/or arms to regimes engaging in state terror; and increasingly, the promotion of counter-terrorist measures as a pretext to engage in state terror. However, the degree to which such means are openly engaged in, and the extent and effectiveness of international response and condemnation, are regarded by Green and Ward to be contingent upon the degree of Western state complicity, state self-interest and political will, alongside the existence of an effective and vocal civil society to oppose and denounce state crime and to organise public intolerance. In the meantime, it is evident that states continue not only to break their own rules, acting illegally, but also to employ deception to conceal breaches of laws and norms from the public, practices which reveal complicity, duplicity and hypocrisy in relation to the commission of genocide, terrorism, and as we shall see within the final section of this chapter, corruption.

Corruption is described by Kofi Annan, in the Foreword of the 'UN Convention Against Corruption', as an 'insidious plague'. Annan argues that such activities have a wide range of 'corrosive effects on societies', undermining democracy and the rule of law with consequences for the violation of human rights, organised crime, terrorism and other security threats. Further consequences mentioned within the Foreword of the convention include market distortion, the undermining of democracy and the erosion of quality of life. The former Secretary General of the United Nations consequently articulates the belief that corruption threatens both the moral principle and ideas, which, we have already mentioned, form the cornerstone of the international liberal society of states. Described as 'evil', the consequences of corruption are presented within the Convention as having a differential impact upon the poor, 'diverting funds intended for development, undermining a Government's ability to provide basic services, feeding inequality and injustice and discouraging foreign aid and investment' (UNODC, 2004: iii). Seen as complementing the United Nations Convention against Transnational Organised Crime, the Corruption Convention is therefore presented as offering a new framework for effective action and international cooperation, introducing 'a comprehensive set of standards, measures and rules that all countries can apply in order to strengthen their legal and regulatory regimes to fight corruption'. As with the frameworks developed to counter terrorism and human trafficking, which will be the focus of Chapters 7 and 8, the anti-corruption regime includes the criminalisation of prohibited acts alongside preventative action requiring multilateral action with both state and non-state actors.

In particular, Chapter III of the Convention, entitled 'Criminalization and law enforcement' advocates that Member States undertake legislative action to create a range of criminal offences relating to corruption. Under articles 15–28, these include the criminalisation of bribery, embezzlement, trading in influence, abuse of functions, illicit enrichment, laundering of proceeds of crime, concealment, obstruction of justice, including attempts to commit an act and participation as an accomplice, assistant or instigator. Green and Ward (2004), in their analysis of corruption as a form of state crime, observe that 'in most but not all cases, corrupt practices directly or indirectly entail violations of human rights'. Reflecting the sentiments expressed by Annan cited above, this may be because corruption diverts resources, depriving individuals of necessities such as food, clean water, health care (Article 25 UNDHR), and education (Article 26 UNDHR), or because corrupt practices facilitate environmental despoilment affecting livelihoods (Article 23 UNDHR). Other examples cited by Green and Ward include where access to human rights is dependent upon payment (including education and health care), with corruption undermining democratic political processes, political participation and access to public services (Article 21 UNDHR).

Scholars working in this area emphasise that the study of corruption muddies the water, obscuring the boundaries between normal political influence on the part of the wealthy and ruling classes and what is viewed as corruption, revealing an interplay between legitimate business activity, state crime, corporate crime, organised crime, atrocity and environmental crimes. Within their discussion of corruption, and drawing upon the work of Della Porta and Meny (1997), Green and Ward (2004: 24) contemplate the relatively indistinct boundary between clientelism, regarded as 'a system of generalised exchange guaranteed by gratitude', and corruption which 'is based on specific exchanges guaranteed by the expectation of a "replay"'. Green and Ward observe an interplay between clientelism, corruption and violence, with consequences for state development and vulnerability to exploitation and victimisation. These themes will be picked up again in relation to the circumstances conducive to atrocity crime, terrorism and human trafficking in the next three chapters.

Significantly, while within the Convention Annan explicitly recognises the connection between economic underperformance, poverty and underdevelopment, and corruption, no reference is made to neo-liberal economic policy, capitalism or structural adjustment, which for Green and Ward (2004: 27) further compound misgovernment and corruption. Thus, they argue, as neopatrimonial regimes become starved of resources, they begin to renege on their obligations to citizens, concentrating patronage on a small network of supporters while at the same time enhancing the likelihood of using violent means to quell opposition and to maintain social control. These observations return us to the comments of Pogge (2008), True (2012) and Tickner (1992, 2014) detailed previously, again serving to alert readers to the relevance of the structure of the present political and economic order (described as built upon a legacy of exploitation), which generates and embeds structural inequalities making particular groups, countries and even regions susceptible to poverty, violence and crime. Thus, while corruption is identified as a key element in economic underperformance and a major obstacle to poverty alleviation and development, the reconceptualisation of corruption as a state crime, and the employment of a symbolic interactionist or social constructivist approach enables a much broader perspective to be adopted: one which enables the examination of linkages between the behaviour of state representatives, liberal economic policies, structural inequalities, crimes and wider social injuries, contextualised historically, socially and politically. Thus, for Michalowski (2010: 29), 'any movement toward true human justice requires significantly constraining, if not dismantling, social systems that allow the exercise of bio-power to harm millions in search for accumulation and/or dominance', arguing further that it is important for scholars to 'reveal the deeper structures through which political power over people and corporate dominance over production and distribution … not only generate crimes and social injuries but also have become so normalized that only in the most egregious instances are they viewed as social problems, let alone as crime' (Michalowski, 2010: 30).

Deconstruction, the challenging of dominant discourses, concepts, ideas, normative and knowledge systems, therefore remain key aspects of state crime scholarship, questioning justificatory narratives, taken for granted assumptions and popular wisdom. This contribution consequently raises questions regarding why particular actions have become criminalised and, why now? Such scholarship consequently asks us to question: whether those promoting and facilitating the criminalisation process were historically engaged in such practices themselves; who the intended recipients of such action are likely to be; what the function and likely consequences of labelling and law enforcement may be; and importantly, whose ends are being served. The UN Convention against Corruption states that it 'will warn the corrupt that betrayal of the public trust will no longer be tolerated', noting that 'it will reaffirm the importance of core values such as honesty, respect for the rule of law, accountability and transparency in promoting development and making the world a better place for all'. The Convention further congratulates itself for making 'a major breakthrough by requiring Member States to return assets obtained through corruption to the country from which they were stolen' taking steps to 'prevent and detect corruption and to return the proceeds'. The anti-corruption regime is consequently regarded as an important step to counter the illicit activities of corrupt officials, particularly for 'developing countries where corrupt high officials have plundered the national wealth and where new Governments badly need resources to reconstruct and rehabilitate their societies'. The convention therefore remains silent regarding the legacy of colonialism, imperialism and decolonialisation, preferring not to dwell upon past histories of corruption by powerful states in the furtherance of their goals, or indeed of the structure of the international society of states, its associated institutions, procedures and economic system, which have facilitated such practices in becoming endemic within and between many nations. The framework therefore remains ahistorical and depoliticised and thus inherently flawed from the perspective of critical state scholarship.

The employment of the symbolic interactionalist perspective from within the disciplines of sociology and criminology, the constructivist approach within international relations scholarship, and the more recent contribution of state crime theorists therefore present alternative perspectives through which to frame contemporary national, regional and international policy responses to corruption, atrocity crimes, terrorism and human trafficking. This work, again, reminds scholars to remain mindful of the social, economic and political context in which strategy is produced. Political agendas, policy objectives, along with the utilisation of particular methods and measures do not occur within a vacuum and reflect choices underpinned by assumptions and motivations. While human rights and victimisation remain a high priority within the current criminal justice infrastructure, reflected within political speeches, statements, legislative frameworks and strategy documents, this chapter has highlighted that not all harm and not all victimisation receives the same treatment. The distribution, extent and seriousness of victimisation does not necessarily equate with social and/or criminal justice. As will be seen within the remaining chapters, the crime control framework that is currently embedded within a liberal model incorporates a normative, legislative and institutional response to collectively defined security threats. While existing strategies continue to embrace a range of situational crime prevention measures and social crime prevention measures to achieve their objectives, the policy responses remain wedded to a liberal institutional framework and in doing so inevitably foreclose the possibility of radical transformative change to the economic, political, gender, class and race hierarchies of the contemporary world order. Critical scholarship consequently directs attention to the power of narrative, hegemonic discourse and knowledge systems, in setting the parameters of action, further alerting readers to the possibility that law, criminal justice and associated strategies may be conceptualised as instruments of social control, directed towards the maintenance of the status quo, preserving existing patriarchal, neo-liberal, political and economic structures, maintaining inequalities and hierarchical structures, and perpetuating injustices.

Chapter 6 consequently focuses on the adequacy of international efforts to prevent instances of atrocity crime. It commences with an examination of the shift in the prevailing view regarding sovereignty and the legal status of humanitarian intervention, moving on to discuss the emergence of the modern humanitarian system. The chapter examines the recent development of the international norm known as 'the Responsibility to Protect' (R2P) and its subsequent revision, questioning the adequacy of the current framework and the prospects for the successful prevention of genocide and atrocity crime in the twenty-first century. Chapter 7 examines the international (UN), regional (EU) and national (UK) counter-terrorism strategies with a view to assessing the adequacy of existing responses to contemporary threats posed by cross-border violent extremism. While both issues, seen from the perspective of critical theory, require political and economic action to tackle the underlying root causes of these human rights violations, the focus upon state deviance (as described within the current chapter), and power politics, remain glaringly absent from official strategy.

Using a gendered lens, following a description of the existing framework to counter the trafficking in human beings, Chapter 8 introduces feminist international political economy, investigating its application to the study of globalisation, neo-liberalism and security. Reconceptualising human trafficking as located within a wider continuum of violence and exploitation, this chapter again implicates state deviance, emphasising the need for a more comprehensive approach to the issue than is offered by the current counter-trafficking regime.

Andreas and Nadelmann (2006) raise the question as to 'what is driving the growth of international criminal law enforcement'. In answering the question, they critique the master narrative, presented as the 'standard view' within official policy debate that conceives this development in terms of a response to the growth in transnational crime in an era of globalisation. This narrative, the authors suggest, is 'at best incomplete and at worst misleading', failing to appreciate the role of power and interest of dominant states in agenda setting and criminalisation processes, also failing to appreciate the significance of moral entrepreneurs and non-state actors within this process. Iadicola (2010) similarly advocates a more nuanced approach. Writing from within the discipline of criminology, Iadicola distinguishes between Empire's criminology and criminology of empire. The former (reflecting Andreas and Nadelmann's description of 'the master narrative' or 'standard view') is considered to focus on crimes that threaten the empire's functioning and control, including common crimes that threaten the distribution of resources 'that come about as the result of economic and political mechanisms of empire', serving to maintain hierarchical relationships within and between societies, in addition to common forms of interpersonal violence. In contrast, criminology of empire places the concept of empire as central to the study of state crime and violence. Thus, for Iadicola, while Empire's criminology serves to maintain and perpetuate the 'criminal regime of the US empire', a more legitimate criminology should include crimes resulting from conquest and incorporation, noting: 'The crimes of aggressive war, genocide and ethnic cleansing, assassinations, torture and repression, state-corporate crimes that devastate the environment and economic crimes of exploitation of labour that result in death and injury, are all part of the process of empire' (Iadicola, 2010: 43). Drawing attention to the impunity surrounding the commission of such crimes, Iadicola suggests that these crimes are set to continue as the empire expands and acts to maintain its control.

As a precursor for Chapters 6, 7 and 8, this chapter has therefore engaged with critical scholarship from within criminology, which has explicitly addressed the normative and political basis of criminalisation and law enforcement. This significant contribution, with its roots within symbolic interactionism, focuses upon the importance of the meaning people give to themselves and to others, with consequences for the processes of criminalisation, societal responses to behaviour and the impact of mechanisms of societal control. Rejecting the legalistic approach, which views crime and law enforcement efforts narrowly in terms of the enforcement of legal norms, the scholarly work detailed here reminds us that crimes, crime control regimes and even the current structure of international politics are socially constructed. The chapter consequently provides an introduction to constructivist theory within international relations and criminology, an approach which places a premium on 'ideas', 'discourse', 'meaning' and 'interpretation'. This contribution, which transcends what Andreas and Nadelmann describe as 'the conventional wisdom' regarding the internationalisation of crime control, permits the inclusion and contextualisation of previously excluded phenomena, provoking attention to the role of knowledge systems and normative frameworks in constructing and maintaining inequalities and relations of production.

References

Aas, K.F. (2007). *Globalisation and Crime.* London: Sage.

Alvarez, A. (2010). *Genocidal Crimes.* London: Routledge.

Andreas, P. and Nadelmann, E. (2006). *Policing the Globe: Criminalization and Crime Control in International Relations.* Oxford: Oxford University Press.

Barnett, M. (2014). 'Social Constructivism', in Baylis, J., Smith, S., and Owens, P. (eds), *The Globalization of World Politics: An Introduction to International Relations*, sixth edition. Oxford: Oxford University Press.

BBC News. (2015). 'IS Yazidi Attacks May be Genocide, Says UN', March. Available online at: www.bbc.co.uk/news/world-middle-east-31962755 (accessed June 15, 2015).

Bellamy, A. (2015). 'The Islamic State and the Case for Responsibility to Protect'. *International Coalition for the Responsibility to Protect.* Available online at: http://protectiongateway.com/2015/04/21/the-islamic-state-and-the-case-for-responsibility-to-protect/.

Blumer, H. (1969). *Symbolic Interaction.* Englewood Cliffs, NJ: Prentice-Hall.

Bowling, B. and Sheptycki, J.W.E. (2012). *Global Policing.* London: Sage.

Chalk, F. and Jonassohn, K. (1990). *The History and Sociology of Genocide: Analyses and Case Studies.* New Haven, CT: Yale University Press.

Chambliss, W., Michalowski, R., and Kramer, R. (2010). *State Crime in the Global Age.* Cullompton: Willan Publishing.

Chomsky, N. (2012). *A New Generation Draws the Line: Humanitarian Intervention and the 'Responsibility to Protect' Today.* Boulder, CO: Paradigm Publishers.

Cohen, S. (1985). *Visions of Social Control.* Cambridge: Polity Press.

Cohen, S. (2001). *States of Denial.* Cambridge: Polity Press.

Deflem, M. (2002). *Policing World Society: Historical Foundations of International Police Cooperation.* Oxford: Oxford University Press.

Della Porta, D. and Meny, Y. (1997). 'Conclusion: Democracy and Corruption: Towards a Comparative Analysis', in Della Porta, D. and Meny, Y. (eds), *Democracy and Corruption in Europe.* London: Pinter. Pp. 166–180.

Findlay, M. (1999). *The Globalisation of Crime: Understanding Transitional Relationships in Context.* Cambridge: Cambridge University Press.

Findlay, M. (2008). *Governing through Globalised Crime.* Cullompton: Willan Publishing.

Foucault, M. (1969). *The Archaeology of Knowledge and the Discourse on Language.* New York: Harper Colophon.

Garland, D. (2002). *The Culture of Control.* Oxford: Oxford University Press.

Goldsmith, A. and Sheptycki, J.W.E. (2007). *Crafting Transnational Policing: Police Capacity-Building and Global Policing Reform.* Oxford: Hart Publishing.

Green, P. and Ward, T. (2004). *State Crime: Governments, Violence and Corruption.* London: Pluto Press.

Iadicola, P. (2010). 'The Centrality of Empire in the Study of State Crime and Violence', in Chambliss, W., Michalowski, R., and Kramer, R. (eds), *State Crime in the Global Age.* Cullompton: Willan Publishing.

Ikenberry, G.J. (2009). 'Liberal Internationalism 3.0: America and the Dilemmas of Liberal World Order', *Perspectives on Politics*, 7(1): 71–87.

Jacobs, S., Jacobson, R., and Marchbank, J. (2000). *States of Conflict: Gender, Violence and Resistance.* London: Zed Books.

Katzenstein, P. (ed.). (1996). *The Culture of National Security.* New York: Columbia University Press.

Levene, M. (1994). 'Is the Holocaust Simply Another Example of Genocide', *African Studies Review*, 41: 3–16.

Madsen, F. (2009). *Transnational Organized Crime.* London: Routledge.

Manis, J. and Meltzer, B. (eds). (1978). *Symbolic Interaction: A Reader in Social Psychology*, third edition. Boston, MA: Allyn and Bacon.

Michalowski, R. (2010). 'In Search of "State and Crime" in State Crime Studies', in Chambliss, W., Michalowski, R., and Kramer, R. (eds), *State Crime in the Global Age.* Cullompton: Willan Publishing.

Onuf, N. (1989). *World of our Making: Rules and Rule in Social Theory and International Relations.* Columbia, SC: University of South Carolina Press.

Partin, G. (2003). International Criminal Law. American Society of International Law, October 4. Available online at: www.asil.org/resource/crim1.htm (accessed December 6, 2003), cited in Reichel, P. (2005) (ed.), *Handbook of Transnational Crime and Justice.* London: Sage.

Pogge, T. (2008). *World Poverty and Human Rights*, second edition. Cambridge: Polity Press.

Ritzer, G. (1996). *Sociological Theory*, fourth edition. Singapore: McGraw-Hill International Editions.

Rose, A. (1962). *Human Behavior and Social Processes.* Boston, MA: Houghton Mifflin.

Sheptycki, J.W.E. (2010). 'The Constabulary Ethic Reconsidered', in Lemieux, F. (ed.), *International Police Cooperation.* Abingdon: Routledge.

Sheptycki, J.W.E. (ed.). (2000). *Issues in Transnational Policing.* London: Routledge.

Smith, C., Zhang, S.X., and Barberet, R. (eds). (2011). *Routledge Handbook of International Criminology.* Abingdon: Routledge.

Sykes, G. and Matza, D. (1957). 'Techniques of Neutralization: A Theory of Delinquency', *American Sociological Review*, 22(6): 664–670.

Tickner, A. (1992). *Gender in International Relations; Feminist Perspectives on Achieving Global Security.* Oxford: Columbia University Press.

Tickner, A. (2014). *A Feminist Voyage Through International Relations.* Oxford: Oxford University Press.

True, J. (2012). *The Political Economy of Violence Against Women.* Oxford: Oxford University Press.

United Nations. (n.d.). *The Universal Declaration of Human Rights.* Available online at: www.un.org/en/documents/udhr/index.shtml.

UNODC. (2004). *United Nations Convention Against Corruption.* Vienna: United Nations Office on Drugs and Crime.

Vold, G., Bernard, T., and Snipes, J. (1998). *Theoretical Criminology*, fourth edition. Oxford: Oxford University Press.

Williams, P. (ed.). (2013). *Security Studies: An Introduction.* London: Routledge.

Part III

Analysis of major international and transnational crimes

6 Genocide and the responsibility to protect

In the first chapter, readers were introduced to the concept of globalisation. Drawing upon the work of Andreas and Nadelmann (2006), evidence regarding the existence of what has been termed 'the standard view of globalisation' was identified within security strategy documentation, also reflecting the presence of a recently altered and expanded notion of security which has moved beyond consideration of state-to-state warfare to include a range of environmental, criminal and developmental threats to nations, regions and international society. This security narrative describes contemporary globalising trends and associated social transformations as facilitating opportunities for crime and terrorism, triggering corresponding law enforcement efforts to counter the threats posed by increasing global independence, technological advancements and population mobility. As revealed in Chapter 3, arguments regarding the temporal frame, the direction and consequences of these developments remain contentious. To reiterate the argument, it has been noted that several academic commentators, and the official discourse employed by the US, UK, EU and UN suggest that the acceleration of transnational law enforcement efforts remains a necessary reaction to increased security threats faced by individual nation-states, regional bodies and internationally. Others, however, present a more ominous picture, in which law enforcement influence and penetration are alternatively conceived as strategic tools of global domination, control and/or imperialism, reflecting power politics and political manoeuvrings within contemporary international relations.

Within the preceding chapters, it has been argued that the theoretical position adopted has implications for projections regarding the prospects of success of current policy and strategy to counter cross-border crime and terrorism. As will be seen in this chapter, these debates emerge once again in relation to international crime with evidence of reliance upon modernisation and liberal approaches which advocate political, legislative and institutional reform, alongside enhanced cooperation and harmonisation, as methods of closing the gap between criminal opportunities and criminal justice responses in the current period of social transformation (whether conceived as processes of modernisation or as globalisation). Marxist informed World Systems Theorists and realist approaches question the progressive optimism of the former perspectives, directing attention to the inherent contradictions and tensions within the contemporary global political and economic system, and the irreconcilable difficulties posed by issues of power, fear, and finite resources within a world order characterised by anarchy (namely, the absence of an overall global authority).

This chapter will introduce students to the emotive issue of genocide and consider the adequacy of international efforts to prevent instances of mass murder and systematic rape committed with intent to destroy, in whole or in part, a national, ethnic, racial or religious group. The chapter will commence with a brief discussion of humanitarian intervention and human rights before moving on to consider the recent development of an international norm known as 'the Responsibility to Protect' (R2P). Engaging with earlier theoretical insights, changes to the early conceptualisation of R2P will be discussed, barriers to successful intervention and encouraging developments highlighted. Reflecting upon continuing challenges facing international society and diverging theoretical interpretations of these developments, including the application of critical state crime scholarship from within the previous chapter, the chapter will conclude with an assessment regarding the prospects for the successful prevention of genocide and atrocity crime in the twenty-first century.

Humanitarian intervention, sovereignty and globalisation

'Massacres of the innocent, forced displacement of populations, large-scale sexual violence and humiliation, and the wanton destruction of civilian property have been going on since the dawn of civilization' (Evans, 2008a: 11). Indeed, as argued by Hafner-Burton and Tsutsui (2007: 407), 'by almost any measure, nearly half of the world's governments today are repressive, systematically abusing human beings living within their borders'. Atrocity crimes continue within the twenty-first century across the globe revealing the continuing failure of states to protect populations in Côte d'Ivoire, the Democratic Republic of the Congo, Kenya, Sri Lanka, the Sudan and the Syrian Arab Republic among others (UN General Assembly Security Council 2013: 16).

Understanding the causes and dynamics of the commission of atrocity crimes is essential to the prevention of future instances, for the design and implementation of effective sanctions packages, and to the apprehension and conviction of perpetrators. With this in mind, it is evident that the international community increasingly recognises the overlap between the risk factors related to armed conflict and those related to atrocity crimes. However, while it is true that atrocity crimes are more likely to occur during armed conflict, particularly internal armed conflict, it is important to note that not all armed conflict generates atrocity crimes and not all atrocity crimes occur within a context of armed conflict. Armed conflicts therefore comprise both a source of risk for atrocity crimes to occur and a consequence of atrocity crime, particularly where past atrocities are left unresolved and justice and reconciliation remain absent (UN General Assembly Security Council, 2013: 3).

The prevailing view of such atrocities, occurring within the sovereign jurisdiction of states, certainly prior to the end of the Cold War, dates back to the emergence of the modern state system in the 1600s. At that time, it was commonly asserted 'that it is no one's business but their own if states murder or forcibly displace large numbers of their own citizens, or allow atrocity crimes to be committed by one group against another on their soil' (Evans, 2008b: 284). This sentiment has been associated with the emergence of the Westphalian concept of sovereignty (detailed in Chapter 3), a notion that underpinned the creation of the modern state system. This model of sovereignty effectively provided states with a legal identity within international society and comprised a principle for organising political space (Baylis, Smith, and Owens, 2014). More recently enshrined in Article 2.1 of the UN Charter, the notion of state-sovereignty signifies the capacity of the state to make authoritative decisions with regard to the people and resources within its territory. Moreover, such authority is contingent upon a corresponding obligation to respect every other state's sovereignty, a reciprocal obligation based on the principal that external powers should not intervene in the domestic affairs of other states. This latter norm of non-intervention is enshrined in Article 2.7 of the UN Charter. The implication of violating this principal of non-intervention is that victim states retain the right of self-defence to defend territorial integrity and political independence thereby providing states with a legitimate exception of the general rule regarding the non-use of force within international relations (ICISS, 2001: 12).

Significantly then, while the associated principles of sovereignty and non-intervention were originally intended to provide order, stability and predictability in international relations, these principles consequently became key obstacles to humanitarianism (conceived as helping and protecting victims irrespective of who and where they are and why they are in need) (Weiss, 2011: 316). The rights associated with the concept of sovereignty have been criticised by commentators as granting sovereign states a licence to kill, with states conceived as the legitimate sovereign authority in control of the population residing within their territory, also bestowed with a right of non-interference from external states and further protected by the principle of sovereign immunity. Informed by this traditional conceptualisation of sovereignty, atrocity crimes were therefore, for a long time, generally reacted to with indifference, denial, renaming or disagreement regarding the appropriate response (Evans, 2008a: 11; Cohen, 2001: xi), a perspective which only recently has been subject to challenge. It is against this backdrop and in the wake of specific atrocity events within two states that, in the 1990s, lively debates unfolded about the right of the community of states to intervene in internal affairs to protect civilians, with some observers contending that there even exists a duty to do so (Weiss, 2011: 267). In the next section of this chapter, the emergence of this new perspective regarding the acceptability of humanitarian intervention and the reconceptualisation of sovereignty will be detailed. Key measures introduced to mobilise political will, to facilitate desirable intervention and to protect against potential abuse will be highlighted before moving on to discuss key changes made to the developing norm and the implications for atrocity crime prevention.

Humanitarian values and the emergence of the modern humanitarian system

The gradual shift in the prevailing view regarding sovereignty and the legal status of humanitarian intervention is associated with the increasing significance and influence of humanitarian values. From the mid-nineteenth century onwards, influenced by direct personal experiences of exposure to death and suffering during periods of war and conflict, perspectives arose which gradually challenged traditional views regarding intervention in response to widespread suffering and loss of life and the acceptability of humanitarian intervention.

The emergence of the modern humanitarian system, which became associated with the principle that the international community has a right/duty to intervene in states to protect civilians, has been dated to the founding of humanitarian institutions which were created in the wake of specific bloody historical events. Whether we view war and internal conflict as a symptom of modernisation, as inherent within the dynamic of global capitalism, or as inherent within human nature, it is evident that a range of bodies responded to the horrors associated with these events, driving forward humanitarian concerns into global consciousness with consequences for the conceptualisation of sovereignty and the organisation of the society of states.

An early example includes the International Committee of the Red Cross (ICRC) created in 1864, following the War of Italian Unification. Significantly, the ICRC later directed governments to adopt the rules of war fulfilling a unique role as the custodian of the Geneva Conventions of 1949 and the additional Protocols of 1977 (Weiss, 2011: 309). Other key international non-governmental organisations were also conceived against the background of conscience-shocking conflict and civil unrest including: Save the Children, in the wake of the First World War and the Russian Revolution; the International Rescue Committee (IRC); Oxfam; Catholic Relief Services (CRS); World Vision and CARE. The emergence of these international humanitarian institutions was originally prompted by concerns regarding the protection of the war wounded (and those who care for them), providing relief such as food and basic supplies to civilians including children suffering the effects of war and aiding victims of civil oppression (regardless of religious or political faith). Bankers, doctors, war correspondents and evangelists were amongst those founding such bodies, highlighting the significance of global mobility and advancements in communication in raising awareness of the consequences of war and conflict, and the role of non-governmental bodies in the generation and mobilisation of political will to 'do something' about such human suffering, thereby lending support for Andreas and Nadelmann's (2006) observation regarding the importance of moral entrepreneurs in mobilising political will and placing particular issues upon the international agenda. Later intergovernmental bodies attached to the United Nations, including the UN Children's Fund (UNICEF) and the UN High Commissioner for Refugees (UNHCR), were created in the aftermath of the Second World War (Weiss, 2011: 266).

The proliferation of non-governmental and intergovernmental organisations fostering humanitarian norms and action, alongside individuals has been described by Weiss (2011: 313) as 'a striking fact of contemporary international society'. This development is associated with advances in information communication technologies and global communications, enhancing public awareness regarding the plight of victims across the globe. Within this context, international human rights norms and instruments have been utilised as measures of accountability, challenging the culture of sovereign impunity, placing political pressure on governments to act, with domestic political costs for inaction and indifference (ICISS, 2001: 6–7). Etzioni (2005), for example, suggests that attentive publics are growing worldwide, predicting increasing demands for legitimacy for state leaders and their representatives in the future. For Etzioni, it is now possible to speak of the emergence of a global public opinion (Etzioni, 2005: 472), with the previously excluded masses entering politics even within undemocratic nations, playing an increasingly significant political role, with unprecedented access to information and a global audience. However, while the increasing number and significance of actors is clearly evident within the humanitarian arena, Weiss (2011: 304) argues that states still remain the most important actors. Thus, for Weiss 'humanitarian values have not superseded traditional conceptions of vital interests but rather have become increasingly central to their definition', reflecting a shift in the conceptualisation of national security discussed in Chapter 1, and representing an evolving definition of national interest. States remain central therefore to the development of international human rights law and to the development of the international humanitarian norms, and it is to these developments we now turn.

International human rights law

According to Dixon (2005: 320–325), until 1945 and the signing of the United Nations Charter, international law was generally concerned only with the rights and duties of states. Individuals were not a major concern of international law, and the overwhelming preoccupation of those who founded the UN was not human rights but rather the issue of states waging aggressive war against each other and state-to-state relations (Evans, 2008b: 284). Within this system, there remained little in the way of rules geared to the protection of individuals, with notable exceptions including: the protection of combatants and civilians during periods of war; the Mandate provisions of the League of Nations Covenant; and, limited rights attached to the Peace Treaties ending the First World War (Dixon, 2005). Over time however, greater protection has been granted to civilians in both internal and international armed conflict, with changes witnessed in relation to individual responsibility and sovereign immunity, which previously protected heads of state from criminal liability for breaches of the laws and customs of war by their armies (Niemann, 2005: 209).

In the aftermath of the Second World War progress was made in challenging the prevailing concept of sovereignty, with individual and group human rights recognised in the UN Charter which committed the UN (in Article 1.3) to 'promoting and encouraging respect for human rights and for fundamental freedoms for all without distinction as to race, sex, language or religion'. As noted by Hafner-Burton and Tsutsui (2007: 407), drawing upon the work of Koh (2002), 'many scholars and policymakers after that time worked to bring offending governments to justice, attempting to hold repressors accountable for their actions and working to stop future abuses', identifying international human rights laws, 'developed in the aftermath of the severe atrocities witnessed during World War II', as among 'the tools available to prevent such repression'. The preamble to the Charter, in its second paragraph, reaffirms a 'faith in fundamental human rights, in the dignity and worth of the human person, in the equal rights of men and women and of nations large and small' with all members of the United Nations pledging themselves, in Article 56, to take 'joint and separate action in co-operation with the Organisation for the achievement of the purposes set forth in Article 55' (Dixon, 2005: 323). In 1945, the Nuremberg Tribunal Charter explicitly recognised the concept of 'crimes against humanity', also introducing the concept of individual criminal responsibility for violation of the Laws and Customs of War. These developments ensured that heads of state could no longer be shielded from liability by sovereign immunity, a position reaffirmed with the signing of the 1948 Convention on the Prevention and Punishment of the Crime of Genocide (Evans, 2008b: 284; Niemann, 2005: 209).

In addition to the UN Charter, the Universal Declaration of Human Rights (1948) similarly embodies the moral code, political consensus and legal synthesis of human rights (ICISS, 2001: 6). Taken together, these tools ensured that respect for human rights became a central subject and responsibility of international relations (Dixon, 2005: 324). Thus, while not intended to be binding and significantly lacking an effective enforcement machinery, the UDHR has been celebrated for creating a general principle of customary international law. Specifically, it has been described as law that has evolved from the practice or custom of states (including, although not restricted to acts and omissions, statements, national legislation and actions of international organisations) with the potential to give rise to binding law. Further sources of international human rights laws include international conventions, or treaties, which are regarded as the most important source of international law (Dixon, 2005). Examples include the International Covenant on Civil and Political Rights (ICCPR) and the International Covenant on Economic, Social and Cultural Rights, which both entered into force in 1976. Both treaties impose binding legal obligations on the State Party requiring each state to adopt legislative measures within their domestic jurisdiction. The former Covenant (ICCPR) establishes a code of civil and political rights similar to those found in the Universal Declaration including: the right to life (Art. 6); the prohibition of torture (Art. 7); the prohibition of slavery (Art. 8); the right to liberty of the person (Art. 9); the prohibition of retroactive criminal legislation (Art. 15); the right of peaceful assembly (Art. 12); the protection of minority rights (Art. 27); the right of recognition as a person before the law (Art. 16); and freedom of conscience and religion (Art. 18) (Dixon, 2005: 325–329).

Together the Universal Declaration and the two Covenants charted the international human rights agenda, providing a benchmark for state behaviour, and influencing the development of provisions in national legislation and international conventions. For Dixon, this legislative framework led to the creation of long-term national infrastructures for the protection and promotion of human rights, with other treaties covering specific human rights matters.[1] International criminal tribunals have also more recently been created to deal with crimes against humanity committed in the Balkans, Rwanda and Sierra Leone, in addition to the creation of the new International Criminal Court in 1998, following the adoption of the Rome Statute by 120 states. Significantly, the court was established to help end impunity for the perpetrators of the most serious crimes of concern to the international community, namely, genocide, crimes against humanity and war crimes.

According to the United Nations, what distinguishes atrocity crime is the deliberate targeting of specific groups, communities or populations, including persons protected under the Geneva Conventions, and sometimes cycles of reaction and counter-reaction between communities (UN General Assembly Security Council, 2013: 3). In the case of genocide, the distinction lies in the intent of the perpetrators to 'destroy in whole or in part' a national, ethnic, racial or religious group. In contrast, war crimes can be committed only in the context of armed conflict or occupation, including the targeting of civilian infrastructures that are not military objectives and of anyone no longer taking an active part in hostilities as well as the use of weapons prohibited under international law. Crimes against humanity are further distinguished by the systematic or widespread nature of the gross human rights violations committed. Significantly, war crimes, ethnic cleansing and crimes against humanity may be committed in the course of the same event or can be precursors to other atrocity crimes (UN General Assembly Security Council, 2013: 3–4).

While not viewed as perfect, particularly in relation to their implementation, this legislative framework has been conceived by advocates as demonstrating that both the substance and process of human rights law is now closer than ever to realising the ideal of universal justice (ICISS, 2001: 6). Societal reform, through the use of law and the development of a normative consensus based upon human rights is therefore viewed as a great achievement of the post-Second World War era, setting new standards of conduct for states and altering expectations about what is and what is not acceptable conduct by states and other actors (ICISS, 2001: 6). The bulk of both customary and treaty human rights law consequently functions to oblige states to refrain from causing 'harm' to their own nationals or other persons within their territorial jurisdiction. Such obligations are not restricted to the prevention of physical harm, but may also extend to include obligations to protect economic, social, legal or intellectual rights. In this sense, Dixon (2005: 322) presents the law of human rights as 'an exception to the absolute exclusive territorial jurisdiction which a state otherwise possesses'; state rights have subsequently become contingent upon the fulfilment of certain duties, an alteration that has served to 'erode the absolute control which a state once exercised over its nationals'. This transformation is accordingly celebrated as a significant achievement of international law, resulting in state responsibility for acts undertaken in its own territory to its own citizens.

Sadly, despite the recent creation of the liberal human rights machinery described above, in general, effective protection for specific individuals in respect of personal violations of their human rights continues to be regarded as the exception rather than the rule. This apparent defect in the enforcement of human rights obligations has led many commentators to lament the 'ineffectiveness' of human rights law and to castigate states for not being prepared to accept compulsory enforcement machinery (Dixon, 2005: 322), prompting the recent creation of an international norm of humanitarian intervention known as 'the Responsibility to Protect' (R2P).

The Responsibility to Protect (R2P)

In 1999, prompted by the deteriorating humanitarian situation in East Timor, the then UN Secretary-General, Kofi Annan, considered international intervention to be in humanitarian crisis, reflecting upon two high profile failures which highlighted significant barriers to international efforts to successfully prevent atrocity crimes and alleviate human suffering.

Kofi Annan's article, submitted in *The Economist* in September 1999, reflected upon the international community's response to Kosovo and Rwanda. Both cases were perceived by Annan as undermining the credibility and standing of the United Nations, serving to highlight significant issues, which were considered to be affecting the effectiveness of the international collective security system. The Kosovo case raised the issue of the 'right authority' to legitimise intervention for humanitarian purposes. In particular, the case raised questions about what to do in instances where the UN Security Council fails to respond within a reasonable time or in the event of the permanent five states (P5 – China, France, Russia, the United Kingdom and the United States) applying their veto power and effectively preventing the adoption of any Security Council draft resolution. In the event, this instance resulted in a group of states intervening in a NATO operation in 1999, significantly, without authorisation from the UN Security Council, raising concerns regarding the possibility of unilateral interference and the potential of abuse of humanitarian intervention. The Rwandan case was subsequently castigated as an example of 'institutionalised indifference', highlighting the need to generate a sense of obligation, duty or political will to activate a timely and effective response to allegations of large-scale loss of human life or ethnic cleansing (Annan, 1999). Both examples served as shameful evidence of UN failure and formed the backdrop against which a new interpretation of sovereignty would be envisaged, and a new international norm of humanitarian intervention developed.

Annan's address to the 54th session of the UN General Assembly in the same month threw down the gauntlet to the member states of the UN to reach a consensus in defence of common humanity, advocating unity 'around the basic questions of principle and processes involved' while simultaneously upholding the principles of the UN Charter. A year later in his Millennium Report to the General Assembly Annan questioned the prevailing view of humanitarian intervention, which held that it was as an assault upon state sovereignty, asking the international community once again to address the issue of how to respond to gross and systematic violations of human rights. Reacting to the challenge, the Government of Canada in association with a number of major international foundations established the International Commission on Intervention and State Sovereignty (ICISS) (ICISS, 2001: vii).

In December 2001, the ICISS published a report co-chaired by Gareth Evans and Mohamed Sahnoun entitled 'The Responsibility to Protect'. Responding to Annan's question, the report was directed to consider 'when, if ever, it is appropriate for states to undertake coercive – and in particular military – action, against another state for the purpose of protecting people at risk in that other state' (ICISS, 2001: vii). This question was viewed by the authors as one of the most controversial and difficult of all international relations questions. It served to divide the international community regarding issues of state sovereignty, territorial jurisdiction and moral conscience. For opponents, the developing norm of humanitarian intervention reflected 'an alarming breach of an international state order dependent on the sovereignty of states and the inviolability of their territory' (ICISS, 2001: vii). Advocates however maintain the long overdue nature of this development and its basis within the UN Charter, international law and indeed within the obligations inherent with the concept of sovereignty itself (ICISS, 2001: xi).

The ICISS report was written in consultation with affected populations, governments, intergovernmental and non-governmental organisations (NGOs), and civil society representatives. It sought to shift the emphasis from the 'right of intervention' (which was viewed as outdated and unhelpful), towards a new focus upon a 'responsibility to protect' (Evans, 2008b: 286). State sovereignty, the bedrock of the international order, previously conceived as the principle that within its territorial boundaries the state is the supreme political authority, along with the associated right of non-intervention, were consequently reconceptualised. Moreover, these rights were now to be regarded as contingent upon the ability of states to fulfil an additional responsibility to protect their own people, directing that if a state is unwilling or unable to protect the rights of its own citizens, it temporarily forfeits a moral claim to be treated as legitimate. Thus, state sovereignty as well as a state's right to non-intervention would be suspended with a residual responsibility necessitating action by external bodies to protect populations at risk. Thus, within the new formulation, set out within the 2001 ICISS document, states are unable to claim the prerogatives of sovereignty unless they are able to meet internationally agreed responsibilities, which include the fulfilment of human rights and providing life sustenance to its citizens (Weiss, 2011: 301–2). Weiss contends that the ICISS's reframing of the central moral issue is noteworthy – replacing the rights of outsiders to intervene with the rights of affected populations to assistance and protection, placing an obligation upon outsiders to come to the rescue (ibid.: 267).

In order to prevent future Rwandas and therefore to generate the necessary political will to respond, the R2P framework made clear individual state obligations and also those of the wider international community in instances of individual state failure. Thus, according to Bellamy (2006: 146), 'The first strategy was to set down the parameters of responsibility – that is, by defining the circumstances in which international society should assume responsibility'. This criterion for action is set out within the 'Basic Principles' and 'Just Cause Threshold' sections of the ICISS report:

> Basic Principles
>
> A. State sovereignty implies responsibility, and the primary responsibility for the protection of its people lies with the state itself.
>
> B. Where a population is suffering serious harm, as a result of internal war, insurgency, repression or state failure, and the state in question is unwilling or unable to halt or avert it, the principle of non-intervention yields to the international responsibility to protect.
>
> (ICISS, 2001: XI)

> The Just Cause Threshold
>
> Military intervention for human protection purposes is an exceptional and extraordinary measure. To be warranted, there must be serious and irreparable harm occurring to human beings, or imminently likely to occur, of the following kind:
>
> A. **large scale loss of life,** actual or apprehended, with genocidal intent or not, which is the product either of deliberate state action, or state neglect or inability to act, or a failed state situation; or
>
> B. **large scale 'ethnic cleansing'**, actual or apprehended, whether carried out by killing, forced expulsion, acts of terror or rape.
>
> (ICISS, 2001: XII)

All acts constituting the crimes and violations related to the responsibility to protect are prohibited under international customary law[2] (UN General Assembly, Security Council, 2013: 3–4). The R2P framework therefore reminded states of their obligations under international law, which are binding on all states regardless of their treaty obligations. The 'Foundations' section of the report further locates the basis of the Responsibility to Protect as: originating within the obligations inherent in the concept of sovereignty, which requires states to protect their people; and also within the responsibility of the Security Council for the maintenance of international peace and security (Article 24 of the UN Charter); and within the developing practice of states, regional organisations and the Security Council itself (ICISS, 2001: XI).

In attempting to respond to the circumstances within Kosovo, characterised by unauthorised regional action, and at pains to distance the R2P norm from unilateral interference in Iraq, the ICISS report also sought to address concerns regarding the potential for abuse of the emerging norm of humanitarian intervention, seeking to challenge the conflation of humanitarian intervention with military intervention, thereby widening the international community's obligations to include action before, during and after situations of compelling human need. Within this framework, three specific responsibilities are viewed as falling to the international community: first, the responsibility to prevent (which is presented as the single most important dimension of the responsibility to protect and requires the international community to address the root causes and direct causes of internal conflict and other man-made crises putting populations at risk). Such prevention may take many forms including development assistance, efforts to provide support for local initiatives to advance good governance, human rights, or the rule of law, in addition to mediation efforts and other measures to promote dialogue or reconciliation. In some cases, international support for prevention efforts may take the form of inducements; in others, it may involve a willingness to apply tough and perhaps even punitive measures. Second, the responsibility to react, including: economic sanctions, targeted sanctions addressing leadership groups and security organisations, arms embargoes, cessation of military cooperation and training programmes, financial sanctions, restrictions on income generating activities, restricting access to petroleum products, aviation bans, restrictions on diplomatic representation, restrictions on travel, restricting membership or expulsion from international and regional bodies; and, third, the responsibility to rebuild: providing full assistance with recovery, reconstruction and reconciliation including security, justice and development assistance (ICISS, 2001).

According to Evans (2008b: 291), the benefit of the proposed framework was that 'reaction does not have to mean *military* reaction'; indeed, military action should be considered a last resort. The Elements and Priority sections of the report therefore require the international community to exhaust the full spectrum of measures, including political, diplomatic, economic and legal pressure. Considering the coercive potential of such activities, Evans argues that this range of measures entails a continuum, from persuasive to intrusive, and from less coercive (e.g. economic incentives, offers of political mediation or legal arbitration) to more coercive (e.g. economic sanctions, political and diplomatic isolation, threats of referral to the International Criminal Court) (Evans, 2008b: 291).

The Just Cause Threshold criteria presented earlier were provided within the report to guide decisions regarding intervention. Again, the purpose of including these principles was to avert future potential Rwandas by making absolutely clear to member states the circumstances in which the principle of non-intervention yields to the international responsibility to protect, thereby creating the necessary conditions for the mobilisation of political will by generating a collective obligation to respond. Military intervention for human protection purposes is therefore presented within the report as an exceptional and extraordinary measure, warranted only in circumstances where there is serious and irreparable harm (entailing large-scale loss of life and/or large-scale 'ethnic cleansing') occurring to human beings, or imminently likely to occur. The provision of criteria therefore addressed critics who pointed to selectivity or inconsistency in responses to humanitarian crisis. The Responsibility to Protect aimed to inhibit the abuse of humanitarian justifications by insisting that intervention was legitimate only in response to mass murder and ethnic cleansing and where the four precautionary principles were satisfied (Bellamy, 2006: 148).

Moreover, the 'Just Cause Threshold' criteria along with four 'Precautionary Principles' and a 'Hierarchy of Authority' were also intended to act as a check upon unilateral action and/or abuse, placing limits upon individual state and regional action and also setting out the appropriate procedure to authorise military intervention. Thus, the precautionary principles included 'Right Intention', ensuring that the primary purpose of the intervention must be to halt or avert human suffering. The precautionary principle of 'Right Intention' therefore addresses the motivation for action, placing a check upon national self-interest and strategic intervention, engaging with the views of sceptics and critics of humanitarian intervention who directed attention to the potential for abuse, with states espousing humanitarian motives as a pretext for action. Military humanitarian intervention is accordingly legitimised by the humanitarian motive to halt or avert human suffering, strengthened by the presence of multilateral operations, regional support and the support of the victims concerned. The second precautionary principle, namely 'Last Resort', advocates employing military action only when every other non-military option has been explored, again acting as a safeguard against abuse and a deterrent against those states seeking to employ military intervention as a pretext for self-interested intervention. The third precautionary principle, 'Proportional Means', places limits upon the scale, duration and intensity of military intervention, thereby responding to arguments which suggest humanitarian intervention can actually cause mass atrocities by encouraging dissatisfied groups to launch rebellions with the intention of triggering a disproportionate response from their government resulting in military intervention. 'Proportional Means' consequently requires intervention to be the minimum necessary to secure the defined human protection objective, thereby providing a further check upon abuse and unauthorised unilateral action. The final precautionary principle, 'Reasonable Prospects of Success', requires that there is a reasonable chance of success in halting or averting the suffering which has justified the intervention, with the consequences of action not likely to be worse than the consequences of inaction (ICISS, 2001: xii).

In addition to the aim of securing political will through the clear articulation of a duty to halt or avert human suffering, the just cause thresholds and precautionary principles also sought to constrain states that may wish to oppose intervention for selfish reasons (Bellamy, 2006: 146), with the ICISS authors further advocating that 'the Permanent Five members of the Security Council should agree not to apply their veto power, in matters where their vital state interests are not involved, to obstruct the passage of resolutions authorising military intervention for human protection purposes for which there is otherwise majority support' (ICISS, 2001: xiii). This proposal was regarded by the report's authors as enhancing the likelihood that like cases would be treated alike, thereby ensuring more consistency regarding the application of humanitarian intervention, reducing the likelihood of unauthorised action in instances of Security Council inaction, and also, serving to enhance the legitimacy and credibility of the UN Collective Security System along the way.

With regard to the appropriate body and procedure to authorise legitimate humanitarian intervention, and to avert future Kosovo scenarios characterised by unilateral or multilateral unauthorised action, the R2P report clearly provides a hierarchy of authority with the United Nations Security Council presented as the appropriate body to authorise military intervention for human protection purposes. Therefore, in addition to the provisions relating to the non-use of veto powers (which have frequently obstructed the passage of resolutions authorising military intervention), the R2P authors created provision to enable the General Assembly to consider the matter under the 'Uniting for Peace' procedure in an Emergency Special Session in the case of Security Council rejection or where an application is subject to delay. Regional or subregional organisations were also permitted to act (subject to authorisation from the Security Council), with unauthorised unilateral or regional action not entirely ruled out in cases of UN Security System failure:

> The Security Council should take into account in all its deliberations that, if it fails to discharge its responsibility to protect in conscience-shocking situations crying out for action, *concerned states may not rule out other means* to meet the gravity and urgency of that situation – and that the stature and credibility of the United Nations may suffer thereby. (ICISS, 2001: xiii)

This is important as the original conceptualisation of the R2P norm (as articulated within the ICISS report) therefore included measures to prevent *undesirable* unauthorised action, but also included a clause effectively allowing for the possibility of *desirable (or at least necessary)* unauthorised action under particular circumstances. Unauthorised military action, unilateral or multilateral (as in the case of Kosovo), was therefore rendered far less likely (although not impossible) as a consequence of the provisions contained in the R2P recommendations. As stated, these included the 'Element Criteria' (which placed responsibilities upon the international community to prevent, react, rebuild); the 'Threshold Criteria' (which required action in relation to large-scale loss of life and/or ethnic cleansing, and therefore placed limitations upon action beyond this remit); the 'Precautionary Principles' (including Right Intention, Last Resort, Proportional Means, and Reasonable Prospects); the 'Hierarchy of Authority' (setting out a hierarchy of authority comprising individual states, Security Council, General Assembly, Regional and sub-regional bodies); and finally, the 'restrictions placed upon the use of the veto power by the five permanent members of the UN Security Council'. As a result of these measures, accusations regarding a perceived selectivity of response by the international community and institutionalised indifference (as characterised within the Rwandan case) were viewed as much less likely.

The original formulation of the R2P norm detailed above (as published within the ICISS report) resulted in cautious optimism as heads of state and government from 150 countries, meeting at the General Assembly in 2005, unanimously accepted:

> not only that sovereign states have a very explicit responsibility to protect their own people from genocide, war crimes, ethnic cleansing and crimes against humanity, but when they manifestly fail in that responsibility – as a result of either incapacity or ill-will – the responsibility falls upon the wider international community to take whatever action is appropriate, including in the last resort, and if the Security Council agrees, military action.
>
> (Evans, 2008b: 284)

In interpreting the developments detailed thus far, it is useful to return to the sociological and international relations perspectives presented in Chapter 3. Here we examine the development of the R2P norm as evidence of progressive reform and adaptation, responding to social strains generated by a period of transformative social change associated with modernity and globalisation.

Theoretical interpretation (Durkheim and modernisation theory)

As discussed in Chapter 3, modernisation models of crime and crime control are based on the ideas of Emile Durkheim (Barak, 2001). To reiterate, writing at the end of the nineteenth century, Durkheim was interested in making sense of the world in which he lived. As a social reformer, he was deeply concerned by some of the changes taking place in society and hoped to offer some positive solutions to some of the problems, defined as 'pathologies', confronting society. Durkheim's theory of societal transformation suggests that rapid social change caused by the increased number, interaction and mobility of people (captured by his notion of 'dynamic density') intensifies conflict by bringing people with different values, norms and beliefs into contact with one another. Thus, as norms and values collide and as traditional mechanisms of social cohesion and solidarity become destabilised (captured by Durkheim's concepts of collective conscience and collective representations), society is viewed as being thrown into a temporary state of disequilibrium (reflecting Durkheim's use of the concept of anomie and the breakdown of common morality) where deviance and crime tend to expand as values clash regarding appropriate norms (Ritzer, 1996: 75–108).

While originally not directly applied to the study of international crime, Durkheimian insights and particularly the notions of social strain and societal control may have relevance for the study of atrocity crime. For Durkheim, problems in modern society were conceived as temporary aberrations and not as inherent difficulties, with the implication that the 'social physician' would be able to 'cure' social ills via structural reform and strategic planning (Ritzer, 1996: 75–108). This position is aligned to the liberal and neo-liberal institutionalist international relations perspectives which advocate consensus building and collective problem solving, utilising institutions within a rule of law framework to tackle common problems within international society (Deudney and Ikenberry, 2009; Dunne, 2014; Ikenberry, 2009, 2011).

The solution for Durkheim entailed the potential to alleviate social pathologies associated with modern egoism, through the cultivation and development of a collective moral system of society, grounded in freedom and communal solidarity (Ritzer, 1996: 75–108). It is here where we may reflect upon the significance of human rights, law and the role of international society in tackling the challenges of the contemporary period.

As noted in Chapter 3, Durkheim's ideas have been used by modernisation theorists to account for changes taking place from the late nineteenth and twentieth centuries through to contemporary developments internationally in the twenty-first century (Barak, 2001). These explanations argue that the destabilisation effects of social changes such as urbanisation, industrialisation and more recently the processes of globalisation are associated with changes in crime and victimisation patterns (Naim, 2002). Viewed as elements of modernisation, rapid social change and population movement have the potential to generate pathologies such as social disorganisation (including internal conflict and war) and anomie, reflecting conflicting values, civilisations and the undermining of social controls and mechanisms of social solidarity. Crime and crime control are therefore primarily viewed by advocates of this position as products of the internal influences of processes of development, with the process of development the same for each society as they undergo the transition from pre-modern, to modern, to late capitalist society.

Durkheim's theory of social transformation highlights how material social facts impact upon non-material social facts which are external to, and coercive of individuals. In this instance, material social facts include those concerned with the morphological components of society such as dynamic density (number of people within society), division of labour and population distribution, which are considered to influence the speed and level of development.

These material social facts are also regarded as important for understanding changes in non-material social facts such as collective morality and the collective conscience (norms and values) and the functioning and effectiveness of collective representations (including institutions such as religion, law and science) and social currents. Changes in material social facts therefore influence non-material social facts which are viewed as underpinning patterns or variation in crime and crime control alongside other individual actions.

Key elements of Durkheim's theory which have been applied to the study of genocide include primarily the concept of strain, associated with sociological positivism, which has been conceived as a facilitating factor for crime. Put simply, it is the idea that something within society has happened to push (normally well-behaved) people towards criminality (in this instance – rapid social change such as urbanisation, industrialisation and globalisation as processes of modernisation). Second, the notion of control is associated with the classical paradigm within criminology which places aside the issue of motivation and instead focuses upon protective or restraining factors (including norms and values and institutions such as the family, law and religion). The idea here is that such factors, which had previously prevented individuals from becoming criminal, have become disrupted, weakened, and/or undermined by the processes of strain associated with development and/or rapid social change.

In accounting for the emergence of the fledgling normative framework and human rights regime, the narrative provided within this chapter details a period of rapid social change marked by state-to-state war and internal conflict, linked to industrialisation and modernisation. Thus, viewed as a symptom of modernity, and as evidence of strain, war and conflict may be interpreted as having kick-started the moral entrepreneurialism of key individuals and groups which led to the generation of the modern humanitarian system, international society and the creation of international laws and norms, namely the purposeful creation of a new collective moral system of modern (global) society, based upon human rights and individual freedom, of which the recent R2P norm may be presented as part. Viewed as a continuation of modernity, Durkheimian theory of societal change anticipates tensions inherent within the quest for modernisation, and the applicability of societal reform, law and structural reforms to alleviate them. Within this perspective, there is reason for optimism, as measures are collectively undertaken to resolve the tensions generated by societal change and to strengthen common morality and societal controls (including international human rights law, judicial and policing cooperation and legislative and judicial harmonisation and other measures contained within the responsibility to 'prevent', 'react' and 'rebuild' detailed previously). Taken as evidence of progress, the emergence of the international legislative framework, the R2P framework, the International Criminal Tribunals and the International Criminal Court point to positive developments, consistent with liberal internationalism, with potential for deterring atrocity crimes, and for the detection and prosecution of perpetrators in the event of large-scale loss of life, or ethnic cleansing.

While usefully applied to account for the development of a normative and institutional framework to prevent and respond to atrocity crime, the utility of this approach has been rendered questionable by subsequent developments. It is significant therefore that the original R2P proposals (as articulated within the ICISS 2001 report) were subject to later revision leading Bellamy to damningly conclude that in 2006, 'Powerful states are no more likely to feel obliged to act to save distant strangers, and there is no more likelihood of agreement about what to do in particular cases' (Bellamy, 2006: 169). We will therefore highlight key changes to the original R2P document before addressing the prospects for humanitarian intervention today and theoretical interpretation of these developments.

R2P: revision and implications

Within his article, provocatively entitled 'The R2P An idea whose time has come and gone', Evans (2008b) describes a rapid initial emergence and acceptance of the concept of R2P by the international society, followed by a subsequent 'denial and evasion' by a number of governments and revision to several of the key elements of the R2P framework. Bellamy (2006) similarly examines a number of critical changes made to the responsibility to protect from its original articulation within the ICISS (2001) report to the 2005 World Summit Outcome Document. In particular, Bellamy argues that 'in order to secure consensus, the concept's advocates have abandoned many of its central tenets, significantly reducing the likelihood of progress in the near future' (Bellamy, 2006: 145–146).

In a convoluted process which endeavoured to negotiate an apparent tension between the Security Council's permanent five, particularly the United States, Russia, and China (who wished to remain unrestricted in such situations), and African and Asian states (who raised concerns regarding the potential for abuse by powerful nations to justify armed intervention against the weak) (Bellamy, 2006: 153), the original R2P language was altered. This change to the original conceptualisation of the R2P norm has been regarded as subsequently reducing the sense of obligation or duty to respond, undermining the original proponents' concern to motivate political will and to avoid institutionalised indifference within future Rwandan-type situations. Bellamy rebuked this change arguing that 'The United States, supported in this endeavour by China and Russia, successfully whittled away the council's responsibility from an obligation to act to a commitment to "stand ready" to act should the prevailing circumstances permit' (Bellamy, 2006: 167). Evans agrees, similarly viewing the failure to include the guidelines for the use of force as 'One of the many disappointments of the World Summit' (Evans, 2008b: 292).

While the just cause thresholds and precautionary principles were originally viewed as pivotal by the proponents of the original R2P formulation, the United States reportedly conceived such criteria as overly prescriptive and restrictive, with Russia and China arguing the reverse, that the criteria were too enabling. Sceptics in some states in the South further argued that the inclusion of criteria would run the risk of encouraging the use of force rather than limiting it. Reservations emanating from the South therefore reflect concerns that powerful states would be free to impose their own culturally determined moral values on weaker members of international society (Bellamy and Wheeler, 2014: 483). The drafters of the World Summit outcome document consequently removed the criteria and discussion regarding the need to consider criteria.

For both Bellamy and Evans, the removal of these guidelines reduced the clarity of when to apply the R2P norm, eliminating vital safeguards against abuse, thereby watering down the sense of obligation to respond to conscience-shocking situations (consequently reducing political will to respond). Perhaps even more significant was the failure to consider the original proposal to refrain from using the veto power 'to obstruct the passage of resolutions authorizing military intervention for human protection purposes for which there is otherwise majority support' (ICISS, 2001: XIII). Rejected as an unacceptable constraint upon the permanent five, the removal of this recommendation has been criticised for retaining the possibility of selectivity of response, creating inconsistency in policy, increasing the possibility that national interest would generate different responses in similar cases and, also, increasing the likelihood of unauthorised unilateral or multilateral action (as in the case of Kosovo), where concerned states circumvent the collective security system with the risk of undermining the United Nations.

Furthermore, the removal of the caveat within the original ICISS report (ICISS, 2001: XIII), which had permitted the General Assembly and regional organisations to act in cases where the Security Council was too slow or deadlocked (thereby providing for flexibility for military intervention outside the scope of Security Council approval), resulted in the rearticulation of a requirement for UNSC authorisation. Thus, as referred to previously, the original ICISS R2P framework included a statement that permitted concerned states to consider (or at least, 'not rule out') 'other means to meet the gravity and urgency' of the conscience-shocking situation at hand.

The inclusion of this statement essentially provided a hierarchy of authority, permitting the General Assembly, regional organisations (and 'concerned states'), to act in prescribed circumstances requiring action, inferring that it was legitimate for states to act outside the UN framework when the scale of the humanitarian catastrophe warranted immediate intervention, also placing a requirement upon states opposed to intervention 'to publicly justify their positions' (Bellamy, 2006: 163). However, as noted by Bellamy, the recommendation regarding the possibility of action outside UN authorisation secured little support particularly in the aftermath of Iraq, with the majority of states arguing that Security Council authorisation remained necessary to warrant legitimate intervention (Bellamy, 2006: 168–169). In considering whether regional or unilateral action would become possible in the event of national and international community failure, Bannon (2006) concludes that the summit agreement strengthens the likelihood of unilateral action outside of UN authorisation but also provides parameters limiting the scope of permissible intervention. Thus, attempts to justify such action on the basis of 'the war against terror', as a means towards democratisation or as a method of 'regime change', fall outside the remit of the R2P norm. Issues surrounding the immediacy of atrocity crimes and the requirement to exhaust all options prior to military intervention and in the case of military action, targeting action to protect populations, are further protections circumscribing US military intervention.

Within this context, rather than acting illegally, states undertaking unilateral action would be acting in a legal void left open by UN non-action (failure), with unsanctioned action conceivably interpreted as the only way of avoiding complicity in the failure to protect (Bannon, 2006: 1163). Bellamy (2006) and Bannon (2006) therefore raise the question as to the legitimacy of regional (and indeed unilateral) action in the absence of UNSC authorisation, alluding to a 'damned if you do, and damned if you don't' scenario where the revised version of the R2P would render unauthorised action, regardless of the heinousness of events, a serious violation of state sovereignty and the principle of non-intervention, yet failure to act would result in a failure to comply with the obligation for action contained within the R2P norm. The current revisions are therefore viewed as ambiguous and unhelpful with the changes to the 'Just Cause Threshold' and 'Precautionary Principles', further presented by Bellamy as a 'backwards step', particularly since the Security Council had previously shown willingness to authorise intervention in cases that fell short of the 'just cause' threshold.

According to Bellamy (2006), the original ICISS formulation of the R2P norm sought to ensure that the Security Council would commit to responding whenever the just cause thresholds were crossed, to submit its decisions to public deliberation about the use of force based on the precautionary principles, and to withhold the use or threat of the veto in humanitarian emergencies other than in cases where a permanent member's vital interests were at stake (Bellamy, 2006: 153). In doing so, the original R2P formulation addressed key challenges including the need to prevent anti-interventionists from blocking collective action, and to prevent potential abuse of humanitarian intervention as a pretext for the pursuit of national self-interest. These considerations, viewed as essential in preventing future Rwandas and Kosovos, and comprising fundamental components of the original R2P formulation, were therefore later disregarded, leading Bellamy to pessimistically conclude that 'in attempting to forge a consensus, the ICISS and its supporters sacrificed almost all of the key elements of their twin strategies' (Bellamy, 2006: 168–169).

Theoretical interpretation (World Systems Theory (WST) and realism)

In applying theoretical insights to the issue of atrocity crime prevention, and in particular to the development and subsequent revision of the R2P norm and to the construction of an institutional framework, alternative perspectives, such as the World Systems approach of Wallerstein (2005), and the realist international relations approach of Moses (2013), have emphasised the need for historical and political contextualisation, placing emphasis upon the salience of economic and power issues in influencing the direction of enforcement and questioning the prospects of the evolving prohibition regime achieving its goal of atrocity prevention and justice for all. As discussed, while Durkheim examined social pathologies arising from industrialisation and urbanisation, urging the need to develop a new normative and institutional framework to strengthen social controls to protect against crime and to act as a deterrent for potential perpetrators, and to secure peace, little consideration is given within Durkheimian and modernisation perspectives regarding relations of power and the geopolitical structure of the contemporary world order. Moreover, as noted by Dunne (2014), the liberal character of this endeavour and the legislative and political institutions comprising the R2P framework is assumed, thereby diverting attention from the normative aspect of this project (Moses, 2013).

Marxist influenced World Systems theorists and realist international relations perspectives challenge this omission, highlighting the salience of key historical transformations and the legacy of colonialism, imperialism, capitalism and power politics upon state vulnerability to crime. Thus, rather than undergoing a temporary period of adjustment caused by processes of global transformation, World Systems theorists contend that civil unrest, internal conflict and mass killings are indicators of a crisis in the contemporary world system, resulting from internal contradictions, and irresolvable problems caused by unequal exchange and the relentless pursuit of capital accumulation. Wallerstein therefore describes the phenomena of terrorism, internal and external conflict, and globalisation as intimately connected, suggesting further that they ought not to be examined in isolation from one another, therefore advocating historical contextualisation and interdisciplinary analysis.

Therefore, while both modernisation theorists and World Systems theorists emphasise the importance of industrialisation within their theorising, they differ in their perspectives regarding the outcome of this process. World Systems theorists question the modernist belief in progress and liberal assumptions regarding the universality of benefits and the inevitability of development, prosperity and equality resulting from liberal social change. By contextualising the processes of industrialisation World Systems theorists emphasise the significance of imperial colonisation, which resulted in the stripping of natural and human resources in colonised states to build the great Western nations who benefited substantially from these relations of exploitation, dominance and subservience. The modern capitalist economic world system is therefore regarded as characterised by unequal relations of production and unequal exchange, which, it is suggested, has led to uneven development both within and across nations, creating inequalities crippling periphery nations and widening the gap between the rich and the poor, a point similarly made by Pogge (2008) as discussed in the previous chapter. WST therefore challenges the taken for granted assumptions implicit within economic liberalism and the globalist perspective relating to the benefits of the free market and of globalisation more generally. For this perspective, neo-liberalism, otherwise known as 'the Washington Consensus', which advocated the removal of barriers to trade, has not resulted in universal benefits for all, reflecting the 'sceptical' position within globalisation theory identified in Chapter 1. Consequently, after the Second World War, orthodox accounts argue that economic integration became a means for promoting peace and prosperity, integrating the world's economies, ensuring interdependence and cooperation. In contrast, WST emphasises the fact that free trade and the free market are myths or ideologies serving to distort reality.

> Free trade, manifestly works only when and as it suits the wealthy; and is 'free' only for those already on the trade train – and yet it continues to be mooted as 'good for us all', on the grounds that liberalisation in trade ensures competition, which is essential for trade and hence development. In short, free/competitive trade works to increase power differentials while supposedly bringing about universal development.
>
> (Schirato and Webb, 2003: 24)

According to Wallerstein and Schirato and Webb then, the complete virtual world market has never functioned freely and fully without interference. Indeed, state interference is regarded as a defining feature of the contemporary global capitalist system, which is based upon unequal exchange and unequal power within the world society of states. World Systems theorists therefore recognise 'globalisation' and the international division of labour as the basis of global inequality, generating economic crises, political instability, identity crisis, social conflict and violence within vulnerable states, already disadvantaged by the legacy of colonialism, imperialism and exploitation. This approach therefore fundamentally questions the Durkheimian and liberal assumption that governments and international institutions can make the system 'fair', also questioning the ability of global governance (as it is currently structured) to resolve contemporary social ills. For Wallerstein, as for Marx before him, governments and international institutions, including international organisations and 'the law', will always reflect interests of capitalists, with both World Systems theorists and realists conceiving international law as intimately bound up with unequal relations of power, and as such, becoming merely tools with which to reproduce and strengthen the gap between the rich and powerful, and the poor and powerless (the position similarly adopted by state crime scholars, presented in the previous chapter, alongside feminist international relations and political economists in Chapter 8).

When considering the effectiveness of the current legal and normative framework to prevent and prosecute atrocity crimes, these alternative perspectives require analysts to examine to whose ends international law (as an institution and as a normative framework) is administered. Marxist influenced scholars and political economic theorists therefore direct attention towards the existence of a continuum of violence, which is viewed as inseparable from processes of globalisation and trade liberalisation associated with the current capitalist global economic world system. Such work emphasises that inequalities and identity crises that fuel violence remain rooted in structures and processes of political economy which are increasingly globalised, with some, more recently, also drawing attention to the gendered dimension of such phenomena (True, 2012: 5; Jacobs, Jacobson and Marchbank, 2000; Tickner, 1992, 2014). Alternative scholarship accordingly requires attention to be focused upon the structure and power relations within the current international society of states and the international political economic system. This work also raises questions regarding the implementation of the R2P framework, the enforcement of international laws, the effectiveness of international tribunals and courts, and the impact of power and state self-interest upon UN Security Council decisions to act.

Drawing upon the work of Morgenthau (1951), Moses (2013) questions the interpretation of increasing interventionism in the post-Cold War period as being indicative of a progressive growing universal conscience of humanity. Applying classical realism to an understanding of the practical and conceptual difficulties of the R2P, Moses argues that the current liberal framework, seeking equal justice under the rule of law, has effectively turned its back on the realities of politics and power, thereby depoliticising the application of the R2P and obfuscating its normative function. Questioning the moral universalism of liberal international law and theory, and drawing upon the writing of Koskennieumi, Moses argues that realists are more inclined to view the development of the R2P as an ideologically driven tool of power politics, which, rather than facilitating peace and justice, in fact intensifies conflict and war, permitting intervention and the total destruction of states designated as 'immoral', particularly those states which reject the liberal, democratic and capitalistic foundation of the existing international order of society of states. Powerful states, Moses reminds us, retain the power of decision over when and how to intervene in crisis-situations in other states, without being subject to the application of the rules themselves and do so, primarily on the basis of their own national interests. The contribution of Moses, the realist perspective and the critical state crime literature detailed within the previous chapter, thereby alert us to the fact that the relatively innocuous use of the term 'international community', to describe the legitimate authority to authorise action, currently serves to hide the fact that it is the USA, China, Russia, Britain and France who retain the decisive power to act or not to act, in contemporary world politics (as the Permanent Five within the UN Security Council and holders of veto power). The R2P is consequently dependent upon the exercise of sovereign power by these states to authorise action within the UNSC and as such, Moses reminds us, the UN serves as a new forum for the pursuit of power politics.

The legalisation of humanitarian intervention within the current framework is consequently viewed 'as a license to such great powers to engage in armed interference whenever it suits their own interests, serving as an expression of an ideologically-driven, imperialist hegemon bent on engaging in a moral crusade' (Morgenthau, 1951: 36 cited in Moses, 2013: 115). By way of example, Moses further reminds us of the humanitarian justificatory narrative espoused by the USA in relation to the 2003 invasion of Iraq, the 2008 Russian intervention in Georgia, and the Chinese incursion in Xinjiang in 2009. Thus, while for modernisation theorists and liberals the emergence of the R2P represents an attempt to resolve conflict and maintain order through the creation of a normative consensus articulated through the rule of law, for Moses, it obscures the continuing salience of power politics in the application of justice in the current world order characterised by anarchy, highlighting the salience of alternative perspectives influenced by Marxism, symbolic interactionist and constructivist insights for the study of crime control.

Looking forward

World Systems theorists and realists therefore call into question the current R2P framework, raising doubts regarding its prospects for adequately preventing atrocity crimes and granting universal access to justice. Despite the significant revision to the ICISS formulation of the R2P, there is, however, recent evidence that the liberal project has retained momentum and continues to be articulated as an appropriate response to this international security issue. While Evans expressed disappointment regarding the alterations to the criteria, language, veto, and hierarchy of authorisation, there is, he argues room for optimism, pointing to the 'steady trickle of good news' since the 2005 World Summit (Evans, 2008b: 286). Bannon (2006) similarly views the Summit agreement as an important contribution to international law, strengthening the development of a new international norm of humanitarian protection. Thus, since 2005, the responsibility to protect has been reaffirmed by the Security Council in its resolutions 1674 (2006), 1706 (2006), 1894 (2009), 2117 (2013) and 2150 (2014). Further embedding is highlighted by Evans pointing to the continued utilisation of the discourse of the responsibility to protect by the UN Secretary General in 2008 in relation to Kenya; Desmond Tutu's (19 February 2008) acknowledgement of limited progress (Tutu, 2008), and the launch of a Global Centre on the Responsibility to Protect in 2008. Action in Burundi has also been cited as 'a perfect example of the concept at work' (Evans, 2008b: 291), alongside the creation of two UN Special Advisor roles (on the Prevention of Genocide and on the Responsibility to Protect).

In 2009, the General Assembly agreed to give ongoing consideration to the concept in resolution (63/308), with the annual reports of the Secretary-General in 2009 (A/63/677), 2010 (A/64/864), 2011 (A/64/877) and 2013 (A/67/929), explicitly examining specific aspects of R2P. The UN Secretary-General's 2010 report (A/64/864), directs the UN Special Adviser on the Responsibility to Protect to develop and refine the R2P concept, advocating political dialogue with member states and other stakeholders to take forward its implementation, thereby highlighting the continuing salience and application of the concept. More recently, the R2P has been applied within Security Council resolutions 2085 (2012) on the situation in Mali; 1996 (2011) on the situation in South Sudan; and 1975 (2011) on the situation in Côte d'Ivoire (United Nations General Assembly Security Council, 11 July 2014: 2). The Special Advisors also issued press releases in 2014, raising concerns in relation to the situation in Kobane, Syria and Sinjar, in northern Iraq, condemning attacks against the lives and physical integrity of populations by terrorist and armed groups such as the Islamic State of Iraq and the Levant (ISIL), stressing the need for the international community to redouble its efforts in order that it may take effective action to resolve the conflict (United Nations Press Release, 10 October 2014; United Nations Press Release, 12 August 2014).

These recent developments may therefore for some be taken as evidence of the bedding down of the current normative liberal institutional framework. For others, however, the process is less certain. Ikenberry (2009, 2011) and Deudney and Ikenberry (2009), for example, address what they see as recent shifts in the underlying circumstances of world politics, with implications for the successful implementation of the R2P framework and the prevention of atrocity crimes, and, as we shall see in the next chapter, also in relation to the adequacy of contemporary counter-terrorist strategy concerned with the threat from Al Qaeda related terrorism. Significant changes that are highlighted within this work include a reported shift in power from the global North and West towards the East and South, alongside an apparent 'emerging challenge' from autocratic states which, they argue, have increasingly called into question liberal internationalist values and ideas which form the basis for the existing international order including: democratisation, free markets and US military power. As noted previously, these scholarly contributions interpret these developments as having led to 'a liberal crisis'. Thus, within this work the emergence of the R2P is presented as a manifestation of wider changes to the principles underpinning the current world order driven by changing security threats, associated with processes of globalisation which increasingly require attention to the domestic governance and practices of states.

For Ikenberry then, the emergence of the 'human rights revolution' detailed within this chapter, and the changes in the conceptualisation of sovereignty observed in Chapter 1, have resulted in a liberal crisis of authority, rule of law and governance, a crisis compounded by the diminishing power of the USA. Thus, while Wallerstein talks of a crisis of the current capitalist world economic system, international relations theorists are speaking of a crisis in the current liberal international order. If, for Wallerstein, the solution is to replace the existing global capitalist world system, the liberal solution, according to these scholars, remains – 'more liberalism', namely, 'a retooled and reinvigorated liberal institutionalism programme' entailing further consensus building, collective problem solving and the utilisation of institutions to that end. However, significantly, for Deudney and Ikenberry (2009: 92) there is an urgent need for international society to acknowledge and respond to the 'historically inherited vulnerabilities and grievances of the rising great powers and autocratic states', referring explicitly to perceived losses and threats to territorial integrity emanating from the geo-political boundaries fixed following decolonialisation and the First and Second World Wars. For this scholarship then, history matters. Indeed, successful resolution to contemporary social ills remains contingent upon efforts to mediate and resolve past grievances and injustices, issues implicated in the commission of both genocidal acts and acts of terrorism for both state and non-state actors.

The liberal world order, which is purportedly suffering from a crisis of legitimacy, is therefore regarded as increasingly subject to challenge by illiberal states and non-state actors seeking to make territorial and ideological adjustments to the established order. At the time of writing, the world continues to witness the expansionist activities of existing states such as Russia and Israel, and has recently confronted the nation-building aspirations of Islamic State. Within this context, it has become increasingly evident that the collective security system, international law and the established territorial boundaries of nation-states are currently under threat. Contemplating the outcome of such events, Ikenberry (2011) suggests that emerging great powers (and non-state actors) within this situation may contest the basic principles and rules of the existing liberal international order. While it is assumed that increasing economic and security interdependence will ultimately result in autocratic-capitalist states embracing the existing order resulting from a need for multilateral action to counter common security threats associated with globalisation alongside national financial interest, this outcome is not guaranteed. Thus, for Ikenberry (2011: 68):

> The coming divide in world politics will not be between the United States (and the West) and the non-Western rising states. Rather, the struggle will be between those who want to renew and expand today's system of multilateral governance arrangements and those who want to move to a less cooperative order built on spheres of influence. These fault lines do not map onto geography, nor do they split the West and the non-West.

If, as suggested by these authors, we are entering a period of instability, described by Wallerstein as a systemic crisis, or as a 'liberal crisis' by Ikenberry and Deudney and Ikenberry, the implications for genocide and internal conflict within states and between them are profound. Historical grievances relating to territorial disputes and the legacy of colonialism, imperialism and global capitalism, compounded by depleting resources, and neo-liberal policies, serve to widen the gap between the rich and the poor. As noted in Chapter 5, other authors, working within symbolic interactionist and constructivist perspectives, have also emphasised the impact of globalising tendencies upon identity, directing attention to the association of genocide with nation-building. Viewing nation-states historically as socially constructed and temporally situated phenomena, Niemann (2005: 219) for example, alongside the realist analysis of Moses, raises serious questions about the suitability of sovereign states as the locus for action within the existing society of states characterised by power politics and self-interest. Thus, Niemann (2005: 219) argues that 'there is a fundamental inconsistency in nominating nation-states as the guardians of international human rights and the prevention of abuses'. This work thoughtfully points to the disturbing association between the development of the nation-state, the corresponding need for states to achieve homogeneity, and resulting acts of genocide, concluding pessimistically that 'diversity and the nation-state do not make happy bedfellows'. For Niemann, contemporary processes of modernisation and globalisation remain intimately associated with trends towards heterogeneity, diversity and difference, and as such, are regarded as generating pathological environments for states with consequences for population vulnerability to atrocity crime. Thus, in an effort to secure national identity, states, it is suggested, may employ nation-building products and symbols, which serve to strengthen nationalist sentiments, also serving to compound differences within communities, arguing further that 'When confronted with social, religious, and cultural diversity, the nation-state has sought to achieve uniformity by annihilation or assimilation' (Niemann, 2005: 219). Adama Dieng, UN Special Adviser on Preventing Genocide, has also recently articulated the atrocity crime of genocide as one of 'identity conflict', a position also evident within the earlier ICISS (2001) report which, similarly, interpreted interstate warfare as a violent 'process of state fragmentation and state formation' serving to transform the international order (ICISS, 2001: 5).

Consequently, for Durkheimian inspired modernisation theorists, internal conflict, as a manifestation of instability, generated by rapid social change associated with modernisation, industrialisation, urbanisation and/or globalising processes, is conceived as a temporary aberration and is therefore not considered insurmountable. The UN and the ICISS, who both employ a liberal internationalist solution, similarly remain optimistic that action may be undertaken to address the sources of strain and the underlying risk factors associated with the commission of atrocity crimes, and also to strengthen institutions to act as a deterrent and to bring perpetrators to justice. UN General Assembly Security Council Report (2013: 3–7), for example, addresses apparent weaknesses in state structures and institutions, arguing that it is vital to strengthen the controls preventing the commission of atrocity crimes. In particular, risk factors identified within the report include the existence of an 'autocratic political regime or one that denies the right to effective participation in public affairs and restricts civil society; weak legislative protection of human rights; and weaknesses in the judiciary, national human rights institutions and the security sector'. For the UN then, lack of liberalism and democracy are defined as *the* risk factors making particular states and groups within states more vulnerable to crimes against humanity. The obvious solution therefore remains more liberalism – namely the strengthening of the legislative and normative framework, democracy and human rights, access controls, financial support, law enforcement and judicial cooperation and the raising of standards through cooperative training and assistance. As already noted, these measures are consistent with the liberal tradition, which advocates cooperation, consensus building and institutional strengthening to promote peace and security and to resolve common problems. For liberals, therefore, common laws and normative consensus contain solutions to conflicting interests as part of a deliberately constructed peace machinery (see Dunne in Baylis, Smith and Owens, 2014: 114–124).

For Niemann (2005) discrimination based upon difference effectively primes communities for genocidal acts, compounded when coinciding with racist propaganda and discourses of hatred against victim groups. For Niemann and for modernisation theorists more generally:

> population mobility, exposure to different norms, values, cultures and life-styles may therefore be seen as increasing vulnerability as political actors within states seek to strengthen national identity, consolidate control and assert their political power and influence both internally, upon dysphoric and excluded civilians within their territories, and externally.
>
> (Niemann, 2005: 219)

In today's rapidly changing world, described by Ikenberry as 'post-hegemonic liberal internationalism', the direction of change is uncertain. At the time of writing, atrocity crimes continue to be committed every day in Syria, Iraq, Yemen and Nigeria with the actions of Islamic State complicating the application of the R2P and blurring the boundaries between atrocity crime and terrorism. For Bellamy (2015), reflecting the salience of Niemann's observations above, 'Islamic State' remains intent upon eradicating Christians, Alawites, Shi'ites, moderate Sunnis, also systematically denying women and girls their fundamental rights, including the right to an education. In doing so, IS presents a challenge to liberal ideas and values, possibly comprising a manifestation of Ikenberry's (2011) 'liberal crisis' or Wallerstein's 'systemic crisis', reflecting the emergence of an alternative illiberal ideology. Though not yet an autocratic state, the salience of non-state actors as security threats and perpetrators of 'state crimes' brings further ambiguity to the fold, destabilising categorisation still further. As noted within the previous chapter, Bellamy, acknowledging the dilemma posed by this recent development, insists on the extension of the application of the R2P, placing responsibility upon non-state armed groups in addition to states, defining this action 'as part of the unfinished conceptual business of R2P'.

The R2P framework can then in many ways be seen as responding to the effects of globalisation. One of these effects has been to challenge the notion of sovereignty, made necessary by the international recognition of the altered nature of security. Epitomised by the IS case, the framework is underpinned by an awareness that current threats to international security not only have to do with traditional issues such as interstate war, but also with threats related to human security, such as poverty, terrorism, refugee flows, the export of drugs, the spread of infectious disease and organised crime (ICISS, 2001: 5). These collective security threats are accepted as interrelated, requiring multilateral action to alleviate them. The R2P framework, serving as an example of such collective action has been described recently by the UN Secretary General as 'a principle that has become a core part of the world's armour for protecting vulnerable populations from the most serious international crimes and violations' (United Nations General Assembly Security Council, 11 July 2014: 20). It has endeavoured to respond to allegations of large-scale loss of human life or ethnic cleansing, requiring preventative action to tackle the deeper causes of such crimes, such as institutional weakness, undemocratic structures, discrimination and poverty and inequality, which, as stated before, have been accentuated by the process of globalisation.

However, from the perspective of World Systems Analysis and the critical scholarship detailed within the preceding chapters, the existing framework remains deficient. In particular, it fails to recognise that inequalities remain rooted in structures and political economic processes. Neither has it addressed how the emergence of the liberal society of states and the development of global capitalism are implicated in the creation of the problems they now wish to solve. Attention is therefore directed towards the global trade in arms, competition for resources and lack of economic security resulting from the legacy of colonialism, imperialism, Cold War geo-politics and neo-liberal economic policy attached to the spread of the global capitalist world system. Critical commentators observe that these developments and those associated with changes to the structure of world order have deepened inequalities and vulnerability to violence. As noted by Weiss (2011: 267) the end of the Cold War generated new conflicts and crises, along with the eruption of long simmering ones held in check by East-West tensions. Without addressing historical grievances, social and economic injustices and power politics, the existing framework, rooted in an ideological liberal and economic project, leaves unchanged underlying structures, reinforcing unequal power relations and perpetuating inequalities which make particular groups susceptible to (perpetration and victimisation) of violence. Aside from radical transformation, as noted by Evans (2008a, 2008b) and De Waal (2007), barriers to implementation remain, including: a lack of trust regarding the motives underpinning humanitarian intervention; resourcing; the present capability of regional and sub-regional bodies; the apparent lack of political will, alongside 'crippling blockages' resulting from P5 use of the veto. Each of these challenges reflects the continuing salience of national-state interest in undermining atrocity crime prevention and prosecution. Thus, for Evans, Bannon and Moses, the manifest failure to address the structure of international relations and the realities of state power within the contemporary world order remain key challenges.

Ikenberry's vision of the post-hegemonic liberal internationalist order requires significant reform to resolve the current liberal crisis, to create legitimacy and authority surrounding the application of the R2P and other mechanisms of international order maintenance. In particular, Ikenberry argues that the United Nations would need to be reformed and the Security Council and international financial institutions such as the IMF and World Bank would need to be reorganised to reflect the power of newly emerging states such as Japan, India, Brazil and South Africa. These steps, it is argued, would lead to a less hierarchical and more legitimate world order. This acknowledgement regarding the need for reform reflects an awareness that the liberal normative project is currently under threat and is perhaps, less espoused than previously, with the future direction less certain than the modernisation assumption of progress would imply. For Dunne (2014: 122), the future is not yet known and the stakes are high. The R2P doctrine is consequently regarded 'as a key test for whether liberalism can endure despite systemic changes to the distribution of material and normative power'. As current crises within the Central African Republic, Iraq, Syria and South Sudan unfold, evidence of 'failure to protect' mounts, reflecting disagreement regarding the application and enforcement of the R2P and the continuing influence of power politics, sovereignty and self-interest. In the meantime, people continue to be killed, girls and women raped and families displaced. Tackling root causes therefore remains an urgent task – factors which re-emerge within the next chapter detailing international, regional and national responses to terrorism.

Notes

1 Examples include: the 1949 Geneva Conventions and 1977 Protocols; the 1984 Convention against Torture and other Cruel, Inhumane or Degrading Treatment or Punishment; the 1979 Convention on the Elimination of All Forms of Discrimination Against Women; the 1973 Convention on the Suppression and Punishment of the Crime of Apartheid and the 1945 Agreement for the Prosecution and Punishment of Major War Criminals and Charter of the International Military Tribunal at Nuremberg (Dixon, 2005: 331).

2 As set out in the Convention on the Prevention and Punishment of the Crime of Genocide and the Rome Statute of the International Criminal Court. Ethnic cleansing, while not defined as a distinct crime under international criminal law, is often a result of a combination of acts that could constitute genocide, war crimes or crimes against humanity (UN General Assembly Security Council, 2013: 3–4).

References

Andreas, P. and Nadelmann, E. (2006). *Policing the Globe: Criminalization and Crime Control in International Relations.* Oxford: Oxford University Press.

Annan, K. (1999). 'Two Concepts of Sovereignty', *The Economist*, September 16. Available online at: www.economist.com/node/324795 (accessed July 2, 2015).

Bannon, A. (2006). 'The Responsibility to Protect: The U.N. World Summit and the Question of Unilateralism', *The Yale Law Journal*, 115(5): 1157–1165.

Barak, G. (2001). 'Crime and Crime Control in an Age of Globalization: A Theoretical Dissection', *Critical Criminology*, 10: 57–72.

Baylis, J., Smith, S., and Owens, P. (2014). *The Globalisation of World Politics*, sixth edition. Oxford: Oxford University Press.

Bellamy, A. (2006). 'Whither the Responsibility to Protect? Humanitarian Intervention and the 2005 World Summit', *Ethics & International Affairs*, 20(2): 143–169.

Bellamy, A. (2015). 'The Islamic State and the Case for Responsibility to Protect.' *International Coalition for the Responsibility to Protect*. Available online at: http://protectiongateway.com/2015/04/21/the-islamic-state-and-the-case-for-responsibility-to-protect/.

Bellamy, A. and Wheeler, N. (2014). 'Humanitarian Intervention in World Politics', in Baylis, J., Smith, S., and Owens, P. (eds), *The Globalization of World Politics: An Introduction to International Relations*, sixth edition. Oxford: Oxford University Press.

Cohen, S. (2001). *States of Denial: Knowing about Atrocities and Suffering*. Cambridge: Polity Press.

Deudney, D. and Ikenberry, J. (2009). 'The Myth of the Autocratic Revival: Why Liberal Democracy Will Prevail', *Foreign Affairs*, 88(1): 77–93.

De Waal, A. (2007). 'Darfur and the Failure of the Responsibility to Protect', *International Affairs*, 6: 1039–1054.

Dixon, M. (2005). *International Law*, fifth edition. Oxford: Oxford University Press.

Dunne, T. (2014). 'Liberalism', in Baylis, J., Smith, S., and Owens, P. (eds), *The Globalisation of World Politics*, sixth edition. Oxford: Oxford University Press. Pp. 113–125.

Etzioni, A. (2005). 'Genocide Prevention in the New Global Architecture', *British Journal of Politics and International Relations*, 7: 469–484.

Evans, G. (2008a). *The Responsibility to Protect*. Washington, DC: Brookings Institution Press.

Evans, G. (2008b). 'The Responsibility to Protect: An Idea whose Time Has Come… and Gone?' *International Relations*, 22: 283–298.

Hafner-Burton, E. and Tsutsui, K. (2007). 'Justice Lost! The Failure of International Human Rights Law to Matter Where Needed Most', *Journal of Peace Research*, 44(4): 407–425.

ICISS. (2001). *The Responsibility to Protect*. International Commission on Intervention and State Sovereignty. Canada: International Development Research Centre.

Ikenberry, G.J. (2009). 'Liberal Internationalism 3.0: America and the Dilemmas of Liberal World Order', *Perspectives on Politics*, 7(1): 71–87.

Ikenberry, G.J. (2011). 'The Future of the Liberal World Order: Internationalism After America', *Foreign Affairs*, 90(3): 56–62.

Jacobs, S., Jacobson, R., and Marchbank, J. (2000). *States of Conflict: Gender, Violence and Resistance*. London: Zed Books.

Koh, H. (2002). 'A United States Human Rights Policy for the 21st Century', *Saint Louis University Law Journal*, 46(2): 293–344.

Morgenthau, H. (1951). *In Defense of the National Interest: A Critical Examination of American Foreign Policy*. New York: Knopf.

Moses, J. (2013). 'Sovereignty as Responsibility? A Realist Critique of the Responsibility to Protect', *Review of International Studies*, 3(9): 113–135.

Naim, M. (2002). *Five Wars of Globalization. The Grotius Lecture Series.* Lecture presented at the American Society of International Law's ('ASIL') 96th Annual Meeting on March 13–16. American University Washington College of Law, the ASIL, and the International Legal Studies Program.

Niemann, G. (2005). 'War Crimes, Crimes Against Humanity and Genocide in International Criminal Law', in Reichel, P. (ed.), *Handbook of Transnational Crime and Justice.* London: Sage.

Pogge, T. (2008). *World Poverty and Human Rights*, second edition. Cambridge: Polity Press.

Ritzer, G. (1996). *Sociological Theory*, fourth edition. Singapore: McGraw-Hill International Editions.

Schirato, T. and Webb, J. (2003). *Understanding Globalisation.* London: Sage.

Tickner, A. (1992). *Gender in International Relations: Feminist Perspectives on Achieving Global Security.* Oxford: Columbia University Press.

Tickner, A. (2014). *A Feminist Voyage Through International Relations.* Oxford: Oxford University Press.

True, J. (2012). *The Political Economy of Violence Against Women.* Oxford: Oxford University Press.

Tutu, D. (19 February 2008). 'Responsibility to Protect', *International Herald Tribune*, 20 February. Available online at: www.responsibilitytoprotect.org/index.php/component/content/article/129-africa/1521-desmond-tutu-taking-the-responsibility-to-protect (accessed January 2, 2015).

United Nations Press Release. (2014). 10 October. Available online at: www.un.org/en/preventgenocide/adviser/pdf/10.10.14%20Statement%20of%20the%20Special%20Advisers%20on%20the%20situation%20in%20Kobane.pdf (accessed January 6, 2015).

United Nations Press Release. (2014). 12 August. Available online at: www.un.org/en/preventgenocide/adviser/pdf/2014-08-12.Statement%20of%20the%20Special%20Advisers%20on%20Iraq.pdf (accessed January 6, 2015).

United Nations General Assembly Security Council. (2014). *Fulfilling Our Collective Responsibility: International Assistance and the Responsibility to Protect.* Report of the Secretary-General, July 11. A/68/947–S/2014/449. United Nations.

United Nations General Assembly Security Council. (2013). *Responsibility to Protect: State Responsibility and Prevention.* Report of the Secretary General, July 9. A/67/929-S/2013/399. United Nations.

Wallerstein, I. (2005). *World-Systems Analysis: An Introduction.* London: Duke University Press.

Weiss, T. (2011). *Thinking About Global Governance.* London: Routledge.

7 Terrorism and counter-terrorist strategies

> The more fully behavioural scientists take account of politics, the more sensible and the more modest their efforts to contribute to peace become.
>
> (Waltz, 1959: 79)

Chapter 1 examined the theorisation of globalisation highlighting the salience of globalisation discourse for contemporary conceptualisation of security and as a tool of political speech. As detailed in Chapter 3, the concept of globalisation has also been central to explanations regarding how and why certain prohibited cross-border activities became criminalised around the world, also becoming central to accounts explaining the internationalisation of crime control and policing (Andreas and Nadelmann, 2006). The earlier modernisation theory, penetrated by the Durkheimian view that the social problems of contemporary society comprise temporary aberrations caused by rapid social change prompted by industrialisation, urbanisation and increasing dynamic density (increasing populations), is a position also evident within recent National Security discourse from within the United Kingdom:

> Social and demographic trends will shape the future. Though Britain's population (like that of the US) is forecast to grow, much of the western world faces the ageing and shrinking of its populations. Overall the world's population will continue to increase. UN projections suggest it will reach 9.2 billion by 2050, compared to 6.9 billion now. In some areas, population growth will outpace the development of stable governance. Poor infrastructure, political exclusion and unemployment, combined with population and resource pressures, caused in part by urbanisation, will increase the risk of instability and conflict. By 2030, population increase will mean that global demand for food and energy will rise by up to 50% and water by up to 30%.
>
> (HM Government, 2010: 17)

Within this narrative, social strain associated with population growth articulated through the discourse of modernisation appear simultaneously with the discourse of globalisation. This discourse emphasises how businesspeople, migrant workers, tourists, goods, services, capital and information are flowing around the globe faster and more extensively than at any point in human history (Bowling and Sheptycki, 2012: 113). Such flows however are a source of insecurity, a contradiction recognised within the 2010 UK National Security strategy. Thus, while aspects of globalisation are viewed favourably, thereby working in the UK's national interest, offering a liberal vision of 'unparalleled opportunities', with the potential for 'lifting billions out of poverty' (HM Government, 2010: 4), globalisation is also presented as creating significant challenges for national governments, making it much harder to isolate states from economic or geopolitical shocks occurring outside of their own territory. Aspects of globalisation are also explicitly identified as generating ideologically driven threats to national security as extremists capitalise on opportunities arising from technological developments, social networking and twenty-four-hour news media (HM Government, 2010: 16).

Processes of modernisation and globalisation are therefore conceived within the UK National Security Strategy, as providing the potential for normative conflict as increased interconnectivity exposes populations to alternative values, norms, cultures and religions:

> We may have to deal with threats motivated by different ideologies which compete with our values. At present only Al Qaeda represents a major ideologically driven threat to the national security of the UK and our allies. But in the future some regionally based ideologies could affect us through our role as an international 'hub', through the engagement of some among our diaspora populations, or through driving conflict which impacts on our interests. It is a realistic possibility that in the next ten years extremists motivated by new ideologies or narratives could cross the line between advocacy and terrorism.
>
> (HM Government, 2010: 16)

Environmental factors are presented within the strategy as 'risk multipliers' exacerbating existing tensions and heightening security risks associated with climate change, failed states, displacement and competition for scarce natural resources. It is against this background that international terrorism is identified as the principle current national security threat (HM Government, 2010: 18) featuring as one of the four highest priority risks facing the United Kingdom (HM Government, 2010: 11). Here, terrorism, development, transnational crime and internal conflict become fused, reflecting the need for a broadened conceptualisation of national security, which extends beyond the traditional concern with state-upon-state conflict, also lending support for the political recognition that national governments are currently ill-equipped to deal adequately with the national security threats in isolation:

> We and our allies are supporting the Government of Afghanistan to prevent Afghan territory from again being used by Al Qaeda as a secure

> base from which to plan attacks on the UK or our allies. Terrorists can also exploit instability in countries like Somalia or Yemen. This instability can spread from one country to another as we saw in the Balkans at the end of the last century. Lawless regions provide a haven for terrorist groups and organised criminal networks alike.
>
> (HM Government, 2010: 13)

Counter-terrorist strategy therefore reflects several of the broader trends identified in Chapter 1, including the influence of the concept of globalisation upon crime and security responses, both as a form of political speech and as a driver of fundamental shifts within the security agendas of nation-states, with implications for the structure and organisation of the contemporary security landscape. As detailed in Chapter 1, international terrorism, epitomised by the tragic events of 9/11, resulted in the blurring of boundaries between internal and external notions of security, foreign policy and national security concerns and served to destabilise traditional distinctions between crime and war, military intelligence and police missions (Aas, 2007; Bigo, 2000). In this chapter, we examine the international (UN), regional (EU) and national (UK) counter-terrorism strategies with a view to assessing the adequacy of existing responses to contemporary threats posed by cross-border violent extremism. The chapter will initially proceed with an examination of the crime prevention approaches adopted within the strategies before assessing their adequacy in the light of the criminological and international relations perspectives presented in Chapter 3. Following Andreas and Nadelmann's (2006) critique of what they term 'the standard view of globalisation', namely an approach which portrays 'the growth of international crime control as simply a natural and predictable response to the explosive growth of transnational crime', we examine the place of historical and political contextualisation within existing counter-terrorism policy before directing attention to broader economic and political structural factors which have been implicated as root causes underpinning terrorist thought and action. The chapter will close with a discussion of the key challenges facing law enforcement agencies and the role of power politics in undermining crime control efforts within this policy domain.

Situational Crime Prevention

Concerned with an analysis of the circumstances giving rise to specific kinds of crime, Situational Crime Prevention (SCP) approaches consist of opportunity-reducing measures introduced through systematic managerial and environmental change to reduce the opportunity for specific forms of crimes to occur (Clarke, 1997). SCP pays tribute to a range of classically informed criminological approaches, based upon the notion of rational and egoistic man, which direct attention to the need to analyse factors underpinning offenders' decision-making processes to engage, persist and desist from particular criminal activities. Such theories emphasise motivational aspects including the satisfaction of various needs (initially economic but later extending to sexual, psychological and social needs), the existence of techniques of neutralisation and moral judgements (introduced in Chapter 5) which, it is suggested, serve to undermine the effectiveness of social controls against crime, and deterrent factors including individual offenders' perception of the costs and risks involved in such activities. The presence of pragmatic facilitators serving to make crime more likely to occur, including the availability of time to commit the crime, individual knowledge of available opportunities and the possession of the necessary skills and techniques to complete the proscribed activity are also focal concerns of such studies, factors viewed as underpinning individual decisions to engage in crime. SCP approaches are also indebted to studies which concentrate upon the environment in which offences occur, directing attention to the presence or absence of social controls (deterrents) and surveillance (capable guardians), also directing attention to the association of particular criminal activities with the lifestyle patterns and routine activities of the population. Concerned with efforts to design out crime, these approaches endeavour to reduce the anonymity of offenders, increase surveillance and reduce escape routes, also exploring seasonal and temporal variation in the commission of crime. Having systematically addressed the commission of the act and the environment in which the act takes place, such approaches also examine the availability of suitable targets or victims, once again identifying patterns with a view to reducing or preventing victimisation. Clarke's (1997) *Situational Crime Prevention: Successful Case Studies* explicitly associates the theoretical indebtedness of SCP approaches to include: Clarke's (1977; 1980) 'choice' model; Newman's (1972) 'defensible space approach'; Jeffery's (1971) 'crime prevention through environmental design' (or CPTED) approach; Goldstein's (1979) 'problem-oriented policing model'; Clarke and Cornish (1985) and Cornish and Clarke's (1986) 'rational choice' perspective on crime; and, Cohen and Felson's (1979) routine activity approach. Drawing upon the insights granted by these studies, Situational Crime Prevention approaches therefore aim to make the commission of crime more difficult and risky, or less rewarding and excusable as judged by a wide range of offenders (Clarke, 1997).

UN, EU and UK counter-terrorism strategy

While it will be demonstrated that situational crime prevention approaches have been particularly influential in guiding counter-terrorism strategy, co-existing alongside dominant narratives of modernisation and globalisation, this approach is not without limitations. Opportunity reduction activities have been challenged for causing spatial, temporal, tactical and/or target displacement, as the introduction of measures serves to alter patterns of criminal behaviour, displace activities to other places, at different times, using different methods, or employing alternative forms of activity (Joyce, 2012: 58–59). Situational Crime Prevention approaches therefore do not necessarily stop the occurrence of a prohibited activity nor do they address the underlying causes of criminal behaviour, which may require attention to be directed towards wider structural factors requiring psychological, social or political interventions (Clarke, 2005: 57, cited in Joyce, 2012: 59).

Here we detail the four work-streams contained within the UN, EU and UK counter-terrorism strategies, each seeking to reduce the risk faced from terrorism, nationally, regionally and internationally. It will be suggested that each approach embraces a liberal framework advocating proportionality, the rule of law and the maintenance and expansion of liberal institutions to better equip states to respond to contemporary security challenges (generated by modernisation and globalisation). Within each strategy, it is evident that measures are introduced to reduce opportunities for terrorist acts and the spread of extremist ideologies, with mechanisms put in place to enhance the risks faced by those involved, while simultaneously seeking to forge a new moral consensus based upon liberal values. Situational Crime Prevention measures therefore will be shown to exist simultaneously alongside modernisation and liberal efforts towards normative consensus building efforts, working to undermine and challenge the existence of justificatory ideologies and techniques of neutralisation, which are viewed as potentially lessening the effectiveness of societal controls upon behaviour.

The final part of the chapter will engage in an assessment regarding the adequacy of these strategies; in the meantime however, it is useful to compare and contrast the UK national and EU regional approaches with the UN international approach to counter-terrorism. While each approach is seen as characterised by consensus building and opportunity reduction measures, placing weight upon Situational Crime Prevention techniques as tools to counter terrorism, it will be suggested that the international approach is more explicitly weighted in favour of social crime prevention methods, in many ways reflecting the broader remit and ambition of the United Nations to address the social, political and economic root causes of the world's contemporary problems and security concerns. However, despite its best efforts, the international framework, which remains tied to the discourses of modernisation and globalisation, remains silent with respect to international relations, power politics and contemporary international history. The chapter will therefore close with a consideration of critical theory and alternative counter-terrorism strategy emanating from within international relations and social science literature.

The development of a comprehensive vision of security

In 2004 the United Nations Report of the High-level Panel on Threats, Challenges and Change, *A more secure world: our shared responsibility* (United Nations General Assembly, 2004, A/59/565) endorsed a broader, more comprehensive concept of security, going further to insist that contemporary threats such as terrorism or civil wars or extreme poverty must not be treated in isolation. The report made clear the interconnectivity of contemporary security threats, highlighting the potential for individual threats such as extreme poverty to generate the conditions necessary for further threats to emerge. Addressing the root causes of security threats was therefore conceived as an essential component of the collective security solution, a vision that highlighted the centrality of the Millennium Development Goals in achieving this objective.

Within the 2004 High-level Panel report, the Secretary General expressed his view that the United Nations had failed to make the best use of its assets in the fight against terrorism. In particular, a lack of consensus in the definition of terrorism was identified as a key obstacle, with the Secretary General pledging to take a lead in promoting a new comprehensive and principled strategy against terrorism (UN, 2004, A/59/565: 1–5). Within the Panel report, terrorism is described as an attack upon liberal values, particularly 'respect for human rights' and 'the rule of law' alongside an attack upon 'the rules of war that protect civilians; tolerance among peoples and nations; and the peaceful resolution of conflict'. These values, we are informed, lie at the heart of the Charter of the United Nations. The international description of terrorism therefore parallels the European Council Framework Decision 2008/919/JHA of 28 November 2008, which amended the earlier Framework Decision 2002/475/JHA on combating terrorism, conceiving terrorism as:

> one of the most serious violations of the universal values of human dignity, liberty, equality and solidarity, respect for human rights and fundamental freedoms on which the European Union is founded. It also represents one of the most serious attacks on democracy and the rule of law, principles which are common to the Member States and on which the European Union is based.
>
> (Council of the European Union, 2008/919/JHA)

As one would expect therefore, both the EU Counter-Terrorism Strategy and the UN recommendation for a global counter-terrorism strategy are aligned with their principle duties of (international and regional) security, to protect 'the values they believe in'. The UK Counter-Terrorism Strategy similarly employs a liberal framework committed to the promotion of a normative consensus around the values of democracy, free speech, tolerance and human rights. This framework, which utilises the rule of law and institutions to generate the conditions necessary for international cooperation, explicitly seeks 'to reduce the risk to the UK and its interests overseas from terrorism, so that people can go about their lives freely and with confidence' (HM Government, 2011a: 9).

Following the High-level Panel report, in March 2005, on the first anniversary of the Madrid train bombings, Kofi Annan set out elements of a global counter-terrorism strategy. The proposed strategy consisted of five pillars: I. Dissuading people from resorting to terrorism or supporting it; II. Denying terrorists the means to carry out an attack; III. Deterring States from supporting terrorism; IV. Developing State capacity to defeat terrorism; and V. Defending human rights (UN, 2006, A/60/825). Later the same month, within the Secretary General's report, entitled 'In Larger Freedom: Towards Development, Security, and Human Rights for All' (United Nations General Assembly, 2005, A/59/2005), Kofi Annan reiterated his call for member states to adopt a strategy along those lines.

The 2005 World Summit Outcome Document (United Nations General Assembly, 2005, A/RES/60/1), referred to in the previous chapter in relation to the R2P norm of humanitarian intervention, further welcomed the United Nations Secretary General's 2004 identification of elements of a counter-terrorism strategy, advocating the adoption and implementation of a strategy to promote a 'comprehensive, coordinated and consistent response, at the national, regional and international levels, to counter terrorism … without delay'. Significantly, the report promoted an approach 'which also takes into account the conditions conducive to the spread of terrorism' (United Nations General Assembly, 2005, A/RES/60/1: 22). This approach reflected the wider ambition of the earlier 2004 High Level Panel report, which recognised wider structural facilitators of terrorism including 'environments of despair, humiliation, poverty, political oppression, extremism and human rights abuse'. Significantly, the Panel report alludes to the centrality of conflict and international relations in the emergence of terrorism, stating 'it [terrorism] also flourishes in contexts of regional conflict and foreign occupation; and it profits from weak State capacity to maintain law and order' (United Nations General Assembly, 2004, A/59/565: 45). However, the report falls short of providing an historical and political contextualisation of these developments (a point to which we shall return shortly).

In September 2006, the United Nations General Assembly adopted Resolution 60/288, which, set out the United Nations Global Counter-Terrorism Strategy and Action Plan. The UN strategy is divided into four components, thereby revising and merging the five pillars identified within the 2006 A/60/825 Report of the Secretary General. These components include: 1. Measures to address the conditions conducive to the spread of terrorism; 2. Measures to prevent and combat terrorism; 3. Measures to build states' capacity to prevent and combat terrorism and to strengthen the role of the United Nations system, and 4. Measures to ensure respect for human rights for all and the rule of law as the fundamental basis of the fight against terrorism.

The 2005 EU Counter-Terrorism Strategy similarly covers four strands of work, although the sequencing and the wording differ. The four work-streams include: 1. 'Prevent': to prevent people turning to terrorism by tackling the factors or root causes which can lead to radicalisation and recruitment, in Europe and internationally (paralleling the 2011 UK Counter-Terrorism Strategy's second strand 'Prevent'); 2. 'Protect': To protect citizens and infrastructure and reduce vulnerability to attack including through improved security of borders, transport and critical infrastructure (paralleling the UK Counter-Terrorism Strategy's third strand 'Protect'); 3. 'Pursue': To pursue and investigate terrorists across our borders and globally to impede planning, travel, and communications, to disrupt support networks, to cut off funding and access to attack materials and bring terrorists to justice (which reflects the UK Counter-Terrorism Strategy's first strand 'Pursue'); and, 4. 'Respond': To prepare ourselves, in the spirit of solidarity to manage and minimise the consequences of a terrorist attack, by improving capabilities to deal with the aftermath, the co-ordination of the response, and the needs of victims (reflecting the content of the UK Counter-Terrorism Strategy's fourth work-stream entitled 'Prepare') (Council of the European Union, 2005).

The Council Framework Decision 2008/919/JHA is informed by the Council and Commission Action Plan, which implemented the Hague Programme on Strengthening Freedom, Security and Justice in the European Union (Official Journal of the European Union, 2005/C 53/01). This work acknowledged that a global response is required to address terrorism advocating that states must focus on different aspects of prevention, preparedness and response to further enhance, and where necessary complement, Member States' capabilities to fight terrorism, concentrating particularly on recruitment, financing, risk analysis, protection of critical infrastructures and consequence management. It is to these aspects of the UN, EU and UK Counter-Terrorism strategies that we now turn, with a view to emphasising the continuing salience of opportunity reduction and risk enhancing measures, underpinned by the narrative of globalisation and modernisation discourse. Measures addressing the conditions conducive to the spread of terrorism, which are also captured within the 'Prevent' work-stream of the UK national and EU regional strategies will subsequently be addressed in the penultimate section of the chapter, paving the way for alternative perspectives regarding the structural root causes of terrorism.

Measures to prevent and combat terrorism

The association of 'Pursue' within both the UK and EU strategies with the classical school of thought is evident in its emphasis on punishment as a deterrent to crime and in its efforts to ensure the certainty and timeliness of punishment. Thus, within the UK strategy, 'Pursue' entails facilitating the 'detection and investigation of threats at the earliest possible stage, with measures aimed at disrupting terrorist activity before it can endanger the public and, wherever possible, prosecuting those responsible' (HM Government, 2011a: 10). Similarly, the 2005 EU Counter-Terrorism strategy endeavours to disrupt terrorist activity, pursue terrorists across borders, further seeking to 'impede terrorists' planning, disrupt their networks and the activities of recruiters to terrorism, cut off terrorists' funding and access to attack materials'.

As with the UK strategy, the EU strategy also aspires to bring perpetrators to justice, reflecting classical concerns with the proportionality and effectiveness of laws, powers and measures. Within both strategies, 'Pursue' is directed towards improvements within investigations and the collection and admissibility of evidence, alongside the promotion of police and judicial cooperation, exchange of information and intelligence and harmonisation in legislative systems. Drawing upon expertise from key police, judicial, national security and intelligence agencies, (including the Joint Situation Centre, Europol, Eurojust, and the Financial Action Task Force, detailed in Chapter 4) and, utilising newly developed instruments such as the European Arrest Warrant and Joint Investigation Teams, the European and UK strategies accordingly endeavour to plug the gap between the emergence of criminal opportunities (which have arisen as a consequence of globalisation), and the measures available to law enforcement and security agencies to protect their populations. Thus, just as technological advancements are identified as having presented criminals and terrorists with criminal opportunities, within both strategies, law enforcement and security agencies are also encouraged to capitalise on such developments, developing new IT systems (such as the Visa Information System and next generation Schengen Information System). The introduction and implementation of legislation to counter money laundering and cash transfers to address terrorist financing, is also promoted, along with measures to restrict access to weapons and explosives and providing technical assistance to enhance the capability of priority third countries.

Both strategies therefore embrace a view of terrorism as but one of several different expressions of a broader phenomenon fuelled by globalisation, where governments are pitted against international networks of stateless civilians, reflecting a perceived interdependency between terrorism, the trafficking of drugs, arms, people, the illegal trade in intellectual property, and money laundering (Naim, 2002). The argument within this position is that the tools and trends of globalisation have done more to empower international criminal networks than governments as they capitalise upon advances in transportation, information and communication technology. The new international threat environment therefore reflects a situation where growing 'security interdependence' results in state security becoming 'increasingly dependent on what goes on elsewhere' (Ikenberry, 2009: 38; Aas, 2007: 104). Recognising state inability to deal with modernisation and the need for transnational cooperation in order to solve common problems, scholars prescribe 'more liberalism' as the solution to the contemporary security challenges. Liberal commentators, therefore, present the growth in interdependence in the realm of security as having generated a demand for a retooled and reinvigorated liberal institutionalism programme; based on consensus building and problem solving (Deudney and Ikenberry, 2009), requiring multilateral rules and institutions (Ikenberry, 2011) with pressure upon the international community to build the capacity and legitimacy to intervene in weak and troubled states (Ikenberry, 2009: 38). The proposed solution therefore adopts an enlarged conceptualisation of security, with implications for the principles of sovereignty and non-intervention. As a proponent of the 'standard view', Naim (2002) for instance, argues that trends of globalisation have rendered obsolete many of the existing institutions, legal frameworks, military doctrines, weapons systems, law enforcement techniques, and even basic definitions and principles on which states have relied for years. Naim contends moreover that states currently need to adapt to new realities, developing more flexible notions of sovereignty and strengthening existing multilateral institutions and devising new mechanisms and institutions to address the altered security climate. Naim's proposed solution therefore fits with the liberal vision of a rule-based system in which states trade and cooperate to achieve mutual gains (Dunne, 2014), strengthening liberal institutions, engaging in cooperative security and collective problem solving to enable progressive change, embracing the normative consensus around democracy and human rights.

The purpose of the UK '*Contest*'s third strand and EU strategy's second strand, '*Protect*' is consequently to strengthen the 'protection against a terrorist attack at home and interests overseas and so reduce vulnerability' (HM Government, 2011a: 12–13). This work-stream involves strengthening defence of key targets and reducing the impact of an attack (Council of the European Union, 2005, 14468/4/05 REV4: 10). '*Protect*' within both the UK and EU Counter-Terrorism strategies consequently reflects the content of the second UN work-stream, which introduces 'measures to prevent and combat terrorism' intending to deny terrorists access to the means to carry out their attacks, to their targets and to the desired impact of their attacks. The second strand of the UN Global Counter-Terrorism strategy therefore merges aspects of the third and fourth pillars of the earlier 2006 UN General Assembly Report of the Secretary General, 'Uniting against terrorism: recommendations for a global counter-terrorism strategy' (United Nations General Assembly, 2006, A/60/825). Thus, in seeking to denying terrorists the means to carry out an attack, the international strategy seeks to reduce opportunities to generate and move finances, to acquire weapons, to recruit and train cadres, and to communicate (particularly through use of the Internet), to deny access to travel and to access intended targets (United Nations General Assembly, 2006, A/60/825: 8–14). This approach therefore recognises that technologies associated with globalisation have been exploited by terrorists, increasing the ability of terrorist groups to work together, share information and reach out to previously unavailable audiences (Kiras, 2014: 358). The UN strategy also requires member states to 'refrain from organising, instigating, facilitating, participating in, financing, encouraging or tolerating terrorist activities', further requiring states to undertake measures to prevent their territories from being used for terrorist installations or training camps, or 'for the preparation or organization of terrorist acts' (United Nations General Assembly, 2006, A/RES/60/288: 5–7). These measures therefore reflect the fourth pillar and the earlier World Summit Outcome requirement for states to refrain from supporting terrorist activities (United Nations General Assembly, 2005, A/RES/60/1; United Nations General Assembly, 2006 A/60/825).

It is evident then that the measures introduced within the '*Protect*' strand within both the UK and EU strategies are therefore broadly aligned with the UN measures to prevent and combat terrorism, embracing situational crime prevention techniques, directed towards securing critical infrastructure, assessing and managing risks to potential target environments and safeguarding hazardous materials, which may be used by terrorists in an attack. Efforts directed towards border, transport and cargo security alongside measures to improve protective security for crowded places feature within these work-streams. Situational Crime Prevention's opportunity reduction techniques including target hardening, access control, entry and exit screening, and surveillance methods are key tools, with '*Protect*' advocating the utilisation of technological advancements and facilitating and improving coordination of law enforcement responses, nationally, regionally and internationally to secure these goals. Technical assistance on protective security is also included within this strand for priority third countries. Practical measures remain wedded to the liberal framework, with the rule of law emphasised within this section, particularly in relation to the legislative framework facilitating the apprehension and prosecution or extradition of perpetrators of terrorist and wider criminal acts (including terrorist financing), promoting mutual judicial assistance and extradition agreements, and strengthened cooperation between law enforcement agencies. The UN's second work-stream also therefore incorporates a number of the fourth pillar elements identified within the earlier Secretary General's Report A/60/825, particularly in relation to the strengthening of the international legal architecture and development and maintenance of an effective and rule of law-based criminal justice system, all the while embracing human rights norms.

Paralleling the EU and UK approaches, the international strategy similarly emphasises the strengthening of border and customs controls, utilising institutions (such as the law) and organisations (e.g. International Civil Aviation Organisation, the World Customs Organisation and the International Criminal Police Organisation – detailed in Chapter 4), to reduce opportunities for potential perpetrators and to act as deterrents, enhancing the risks of detection and prosecution. Measures contained within this work-stream again endeavour to strengthen the defence of vulnerable targets, such as infrastructures and public places, and reducing the impact of an attack, assessing and managing risks to potential target environments and safeguarding hazardous materials. The strategy therefore advocates the utilisation of a range of Situational Crime Prevention opportunity-reducing measures to control facilitators and harden targets against attack, enhancing the security of manufacturing and document security and introducing access controls (for example, travel bans introduced under the United Nations sanctions regime and applied via UN Special Notices). Civil protection measures are also included to 'prevent and combat' terrorism, introducing measures to respond to terrorist attacks and other disasters.

Measures to Prevent therefore reflect a liberal criminal justice framework, emphasising the cooperative strengthening of the existing domestic and international legislative and institutional framework, employing situational crime prevention measures to reduce terrorist opportunities and access to targets. These measures are articulated within a globalisation and modernisation narrative, revealing the presence of Andreas and Nadelmann's 'standard view of globalisation' which suggests the intensification of contemporary crime control infrastructure is a logical response to enhanced criminal threats emanating from the opportunities provided by globalising processes.

Measures to build states' capacity to prevent and combat terrorism and to strengthen the role of the United Nations system

The UN's third strand introduces 'measures to build States' capacity to prevent and combat terrorism and to strengthen the role of the United Nations system' (United Nations General Assembly, 2006, A/RES/60/288: 7–8). The third strand consequently reflects the Secretary General's earlier A/60/825 fourth pillar which recommended seven priority areas directed towards capacity enhancement: 1. Promoting the rule of law, respect for human rights, and effective criminal justice systems; 2. Promoting quality education and religious and cultural tolerance; 3. Countering the financing of terrorism; 4. Ensuring transport security; 5. Harnessing the power of the Internet to counter terrorism; 6. Improving the protection of soft targets and the response to attacks on them; 7. Strengthening state capacity to prevent terrorists from acquiring nuclear, biological, chemical, or radiological materials, and ensuring better preparedness for an attack with such materials. Pillar four also emphasised resourcing and governance arrangements of the international response, information sharing, reporting mechanisms, and steps to institutionalise the Task Force within the Secretariat (United Nations General Assembly, 2006, A/60/825: 15–22).

It is evident therefore that several of the original fourth pillar priority areas were later reallocated within the UN Global Counter-Terrorism Strategy to be included within 'measures to prevent and combat terrorism', detailed previously. The priority areas that were retained in the final version under the banner of 'measures to enhance states' capacity' included resourcing and governance capacity-building measures encouraging states to enhance their voluntary contributions to United Nations counter-terrorism cooperation and technical assistance projects.

Fourth pillar concerns with strengthening the international legal architecture and development of an effective and rule of law-based criminal justice system are also apparent within the third strand's emphasis upon enhanced cooperation, technical assistance and the sharing of best practice. In this regard, the third strand of the UN strategy encourages the utilisation of the skills and expertise of key institutions and agencies. Thus, the Secretariat is allocated the role of ensuring overall coordination and coherence of the UN response, with a range of further bodies responsible for working in consultation with the Counter-Terrorism Committee and its Executive Directorate. Examples include: the UN's Counter-Terrorism Implementation Task Force; the Terrorism Prevention Branch of the UN Office on Drugs and Crime; the International Monetary Fund; World Bank; International Criminal Police Organisation; International Atomic Energy Agency; the Organisation for the Prohibition of Chemical Weapons; World Health Organisation; International Maritime Organisation; the World Customs Organisation; and, the International Civil Aviation Organisation (detailed in Chapter 4).

These bodies build international, regional and national capacity through the advancement of cooperation in the provision of technical assistance, the implementation of international conventions and protocols related to the prevention and suppression of terrorism, including efforts directed towards the fourth pillar concern to create an adequate anti-money-laundering regime, also tackling the financing of terrorism. Expertise is also drawn upon to identify and address national shortfalls in areas of transport security, border security, and to prevent and prepare for terrorist attacks, revealing an overlap between the measures to 'prevent' and those designed to 'build capacity'.

The fourth, and final strand of the UK strategy *Contest*; entitled '*Prepare*', aims to provide an efficient and effective response to attack and to enhance preparedness. Within the EU strategy, these issues feature under the heading of '*Respond*'. Despite the divergence in terminology, both strands aim to mitigate the impact of a terrorist attack, including efforts to bring a terrorist attack to an end, and to increase resilience to enable recovery (HM Government, 2011a: 13). This strand entails the creation of crisis coordination arrangements and operational procedures (Council of the European Union, 2005, 14468/04/05 REV4: 15) enhancing information sharing, media and communication coordination and interoperability between emergency services and enhancing capabilities and resources. Again, technical assistance to priority third countries also features within this strand with the European Strategy further directing attention to the role of key European institutions including the Commission in managing consequences of terrorist attack.

While it is evident that there remains overlap between the two sections detailed above and some confusion stemming from the reorganisation of priority areas between the April 2006 recommendation report (UN A/60/825) and the final Global Counter-Terrorism strategy (UN September 2006, A/RES/60/288), it is nevertheless clear that the international strategy remains underpinned by a liberal framework, emphasising the utility of building institutional capacity to counter terrorism, advocating multilateral action and technical assistance to strengthen the legislative framework and instruments to better prevent, prepare and respond to attack. Focusing upon the sharing of information and best practice, the UN's third strand therefore claims to build capacity through multilateral cooperation, enhancing the coordination and coherence of the international counter-terrorism response.

Measures to ensure respect for human rights for all and the rule of law as the fundamental basis of the fight against terrorism

The fourth strand of the UN Counter-Terrorism Strategy contains 'measures to ensure respect for human rights for all and the rule of law as the fundamental basis of the fight against terrorism' (United Nations General Assembly, 2006, A/RES/60/288: 9). This focus reflects the fifth pillar of the earlier Report of the Secretary General, which stated:

> Only by placing counter-terrorism within a rule-of-law framework can we safeguard the internationally valued standard that outlaws terrorism, reduce the conditions that may generate cycles of terrorist violence, and address grievances and resentment that may be conducive to terrorist recruitment. To compromise on the protection of human rights would hand terrorists a victory they cannot achieve on their own. And when human rights are abused as part of a campaign against terrorism, terrorists exploit the abuse to mobilize recruits and seek to further justify their actions.
>
> (United Nations General Assembly, 2006, A/60/825: 22–23)

The 2006 UN Global Counter-Terrorism Strategy therefore reminds states of their obligations under international law, promoting implementation of core international instruments on human rights law, refugee law and international humanitarian law and offering assistance to ensure due respect for human rights and fundamental freedoms while countering terrorism. This strand also seeks to promote the creation and implementation of domestic legislative frameworks for terrorist acts. Both the UK strategy and the EU strategy similarly express a commitment to human rights and the rule of law, recognising a link between human rights violations, resentment and the potential for radicalisation (HM Government, 2011a: 33; Council of the European Union, 2005, 14469/4/05 REV4: 6).

The UN strategy, as one might expect, is therefore consistent with the rule-based liberal framework contained within the 2005 EU and 2011 UK Counter-Terrorism Strategies. Each strategy seeks to forge a moral consensus condemning terrorism as a violation of human rights in all its forms and manifestations, advocating action to prevent and combat terrorism, particularly through the rule of law. Reflecting hallmarks of liberal internationalism, the international framework advocates intergovernmental arrangements and multilateral rules and institutions as solutions, requesting that member states make use of existing international conventions, protocols and resolutions against terrorism, and reach an agreement on a comprehensive convention on international terrorism. In this regard, each approach recognises that human rights violations may be both the product of terrorist acts, and also, potential motivating factors underpinning terrorist acts, a view that places liberal values and principles as 'universal' and 'under threat'. These assumptions regarding the universality of liberal values, norms and principles have recently become subject to challenge as detailed within the previous chapter, a point to which we shall return shortly.

Following Durkheimian theory, human rights may be interpreted as a new form of collective conscience, offering a possible solution to the global disequilibrium caused by industrialisation and urbanisation (later identified as processes of modernisation and more recently as processes of globalisation). As detailed in Chapter 3, within this approach rapid social change is believed to generate social strain as people with different norms, values, cultures and religions come into contact with one another, undermining traditional societal controls upon behaviour.

Durkheim's solution to modern egoism entailed the creation of a new moral system of society grounded in freedom and communal solidarity, a modern form of collective conscience guided by a morality which requires them to give due recognition to the inherent dignity, rights and freedom of the individual (Ritzer, 1996). It is evident from a cursory examination of contemporary counter-terrorism strategy that human rights today comprise a central component of the liberal rule of law framework employed within the international, regional and national approaches. Counter-terrorism strategies embrace the spread of an international normative system of human rights, alongside liberal principles of 'democracy' and the 'rule of law', which, as mentioned earlier, are presented as 'universal' yet 'under attack'. This component of the international counter-terrorism strategy is consequently normative, underpinned by progressive notions of societal change and the inevitability of further liberalism, integration and cooperation. Human rights, within the liberal framework, accordingly serve as a form of socialising agent, creating norms and expectations and acting as a guide for relations between the international society of states and between states and their citizens. For Dunne (2014: 123) advocates of liberalism believe 'that there is only one path to modernisation and that illiberal voices will be drowned out by the imperatives to open markets and hold governments accountable'. Counter-terrorism strategies, underpinned by liberal assumptions regarding the universality of human rights and their legitimacy as the normative foundation for the current world order, do not therefore engage with the 'liberal crisis' thesis presented by Ikenberry discussed in the previous chapter. Within discussions of human rights, none of the strategies currently acknowledges that liberal values or ideas are under threat (from autocratic states or from non-state actors), or indeed that they themselves are historically situated, socially constructed phenomena. Ahistorical and depoliticised, human rights are therefore not conceived within such orthodox accounts as part of an 'ideologically driven', moral imperialistic project of liberalism, but rather, taken as given, namely, *the* moral foundation of global international society.

The conceptualisation of human rights within the counter-terrorism strategies is important given its relevance for the interpretation of ideologically driven threats which feature within the '*Prevent*' work-streams of the EU and UK strategies, and within 'Measures to address the conditions conducive to the spread of terrorism' within the UN Global Counter-Terrorism approach. The fourth and first strands of the international approach therefore move beyond the Situational Crime Prevention approach highlighted earlier, touching upon perceptions of grievances and resentment motivating individuals to become radicalised, recruited, or supporters of terrorist groups. Each of the strategies mentioned within the present chapter therefore moves uneasily into the area of social crime prevention, although as will be discussed in the final section of this chapter, the extent to which the current counter-terrorism strategies manage adequately to address the underlying social and economic causes of terrorist behaviour is subject to debate. Within the current strategies, human rights reflect the liberal imperative towards consensus building, utilising the rule of law to prohibit terrorist acts and to provide protections of due process within criminal justice processes. The question remains as to whether current approaches encompass a broad enough agenda in order to eliminate the terrorist security threats currently facing the United Kingdom, the European Union and the international community. It is to this assessment we now turn.

Measures to address the conditions conducive to the spread of terrorism

The first strand of the 2006 UN Global Security Strategy contains 'Measures to address the conditions conducive to the spread of terrorism'. This work-stream is consistent with the EU and UK '*Prevent*' category, all of which seek to identify the social and economic conditions underpinning 'radicalisation and recruitment'. This strand consequently alludes to a more social approach to crime prevention, endeavouring to tackle the underlying causes of terrorism.

The social and economic conditions identified within the EU strategy include: 'poor or autocratic governance, rapid or unmanaged modernisation, lack of political or economic prospects, lack of educational opportunity, discrimination and inequality' (Council of the European Union, 2005, 14468/4/05 REV4: 9). The condition of poverty is also explicitly identified within the 2011 UK Strategy, which, reportedly allocated 30 per cent of Official Development Assistance (ODA) by 2014/15 to support conflict-affected and fragile states, including countries such as Pakistan, Yemen and Somalia. The UK position thereby recognises the interdependence of poverty reduction efforts with counter-terrorism, viewing such action as within the UK national security interest (HM Government, 2011a: 71).

Within the UN, 'a lack of good governance, socio-economic marginalisation, discrimination and political exclusion' are identified as facilitating factors of terrorism, paralleling the EU strategy and reflecting risk factors for atrocity crime detailed within the previous chapter. Further similarities are also apparent between the UK national, EU regional and UN international strategies, particularly in relation to the significance of an absence of 'the rule of law' and 'violations of human rights', as discussed in the previous section of this chapter. Having identified social and economic 'root causes' of radicalisation, the solution to the problem within each approach is subsequently presented as 'the pursuit of good governance, human rights, democracy', 'as well as education and economic prosperity' (Council of the European Union, 2005, 14468/4/05 REV 4: 9). We see here then a number of liberal assumptions underpinning the proposed solution, particularly the liberal internationalist vision of an open, rule-based system in which states trade and cooperate to achieve mutual gains to solve security dilemmas, pursue collective action and gain greater prosperity and freedom (Dunne, 2014). The UN therefore reaffirms its commitment to eradicate poverty and promote sustained economic growth, sustainable development and global prosperity for all, advocating the achievement of the Millennium Development Goals with this objective (United Nations General Assembly, 2006, A/RES/60/288: 4–5).

The second strand of the UK strategy, and the first component of the EU strategy, both of which are referred to as '*Prevent*', similarly explicitly aim to address 'radicalisation to all forms of terrorism' (HM Government, 2011a: 12). Radicalisation and recruitment to groups such as Al Qaeda (and more recently IS) are identified as representing the main threat to the European Union as a whole (Council of the European Union, 2005, 14468/4/05 REV 4: 6). Within the UK Counter-Terrorism strategy, the threat from Al Qaeda, its affiliates, and associated groups, along with the continuing threat from Northern Ireland related terrorism are identified as the predominant concerns (HM Government, 2011c). Within both the EU and UK strategies, '*Prevent*' entails efforts directed towards challenging extremist ideas that are conducive to terrorism and promoting measures to identify and counter the methods, propaganda and conditions conducive to terrorist radicalisation and recruitment. The UN Global Counter-Terrorism strategy similarly includes measures to counter the 'dehumanisation of victims of terrorism', as factors underpinning radicalisation and recruitment, highlighting the need for education along with the need to facilitate inter-faith and cultural dialogue, social inclusion and the promotion of a global consensus against terrorism (United Nations General Assembly, 2006, A/RES/60/288: 4–5). '*Prevent*' within the EU and UK approaches, and the UN work-stream entitled, 'Measures to address the conditions conducive to the spread of terrorism', are consequently clearly concerned with the modernisation and liberal imperative to generate normative consensus, with the UK explicitly acknowledging that its success, in part, is dependent upon the implementation of 'a successful integration strategy, which establishes a stronger sense of common ground and shared values, which enables participation and the empowerment of all communities and which also provides social mobility' (HM Government, 2011a). '*Prevent*', therefore, seeks to address ideologically driven threats mentioned earlier, reflecting the Durkheimian vision to create a modern form of collective conscience, or moral framework (Ritzer, 1996). The normative framework or moral consensus being promoted internationally, regionally and nationally is therefore one which embraces the liberal values of human rights, democracy and the rule of law; it is also a consensus which explicitly rejects the legitimacy of violence as a tool of political action. It is at this point that we can observe that liberal discourse is again conflated with that of modernisation, with aspects of globalisation implicated as potential facilitating tools within this process:

> The ability to put ideas into action has been greatly enhanced by globalisation: ease of travel, transfer of money and communication –

> including through the internet – mean easier access to radical ideas and training.
>
> (Council of the European Union, 2005, 14468/4/05 REV 4: 8)

In this regard, the revised UK Counter-Terrorism Strategy, which takes on board the 2011 Lord Carlile 'Independent Prevent Strategy' review recommendations, endeavours to challenge the opportunities provided by the internet to espouse extremist ideologies, promoting cooperation with internet service providers, including the United States, from which a great many offending sites originate (HM Government, 2011b: 8). Thus, within the UK strategy, while there is clearly an attempt to strengthen social controls through the creation of a moral consensus, reflecting a more social approach to crime prevention, '*Prevent*' also advocates the utilisation of powers to exclude individuals seeking to enter the UK from overseas with the intention of engaging in activity in support of extremists. Such measures include efforts to expel controversial imams or deny visas to extremist preachers. '*Prevent*' is therefore, evidently, also aligned with the Situational Crime Prevention (SCP) approach, which introduces measures aimed at opportunity reduction including efforts to deflect potential perpetrators and the use of access controls. Using the language of SCP, measures include efforts directed towards the control of psychological disinhibitors, particularly the dissemination of propaganda, which can be directed at the dehumanisation of target groups and further used as a recruitment tool serving to radicalise others (Clarke, 1997). The objective of '*Prevent*' is therefore explicitly stated as responding to the ideological challenge of terrorism and the threat faced by the UK from those who promote it. However, the framing of the debate remains outside the contours of the 'liberal crisis' thesis as detailed by Ikenberry and neither does it engage with the 'systemic crisis' thesis of Wallerstein. Consequently, the legitimacy and universality of the liberal framework remains intact, with those recruited conceived as 'radicalised' and 'illegitimate' rather than presented as expressing alternative ideologies that reject liberal ideas, values and rules. This position consequently fails to engage with symbolic interactionist and constructivist perspectives and the critical state crime scholarship, detailed in Chapter 5, which reminds us of the importance of power in setting agendas, criminalising acts and enforcement, further directing attention to the motives and interests of those who have 'the power to define' (Green and Ward, 2004; Michalowski, 2010). Within the existing counter-terrorist strategies then, the objective is limited to prevention of people from being drawn into terrorism, providing advice and support directed to those ends. Accordingly, tackling the decision-making processes of would-be perpetrators entails the incorporation of SCP opportunity reduction techniques including efforts directed towards reducing temptation, and those directed towards the stimulation of feelings of conscience at the point of contemplating the commission of a specific kind of offence (Clarke, 1997). Such techniques are underpinned by the classical assumption that individuals remain guided by a pleasure–pain principle by which they calculate the risks and rewards involved in their actions, and that the provision of information and support will divert those at risk and challenge values and techniques of neutralisation which provide justificatory narratives for such action.

Within the UK strategy, the third objective of '*Prevent*' incorporates the liberal and situational crime prevention concern with cooperative methods of problem solving, promoting public, private and civil society and cross-sector collaboration and coordination, to identify and tackle risks of radicalisation. This method, also evident within the collaborative and cross-departmental work of the EU and UN again reflects the acknowledgement that states are ill-equipped to deal with security threats in isolation and that multilateral efforts are increasingly necessary to combat security threats. The existence of illiberal or conflicting values alongside the opportunities generated by advancement in information communication technologies, transportation and social media enabling their dissemination are therefore key aspects of 'root causes' identified within each counter-terrorism strategy, a point to which we shall return shortly when discussing the effectiveness of current counter-terrorism strategies.

One further point of similarity between the strategies worthy of mention is the recognition of 'unresolved conflicts' as a further root cause of terrorism (United Nations General Assembly, 2006, A/RES/60/288: 4). Indeed, within the earlier April 2006 'Recommendations for a global counter-terrorism strategy' report, the UN Secretary General observed:

> There has been ongoing discussion among Member States about whether terrorism can be traced to certain so-called 'root causes'. For the purposes of moving forward on an operational strategy to counter terrorism I hope that Member States will recognise that terrorist acts do not occur in a social or political vacuum. Let us agree, however, that there is no excuse for terrorism and that all terrorism is unacceptable. But let us also agree that we must address conditions conducive to exploitation by terrorists.
> (United Nations General Assembly, 2006, A/60/825: 3)

Later within the same report, Annan provided further details of the political circumstances motivating terrorist action:

> Many terrorist groups have emerged in the context of local or regional violent conflicts, some of which serve as a rallying cry for terrorist leaders in faraway regions. Prolonged unresolved conflicts in particular often create conditions conducive to exploitation by terrorists and as such must not be allowed to fester, however intractable they might seem. In addition, suicide terrorism campaigns often occur in the context of foreign occupation or perceived foreign occupation. It follows that successful conflict resolution efforts and attention to issues arising in the context of

> foreign occupation or perceived occupation can help to reduce the prevalence of terrorism in the long term.
>
> (United Nations General Assembly, 2006, A/60/825: 6)

Within the UK National Security Strategy, *A Strong Britain in an Age of Uncertainty*, the perceived objectives of Al Qaeda terrorists are clearly articulated:

> Al Qaeda wants to use violence to overthrow governments in the Middle East to create a caliphate, a unified government for the Muslim world based on an extreme interpretation of Islam. By launching terrorist attacks against the US and its allies, Al Qaeda hopes to remove western influence from the Islamic world.
>
> (HM Government, 2010: 14)

The UK government's statement regarding the aims of Al Qaeda broadly reflects the objectives set out in Osama bin Laden's statement issued in October 2001 on Al-Jazeera television, after the September 11 bombings. In this statement, bin Laden presents a context of vengeance, implying that the bombings were an act of revenge for what is described as 'humiliation and contempt' over an eighty-year period. Bin Laden's commentary explicitly cites civilian deaths in Iraq, Nairobi, Dar es Salaam and Afghanistan, resulting from Western military action, and Israeli action in Palestine, Jenin, Ramallah, Rafah, Beit Jala and other Islamic areas. Bin Laden's statement refers directly to attacks upon Islamic holy places as motivating factors underpinning Al Qaeda action and alludes to Western hypocrisy referring to the hundreds and thousands of Japanese deaths during the final stages of the Second World War. The statement ends with a sinister warning, claiming that neither the United States nor those residing in the United States would enjoy security before it is seen as a reality in Palestine, and before 'all the infidel armies leave the land of Mohammed'.

The UK position acknowledges the political motivation for Al Qaeda terrorism, however refuses to be drawn into discussions regarding the legitimacy or otherwise of such narratives. Again, the debate falls short of the identification of a 'liberal crisis' or the emergence of alternative autocratic regimes (Ikenberry, 2009, 2011). Thus, while the UK Counter-Terrorism Strategy explicitly acknowledges that 'radicalisers exploit grievances', identifying the 'perception of UK foreign policy', 'experiences of Islamophobia' and 'a perception that the west is at war with Islam' as examples of grievances underpinning Al Qaeda inspired terrorism in particular, the UK strategy falls short of providing historical and/or political contextualisation of these viewpoints. Indeed, the strategy adds, 'these grievances may be real or perceived although none of them should provide justification for the use of terrorism' (HM Government, 2011a: 60).

Returning to the symbolic interactionist and constructivist emphasis upon the importance of ideas, discourse, meaning, interpretation and power in the social construction of reality, Findlay (2008: 93) identifies a common practice within dominant political alliances of denying purpose to the terrorist, 'or at least any purpose which can claim rationality and hence that it is legitimate'. Arguing further that such a strategy aims 'to devalue the currency of the ideology in contest', noting 'when religious fundamentalists talk about terror attacks as holy war, the victim cultures retaliate by reinterpreting these acts as illegitimate violence'. A central device in such a process of neutralisation is therefore to define the actions of the opposition as only criminal (Matza, 1964), and 'hence to devalue or delegitimise the claims of proponents who cite provocation by victim cultures as the inevitable reason for violence'. Hence, for Findlay, if terrorism is deemed to challenge the legitimacy of the state, 'governments will move to counter the challenge by neutralising the ideological impetus of the opposition, as much as it will move to neutralise the active threat posed thereby' (Findlay, 2008: 75). A similar point is made by Bowling and Sheptycki (2012: 115), who suggest that in defining 'true terrorism', images of the barbarian are created in an effort to 'symbolically reaffirm and secure civilisation'.

This is a position reflected within the international strategy, which strongly asserts that there is never any legitimate justification for terrorism, thereby endeavouring to secure a consensus regarding the illegitimacy of terrorism, regardless of circumstance. However, significantly, within the 2006 UN recommendation document, Annan alludes to the presence of what are termed 'legitimate grievances', advocating nevertheless, alternative, non-violent means for resolution:

> A civil society campaign will need to work to convince those with *genuine grievances* that there exist alternative, non-violent strategies, and that these have in most cases proved more effective. Recent history offers numerous examples of non-violent opposition movements leading to significant change. Such success stories deserve to be highlighted more.
>
> (United Nations General Assembly, 2006, A/60/825: 4)

As discussed in Chapter 3, modernisation theory and, more recently, the globalisation thesis present crime and crime control as consequences of modernising and globalising tendencies linked with rapid social changes associated with increasing populations, industrialisation and urbanisation. These developments, it is argued, have served to increase opportunities resulting from advances in information communication technologies, transportation, and the mobility of goods, people and money serving to make the world more interconnected and interdependent. This view, described by Andreas and Nadelmann as 'the standard view', has however become subject to challenge from a range of authors who have pointed to the ahistorical and depoliticised nature of such theorising. With Annan's comments in mind, it is to these perspectives we now turn.

World Systems Analysis: economic root causes of terrorism

As detailed in Chapter 3, Wallerstein, a key proponent of World Systems Analysis, advocates historical contextualisation of the developments associated with modernisation and globalisation, advocating interdisciplinary analysis. As with the approaches discussed thus far, Wallerstein identifies an interrelationship between globalisation, terrorism, internal and external conflict. However, taking the emergence of capitalism in the sixteenth century as his starting point, he argues that theorists must substitute the nation-state as the focus for study, presenting what is termed 'the world system' as the most appropriate unit of analysis.

The contemporary international society of states, bound together through international institutions such as the United Nations and regional bodies such as the European Union, are therefore examined as historically and temporally bounded constructions which form the most recent chapter of a World System, which transformed from 'one based upon world empires' to 'one based upon world economies'. For Wallerstein, the modern world economy is a capitalist world economy based upon market exchange and the accumulation of capital, a large geographic zone characterised by the internal exchange of goods and flows of capital and labour. Significantly, while modernisation theorists and World Systems theorists both emphasise the importance of industrialisation as a driver for social change and as an explanatory variable through which to make sense of social problems such as crime, each perspective differs with respect to their understanding of the outcome of this process. Modernisation theory (which is linked to economic liberalism) suggests that state dependence and underdevelopment are temporary conditions, mid-stages in a modernising process that will ultimately result in development, prosperity and equality. In challenging the assumption of progress underpinning this approach, and through a contextualisation of industrialisation and capitalist development, World Systems theorists assert instead, that Western societies have developed to the degree that they have done to the detriment of the third world, or lesser developed states (Barak, 2001). For Wallerstein, the current world economy which is described as containing 'many political units, tied loosely together in the modern world in an interstate system, representing multiple religions and cultures', is also underpinned by the legacy of imperial colonisation. Characterised by relations of exploitation, dominance and subservience, it is argued by Wallerstein that nations were stripped of natural and human resources in order to build Western nations, resulting in uneven development and long-standing inequalities, the legacies of which form the basis of many of the social ills of today, compounded by the legacy of geo-political conflict relating to the First and Second World Wars, and the Cold War.

The modern capitalist economic world system is therefore described as characterised by an uneven expansion of the capitalist mode of production, unequal relations of production, unequal exchange and unequal power within the world society of states. For Wallerstein, this system is not sustainable, with our capitalist world economy, the current world system, described as nearing its end and currently experiencing systemic crisis. Reflected in the manifestation of internal and external state instability and anxiety, Wallerstein argues that this situation has created 'violence as people try to preserve acquired privileges and hierarchical rank in a very unstable situation'. Social conflicts are therefore interpreted as a consequence of the systemic failure of the capitalist world system, a process 'that take[s] quite an unpleasant form' and of which terrorism, crime and atrocity offences remain a constituent part (Wallerstein, 2005: 77). Terrorism and atrocity crimes are therefore regarded as consequences of unresolved questions regarding territorial boundaries and ideological competition generated by imperial collapse, decolonialisation and the First and Second World War territorial and jurisdictional changes. Instances of terrorism, genocide and crime are therefore presented as integrally linked with relations of production, inequality and exploitation which only political action may counter.

Within this account, the UK national, EU regional and UN international approaches, with their concern to forge a new moral consensus around liberal values and human rights, together with opportunity reducing and risk enhancing situational crime control measures (and their interest in maintaining the status quo), may not be sufficient to address the underlying structural causes of terrorism. Rather, for Wallerstein, such causes remain the inherent tensions and contradictions implicit within the global capitalist economic system and the legacy of tensions emanating from relations of exploitation and inequality. Further, recognising globalisation and the international division of labour as the basis of global inequality, Wallerstein questions the notion that governments and international institutions can remedy social problems. Viewed as reflecting the interests of capitalists, international institutions are conceived as part of the problem, reproducing patterns of exploitation and inequality, trapping underdeveloped or peripheral countries in a state of underdevelopment. Consequently, for Wallerstein as for Marxists and critical scholars more generally, violent conflicts will persist until economic and power imbalances are removed, a point similarly made within the previous chapter referring to Ikenberry (2009, 2011). The system must therefore be substantially reorganised or replaced (see also Fanon, 1990). Wallerstein therefore leaves his readers with the question:

> As we are entering into this period of transition, marking the end of the global capitalist world system and its replacement with another world system, the future is not yet determined. We have a choice to make. Do we wish to retain a hierarchical system based upon privilege and rank, or will we move towards a truly democratic and egalitarian system?
>
> (Wallerstein, 2005)

Liberal internationalist reform

As noted in the previous chapter, more recently, liberal internationalists have also raised questions regarding the contemporary period of transition, also acknowledging that we have entered a period of crisis. However, this scholarship replaces Wallerstein's focus upon the global economic system with a concern for the relations between states in the current world order. Ikenberry (2009, 2011), for example, reflects upon the recent decline in the relative power of the US and EU, and the shift in power from North and West to East and South, asking what such developments mean for the future and raising questions regarding the kind of world order that will emerge.

As detailed previously, within the discipline of international relations, a range of analysts have raised the possibility that the existing political structure we know of as 'international society' is currently facing a crisis of legitimacy. This position is reflected by growing pressure to reform, reorganise and strengthen the liberal institutions governing the global society of states so that individual state power and capacity become a less significant determinant of stability (Ikenberry, 2009) reflecting World System theorist and realist observations regarding the continuing salience of dominant state interest and relations of power. Ikenberry (2009) argues that the liberal international order will need to become 'more universal and less hierarchical', with the US ceding authority and control to a wider set of states and giving up some of its hegemonic rights and privileges. Recent liberal theory therefore acknowledges that within the current liberal framework, peace and security is currently being undermined by the economic power exerted by the West; by power politics asserted within the United Nations Security Council; and, through the application of the veto system with international institutions perpetuating structural inequality, dominance and dependence (Dunne, 2014). Findlay (2008: 8) agrees, emphasising the differential responses to terrorism, particularly state-sponsored terror, or where the aggressor is otherwise politically or economically aligned to the West. Such work directs attention to hypocrisy, inconsistency and outright abuses of power, noting that such 'savage terrorist incursions pass either unrecognised for what they are or only receive mild administrative sanction' (Findlay, 2008: 8; see also Chomsky, 2011 and Cohen, 2001: 157–159). Drawing upon the work of Baxi (2007), Findlay reminds us of the more significant risks of terror within past phases of globalisation linked to industrialisation, emphasising the work of feminists and other critical theorists who detail the application of terror upon women and indigenous peoples, raising questions as to how and why insurgent terrorism has been prioritised within the risk/security nexus (Findlay, 2008: 49).

Deudney and Ikenberry (2009) and Ikenberry's later (2011) work also explicitly point to the need for international society to acknowledge and respond to 'historically inherited vulnerabilities and grievances of the rising great powers and autocratic states', arguing that US and liberal state foreign policy 'should not exacerbate these grievances and vulnerabilities but rather mollify and ameliorate them' (Ikenberry, 2011: 92). In order to become better equipped to face the challenges of the contemporary period, and as a means of addressing the resentments and grievances directed towards the structure and functioning, and ultimately the legitimacy, of the current international order and institutions, both reform *and* conciliation are viewed as required, thereby acknowledging and responding politically to both historically inherited legacies and legitimate grievances.

Conciliation and political action: necessary components in counter-terrorism strategies

Reform of institutions alongside dialogue are therefore viewed as necessary to readdress the shift in the balance of power within the contemporary world order and to restore the legitimacy and capability of international governance structures. Ikenberry's observations therefore reflect the endorsement within the fourth pillar of the Secretary General's recommendation report in which he introduced measures to promote shared values, tolerance, understanding, critical thinking and dialogue (A/60/825: 15–22) to uncover and address the underlying root causes of terrorism. Arrigo's (2010) work embracing the symbolic interactionist concern with meaning and interpretation, which explores the relevance of 'Critical Restorative Justice methods' (CRJM) for de-escalating international episodes of terrorism, is interesting in this regard. This work addresses Hamas specifically and efforts by Egypt's Muslim Brotherhood to address Israeli occupation of the Gaza Strip, the West Bank and Golan Heights and the use of violence to obtain sovereignty, self-determination and justice. Arrigo argues that the integration of critical restorative justice along with symbolic interactionism raises provocative challenges for mediating global disputes of terrorism and for advancing criminological understanding. This approach, we are informed, comprises a form of 'moral engagement without condemnation or vilification of those in dispute'. The aim is to de-realise the offence while humanising the participants, allowing possibilities for insight, change and renewal. Critical Restorative Justice, by enabling parties to tell their own story, is therefore regarded as a useful way forward in dialogue exchange, making 'radical transformation' possible and entailing 'pivotal "breakthroughs or epiphanies" employing a language of healing [and] restoration' and generating the prospect for 'transformative justice' (Arrigo, 2010: 777). Essentially, the conceptual framework outlined in Arrigo's paper is viewed as a potential way of negotiating peace between polarised positions, validating the narratives of both parties to a conflict, including personal descriptions, cultural mythology, oral histories, critical memories and ancestral legends since these forms are viewed as comprising the multiple sites of knowledge production, perpetual differences and competing truth claims. Within this work therefore, the legitimacy of the dominant liberal narrative is no longer taken as given, providing space for alternative perspectives to become articulated.

Speaking at the BBC Radio 4 Reith Lecture series entitled 'Securing Freedom' in 2011, during the tenth anniversary of 9/11, former Director-General of the UK Security Service (MI5), Eliza Manningham-Buller, also acknowledges the need for dialogue, political solutions and efforts directed towards conciliation in order to achieve 'long term success and a reduction in the threat'. Within her speech, terrorism is defined as 'a violent tool used for political reasons to bring pressure on government by creating fear in the populace' and as such must 'be resolved by politics and economics, not through arms and intelligence, however an important role these play'. These observations are also evident in the work of Bowling and Sheptycki (2012: 117), who similarly assert that 'technical-enforcement imposing a world system lock-down cannot ultimately solve the problems of social ordering in that system. However that is what is being attempted.' For Bowling and Sheptycki, as for Manningham-Buller, while policing, intelligence and security responses must respond to immediate threats, pointing to the achievements made utilising situational crime prevention methods, law and order, institution and capacity building and so forth, policing, it is argued, must also respond to the longer-term issues, giving way to diplomatic and socio-cultural solutions.

Reiterating the need for a politicised and historical understanding of the root causes of terrorism, Manningham-Buller forcefully asserts within her lecture that 'politics and especially foreign policy have to play their crucial parts', arguing that 'how a nation conducts its foreign policy has a direct bearing on its chances of success in the search for conciliation'. To contextualise the debate, Manningham-Buller identifies the three articulated aims of Al Qaeda: (1) the removal of the US and its allies from the Arab lands; (2) to depose apostate rulers; and (3) to restore the Islamic form of government known as the Caliphate. Her speech consequently reflects the contents of Bin Laden's speech made on Al-Jazeera television referred to previously. Manningham-Buller confesses that there was an explicit recognition within the UK Security Service in 2001 regarding the intertwining of national security, foreign policy and the roots of extremism, recalling:

> one of those present argued that the Peace process between Israel and Palestine needed to be revived – an explicit recognition that the west needed to readdress the open sore in the Middle East that could well have contributed to these events.
>
> (Manningham-Buller, 2011)

Chomsky (2011), a well-known and controversial critic of US foreign policy, similarly directs attention to Palestine and Israel, focusing on United States support for Israeli settlement expansion and occupation contrary to international law, blocking diplomatic settlements and peace plans, also hindering the dispatch of international monitors to the dispute, through the use of their veto power privileges within the UN Security Council. This work therefore recognises that power politics and state self-interest currently hinder efforts to counter terrorism, a point similarly made within the previous chapter examining responses to atrocity crime. In addressing the solution to the unresolved Israel/Palestine conflict, Chomsky observes that there is almost universal agreement on what the solution should be, backed by the Arab League; by the Organization of Islamic States (including Iran); by Europe; by the United

Nations; and by international law. The solution, Chomsky argues, is for the United States to change policy, suggesting that if the United States 'decides to join the world, Israel will have no option but to go along' (Chomsky, 2011: 195).

Importantly, while the military responses in Iraq and Afghanistan, alongside the police and intelligence work (underpinning the situational crime prevention techniques discussed earlier in this chapter) may well be successful in preventing and reducing opportunities for attack, and to better equip states to respond to attack, and while such efforts may be useful in informing governments and anticipating risks, such measures are not viewed by Manningham-Buller as sufficient in resolving divisions. Rather she argues, this work must comprise part of wider political, diplomatic and economic solution including dialogue with those who executed the terrorist campaign.

Again, rejecting the validity of violence as a tool of political persuasion, Manningham-Buller clarifies:

> Talking does not mean approval, it means attempting to reduce the threat by addressing, if possible, its causes. It is a way of exploring peaceful options, probing possibilities and identifying whether there is room to manoeuvre and what compromises, if any, may be reached, what political grievances can be acknowledged, or even, in rare cases, accommodated. It is also the opportunity for governments to express their own positions.
> (Manningham-Buller, 2011)

This position therefore reiterates Arrigo's earlier recommendation for dialogue and narrative expression without vilification (admittedly made all the more difficult as terrorists employ ever more abhorrent techniques to instil fear and terror to secure their objectives, and as ever more non-combatants lose their lives as 'collateral damage' as a consequence of military and security initiatives). Here, the package of situational crime prevention measures detailed earlier, which comprise the bulk of the measures included within the current strategies to counter terrorism, remain an important dimension of a comprehensive package of measures, but it is argued, must not be substituted for engagement with the wider policy context, political and economic solutions and conciliatory dialogue. Although, as Manningham-Buller, rather pessimistically, acknowledges, 'even with the addition of such methods the outcome is far from certain' and 'may well prove fruitless'.

However, historical and political contextualisation and the requirement of quiet diplomacy and sensitive foreign policy still, in many ways, sidestep the issue relating to the existence of alternative ideologies that reject liberal ideas and values. These proposals work from within the existing framework and therefore fall short of proposing radical structural change to the global capitalist world economy, or to the current world political order. While providing a welcome addition, the approach taken above still takes for granted the existence and expansion of a liberal moral consensus denouncing the legitimacy of terrorist acts and the universality of human rights, the rule of law, democracy and liberalisation in trade, as reflected within the 'standard view' espoused by the liberal, modernisation and globalisation perspectives.

As noted by Manningham-Buller, the justificatory narratives which have recently been articulated by those perpetrating and convicted of Al Qaeda related terrorism include reports of: 'avenging deaths'; 'revenge at Western support of autocratic rulers'; 'Western exploitation and occupation of Muslim lands and resources'; with American military bases stationed in the holy lands of Saudi Arabia also commonly identified as having first motivated Osama bin Laden to attack the West, especially the USA and to launch a global Jihad. These grievances (legitimate or not) may indeed be subject to conciliatory efforts embracing diplomatic, economic and political initiatives. However, the alternative motives, namely the frequently cited narrative of contempt for Western materialism and immorality and the intense dislike of democracy, free speech and human rights, require more fundamental resolutions, challenging the very liberal values underpinning the international institutions and international political order of the contemporary global society of states. The advocates of such a position, described by Cronin (2003: 41) cited in Kiras (2014: 363), as 'religious terrorists', do not seek to modify but rather replace the normative structure of society. To address the root cause of this narrative would consequently entail engagement with visions of an alternative world order or alternative world system currently viewed as unimaginable from those national, regional and international organisations operating within the existing system, and unlikely (although not impossible), given the conflation of economic and security agendas by contemporary liberal internationalist theorists. As with our previous chapters then, the adequacy and criteria by which counter-terrorism strategy is judged remain contingent upon the particular lens through which the phenomenon is viewed and whether one permits historical and political considerations to come to the fore.

In June 2014, ISIS overran the city of Mosul, subsequently advancing towards Baghdad and declaring the creation of a caliphate and changing its name to Islamic State. As a collection of organisations espousing illiberal values, running counter to the liberal ideas of democracy, human rights, and freedom of speech, Al Qaeda, al-Qaeda in Iraq (AQI), Islamic State in Iraq (ISI) and Islamic State in Iraq and the Levant (Isis) currently employ brutal tactics – including mass killings and abductions of members of religious and ethnic minorities, as well as the beheadings of soldiers and journalists. As heinous as their activities are, uncertainty remains regarding the prospects of such groups achieving their ambition and what the possible outcome would mean for the long-term future of the post-hegemonic liberal international order. As detailed, several possibilities are imaginable.

Conceived as temporary aberrations, such events may be interpreted by modernisation scholars as evidence of terrorists capitalising on social disorganisation caused by rapid social change and modernisation facilitated by the Arab Spring (in Tunisia, Libya, Algeria, Lebanon, Jordan, Sudan, Oman,

Saudi Arabia, Egypt, Syria, Morocco, Yemen, Bahrain, Kuwait), and the associated calls for better living conditions. As such, these developments may be viewed as part of an inevitable march toward further liberalism, human rights and global prosperity. The solution within this perspective is to continue with the agenda of forging an international moral consensus, rejecting the legitimacy of terrorist action and the use of violence as a political tool, and further strengthening the liberal values of human rights, the rule of law, democracy and free speech. A further dimension to this approach is through the strengthening of societal controls supporting the globalisation thesis position, which calls for measures to reduce opportunities for terrorism and raise the risks to those involved, and symbolic interactionist insights regarding the need to challenge justificatory narratives and techniques of neutralisation that free terrorists from social control. The modernisation and globalisation perspectives are therefore consistent with recent liberal internationalist proposals to strengthen and expand the current liberal governance structures and associated institutions to ensure that they are fit for purpose. The solution is therefore to reform existing structures to generate a more universal, less hierarchical and more equitable international order, capable of applying (and enforcing) moral and legal standards fairly and consistently, thereby removing the source of existing grievances, and offering the potential of social and economic prosperity and collective security for all. A reformed United Nations and Security Council and revised international economic institutions like the IMF and World Bank would therefore remove some of the barriers shaped by power politics and national self-interest, enhancing the legitimacy of the international order and bestowing the capabilities to intervene inside states for security and human rights reasons. These solutions, creating the trust necessary for enhanced police and judicial cooperation and harmonisation, raise the possibility of effective collective multilateral action to tackle Al Qaeda related terrorism, containing or eliminating the threat over the longer term as international society sees through its commitment to eradicate poverty and promote sustained economic growth, sustainable development, global prosperity and justice for all.

For Waltz, however, the assumption of liberals, namely that history moves relentlessly towards progress, is viewed as simplistic and ultimately refuted by an international environment that makes it difficult, if almost impossible, for states to behave in ways that are progressively more moral (Waltz, 1959: 233). Waltz's realist view emphasises the framework of world politics and the condition of anarchy as undermining cooperative and multilateral solutions to the world's ills. For Waltz, in the absence of a consistent, reliable process of reconciling the conflicts of interest that inevitably arise among similar units in a condition of anarchy, each state pursues its own interests, with force remaining a means of achieving the external ends of states. While for Waltz, states alone have a monopoly on the legitimate use of physical force, thereby conceiving terrorist use of violence illegitimate, as revealed in Chapters 2 and 5, others have called into question the state/terrorist; crime/war and police/military dichotomies (Aas, 2007: 105; Findlay, 2008), highlighting the interweaving of conflicts, organised crime and terrorism. Within this climate, terrorist groups may alternatively be regarded as part of a continuum towards statehood, which may or may not come into fruition. Indeed, literature discussing the contentious definition of terrorism frequently points to the numerous examples of countries founded upon national resistance movements. This distinction is not inconsequential, as Aas (2007: 106) reminds us. Thus, 'as a crime, terrorism falls under the auspices of law enforcement agencies and due process of law, whereas as an act of war, it merits a military response.' As recent events make clear, as a non-state actor, Al Qaeda were effectively viewed as waging war on the USA, who responded with military action, action that served to conflate military, police and penal contexts, destabilising established principles of international order, thereby muddying the distinction further and exposing the 'high policing' or order maintenance function of law, criminal justice and military action.

Just as the R2P doctrine has been described as a key test for whether liberalism can endure despite systemic changes to the distribution of material and normative power (Dunne, 2014: 122), it may be speculated that the endurance and transformation of Al Qaeda may similarly either strengthen or undermine the liberal goal of preserving and extending liberal institutions, acting as a catalyst or check upon those with alternative ideologies or with visions of territorial or ideological readjustment.

Cultural explanations therefore point to the use of violence as a means of regaining or preserving cultural identity, traditions and values against Westernisation, American imperialism and materialism, particularly by those who perceive themselves as losers in the contemporary international system (Kiras, 2014: 362; Barber, 2003; Huntington, 1996). Findlay (2008: 77) similarly observes that in conflict-ridden and post-conflict cultures, terrorism can be a force in state formation, explaining that an important feature of para-political analysis is to treat as state-like entities a whole range of organisations and institutions, which at first may not conventionally be classified as states. The transition from Al Qaeda to Islamic State therefore raises questions regarding the future. Viewed simultaneously as revolutionary religious movements or as terrorist movements, it is evident that IS are currently dedicated to overthrowing authorised states, seeking territorial control and sovereignty as well as eventual moral and legal standing, albeit outside of the dominant liberal order of the contemporary society of states known as international society.

Tickner (2014: 154) has recently argued that the re-emergence of conservative religious movements (both Christian and Islamic) challenges the predictions of modernisation theory and the universal acceptance of a liberal world order, reminding us that the Treaty of Westphalia, which has been conceived as 'a landmark in the origins of the modern state system', also marked the defeat of religion as a scheme for organising international authority. For Tickner then, the radical revival of Islam represents an attempt to replace the secular state system and Western-led international institutions with an Islamic system under God's rule. Tickner further directs attention to the misogynistic objectives underpinning this aspiration, bringing into focus the omission of gender politics within consideration of globalising discourses, which have been used to further the study of atrocity crime, terrorism and other aspects of violence (an issue to which we shall return in the next chapter in relation to strategic responses to human trafficking).

Terrorist groups have the capacity to evolve in the methods employed, in nature, and in form. However, the success of such groups to achieve their goals over the longer term, and whether they will eventually become integrated within the existing liberal institutional framework, or remain an autocratic outsider espousing an alternative ideology, is likely to be dependent upon forging a greater degree of homogeneity than presently exists within the Islamic world and between the different groups fighting within Iraq and Syria. It will also remain contingent upon whether the existing order is prompted to enact political and economic change as a means of responding to and circumscribing the current threat. As it stands, from the perspective of critical theory, the existing counter-terrorist framework is found wanting, ill-equipped to respond to these challenges, with counter-terrorist strategy currently masking its true normative and ideological intentions.

References

Aas, K. (2007). *Globalisation and Crime.* London: Sage.

Andreas, P. and Nadelmann, E. (2006). *Policing the Globe: Criminalization and Crime Control in International Relations.* Oxford: Oxford University Press.

Arrigo, B. (2010). 'Identity, International Terrorism and Negotiating Peace: Hamas and Ethics-Based Considerations from Critical Restorative Justice', *British Journal of Criminology*, 50: 772–790.

Barak, G. (2001). 'Crime and Crime Control in an Age of Globalization: A Theoretical Dissection', *Critical Criminology*, 10: 57–72.

Barber, B. (2003). *Jihad vs. McWorld.* New York: Corgi Books.

Baxi, U. (2007). *Revisiting Social Dimensions of Law and Justice in a Post-human Era.* Keynote Address, Julius Stone Centenary Conference, University of Sydney.

Bigo, D. (2000). 'When Two Become One: Internal and External Securitisation in Europe', in Kelstrup, M. and Williams, M.C. (eds), *International Relations Theory and the Politics of European Integration*. London: Routledge.

Bowling, B. and Sheptycki, J.W.E. (2012). *Global Policing*. London: Sage.

Chomsky, N. (2011). *Power and Terror: Conflict, Hegemony, and the Rule of Law.* London: Pluto Press.

Clarke, R.V. (ed.). (1997). *Situational Crime Prevention: Successful Case Studies.* Second Edition. New York: Harrow and Heston Publishers.

Clarke, R. (2005). 'Seven Misconceptions of Situational Crime Prevention', in Tilley, N. (ed.), *Handbook of Community Safety and Crime Prevention.* Cullompton: Willan Publishing.

Cohen, S. (2001). *States of Denial.* Cambridge: Polity Press.

Council of the European Union. (2005). *The European Union Counter Terrorism Strategy.* Brussels, 30 November. 14468/04/05/REV4.

Council of the European Union. (2008). Council Framework Decision 2008/919/JHA of 28 November amending Framework Decision 2002/475/JHA on combating terrorism.

Cronin, B. (2003). *Institutions for the Common Good: International Protection Regimes in International Society.* Cambridge: Cambridge University Press.

Deudney, D. and Ikenberry, J. (2009). 'The Myth of the Autocratic Revival: Why Liberal Democracy Will Prevail', *Foreign Affairs*, 88(1): 77–93.

Dunne, T. (2014). 'Liberalism', in Baylis, J., Smith, S., and Owens, P. (eds), *The Globalisation of World Politics*, sixth edition. Oxford: Oxford University Press. Pp. 113–125.

Fanon, F. (1990). *The Wretched of the Earth*, trans. Constance Farrington. London: Penguin.

Findlay, M. (2008). *Governing Through Globalised Crime.* Cullompton: Willan Publishing.

Green, P. and Ward, T. (2004). *State Crime: Governments, Violence and Corruption.* London: Pluto Press.

HM Government. (2010). *A Strong Britain in an Age of Uncertainty: The National Security Strategy.* London: The Stationery Office.

HM Government. (2011a). *Contest: The United Kingdom's Strategy for Countering Terrorism.* London: The Stationery Office.

HM Government. (2011b). *Report to the Home Secretary of Independent Oversight of Prevent Review and Strategy.* London: The Stationery Office.

HM Government. (2011c). *Prevent Strategy.* London: The Stationery Office.

Huntington, S. (1996). *The Clash of Civilizations and the Remaking of World Order.* London: Simon and Schuster.

Ikenberry, J. (2009). 'Liberal Internationalism 3.0: America and the Dilemmas of Liberal World Order', *Perspectives in Politics* 71(1): 71–87.

Ikenberry, J. (2011). 'The Future of the Liberal World Order: Internationalism After America', *Foreign Affairs*, 90(3): 56–68.

Joyce, P. (2012). *Criminology: A Complete Introduction.* London: Hodder and Stoughton.

Kiras, J. (2014). 'Terrorism and Globalisation', in Baylis, J., Smith, S., and Owens, P. (eds), *The Globalisation of World Politics: An Introduction to International Relations.* Oxford: Oxford University Press. Pp. 357–371.

Manningham-Buller, E. (2011). *Terror. The Reith Lectures 'Securing Freedom'.* www.bbc.co.uk/programmes/b0145x77#auto.

Matza, D. (1964). *Delinquency and Drift.* New York: John Wiley.

Michalowski, R. (2010). 'In Search of "State and Crime" in State Crime Studies', in Chambliss, W., Michalowski, R., and Kramer, R. (eds), *State Crime in the Global Age.* Cullompton: Willan Publishing.

Naim, M. (2002). *The Five Wars of Globalisation.* The Grotius Lecture Series, American Society of International Law's ('ASIL') 96th Annual Meeting on March 13–16.

Official Journal of the European Union. (2005). The Hague Programme: Strengthening Freedom, Security and Justice in the European Union. 2005/C 53/01.

Ritzer, G. (1996). *Sociological Theory*, fourth edition. Singapore: McGraw-Hill International Editions.

Tickner, A. (2014). *A Feminist Voyage Through International Relations.* Oxford: Oxford University Press.

United Nations General Assembly. (2004). *Report of the High-Level Panel on Threats, Challenges and Change: 'A More Secure World: Our Shared Responsibility'*, December 2. A/59/565.

United Nations General Assembly. (2005). *Report of the Secretary General: 'In Larger Freedom: Towards Development, Security and Human Rights for All'*, March 21. A/59/2005.

United Nations General Assembly. (2005). *Resolution Adopted by the General Assembly. 60.1. World Summit Outcome*, October 24. A/RES/60/1.

United Nations General Assembly. (2006). *Report of the Secretary General 'Uniting against terrorism: recommendations for a global counter-terrorism strategy'*, April 27. A/60/825.

United Nations General Assembly. (2006). *Resolution Adopted by the General Assembly. 60/288. The United Nations Global Counter Terrorism Strategy*, September 20. A/RES/60/288.

Wallerstein, I. (2005). *World-Systems Analysis: An Introduction*. London: Duke University Press.

Waltz, K. (1959). *Man, the State and War*. New York: Columbia University Press.

8 Human trafficking

In the previous chapter, discourses of modernisation and globalisation were seen to have penetrated counter-terrorism strategy at the international (UN), regional (EU) and national (UK) levels. Here, focusing specifically upon the issue of human trafficking, it will become evident that within political, theoretical and popular imagery, processes of globalisation are similarly implicated as generating opportunities for crime and victimisation with respect to the proliferation of the trafficking in persons, and with it, this discourse is also used to account for the emergence of an ever-growing, counter-trafficking regime. Anthias (2014: 164) for example, presents trafficking as a phenomenon which 'lies at the crossroads of migration, gender, policies and crime, in the context of globalisation'. Iñiguez de Heredia (2008: 302–303) similarly locates trafficking within this broader context, pointing to improvements in communication and transportation, the development of tourism, and also the spread of transnational crime as facilitating 'the flourishing of trafficking'. Writing in a similar vein, Aas (2007: 43) too argues that the increasing flows of tourists and the internet have had a profound impact on the pattern of commercial sex across the globe, further implicating wider social and political factors such as the collapse of communism, the rise of neo-liberalist policies, alongside cultural shifts in attitudes to extramarital sex.

Aspects of globalisation are also explicitly recognised within the United Kingdom's 2011 Human Trafficking Strategy. Thus, the strategy emphasises 'the ease of international travel [that] has led to the opportunity for increased movement of people across borders, both legally and illegally, especially from poorer to wealthier countries such as the UK' (HM Government, 2011: 6). Within the foreword of the UNODC (2004: iii) *United Nations Convention Against Transnational Organized Crime and Protocols Thereto*, Kofi Annan (the previous Secretary General of the UN) similarly castigates 'uncivil society' for their exploitation of 'the openness and opportunities of globalisation', presenting terrorists, criminals, drug dealers and traffickers in people, as examples of 'uncivil society', and collectively condemning them as 'enemies of progress and human rights'. Discourses of globalisation and modernisation are therefore fused within contemporary policy narratives directed towards the eradication of trafficking in persons.

This chapter will proceed in two parts. Initially, counter human trafficking responses at the international (UN), regional (EU) and national (UK) levels will be examined in relation to their approach, priorities and underlying assumptions. Engaging with feminist scholarship from within international relations, criminology and international political economy, the limitation of the existing counter-trafficking framework will be explored, engaging with debates regarding the conceptualisation of human trafficking, state, corporate and military complicity, and the significance of wider structural economic and social conditions associated with trade liberalisation and the contemporary structure of the international society of states.

International, regional and national responses to human trafficking

People trafficking is a multidimensional issue involving the sale, transportation and exploitation of people (Iñiguez de Heredia, 2008: 313). It is frequently presented as a stain on humanity and, more recently, cited as evidence of the 'dark underside' of globalisation or migration and as an abrogation of human rights (True, 2012). A cursory look at the increasing literature examining human trafficking will immediately inform the newcomer that although human trafficking is commonly regarded as having intensified over the past thirty years, it is not a new phenomenon, with concerns raised with respect to prostitution and the 'trafficking in women' going back to 'anti white-slavery' campaigns at the turn of the century (Iñiguez de Heredia, 2008: 299; Aas, 2007: 29; Jahic and Finckenauer, 2005: 24; Doezema, 2000: 23).

The United Nations Convention against Transnational Organized Crime (UNTOC) and its Protocols were adopted by the General Assembly on 15 November 2000. The Convention's Protocol to Prevent, Suppress and Punish Trafficking in Persons, especially Women and Children and the Protocol against the Smuggling of Migrants by Land, Sea and Air are described as the only universal instruments that address these crimes in a comprehensive and integrated manner, providing a framework for international action (UNODC, 2012: 8). Iñiguez de Heredia (2008: 305) describes the Trafficking Protocol as a watershed in the history of the international fight against trafficking in human beings, marking 'an important step forward'. Agreed to in 2000 and in force since 2003, the Trafficking Protocol is credited with providing a definition of trafficking and directing attention to causes, such as poverty and inequality, that are presented as the root of the problem, as well as introducing preventative and post-trafficking measures to support victims of trafficking (Iñiguez de Heredia, 2008: 313).

The international approach to counter-trafficking in persons, as one might expect, remains consistent with the international approach to counter-terrorism detailed within the previous chapter. As will be demonstrated, this approach utilises a liberal framework, employing collaborative multilateral action advocating both situational and social crime control measures to provide 'effective action to prevent and combat trafficking in persons, especially women and children' (UNODC, 2004: 41). In doing so, the Protocol explicitly recognises that human trafficking primarily affects women, and in response advocates a gendered and contextually sensitive approach to the issue advocating action 'in the countries of origin, transit and destination', to pursue measures to 'prevent', 'punish' and 'protect'.

The purpose of the UN Protocol to Prevent, Suppress and Punish Trafficking in Persons, Especially Women and Children, as set out within its statement of purpose, are:

a to prevent and combat trafficking in persons, paying particular attention to women and children;
b to protect and assist the victims of such trafficking, with full respect for their human rights; and
c to promote cooperation among States Parties in order to meet those objectives.

The UNODC's 2012 'Comprehensive Strategy to Combat Trafficking in Persons and Smuggling of Migrants' presents the UNODC as 'the guardian of the Organized Crime Convention and its Protocols', and as such, fulfils 'a leading role in strengthening and coordinating the criminal justice response to human trafficking and smuggling of migrants'. The Protocols provide clear mandates to UNODC to support efforts to undertake action in line with points (a), (b) and (c) above, adding a further objective: 'To prosecute those who traffic persons and smuggle migrants, upholding justice and ensuring an effective criminal justice response'.

At a regional level, the European Union Directive (2011/36/EU) of 5 April 2011 on 'preventing and combating trafficking in human beings and protecting its victims'[1] advocates action 'with a view to raising awareness, reducing vulnerability, supporting and assisting victims, fighting the root causes of trafficking and supporting those third countries in developing appropriate anti-trafficking legislation'. The objectives are therefore broadly similarly to the measures contained within the UN framework and are later translated into five priority areas in the 2012 EU Strategy towards the Eradication of Trafficking in Human Beings 2012–2016 (European Commission, 2012, COM (2012) 286 final):

(A) Identifying, protecting and assisting victims of trafficking.
(B) Stepping up the prevention of trafficking in human beings.
(C) Increased prosecution of traffickers.
(D) Enhanced coordination and cooperation among key actors and policy coherence.
(E) Increased knowledge of and effective response to emerging concerns related to all forms of trafficking in human beings.

At a national level within the United Kingdom, as detailed within the 2011 Human Trafficking Strategy, four key aims are identified:

1 international action to stop trafficking happening in the first place;
2 a stronger border at home to stop victims being brought into the UK;
3 tougher law enforcement action to tackle the criminal gangs that orchestrate the crime; and
4 improved identification and care for the victims of trafficking (HM Government, 2011: 3).

However, within the UK Strategy, there is a notable lack of consistency in the terminology and sequencing used with regard to the key aims, thus later within the document the aims are reproduced in a different order with the law enforcement and border control elements articulated somewhat differently:

1 improved victim care arrangements;
2 enhanced ability to act early, before the harm has reached the UK;
3 smarter multi-agency action at the border;
4 better coordination of our law enforcement efforts within the UK (HM Government, 2011: 7).

For the newcomer to this policy area, while the themes are broadly in line with one another at the international, regional and national levels, it is important to highlight that there is a marked lack of consistency in the terminology used within the different documents and also considerable variation in the prioritisation and sequencing of the strategic aims. It is also worthy of mention that particular measures included within the headings between protocols and directives and their subsequent strategies within the UN and EU are subject to variation, with the UNODC presenting their strategic approach in relation to three interrelated themes. This lack of consistency serves to obfuscate comparison and provides a challenge to those wishing to build a picture of the strategies and methods utilised to counter human trafficking.

The inconsistencies revealed within the legal instruments and strategic documents at the international, EU regional and UK national levels highlight the rather superficial and overlapping nature of the categories currently utilised to demarcate existing work-streams and particular measures within this field. In order to clarify the measures used and to provide a degree of consistency with our previous chapter, the work-streams detailed above will therefore be re-examined using our previous classification:

1 measures to prevent and combat (human trafficking);
2 measures to build states' capacity to prevent and combat (human trafficking);
3 measures to ensure respect for human rights for all and the rule of law as the fundamental basis of the fight (against human trafficking);
4 measures to address the conditions conducive to the trafficking (in human beings).

As with our previous chapter, the purpose will be to examine the particular approaches adopted within the strategies, and to identify particular situational and social crime prevention measures that are advocated within them. This will be followed by an assessment of the adequacy of the national, regional and international strategies, incorporating the views of feminist scholars working within international relations, international political economy and criminology. An additional aim of the present chapter is therefore to direct attention to wider structural factors influencing human trafficking, raising questions regarding the adequacy of the existing counter-trafficking framework and dominant interpretation of the underlying root causes and conditions conducive to the trafficking in persons.

Measures to prevent and combat human trafficking

In Chapter 7, it was argued that the first category, '*Measures to prevent and combat*' should be viewed as associated with the classical school of thought, associated with social contract philosophers of the seventeenth and eighteenth centuries, including the principles of Beccaria. To reiterate, as a social reformer Beccaria sought to eradicate injustice and inconsistency within the criminal justice system, promoting proportionality, promptness and certainty in punishment (Vold, Bernard and Snipes, 1998: 14–26). Emphasising punishment as a deterrent to crime and viewing perpetrators as rational and freethinking individuals who weigh up the benefits of their crimes against the possible risks and costs of their actions, the classical paradigm within criminology directs attention to decision-making processes, providing a legislative basis for detection, investigation and prosecution.

Infused by both the discourse of modernisation and of globalisation, efforts within this work-stream are concerned with providing a normative consensus against the trafficking of persons, entailing the criminalisation of particular prohibited acts and strengthening the legal architecture, at national, regional and international levels. This action is undertaken in order to deny potential offenders the means of committing their offence, reducing opportunities for crime and victimisation to occur, and ensuring that proceeds of crime may be recovered and confiscated. The aim therefore is to deny the potential offender the benefits of their crime and, as such, remove any financial incentive which may motivate the offender in the first instance. Such measures are therefore consistent with opportunity theories and rational choice perspectives on offending. These retain the Durkheimian emphasis upon the strengthening of societal controls against crime and place confidence in the liberal belief regarding the utility of law and punishment as effective deterrents against crime (Vold, Bernard and Snipes, 1998: 153).

At an international level, within the *General Provisions* section of the UN Protocol to 'Prevent, Suppress and Punish Trafficking in Persons, Especially Women and Children', Article 5, under the heading '*Criminalisation*', introduces a requirement for each State Party to adopt legislative measures to establish criminal offences. In particular, the Protocol advocates the creation of legislation with regards to: 'attempts to commit an offence'; 'participating as an accomplice'; and, 'organizing or directing other persons to commit an offence relating to the trafficking in persons'.

At a regional level, within the EU, trafficking in human beings is specifically prohibited by Article 5 of the Charter of Fundamental Rights of the European Union, with further significant instruments including the Council Framework Decision 2002/629/JHA of 19 July 2002 on combating trafficking in human beings (OJ L 203, 1.8.2002); the EU Plan on best practices, standards and procedures for combating and preventing trafficking in human beings (OJ C 311, 9.12.2005); and the Stockholm Programme (OJ C 115, 4.5.2010). Significantly, each instrument prioritises the fight against trafficking in human beings and advocates the development of appropriate anti-trafficking legislation.[2] The frameworks cited above reveal a concerted effort at regional and international level to strengthen the legal architecture available to law enforcement agencies to detect, investigate, prosecute and punish would-be human traffickers.[3]

Thus, Article 2 of EU Directive 2011/36 directs Member States to:

> take the necessary measures to ensure that the following intentional acts are punishable:
>
>> The recruitment, transportation, transfer, harbouring or reception of persons, including the exchange or transfer of control over those persons, by means of the threat or use of force or other forms of coercion, of abduction, of fraud, of deception, of the abuse of power or of a position of vulnerability or of the giving or receiving of payments or benefits to achieve the consent of a person having control over another person, for the purpose of exploitation.
>
> (Official Journal of the European Union, 2011, Directive 2011/36/EU)

Article 3 of the directive further extends to cover offences of incitement, aiding and abetting, and attempt to commit an offence referred to in Article 2, demonstrating consistency with the UN Protocol detailed previously.

While the United Kingdom originally decided not to adopt EU Directive 2011/36 remaining outside of its jurisdiction, more recently, within the 2011 Strategy, the UK expressed its commitment to working with other countries in Europe, formally applying to opt in. In the meantime, the UK has been active in developing and reviewing existing legislation with a view to ensuring effective prosecution of traffickers. Thus, the Modern Slavery Act 2015, which received Royal Assent on 26 March 2015, consolidates earlier offences relating to trafficking and slavery, creating an offence of 'Slavery, servitude and forced or compulsory labour' and another offence of 'Trafficking' (Home Office, 2015).

Legislative frameworks have therefore been strengthened at national, regional and international levels, creating new laws, granting new powers and measures to deter human trafficking and enhance prosecution, including efforts directed towards the identification, tracing, freezing, seizure and confiscation of the proceeds of crime and the implementation of anti-money laundering legislation and instruments to enhance financial investigation.[4] Such measures have been undertaken 'to raise the risks faced by traffickers', with efforts directed toward the confiscation of profits seeking 'to drive traffickers out of business and to stop more vulnerable men, women and children becoming trafficking victims' (HM Government, 2011: 7).

Associated with this development, activities within this work-stream are directed at a regional and national level towards effective 'detection, investigation and prosecution', entailing measures to enhance law enforcement and judicial cooperation, including bodies such as Europol, Eurojust and the European Police College (detailed in Chapter 4), that are directed towards information exchange and the sharing of best practice, alongside the use of joint investigation teams (European Commission, 2012, EU Strategy COM (2012) 286 final: 9–11; HM Government, 2011: 22). With this in mind, liberal concern with due process and the rule of law also require legislative basis for the investigative tools utilised in the investigating and prosecution of offences relating to human trafficking. When considering measures to prevent and combat human trafficking then, efforts are also governed towards provision of the means of obtaining, and the admissibility of evidence including communication interception, covert surveillance and the monitoring of bank accounts to facilitate proactive financial investigation of human trafficking cases (Official Journal of the European Union, 2011, EU Directive 2011/36). These measures are consequently concerned to enhance consistency in approaches and procedures, advocating harmonisation in legislative systems and an approximation of penalties (Article 4 of EU Directive 2011/36).

Efforts to prevent and combat human trafficking consequently endeavour to plug the gap between the emergence of criminal opportunities and the measures available to law enforcement and security agencies to protect their populations. Examples include responding to the early critique and increasing awareness regarding the salience of internal trafficking from one place to another within a country, which had originally remained outside of the UN Protocol and retained a focus upon the 'international' and 'organised crime' aspects of trafficking (European Commission, 2012, EU Strategy COM (2012) 286 final: 9–11; HM Government, 2011: 4). Efforts have also recently become focused upon the criminalisation of service users as a form of deterrence and demand reduction[5] again reflecting the expanding remit of legislative efforts.

Within the previous chapter, which addresses strategic responses to threats of terrorism, it is evident that measures within this category sought to strengthen the defence of key targets including vulnerable populations and critical infrastructure. Terrorism prevention consequently entailed the use of situational crime prevention measures such as target hardening, access control, entry and exit screening, and surveillance methods. Human trafficking prevention measures remain in line with those advocated for the prevention of terrorism. Thus, within the UN, EU and UK strategies and legislative frameworks, measures are introduced in order to strengthen border and customs controls. Part III of the UN Protocol for example, under sections 11–13, advocates the strengthening of border measures including efforts to ensure the integrity and security of travel documents alongside measures to enable the denial of entry and the revocation of visas of persons implicated in the commission of offences established in accordance with the Protocol. Alongside requirements upon nation-states to develop appropriate legislative measures, the Protocol also requires states to create an obligation on the part of commercial carriers, including any transportation company or the owner or operator of any means of transport, to ascertain that all passengers are in possession of the necessary travel documentation. Further measures are introduced within this section. However, given that the Protocol merges preventative measures with efforts to enhance cooperation and coordination, these will be addressed within the next section, which examines measures to build state capacity.

On a national level, within the UK, efforts to strengthen border controls similarly consist of access controls, explicitly referring to the capitalisation of developments within technology, utilising biometrics and advance travel information to create 'an offshore line of defence', in order 'to check individuals at the point of departure and through each stage of their journey' (HM Government, 2011: 17). Alongside technology, the UK strategy utilises what are termed 'juxtaposed controls', namely immigration controls performed outside the UK by UK immigration staff, in ports, at international rail terminals and on board Eurostar services to prevent illegal immigrants before they get to the UK (HM Government, 2011: 19). Border controls also relate to the work of the UK Border Agency's Risk and Liaison Overseas Network (RALON), which currently operates in over fifty locations worldwide, working with airlines and local border control to identify and reduce the threats to the UK and to ensure passengers hold the right travel documents before they travel (HM Government, 2011: 15).

As with the international approach, there is a blurring within the UK strategy between cooperation, coordination and prevention measures to facilitate 'smarter multi-agency action at the border'. More on this shortly. Suffice to say, as with counter-terrorism methods employed within the '*Protect*' work-stream, the measures detailed above comprise practical situational crime prevention measures aligned with the liberal framework, emphasising the rule of law through the development of an effective legislative framework to facilitate the apprehension, prosecution and disruption of perpetrators of human trafficking acts (Ikenberry, 2009, 2011; Deudney and Ikenberry, 2009). Furthermore, within this section we can observe the development of a normative framework conceiving human trafficking as a violation of human rights, with law enforcement, immigration and security personnel working collaboratively with a range of partners, both within their own borders and externally, to address border, transport and documentation security deficits. Within this approach, which reflects the impact of globalising trends upon the conceptualisation of security, altered working patterns and governance arrangements, law enforcement and security responses capitalise upon technological developments to reduce opportunities available for potential perpetrators to obtain access to their targets and proceeds of their crimes. Globalising processes are consequently implicated in the generation of criminal opportunities but are also regarded as facilitating crime control responses, thereby lending support for Andreas and Nadelmann's (2006) observations regarding the existence of a 'standard view of globalisation', and the plurality of the newly emerging security field, detailed previously (Bigo, 2000; Johnston, 2000; Sheptycki, 1995; Loader and Walker, 2007) (see Chapter 4).

Measures to build states' capacity to prevent and combat human trafficking

The UN Protocol's third strand is entitled 'Prevention, cooperation and other measures'. The measures contained within this section include a number of social crime prevention approaches which we shall address later within the section entitled 'Measures to address the conditions conducive to the spread of human trafficking', along with the situational crime prevention measures contained within Articles 11–13 concerned with border and document security (detailed within the previous section). There is, therefore, a merger within the UN Protocol of a variety of courses of action, which have received separate treatment within the later 2012 UNODC Strategy; the EU Directive 2011/36/ EU; 2012 EU Strategy; and, the 2011 UK Strategy. Despite the lack of consistency however, similarities are apparent, again reflecting the liberal imperative for the maintenance and development of institutions, and for cooperative problem solving for collective security issues.

Article 9 of the Protocol, for example, refers to the need to develop policies, programmes and other measures, including cooperation with non-governmental organisations, other relevant organisations and other elements of civil society. The Protocol consequently advocates bilateral and multilateral action to alleviate the factors underpinning vulnerability to victimisation and to discourage demand. Article 10 considers law enforcement, immigration and other relevant authority cooperation with respect to information sharing and training, together with wider partners, with Article 11 explicitly referring to border agency cooperation and communication. These issues, contained within the UN Protocol, are reflected within the third component of the UNODC's Strategic Approach to combating trafficking in persons and the smuggling of migrants. In particular, the UN Strategy refers explicitly to the contribution of the UN System Task Force on Transnational Organized Crime and Drug Trafficking and its efforts to promote a comprehensive framework for UN System action against transnational organised crime and drug trafficking, including action against human trafficking and migrant smuggling. Cooperation and coordination in the area of human trafficking are also detailed with reference to the work of the

UNODC, a body tasked to 'ensure efficient coordination at the UN level', through the Inter-Agency Coordination Group against Trafficking in Persons (ICAT) and UN.GIFT. This work is reportedly undertaken in order 'to strengthen inter-agency coordination and cooperation at both the policy and operational levels', with the Global Migration Group (GMG) further tasked to strengthen interagency cooperation and ensure greater consistency in policy formulation, particularly in the area of migration. Cooperation and coordination are consequently related to the work of these bodies together with their civil society and private sector partners (UNODC, 2012: 22) and, also, in relation to the work of the UNODC in managing the activities of the United Nations Voluntary Trust Fund for Victims of Trafficking in Persons.

Enhanced coordination and cooperation and policy coherence are reiterated as key priority areas at a regional level within the 2012 EU Strategy. These measures entail action to strengthen the EU Network of National Rapporteurs or Equivalent Mechanisms; coordinating EU External Policy Activities; promoting the establishment of a Civil Society Platform; reviewing projects funded by the EU; strengthening the fundamental rights in anti-trafficking policy and related actions; coordinating training needs in a multidisciplinary context (European Commission, 2012, EU Strategy COM (2012) 286 final: 11–13). Within the EU Strategy, 'cooperation and coordination' consequently refers to the development of institutional mechanisms to undertake monitoring, data collection and assessment functions, also working to strengthen and formalise partnerships with priority third countries, international organisations and civil society. The measures contained within this work-stream also include the coordination and monitoring of anti-trafficking projects and programmes (internally and externally) and mainstreaming fundamental rights within anti-trafficking legislation and policy. Within this priority area, cooperation and coordination further extend to the facilitation of consistent judicial and cross-border law enforcement training including the development of training frameworks for transition and developing countries through the activities of the European Training Foundation, the European Police College, Frontex, and the European Asylum Support Office. This work-stream is therefore consistent with EU Directive 2011/36, which required that 'law enforcement officials and prosecutors should be adequately trained, in particular with a view to enhancing international law enforcement and judicial cooperation'.

At the national level, within the UK Strategy, cooperative action features both within the multi-agency work contained in the third priority area 'Smarter multi-agency action at the border' and the fourth priority area addressing 'Better coordination of our law enforcement efforts within the UK'. This work again relates to the liberal preoccupation with the creation of new institutions such as UK Border Agency, the National Crime Agency, and the Organised Crime Coordination Centre, to facilitate cooperation and coordination between law enforcement, customs, immigration and visa staff, to better identify organised criminals and to ensure a more coordinated response (HM Government, 2011: 21). Consequently, the UK works with European institutions such as

Frontex, Europol and Eurojust (detailed in Chapter 4), who provide risk profiles for victims and profiles for traffickers to be used during border control activities and targeted operations across Europe (HM Government, 2011: 17).

The UK Strategy also advocates the strengthening of existing bodies, incorporating the UK Human Trafficking Centre into the newly created National Crime Agency (to collate and analyse intelligence from police forces, the UK Border Agency, the Child Exploitation and Online Protection Centre, and the Gangmasters Licensing Authority), further drawing upon public, private and voluntary sector partners to assess the threats, harms and risks to the UK (HM Government, 2011: 7–8). These developments within the UK are therefore consistent with the EU requirement for Member States to establish national multidisciplinary law-enforcement units on human trafficking to function as contact points for EU agencies, to improve the detection of human trafficking and the collection and analysis of information on the subject (European Commission, 2012, EU Strategy COM (2012) 286 final: 9–11).

Collaborative working, the creation of institutions and strengthening, enhanced coordination at policy and operational levels and judicial, law enforcement and immigration cooperation are therefore dominant strategic responses for each level. Related to these efforts to facilitate institutional cooperation, the second component of the UNODC 2012 Strategy entails measures to promote the Protocols on Trafficking in Persons and Smuggling of Migrants and capacity-building activities. The multi-agency, inter-departmental, cross-sector and cooperative mechanisms identified above therefore seek to build international, regional and national capacity. This is achieved through the advancement of cooperation in the provision of information sharing, best practice and training, facilitating the implementation of international conventions and protocols and also providing technical assistance to generate an effective anti-trafficking regime, underpinned by the rule of law and human rights. As discussed within the previous section, this work also extends to include the confiscation of criminal assets and the prevention of money-laundering, thereby paralleling capacity-building efforts within counter-terrorism responses, detailed within the previous chapter.

Significantly, while such cooperative work is described as strengthening existing international, regional and national responses to human trafficking, the 2012 UNODC Strategy acknowledges that states cannot afford to be complacent. The UNODC warns that contemporary efforts are presently hindered by under-resourcing, also acknowledging that the goal of universal ratification of the Convention and Protocols has not yet been achieved, asserting: 'The ratification of the Protocols has been uneven geographically and gaps in ratification continue to make cooperation difficult and risk encouraging impunity' (UNODC, 2012: 15). Gaps evidently remain, with the UNODC acknowledging that even when states have reported criminalising trafficking in persons, not all of this legislation fully implements the international obligations of states under UNTOC or its Protocols. The mere existence of domestic laws is not therefore viewed as sufficient to ensure that they are used in practice, pointing to low prosecution rates and concluding, 'much work remains to be done to strengthen the capacity of national criminal justice systems to respond to human trafficking and migrant smuggling' (UNODC, 2012: 8). Responding to such challenges, the UNODC therefore promotes the implementation of the Organized Crime Convention and its Protocols on Trafficking in Persons and Smuggling of Migrants (with the aid of its Omnibus software), an objective placed within the remit of its cooperative and coordination activities (UNODC, 2012: 4).

Technical assistance and capacity building for member states also feature within this component of the UN Strategy, with the explicit objective of bringing national legal frameworks in line with international conventions, including: legislative assistance; extradition and the confiscation of proceeds of crime and other assets; the development of national policies and strategies; criminal justice responses in investigating and prosecuting crimes of human trafficking and migrant smuggling (by facilitating information exchange and joint action); victim support; the protection of the rights of migrants; and international cooperation (UNODC, 2012: 17; 21). Technical assistance and capacity-building activities are therefore predominantly concerned with extending the rule-of-law framework consistent with the classical imperatives to reduce opportunities, enhance risks and cost, preventing access to benefits in the form of proceeds of crime, also enhancing legislative and procedural harmonisation and an approximation of penalties. UNODC cooperative action further extends to state and non-state actors 'such as law enforcement, judiciary and victim service providers in countries of origin, transit and destination with the aim to improve transnational referrals and victim support' (UNODC, 2012: 20).

At a national level, within the UK enhanced cooperation and the provision of technical assistance is discussed within the second work-stream promoting action to enhance the ability to act early, before the harm has reached the UK.

> Evidence suggests that some countries top the list repeatedly as areas of concern for trafficking. We will therefore focus on those transit and source countries from where the greatest threat originates ... Through closer working we will engage with foreign governments to ensure that common challenges are identified, and that they work with us to address those challenges through, for example, capacity building.
>
> (HM Government, 2011: 13)

With this objective in mind, the UK strategy details collaborative work with international partners, including Interpol, European bodies such as Europol and Frontex, alongside overseas governments in source and transit countries to improve the enforcement and awareness-raising response to human trafficking. The UK also engages with the Council of Europe and EU Member States, 'to share intelligence and law enforcement expertise, exchange best practice on investigation and prosecution of traffickers, and share resources' (HM Government, 2011: 12), extending further to include the

Five Country Conference (FCC), which entails the UK working with the United States, Canada, Australia and New Zealand on common immigration-related challenges.

Capacity building therefore entails the facilitation of situational crime prevention measures, including access controls and target removal activities, which are seen to coincide with demand reduction activities. These have the potential to include social crime prevention measures, addressing the root causes of trafficking underpinning the conditions conducive to human trafficking, which will be presented shortly. Citing diplomatic measures and training assistance, the UK Strategy advocates working with transit and source countries to improve the ability of overseas investigators and prosecutors in case building and prosecution, and to ensure that appropriate local action is taken to address specific risks and threats with implications for the UK. The focus is therefore again consistent with classical concern with enhancing the certainty of detection, prosecution and punishment, also remaining consistent with opportunity and rational choice theories, which directs attention to risk enhancing measures and opportunity reducing activities.

It is perhaps interesting to note that within the previous chapter on counter-terrorism responses, a further component of the capacity-building work-stream was directed towards the creation of crisis coordination arrangements and operational procedures, to ensure interoperability between emergency services, and to enhance capabilities and resources to facilitate resilience to enable recovery in the event of a terrorist attack. With respect to counter-trafficking strategy, at an international level, the protection and support of victims of trafficking and smuggled migrants is included within the 'promotion of the Protocols and capacity building' section, detailed under the sub-heading 'technical assistance and capacity building'. Resilience and recovery are therefore conceived in terms of enhancing state capacity to respond to the needs of victims, aiding recovery and reintegration and facilitating coherent, coordinated and consistent responses in the identification, referral, processing and care provided to the men, women and children who become victims of trafficking. This reveals consistency with the counter-terrorism strategy detailed previously.

The explicit aim of the UNODC Strategy is therefore to enhance state capacity to accurately identify victims (directing attention to the sharing of best practice between law enforcement, border control, social services and judicial authorities, with regard to interviewing techniques and the use of forensics) and to provide support and protection (referring to the work of NGOs), to ensure that victims achieve full physical and psychological recovery. Support and protection are defined as including health care, psychological assistance, emergency protection and help in reintegration, with these measures explicitly tied to the objective of protecting victims. However, recognising the necessity of victim cooperation to ensure successful prosecution of traffickers and smugglers, the UNODC Strategy further requires states to ensure that they have sufficient law enforcement, administrative and immigration measures in place to identify, support, assist and protect victims and witnesses, and to ensure that victims have access to compensation for damage suffered. The UN Action Point which relates to the protection of victims stresses the provision of technical assistance in the form of guidance notes, the training of field staff and the provision of advice and expertise in the development and implementation of programmes, in close cooperation with UN key partners, multilateral and bilateral agencies (UNODC, 2012: 21–22). This aspect of capacity building therefore incorporates Articles 6–8 of the second element of the UN Protocol to Prevent, Suppress and Punish Trafficking in Persons, Especially Women and Children, entitled 'Protection of victims of trafficking in persons'.

At a regional level, Articles 11–17 of the EU Directive 2011/36 are similarly concerned with the provision of assistance and support for victims, which, it is stated, should not be conditional on the victim's willingness to cooperate or act as a witness in the criminal investigation, prosecution or trial (marking a divergence from the UN approach which had been subject to criticism for placing the needs and rights of victims below that of successful prosecution). Within the Directive, assistance and support again refer to the provision of appropriate and safe accommodation and material assistance, as well as necessary medical treatment including psychological assistance, counselling and information, and translation and interpretation services where appropriate. Moreover, such assistance and support should be available 'before, during and for an appropriate period of time after the conclusion of criminal proceedings'. These measures are reiterated within Article 6 of the UN Protocol. However, it is evident that the EU Directive omits the provision of 'employment, educational and training opportunities' from within the scope of their definition of assistance and support, a point to which we shall return later, and which has been identified as having a vital role in tackling the root causes of trafficking and for achieving human rights to equality between men and women with regard to employment, work and pay, alongside the right to choose an occupation and engage in work (Article 15 and 23 EU Charter). Article 12 of the EU Directive includes measures to provide victims with legal counselling, legal representation and compensation, also including witness protection, and measures to prevent secondary victimisation during investigation, prosecution or trial proceedings. Articles 13–16 are concerned explicitly with the provision of assistance and protection for child victims, with Article 17 addressing compensation. These measures are translated within the first priority area of the EU Strategy entitled '*Identifying, protecting and assisting victims of trafficking*'. As with the UN Protocol, UNODC Strategy and EU Directive, the EU Strategy prioritises the identification of victims to facilitate the investigation and prosecution of traffickers, also emphasising the necessity of attending to what are termed the 'five broad needs of victims', namely, 'respect and recognition, assistance, protection, access to justice and compensation'. Reiterating the focus of the 2011 Directive and UN Protocol, the EU Strategy further includes mechanisms to protect, assist and socially include victims of trafficking, measures which again omit the Protocol's suggestion for the provision of employment, educational and training opportunities. With regard to efforts to build capacity within EU Member States, this work-stream requests the development of national referral mechanisms to better identify, refer, protect and assist victims, also addressing compensation and the safe return of victims. The majority of the measures introduced within this section relate to the provision of guidelines and information covering the identification of victims, child protection systems and access to information on labour, social, victim and migrant rights within the EU and national level (EU Strategy COM(2012) 286 final: 6–8).

Within the UK Strategy, 'improved victim identification and care' feature as the first priority area, reiterating the regional focus upon the provision of a national referral mechanism and the need to better identify victims of trafficking. Citing the 2009 Europe Convention on the Trafficking in Human Beings, the UK strategy refers to the provision of a 45-day recovery and reflection period and the granting of residence permits for conclusively identified victims 'in certain circumstances'. Significantly, access to support within the UK Strategy adheres to the UN Protocol definition, thereby including the provision of education and training but again falling short of employment. As with the EU and UN approaches, information sharing, access to advice, accommodation and support, the provision of awareness training and guidance for practitioners, and those likely to come into contact with victims, exists alongside details of altered funding arrangements for victim service providers, with a particular emphasis upon child victims. As an indication of commitment to tackling human trafficking and providing support for victims, the UK Strategy further announces an intention to sign and implement the EU Directive by 2013.

Part 5 of the UK Modern Slavery Act 2015 provides a defence for slavery or trafficking victims who commit an offence. This provision therefore adheres to Directive 2011/36 which asserted that victims of trafficking in human beings should be protected from prosecution or punishment for criminal activities (including the use of false documents, or offences under legislation on prostitution or immigration), that they have been compelled to commit as a direct consequence of being subject to trafficking. The Act also introduces special measures for witnesses in criminal proceedings, civil legal aid for victims of slavery alongside provisions to enable 'independent child trafficking advocates' to be available to represent and support child victims of human trafficking facilitating access to legal or other advice, assistance and representation. The Act further includes measures relating to the issuing of guidance to public authorities with regard to the identification of victims; arrangements for providing assistance and support to victims; and, guidance concerning arrangements for determining whether there are reasonable grounds to believe that a person may be a victim of slavery or human trafficking. The Act places a requirement upon public sector bodies to notify the Secretary of State about suspected victims, also placing a requirement upon immigration rules to make provision for leave to remain in the United Kingdom to be granted to overseas domestic workers who have been determined to be a victim of slavery or human trafficking.

The measures contained within this section therefore reveal similarity with those detailed in relation to the cooperative and coordination efforts to counter terrorism referred to within the previous chapter. The liberal institutional focus upon collaboration and collective problem solving is evident with measures promoting law enforcement and judicial cooperation, multi-agency and cross-sector partnerships. Cooperation and coordination are seen here to be focused upon enhancing national, regional and international capacity within both policy and operational arenas, creating new institutions and strengthening existing ones, enhancing training, data collection and analysis, the sharing of best practice and information sharing alongside crisis coordination efforts, facilitating resilience, recovery and consistency with regard to the service and support provided to victims. Capacity building and cooperation further extend to the provision of technical assistance to facilitate the harmonisation of criminal justice responses to trafficking and approximation in sentencing.

Measures to ensure respect for human rights for all and the rule of law as the fundamental basis of the fight against human trafficking

In the Foreword of the Organized Crime Convention and its Protocols on Trafficking in Persons and Smuggling of Migrants (UNODC, 2012: iv), Kofi Annan, the former Secretary General of the UN, articulates his belief that 'the trafficking of persons, particularly women and children, for forced and exploitative labour, including for sexual exploitation, is one of the most egregious violations of human rights that the United Nations now confronts'. Employing the discourse of globalisation, Annan recognises that human trafficking is both 'widespread and growing' and as such, is regarded as comprising 'an affront to human dignity and a challenge to every State, every people and every community'. Within this narrative, Annan conceives the perpetrators of people trafficking 'as enemies of progress and human rights exploiting the openness and opportunities of globalisation for their purposes'.

Within the previous chapter, measures to ensure respect for human rights for all and the rule of law were included as the fourth strand of the UN Counter-Terrorism Strategy, comprising the fundamental basis of the fight against terrorism. To reiterate, it was explicitly argued that only by placing counter-terrorism within a rule-of-law framework can the internationally valued standard that outlaws terrorism be safeguarded (United Nations General Assembly, 2006, UN A/60/825: 22–23). Counter-trafficking strategies at the international, regional and national levels are similarly placed within a rule-of-law framework, as detailed previously with regard to the adoption and implementation of the legislative framework within the previous section. The UNODC strategy therefore urges member states to ratify the United Nations Convention against Transnational Organized Crime and Protocols, reminding states of their obligations under human rights law, refugee law and international humanitarian law, further promoting the creation of domestic legislation to tackle the threat of trafficking. EU Directive 2011/36 similarly reminds Member States of their obligations, referring specifically to the 1989 United Nations Convention on the Rights of the Child, in addition to Council Directive 2004/81/EC of 29 April 2004[6] and Directive 2009/52/EC of 18 June 2009.[7] However as noted within the EU Strategy (European Commission, 2012, COM(2012) 286 final: 4) not all Member States have ratified these legal instruments, or others securing the rights of women, domestic workers and those concerned with child and forced labour.[8]

International norms prohibiting slavery and trafficking are articulated within the Universal Declaration of Human Rights (UDHR), the Charter of Fundamental Rights of the European Union, and the UK Human Rights Act 1998. Thus, with respect to Annan's comments cited above, Article 1 of both the EU Charter of Fundamental Rights and the Universal Declaration recognise the inherent dignity and the equal and inalienable rights of all members of the human family. Indeed, within the Preamble of the UDHR, this is described as 'the foundation of freedom, justice and peace in the world', with the Preamble of the Charter of Fundamental Rights (2000/C 364/01) similarly 'resolved to share a peaceful future based on common values', particularly the 'universal values of human dignity, freedom, equality and solidarity' in addition 'to the principles of democracy and the rule of law'.

Once again, the Durkheimian aspiration for an 'international' collective conscience based upon individual freedom is observed, coexisting with the assumption articulated within the Democratic Peace thesis, which contends that liberal democratic states are pacific in their international relations with other liberal states. Modernisation theory and the liberal economic assumption that market-driven economic exchange are the roots to social progress and better standards of life in larger freedom are therefore clearly articulated within the UN Declaration of Human Rights, underpinning the legal and institutional framework of international relations following the Second World War. Human rights are, therefore, based on the principle of respect for the individual, rights to which everyone is entitled by virtue of being human.

Significantly, slavery or servitude is explicitly prohibited in all forms within Article 4 of the UNDHR, and this prohibition is reiterated within Article 5 of the EU Charter, which further adds forced labour and the trafficking in human beings to its remit. Article 5 of the UNDHR and Article 4 of the EU Charter prohibit torture or cruel, inhuman or degrading treatment or punishment, with Article 3 of the UNDHR, and Article 6 of the EU Charter, further assuring the individual right to liberty and security. These measures are also contained within the Human Rights Act 1998, which came into force in the United Kingdom in October 2000 and codifies the protections in the European Convention on Human Rights into UK law. Further protections, which also have relevance for labour, sexual and organ exploitation, include: those pertaining to the right to the integrity of the person (Article 3 EU Charter); the right to move and reside freely (Article 13 UNDHR; Article 45 EU Charter);

to the rights of the child (Article 24 EU Charter); the prohibition of child labour and protection against economic exploitation (Article 32 EU Charter); and, the right to fair and just working conditions, respecting health, safety and dignity and entitlement to rest periods and leave (Article 23 and 24 UNDHR; Article 31 EU Charter).

This framework therefore provides the basis for a moral consensus condemning slavery, servitude and trafficking in persons as a violation of human rights and as such comprises a central component of the liberal rule-of-law framework employed within international, regional and national counter-trafficking strategies, reiterated within EU Directive 2011/36. Again, while victims are obviously central to this legislative framework, it is also important to note that human rights protections are also extended to those accused of perpetrating acts of trafficking, with the human rights framework offering further protections relating to the right to have a fair trial and the principles of the legality and proportionality of criminal offences and penalties (Article 47, 48, 49 EU Charter; Article 9, 10, 11 UNDHR). Protections extend further, ensuring that in the event of removal, expulsion or extradition, individuals would not be subject to the death penalty, torture or any other inhuman or degrading treatment or punishment (Article 19 EU Charter). These measures preventing arbitrary arrest, detention or exile, ensure that defendants are presumed innocent, and have access to an impartial and public hearing and fair trial, subject to proportionate penalty. This framework therefore reflects the continuing resonance of classical principles protecting against the arbitrary application of justice and inconsistency in the administration of punishment (see Chapter 3). With regard to the previous chapter, which examined counter-terrorism strategy, these measures of due process that work to protect the rights of defendants are essential. Thus, we are reminded of an association between the failure to protect human rights, with wider claims of legitimacy for the structure of international society and individual nation-states and terrorist recruitment:

> To compromise on the protection of human rights would hand terrorists a victory they cannot achieve on their own. And when human rights are abused as part of a campaign against terrorism, terrorists exploit the abuse to mobilize recruits and seek to further justify their actions.
>
> (UN General Assembly, 2006: 23)

Significantly, with respect to terrorism, violation of human rights is regarded as central to the creation of justificatory narratives underpinning recruitment and ideological support, but is also key to understanding the underlying conditions generating cycles of violence and explanatory variables with regard to grievances and resentment viewed as conducive to terrorist recruitment. Within counter-terrorist strategy, violations of human rights are accordingly implicated in the motivation for terrorist action and wider ideological support facilitating perpetration. Drawing a parallel between the international, regional and national responses to counter-trafficking and terrorism, it is therefore helpful to examine the portrayal of trafficking motivation and the underlying causes of trafficking as detailed within the strategies. In particular, it is interesting to examine whether such a discourse (which implicates the violation of the human rights of individuals vulnerable to perpetration) is similarly evident within the policy rhetoric examining human trafficking. While recent political discourse has explicitly alluded to the need to engage with wider economic and political resolutions to the international threat of terrorism, it is also interesting to examine the place of wider structural factors within discourse relating to the factors conducive to the perpetration of trafficking and victimisation. It is to this task we now turn before engaging with theoretical assessment regarding the adequacy of contemporary approaches to counter the trafficking in human beings.

Measures to address the conditions conducive to the spread of human trafficking

It is a central argument of this chapter, that international, regional and national counter-trafficking strategies currently reflect the liberal internationalist vision of a normative, rule-based system. This system, it is argued, is based upon the rule-of-law and human rights, utilising domestic and international institutions to protect common values and as a means of responding to the criminal opportunities resulting from social change associated with processes of modernisation and globalisation. Within the '*measures to prevent and combat trafficking*', efforts to criminalise prohibited acts and to strengthen legal architecture are apparent. Thus, emphasis is placed within the existing counter-trafficking framework, upon the employment of situational crime prevention measures to deny potential perpetrators the means of committing offences relating to the trafficking in persons, alongside measures to reduce opportunities to access targets (victims), in addition to measures to recover and confiscate the proceeds of crime. Utilising new technologies and enhancing law enforcement and judicial cooperation, action is taken to strengthen the controls against crime, enhancing document, transport and border and customs security, implementing access controls, screening and surveillance, engaging in information exchange, sharing good practice and engaging in joint operations. The objective, also evident within the '*building state capacity*' measures, is to facilitate the harmonisation of legislative systems and the approximation of penalties pertaining to trafficking, enhancing cooperation and coordination, including data collection, monitoring and assessment, thereby reflecting the liberal belief in collective security and collaborative action to counter common problems.

State capacity-building measures within anti-trafficking strategy witnessed in efforts to ensure the recovery and reintegration of victims following the violation of their human rights, with such rights embedded within a moral and legislative framework as detailed above. However, such measures are also integrally linked with crime control efforts to secure victim cooperation with authorities to facilitate effective investigation, prosecution and sentencing of perpetrators. Each of the measures detailed thus far is therefore consistent with the classical emphasis upon the deterrent effect of punishment as a form of crime prevention. However, as with counter-terrorism strategy, social crime prevention measures are also detected within the anti-trafficking strategy. Thus, in the foreword of the UN Convention Against Transnational Organized Crime, the former Secretary General, Kofi Annan, locates the root of trafficking of persons for forced and exploitative labour, including for sexual exploitation, within the 'social and economic conditions in the countries from which the victims come, facilitated by practices that discriminate against women and driven by cruel indifference to human suffering on the part of those who exploit the services that the victims are forced to provide' (UNODC, 2004: iv). Similarly, the 2012 EU Strategy describes the trafficking in human beings as:

> a complex transnational phenomenon rooted in vulnerability to poverty, lack of democratic cultures, gender inequality and violence against women, conflict and post-conflict situations, lack of social integration, lack of opportunities and employment, lack of access to education, child labour and discrimination.
>
> (European Commission, 2012, COM (2012) 286 final: 3)

As with efforts to counter terrorism then, counter-trafficking efforts at the international and regional level acknowledge the significance of social and economic conditions conducive to trafficking, with Annan emphasising the significance of achieving the Millennium Development Goals as a means of eradicating poverty, promoting sustained economic growth, sustainable development and global prosperity for all. Social crime prevention measures are therefore also alluded to, with the UN Strategy advocating that States Parties employ bilateral or multilateral cooperation to alleviate the factors that make persons vulnerable to trafficking, such as poverty, underdevelopment and lack of equal opportunity. Thus, within the 2012 UN Strategy, the livelihood creation and skill development activities of the UNODC's Drug Prevention and Health Branch are detailed, particularly efforts directed towards the provision of health care, sustainable livelihood opportunities and outreach services to populations that are vulnerable to human trafficking (UNODC, 2012: 14).

Alongside economic factors such as poverty reduction and global economic growth, the *Prevent* work-stream within the counter-terrorism strategy also included efforts to address the recruitment and radicalisation of terrorists and normative work to challenge techniques of neutralisation resulting in the dehumanisation of victims and justificatory narratives providing support for the use of violence as a means of generating political change. Although reformulated, these aspects are also evident within the preventative measures contained within the national, regional and international strategies. Thus, within the UN Protocol, within the work-stream entitled, 'III. Prevention, cooperation and other measures', the situational crime prevention measures detailed previously exist alongside a range of social crime prevention measures advocating measures to 'conduct research', 'information exchange', 'mass media campaigns', in addition to those directed towards the generation of social and economic initiatives to prevent and combat trafficking in persons. Prevention within the Protocol also extends to the creation of policies and programmes to alleviate poverty, underdevelopment and lack of equal opportunity and measures to 'discourage the demand that fosters all forms of exploitation of persons, especially women and children that leads to trafficking'. Here, measures relating to the need to improve the quality and availability of information on trafficking, and those relating to awareness raising, comprise the first component of the UNODC's 2012 Strategy which refers explicitly to measures to expand UN.GIFT's Knowledge Hub with the aspiration of becoming 'the primary UN portal on human trafficking'; the promotion of the Blue Heart Campaign as an awareness-raising and advocacy tool; media coverage, website, Facebook and social media usage to raise awareness and mobilise support for action; and, also, the use of UN Goodwill ambassadors to bring awareness to key issues.

Much of this 'preventative' work therefore entails efforts to prevent people from becoming victims of trafficking through the provision of crime prevention advice and support directed to those ends. For example, in relation to migrant smuggling, the UNODC (2012: 8) strategy cites research which concludes that 'migrant smuggling is best prevented by informing potential migrants that being smuggled is not worth the expense and the risk, as well as enforcing laws against the exploitation of foreign labour'. As with such efforts directed towards terrorist recruitment, these measures are also directed toward the decision-making processes of would-be perpetrators entailing the incorporation of SCP opportunity-reduction techniques including efforts directed towards reducing temptation, and those directed towards the stimulation of feelings of conscience at the point of contemplating the commission of specific kinds of offence (Clarke, 1997). Reflecting classical assumptions regarding human nature, again, it is assumed that would-be offenders (and potential victims) rationally calculate the risks and benefits of their action, and that the provision of information and support will divert those at risk and challenge values and techniques of neutralisation, which provide justificatory narratives for those engaging in trafficking. The provision of information, research, awareness raising and education programmes are also key components of the EU Directive 2011/36 preventative action under Article 18, as are actions promoting practitioner training and multi-agency, cross-sector collaboration to those ends. Criminalisation is also included as a key aspect of prevention within Article 18, suggesting that Member States should consider taking measures to establish a criminal offence of the use of services which are the objects of exploitation.

Other aspects of demand reduction, evident within the 2011 EU Strategy include research and the sharing of best practice, building upon work undertaken in relation to public awareness campaigns, targeting consumers and users of services and initiatives aimed at eliminating human trafficking from the supply chains of businesses, through the implementation of corporate social responsibility and codes of conduct. Similarly, within the UK Strategy emphasis is placed upon the need to tackle 'the demand for inexpensive, unprotected and often illegal labour'. As with the EU Strategy, this objective is pursued by encouraging greater corporate moral and social responsibility within the private sector 'to build an environment where this kind of labour is neither desired nor readily available' (HM Government, 2011: 23). Such efforts reflect the desire to generate a normative consensus prohibiting exploitation, thereby emphasising the harm of the victim, further tackling justificatory narratives and the dehumanisation of trafficked men, women and children.

Private sector engagement is also highlighted as a key aspect of prevention within the EU Strategy, alongside the previously mentioned awareness campaigns aimed at vulnerable groups at risk from victimisation. Prevention within the UK Strategy is captured in the heading 'Enhancing our ability to act early' emphasising collaborative efforts to raise awareness, alongside enforcement to 'disrupt and deter' potential traffickers. This aspect of the UK Strategy reveals similarity with the regional and international approaches in its emphasis upon data collection and analysis and international cooperation, 'targeting traffickers before they reach the UK and, preventing more people from becoming victims in the first place' including awareness raising in source and transit countries to reduce the supply of potential victims to the UK (HM Government, 2011: 12). The UK strategy further employs border and access controls, which are viewed as comprising an essential aspect of the UK preventative strategy including the use of e-Borders and juxtaposed controls to improve the security, efficiency and effectiveness of the border, as well as using intelligence, immigration powers and visa applications to deflect potential offenders and to exclude individuals seeking to enter the UK.

To summarise then, awareness-raising activities are therefore emphasised in order to counter the dehumanisation of victims and also as means of target reduction, while efforts to strengthen criminal justice responses serve to enhance the risks for would-be perpetrators (enhancing the certainty of detection, investigation, prosecution and penalty), reducing benefits through the removal of financial incentives through the confiscation of proceeds of crime. Situational crime prevention measures are used to strengthen controls, denying offenders the means of committing crime and reducing the opportunities available.

As with the counter-terrorism strategies however, the issue of motivation remains relatively absent reflecting an assumption regarding the financial motive of offenders to engage in trafficking. Thus within the UK strategy it is asserted that 'Offenders are primarily driven by profit', citing the UK Threat Assessment judgement that 'organised immigration crime is lucrative enough to attract and maintain the interest of organised criminals' (HM Government,

2011: 6). Significantly, while engagement with perpetrators is briefly referred to within a wider discussion regarding the need to enhance an understanding of how and why people become victims of trafficking (thereby raising the prospect of engaging with the motivation of offenders in their decision to perpetrate acts of trafficking), this promise is short-lived. Thus, the UK Strategy advocates the need to standardise de-briefing practices for victims and traffickers as a means of building intelligence, but restricts such engagement to a limited range of 'necessary intelligence gathering', focusing upon securing details of recruitment, transit routes, methods of crossing the UK border, and activities within the UK (measures reflected within Article 10 of the UN Protocol). Similarly, while aspects of globalisation are also implicated as having generated opportunities for both the legal and illegal movement of people across borders, particularly the ease of international travel, and while it is acknowledged that traffickers use poverty, war, crisis and ignorance to lure vulnerable migrants to the UK for exploitation, the counter-terrorist strategic emphasis upon the need to facilitate dialogue, social inclusion, education and the need to challenge extremist ideas remain conspicuously absent from counter-trafficking discourse. Victims, we are informed, may travel to the UK willingly in the belief they are destined for a better life, moving from poorer to wealthier countries, with the UK Strategy further acknowledging that 'some countries top the list repeatedly as areas of concern for trafficking'. Yet, there is little engagement with the historical context underpinning the wider structural factors located as the root of these developments, and again, there is little engagement with political resolutions, which, it seems, remain beyond the scope of UK action. The violation of human rights which featured as a possible motivating factor in the recruitment of terrorism and the prevalence of alternative ideologies which require challenging, again remain absent from discussions of human trafficking. It is to these omissions, and to others, emphasised by feminist international relations and political economic scholars, that we now turn.

Challenging the status quo – global economy and feminist reimagining

While the UNODC Strategy, EU Directive 2011/36, EU Strategy and UK Strategy claim to adopt a contextual understanding and sensitivity to the underlying causes of the different forms of trafficking, purporting to generate measures to prevent trafficking, protect victims, and prosecute perpetrators, it is also evident that a growing literature remains critical of current policy responses within this area. Jahic and Finckenauer (2005) for example argue that the theorisation of trafficking has become a conflict zone reflecting tension between different political agendas and interests. Their work subsequently identifies four different conceptualisations or themes evident within the existing literature and policy responses to trafficking as 'illegal migration', as 'prostitution', as 'forced labour' and as 'involving criminal activity' (Jahic and Finckenauer, 2005, 24–40). For Jahic and Finckenauer (2005: 37), while there has been a tendency to simplify and isolate such themes, trafficking entails all of these issues and consequently there is a need to generate a response capable of grasping all aspects.

For True (2012) the dominant international approach to trafficking has entailed conceptualising the problem as a criminal justice issue. This approach, it is argued, primarily seeks to identify and prosecute traffickers, and to maintain the sanctity of national borders, despite evidence regarding the ineffectiveness of criminal prosecution as a deterrent. True joins a number of authors who implicate intensified international integration and US hegemony as influencing the development of the criminal justice approach towards human trafficking (Papanicolaou, 2008: 381; Snajdr, 2013; Hughes and Denisova, 2001). This trend has been located as following initial collaboration and lobbying by abolitionist feminists and conservative Christian groups in the United States, who sought to eradicate prostitution and whose efforts resulted in the Victims of Trafficking and Violence Protection Act (VTVPA) in 2000. Papanicolaou and Snajdr regard the related TIP report stemming from the act as a strategy on the part of the US government to manage and shape the criminal justice landscapes of transitional states, presenting the report as a tool of foreign policy, applying international political pressure and ensuring compliance through a ranking of countries attached to threats of US sanctions. US influence is further illustrated by these authors in the funding arrangements of international and domestic NGOs alongside assistance in the form of law enforcement and judicial training around the globe. This work is therefore aligned with the state crime literature within Chapter 5 and the statecraft literature within Chapter 2, which interprets law and criminal justice as a manifestation of power and social control, and, influenced by symbolic interactionism and constructivism, reinterprets both crime and crime control as socially constructed phenomena.

As detailed previously, Andreas and Nadelmann (2006: 253) similarly call into question dominant discourse, which presents the internationalisation of crime control as a natural and predictable response to the growth of transnational crime resulting from globalising tendencies. This work implicates transnational moral entrepreneurs, such as those identified by Papanicolaou and Snajdr, in addition to powerful states (such as the United States), in promoting and imposing 'their criminal norms on others'. This work consequently points to the centrality of the USA in setting the international agenda and framing the debate, resulting in a merger between the strategic conceptualisation of human trafficking as organised crime, prostitution and trafficking. To illustrate the point, the UNODC Strategy argues that the trafficking in persons and smuggling of migrants are 'generally committed by organized criminal groups of varying degrees of scale and organization' (UNODC, 2012: 20) with the UK Strategy similarly acknowledging that 'most traffickers are organised criminals' (HM Government, 2011: 6). Efforts are therefore concentrated around capacity building to strengthen the investigation, prosecution and adjudication of such cases employing advanced techniques including intelligence-led policing, financial investigations and the use of forensics, enhancing document and transport security and tackling the money laundering aspects of such crimes.

Snajdr (2013) examines this 'prevailing anti-trafficking master narrative'. This project, he argues, is driven by the USA, and is underpinned by three basic propositions, first, that trafficking-in-persons exists on a massive and ever-increasing scale (a view espoused by Kofi Annan within the Foreword to the Protocol, where he describes trafficking in persons as 'widespread and growing'). The second assumption identified by Snajdr is that human trafficking is the result of a set of legal shortcomings on the part of other states (a view again evident within each of the strategies detailed earlier with regard to capacity building, assistance and cooperation). The final assumption recognised by Snajdr is the view that the appropriate response to trafficking is to strengthen laws and law enforcement and to encourage the non-profit sector to assist with helping victims (again evidenced within the strategic documents detailed previously with respect to the measures included to prevent and combat trafficking, build capacity, and embed human rights). For Jahic and Finckenauer (2005: 37), this emphasis upon the organised crime aspect of trafficking has been detrimental to victim safety and well-being, which, they argue, are sacrificed to the prioritisation of prosecution imperatives. Papanicolaou (2008: 379) further challenges the ideological conceptualisation of trafficking as organised crime, suggesting that it acts 'as a diversion from more substantive paths of inquiry', particularly the 'structures of national economy ... that bear upon patterns of labour exploitation'. In Hughes and Denisova's (2001: 63) study of trafficking in the Ukraine, while accepting the prevalent role of organised crime networks, it is further argued that it is also important to direct attention to the collaboration of individual criminals and organised crime groups with corrupt police and government officials, foreign governments and NGOs, which together comprise a 'transnational criminal nexus'. Governments of the destination countries are consequently viewed by Hughes and Denisova as complicit in this process, 'often open and unapologetic about their demand for foreign women and their intention to legalize the flow of women from sending countries', suggesting moreover, that countries with legal or tolerated sex industries create the demand (a point responded to recently with the criminalisation of service users within the UK Slavery Act 2015 and EU Directive 2011/36/EU). Critical theorists consequently emphasise the blurring of boundaries between legitimate and illicit enterprise and state complicity emphasising continuity and interdependency with other sectors of the labour market. Papanicolaou (2008: 402), for instance suggests that:

> Whereas standard accounts conjure up an image of all powerful, control hungry, mafia-type transnational organisations, the consideration of the available information so far points to rather small groups, which are perhaps interconnected and heterogeneous overall, but which possess significant ties with legitimate endpoints, such as bars, night clubs, or strip clubs, where a strong indigenous presence is indispensable to the whole process.

For Papanicolaou, it is essential to examine the local and domestic context of trafficking, examining the 'entire circuit of exploitation' as it is embedded within wider economic and social conditions.

The 'organised crime' narrative has also been challenged for failing to attend to political, military and corporate complicity, with recent studies highlighting a continuity of violence between peacetime, wartime, post-war and post-crises situations. Scholars have therefore examined the relationship between military presence and the emergence of domestic sex industries and trafficking for sexual exploitation. This includes work which has highlighted the role of UN peace-keepers, sub-contractors and law enforcement personnel in the sexual exploitation of both women and children within countries, including: Angola, Bosnia, Cambodia, Croatia, Mozambique and Rwanda and Thailand (Enloe, 1990; Kelly, 2000: 57–59; Snajdr, 2013: 245; Human Rights Watch, 2002; Arnold and Bertone, 2002: 30; Iñiguez de Heredia, 2008: 307; Tickner, 1992).

Jacobs, Jacobson and Marchbank (2000: 1) similarly draw attention to the role of states in creating and perpetuating conflict and violence, as well as their potential for creating the conditions in which conflicts, especially engendered ones, might be curbed or ameliorated. This point is also made by True (2012), who identifies a direct association between state failure to protect women's economic and social rights (by monitoring labour standards and ensuring access to adequate housing, education and alternative employment opportunities), and violence against women (True, 2012: 58).

Critics of the dominant 'organised crime/criminal justice' policy response, therefore question the accuracy of the organised crime narrative, suggesting that the contemporary focus upon transnational organised networks fails to engage with situations where participants are not organised and where the event occurs within domestic boundaries (Iñiguez de Heredia, 2008: 307), also ignoring state complicity and diverting attention away from a wider range of actors central to the exploitation of human beings. With this in mind, failings identified within the UN Trafficking Protocol with regard to the domestic dimension of trafficking have, it seems, been recognised and responded to recently (UK Modern Slavery Act 2015; Official Journal of the European Union, 2011, EU Directive 2011/36/EU; European Commission, 2012, EU COM(2012) 286 final: 9–11; and HM Government, 2011: 4). Thus, the Modern Slavery Act defines Trafficking as follows: 'A person commits an offence if the person arranges or facilitates the travel of another person ("V") with a view to V being exploited'. Here, 'travel' includes 'within any country', thereby widening the scope of the trafficking framework to include domestic cases.

Further encouraging signs have been evidenced through increasing academic and political awareness regarding the difficulty in obtaining accurate figures of trafficking, with commentators noting wide variation in the estimates provided, and the data utilised. This recognition reveals an unwillingness to unthinkingly cite TIP (Trafficking in Person) estimates, with the UK Strategy explicitly acknowledging such difficulties, and with the EU including 'knowledge and research generation' as explicit objectives within its strategy. Academic literature further alludes to a growing awareness regarding the questionable nature of frequently cited statistics, emphasising that such data may not represent the same things, and highlighting a tendency for governments, law enforcement agencies and NGOs to conflate victims of trafficking with victims of labour exploitation, thereby failing to differentiate between trafficking and smuggling, rendering meaningful conclusions practically impossible (Aas, 2007: 37; Arnold and Bertone, 2002; Jahic and Finckenauer, 2005: 28; UNODC, 2012: 8; Iñiguez de Heredia, 2008: 300; Snajdr, 2013).

Data limitations aside, for Snajdr, the prevailing master narrative has constructed human trafficking as a global crime which places the 'rule of law' societies of Western Europe and North America as victims, alongside predominantly, women and children. This discourse, he suggests is highly selective, failing to include important details regarding the context that fosters sexual exploitation and fails to include key experiences, particularly those which depart from the grand narrative. These concerns regarding the accuracy of trafficking data and the representation of 'the trafficked' are reiterated within a body of literature which takes exception to the addition of prostitution within the organised crime 'criminal justice' orientation of current counter-trafficking responses. In particular, this merger has been viewed by several commentators as inadequate, leading to confusion and the misrepresentation of trafficking victims, resulting in punitive and morally charged crime control responses which criminalise traffickers and prostitution clients and which fail to adequately address human rights and labour protection (Iñiguez de Heredia, 2008: 313; Bernstein, 2012: 236–242).

The root of this confusion has been located within an ideological divide between two opposing feminist positions regarding prostitution. Both positions, it is argued, have become significant in influencing policy, also highlighting the salience of moral entrepreneurialism for the development of the international, regional and national legislative framework for counter-trafficking. As detailed by Doezema (2000: 33), the first perspective is described as 'the neo-abolitionist position'. This presents prostitution as a form of violence against women, comprising a form of 'sexual exploitation' and more recently, as a violation of human rights. Within this position, every act of prostitution is regarded as involving coercion and exploitation due to the cultural and social inequalities between men and women. Anti-trafficking legislation within the US incorporated the views of feminists and conservative Christians who sought to eradicate prostitution. Trafficking, prostitution and organised crime thereby became fused, resulting in what Jahic and Finckenauer (2005: 33) have described as the 'trafficking as prostitution' position. The later iteration of this neo-abolitionist position consequently encompassed the view that trafficking constitutes another form of commodification of women's bodies, and therefore it is impossible to separate prostitution and trafficking. Within this perspective, both prostitution and trafficking entail the 'purchasing' of a woman's body, albeit under slightly different conditions and, therefore, there is no legitimate foundation for separating voluntary and involuntary prostitution. For Jahic and Fickenauer, this position therefore requires that every sex worker should be regarded as a trafficking victim requiring protection and assistance.

The second view of prostitution distinguishes between 'trafficking in women' and 'forced prostitution' on the one hand and 'voluntary prostitution' on the other (Doezema, 2000: 33). The issue of consent and agency is therefore extremely important within this perspective, with proponents of this view emphasising women's right to choose to sell sex as a profession and questioning the earlier perspective which regards all kinds of commercial sex as involving victimisation (Aas, 2007: 44–45). Scholars note that the legacy of this tension between feminist perspectives on prostitution remains evident within discussions of human trafficking today. The diverging positions are consequently reflected in law, which conflates prostitution with human trafficking, criminalising traffickers and prostitutes' customers (emphasised within the legislative framework and strategies detailed previously). This position is contrasted against calls to decriminalise and to destigmatise women's sexual labour, and to gain rights and protections for sex workers.

While the UN Protocols make a distinction between trafficking in persons[9] and the smuggling of migrants,[10] commentators have argued that existing instruments compound confusion by failing to define prostitution and sexual exploitation, resulting in a failure to distinguish clearly between these issues and trafficking (Iñiguez de Heredia, 2008: 310). The merger of prostitution and trafficking has also been criticised for placing disproportionate emphasis upon sexual violation rather than the structural conditions of exploited labour more generally (Bernstein, 2012: 242; Aas, 2007: 39). Jahic and Finckenauer (2005: 34) reiterate this point, asserting that the link between prostitution and trafficking has been stressed so single-mindedly at times, that the possibilities that trafficking may not always or necessarily involve sexual exploitation, and that not all sex workers are trafficking victims, have become lost. Thus, UNODC's 2012 'Comprehensive Strategy to Combat Trafficking in Persons and Smuggling of Migrants' identifies exploitation for sexual purposes as the most visible form, reporting that approximately 79 per cent of trafficking victims are trafficked for sexual exploitation, with 18 per cent being trafficked for forced labour (UNODC, 2012: 6). These finding are consistent with the EU Strategy, which similarly reports that 'three quarters of registered victims were trafficked for sexual exploitation (an increase from 70 per cent in 2008 to 76 per cent in 2010) and the rest for labour exploitation (a decrease from 24 per cent in 2008 to 14 per cent in 2010), forced begging (3 per cent) and domestic servitude (1 per cent)' (European Commission, 2012, 286: 2–3). However, within the 2011 UK Strategy, it is suggested that whilst historically, 'most adult victims identified were women trafficked for sexual exploitation' more 'recent trends suggest that trafficking for labour exploitation could become more prevalent than other forms of trafficking', thereby predicting an alteration in this pattern over the longer term. This recognition within the UK strategy therefore reiterates academic observation that the conflation of trafficking with prostitution and sex work has resulted in an excessive amount of attention on the sexual exploitation aspect at the expense of trafficking for other purposes, also leading to moralistic undertones entering policy discussions (Jahic and Finckenauer, 2005: 25).

Despite limited evidence of progress, Doezema (2000: 24) and Jahic and Finckenauer (2005: 27) suggest that trafficking victims continue to be portrayed as 'innocent', 'deceived and unwilling', 'young', 'naïve', and 'in need of protection', a representation which is viewed by such authors as reflecting a minority of those trafficked and distorting policy responses and understanding of the dynamics of the phenomena. Drawing a parallel between earlier myths surrounding 'white slavery', and more recently in relation to 'human trafficking', commentators have located the misrepresentation of victims and early legislative instruments as grounded in the perceived need to regulate female sexuality, mobility, and independence, and responding to 'perceived threats to the "purity" or chastity of certain populations of women' (Iñiguez de Heredia, 2008: 304). This observation therefore adds a gender dimension to the social control function of law and criminal justice, as discussed within Chapters 2 and 4. For Doezema (2000: 24–26) this has been achieved under the guise of protecting women, comprising a metaphor for a number of deeper fears and anxieties concerning national identity, women's increasing desire for autonomy, foreigners, immigrants and colonial peoples. Bernstein (2012: 242–245), similarly, in accounting for what is described as the 'recent "carceral" turn in anti-trafficking policy', views this configuration as a new social strategy for regulating race and class others. Anti-trafficking policy is therefore described as having witnessed a fundamental shift in focus from 'bad men inside the home' to 'sexual predators outside of it' and from concern with 'sexually improper women' to sexually improper (often racially coded as non-white and foreign) criminal men, and unscrupulous organised crime networks. Within such scholarship, contemporary strategies are regarded as serving to manage the racialised poor, delegitimising markets in female sexual labour and the commercialisation of sexuality. For Bernstein, this comprises part of a neo-liberal gender strategy, espousing a moralistic sexual politics based upon an ideology that is 'pro-marriage', 'pro-family' and 'anti-non-procreative sex'. The symbolic interactionist and constructivist concern with discourse, meaning, interpretation and power, therefore becomes significant within this analysis. What is particularly worrying for Bernstein is that this approach restricts an understanding of 'women's human rights' to questions of sexual violence and to bodily integrity, thereby obfuscating the gendered dimensions of broader structural social, economic, and cultural issues, individualising trafficking and removing responsibility from state and international institutions.

Pointing to the portrayal of illegal immigrants and prostitutes, who are represented as typically bad, undeserving of protection and subject to public vilification and criminalisation, theorists examine human trafficking agendas as a means of societal control, setting the parameters of idealised femininity and functioning as a tool for migration control and as a means of governing through crime (Papanicolaou, 2008: 381; Aas, 2007: 33; Bernstein, 2012: 235). This work suggests that the representation of victims as innocent and/or duped reflects simultaneous efforts to protect some, while punishing those who do not meet the criteria, further serving to suppress unregulated migratory flows. Academics adopting this position point out that the majority of trafficking victims are aware that the employment offered to them is in the sex industry, voluntarily entering into such activities, only later discovering the horrendous conditions under which they are expected to work. With this revised portrayal of trafficking victims, it becomes necessary to regard women as independent actors endowed with rights and reason, a realisation which scholars have argued has resulted in an uneasy compromise within the UN Protocol to Prevent, Suppress and Punish Trafficking in Persons, Especially Women and Children. Within the Protocol, the consent of a victim of trafficking to the intended exploitation is accordingly deemed 'irrelevant' (UNODC, 2004: 43). For Iñiguez de Heredia (2008: 310) and Doezema (2002: 20), the inclusion of this statement within the Protocol reflects an effort to engage with the two contrasting ideological positions identified above (prostitution as an abuse of women's human rights versus sex work as legitimate labour).

This approach therefore sidesteps wider structural issues including the global economic and political aspects of migratory flows, and the role of power and unequal relations in setting the parameters for employment and social inclusion.

As observed by Jahic and Finckenauer (2005: 36), '[i]n practice, it is hard to make these distinctions and to differentiate between exploited and coerced trafficking victims on the one hand, and migrants who are willing to endure considerable hardship on the other'. However, in failing to differentiate between trafficking and migration for sex work, Iñiguez de Heredia (2008: 310) notes that the Protocol 'is likely to make life even more difficult for Third World women who are most likely to travel for sex work'. The Convention therefore grapples uneasily with the distinction between 'smuggling', 'sex trafficking' and 'prostitution'. For Iñiguez de Heredia (2008: 310), 'the clause "irrelevant consent" is there to take the weight off the victim in proving that there was force involved, and also acknowledges that the majority of victims know that they will be involved in some kind of illegal activity though they are enslaved in the end'.

For Doezema (2000: 45–46) the social stigma and legal restrictions surrounding prostitution mean that women and men in the sex industry are denied the legal protection granted others as citizens and as workers. Thus according to Anthias (2014: 165), their over-riding problems are therefore linked to illegality as migrants and the illegal nature of the sex trade itself in many countries, making them doubly vulnerable. Extending the international and national labour and human rights standards to the sex industry and other informal labour sectors is therefore regarded as the most promising method of ensuring the rights of those involved. For Doezema, the generation of 'new laws that target "guilty" women at the expense of "innocent" comprises a position that restrict women's ability to migrate and are based more on states' interests in controlling immigration and women's sexuality'. Doezema argues 'that policies towards "trafficking" must be based on the recognition of women's and migrant's rights' (Doezema, 2000: 45–46). Doezema concludes by spelling out the unpalatable truth: 'Once it is recognised that debt-bondage and other slavery-like practices, when they occur, are actually problems for women who are already sex workers, or who plan to be, it is impossible to get around the fact that these are abuses of sex workers' rights' Doezema (2000: 48).

Retaining the focus upon labour and human rights standards and moving from consideration of sex work to labour exploitation more generally, Arnold and Bertone (2002: 31), citing the work of Marshall (2001: 8), recognise that trafficking of people follows irregular migration flows into industries where there is a demand for cheap labour. Moreover, this pattern is thought to mirror irregular migration flows all over the world. Along with the social, political, and economic circumstances, characteristics of such work include exploitation in the form of debt bondage, low or no wages, excessive working hours, and unsafe working conditions. Industries characterised by a high proportion of irregular migrants include factory work, fisheries, and domestic labour. Significantly, and reflecting the observations made in relation to sex workers, the degree of exploitation is thought to vary, with Arnold and Bertone recognising that it may often not even be seen as such by the 'victim', who may see themselves as being no worse off than if they had stayed home.

As mentioned in the previous section detailing strategic measures to counter the conditions conducive to trafficking, it is generally recognised at each level (the international, regional and national), that poverty is a vital underlying factor associated with human trafficking. Indeed, within the Foreword of the UN Protocol, Annan asserts 'it is rooted in social and economic conditions in the countries from which the victims come, facilitated by practices that discriminate against women and driven by cruel indifference to human suffering on the part of those who exploit the services that the victims are forced to provide'. This statement appears at first sight to recognise that 'inequalities, poverty and lack of opportunities affect men and women differently' (Iñiguez de Heredia, 2008: 303). Indeed, EU Directive 2011/36/EU explicitly recognises what is termed 'the gender-specific phenomenon of trafficking', acknowledging that women and men are often trafficked for different purposes and advocating gender-specific assistance and support measures 'where appropriate'. The 2012 EU Strategy elaborates further, stating that 'vulnerability to trafficking and to different forms of exploitation is shaped by gender', recognising that 'women and girls tend to be trafficked for exploitation in the sex industry, in domestic work or the care sector', with 'men and boys' tending 'to be victims of forced labour, in particular in agriculture, construction, mining, forestry sectors and on fishing fleets'. Gender may therefore, we are informed, impact the short- and long-term consequences for victims with implications for the support and assistance provided. Within the EU Strategy, action is therefore advocated to undertake research into the gender specificities of the way men and women are recruited and exploited, also committing to increase understanding of vulnerable 'high-risk' groups including children, especially early school leavers, children left behind, unaccompanied children, and children with disabilities, as well as people in the Roma community.

While gender inequality and discrimination against women feature within the international narratives of contemporary counter-trafficking strategies, scholars have recently called into question the adequacy of these 'gender-specific' approaches. True (2012), for example, who employs a feminist political economy approach to the study of violence against women, suggests that the present 'gendered law-and-order approach' evident within contemporary anti-trafficking strategies, remains problematic. Such an approach, she argues requires a clear delineation between trafficking victims and illegal migrants. However, as we have already noted, such a distinction is extremely ambiguous. The result, for True, is that most women appear to fall outside of formal victim processes, resulting from officer discretion influenced by gender and racial stereotyping and the prejudices and imperatives of states, shaped by wider geo-political and economic interests (see also, Crawley, 2000: 87–104). Victims are therefore often subject to restricted migration possibilities, criminalisation and/or deportation as illegal non-citizens, with access to assistance, welfare, or victim migration status dependent upon formal identification processes and/or cooperation and willingness to act as witnesses within any subsequent criminal trial (Doezema, 2000: 39; Bowling and Sheptycki, 2012: 115). For True (2012: 71), this downplays the objective of protecting human rights and emphasises the failure of states to locate trafficking in broader patterns of global migration, uneven development and gendered inequalities. Furthermore, contemporary counter-trafficking strategies are chastised for their failure to acknowledge the broader issue of abuse, exploitation, and unfair and unequal treatment of migrant workers, particularly with respect to the domestic service sectors, where women and girls predominate (True, 2012: 76).

True's contribution directs attention to a small but growing body of literature which challenges the dominant conceptualisation of security within international relations and policy discourse, and which directs attention to the significance of gender to the emergence of the state system, imperialism, capitalism, modernisation and globalisation (Enloe, 1990; Tickner, 1992, 2014; Jacobs, Jacobson and Marchbank, 2000). In *Gender in International Relations,* Tickner's (1992) groundbreaking analysis examined the implications of a feminist perspective on international relations, challenging traditional accounts for their failure to explicitly address gender as a category of analysis, arguing further, that little attention has been paid to women's particular needs with respect to security or to how women are affected by global politics or the workings of the world economy. Identifying the ambiguous role of women within the dominant conceptualisation of security, Tickner (1992: 28) asserts that while women have traditionally been defined as those whom the state and its men are protecting, women retain little control over the conditions of their protection. For Tickner, feminist reformulations of the meaning of security are required to redirect attention to the relationship of hierarchical gender relations to other forms of domination, and as a source of domination themselves. Doezema (2000: 45) for example, identifies the broadening focus of 'trafficking in women' to have expanded to include domestic labour and marriage, serving to link trafficking to wider issues of labour migration and the lack of informal-sector labour regulation, thereby highlighting the complexity and reality of female labour migration.

While for Jahic and Finckenauer (2005: 37), broadening the definitional scope of trafficking risks diverting attention away from 'real' victims and their needs, resulting in unfocused programmes and watered down policies, others have examined the structures which lead to poverty, inequality and gender division, emphasising continuity and a continuum of violence and exploitation. In doing so, such studies reflect again the first ideological perspective regarding prostitution, detailed previously, which emphasises both prostitution and human trafficking as violations of human rights. However, grappling with the second ideological position, which rejects the notion of victimisation and retains the notion of agency and employment choice, this new body of thought introduces the notion of survival strategies and the concept of socially and economically constrained choice. Brennan (2003: 156), cited in Aas (2007: 44–45), for example, points out that sex workers can be 'at once independent and dependent, resourceful and exploited. They are local agents caught in a web of global economic relations'. Similarly, for True (2012: 62–63), poverty undermines neo-liberal notions of individual choice by eliminating or criminalising alternative means of survival, thereby pushing women to choose migration as a way to escape oppressive economic and social conditions (see also Bernstein, 2012: 241). This position acknowledges that not all trafficked victims are victims in the traditional sense, noting 'often migration was their decision as an economic agent pursuing better access to productive resources and independence'. For Iñiguez de Heredia (2008: 300–301) the underlying causes of trafficking, including gender, race and class discrimination and violence must be contextualised with respect to people's own struggles against those circumstances that make them a target of such discrimination and violence.

True therefore joins a growing number of authors who direct attention to the existence of a multidimensional continuum of violence, a position similarly adopted within the state crime literature discussed in Chapter 5 (see Michalowski, 2010: 23). Thus, in 1992, Tickner highlighted the interconnection between structural violence associated with imperialism, militarism, racism and sexism, arguing that 'the behaviour of individuals and the domestic policies of states cannot be separated from states' behaviour in the international system' (Tickner, 1992: 56). More recently, feminist scholars have argued that the continuum of violence extends from 'violence in the home, to the structural violence of poverty, to the ecological violence associated with the depletion of our planetary resources and natural disasters, to the violence of war and its aftermath' (True, 2012: 5). Violence at all levels of society is therefore reconceptualised as interrelated and embedded in the gender, class and race hierarchies of dominance and subordination. This body of work therefore advocates a gendered corrective to dominant paradigms within international relations and criminal justice theorising, requiring a reorientation of attention to the perspective of women's experience of insecurity rather than the security agendas of states. True (2012) therefore examines gendered forms of labour exploitation in the global political economy to which women are especially susceptible, including transnational domestic labour, trafficking for sex, prostitution and other indentured labour, also exploring gender violence within free trade zones, special economic areas and transition countries as a result of liberalisation and the deregulation of markets. By widening the definition of violence, True is able to examine the perpetuation of gender-based violence resulting from the activities of international financial institutions which have resulted in economic and social austerity, providing a much needed link to violence within the household, extending her analysis to within the context of armed conflict, post-conflict and post-crises situations.

This work acknowledges both female perpetration and male victimisation, emphasising structural constraints upon efforts to extract oneself from exploitative situations in addition to heightening vulnerability and susceptibility to both victimisation and perpetration. As noted previously, when discussing strategic approaches towards terrorism, the violation of human rights became implicated as a potential underlying factor influencing terrorist recruitment, generating resentment and grievances with consequences for the emergence of justificatory narratives and techniques of neutralisation to qualify such behaviour towards others. While issues such as poverty and the socio-economic conditions of individuals and states enter within the strategic narratives for counter-trafficking in relation to the recruitment and migration of potential victims of human trafficking, such discussions are omitted in relation to potential perpetrator motivation. Drawing upon the work of Shannon (1999), Iñiguez de Heredia (2008: 302) reminds us of the salience of structural inequalities that underlie the problem of trafficking, identifying poverty and cultural attitudes including the conceptualisation of 'women and children as second-class citizens' as the wider context which ultimately cultivates the ground for both victims and criminals and their attempts to escape these realities. Ideas, ideology, discourse, meaning, interpretation and power therefore matter, reflecting again the salience of symbolic interactionist and constructivist insights. Within this work, attention is consequently directed toward gender inequality and the violation of human rights (including social and economic rights) as a significant contributing factor underlying the trafficking in persons.

Noting the sidelining of gender within dominant discourses of globalisation, Jacobs (2000) is one of a growing number of scholars recognising the differential impact of globalising tendencies upon men and women, remaining sensitive to other social cleavages such as class and race. Thus, while many have noted the deepening global inequality accompanying globalisation (Wallerstein, 2005), with some drawing attention to the existence of a hierarchy of countries in the world resulting in increasing exploitation and economic disadvantages faced by many third-world economies and societies, few have taken issues of gender as the object for study. Those that have recognise that women have been disproportionately affected by the detrimental effects of globalisation (Anthias, 2014: 162), with others pointing to 'the feminisation of poverty' and the 'feminisation of migration' (True, 2012: 33, 55; Jacobs, 2000: 220; Aas, 2007: 42). Such developments, it is suggested, have consequences for mobility, opportunity, resistance and human rights, in addition to community and individual identities (Doezema, 2000: 46). Thus, for True (2012: 59), trafficking is regarded as a dark underside of migration, inseparable from processes of globalisation and trade liberalisation. Within this wider political and economic context, True directs attention to the significance of informal economic activity, including 'feminized economies such as the sex and domestic workers trade, and unpaid work in the home', which are presented as comprising 'major parts of the globalisation story' (True, 2012: 29). True therefore follows Tickner in the view that it is imperative to examine wider patterns of exploitation including unpaid or underpaid labour, to fully appreciate the continuum of violence of which trafficking and smuggling are a part. For Tickner (1992: 134), such work was crucial for the expansion of the capitalist world economy, with subsistence labour, volunteer work, household work, and reproduction remaining economic activities performed primarily by women, taking place on the periphery of the world economy and discounted or devalued by wider society, with implications for female participation, employment, opportunity and security today (Tickner 1992: 93). Feminist scholars have therefore recently highlighted the inadequacy of strategies which separate trafficking and smuggling from wider consideration of labour exploitation, examining connections between global economic institutions, notions of security and the political-economic causes of violence (Jacobs, Jacobson and Marchbank, 2000: 3).

True (2012), Jacobs, Jacobson and Marchbank (2000), and Tickner (1992, 2014), consequently examine the impact of globalising tendencies and neoliberal economic policy upon women, also exploring the consequences for men. Jacobs (2000: 218) describes the globalisation project as 'the centralised and market-based management of market rules by G-7 states, implemented by the IMF, the World Bank and the WTO and concentrated in the market power of transnational corporations'. True agrees, arguing that this international economic and political framework, which comprises the political economy of globalisation, encourages migration for employment without attending to minimum social and labour standards that would protect against exploitation and violence, with Jacobs further suggesting that societies are therefore subordinated to these global forces. Critics consequently emphasise the gender bias implicit within the dictates of macro-economic policy, which has resulted in job losses, welfare cuts, and reduced health and labour standards (associated with austerity and structural adjustment and deregulated investment conditions), a situation further compounded by the differential impact of development aid and export led strategies, which have cumulatively served to reduce the status of women, and exacerbate inequalities in income, thereby degrading the living conditions of low income populations even further (Broadhead, 2000: 36).

These authors point to the gendered consequences of global competition, which generates an expanded demand for cheaper female labour, both within formal manufacturing economies and in informal economies associated with domestic and intimate services, resulting in lower pay, job losses, reduced labour standards and employees' rights. Other literature highlights the association of such developments with the introduction of tighter visa requirements, immigration and asylum policies and the rise in clandestine migrants (Aas, 2007: 32).

Scholarship continues to suggest that trafficking flows are generally from underdeveloped regions and states to more affluent regions and states. Within the EU Strategy, the most common states of origin for victims from within the EU are listed as Romania, Bulgaria, Poland and Hungary, with most reported victims from non-EU countries coming from Nigeria, Vietnam, Ukraine, Russia and China (European Commission, 2012, COM (2012) 286 final: 3). The UK Strategy similarly recognises China, South East Asia and Eastern Europe as the countries of origin for most adult victims within the UK, with child victims originating from Vietnam, Nigeria, China and Eastern Europe (HM Government, 2011: 5). Yet, little is made of the socio-economic or geo-political circumstances of these nations, past or present, and no details are provided of the individual narratives of these victims, their traffickers or the wider circumstances leading to their identification.

In Chapter 3, Wallerstein's World Systems Analysis was introduced, a position that acknowledged the interconnection between globalisation, terrorism, and internal and external conflict. To reiterate, Wallerstein's historical contextualisation of the developments associated with modernisation and globalisation challenged the assertion expressed within modernisation theory and liberal economic thought that modernisation will inevitably lead to development, prosperity and equality. For Wallerstein, the current world economy must be examined with respect to the legacy of imperial colonialisation and, as such, is regarded as characterised by relations of exploitation, domination and subservience, resulting in uneven development and longstanding inequalities.

Significantly, while Wallerstein recognised unequal relations of production, unequal exchange and unequal power, also acknowledging the inevitability of conflict and violence 'as people try to preserve acquired privileges and hierarchical rank in a very unstable situation', identifying internal and external state conflict, genocide and terrorism as illustrations of systemic crisis within the current capitalist world system, serious consideration of gender relations is absent from his analysis. Feminist scholars, while crediting such approaches for politicising exchange relationships and making power structures visible, point to the significance of gender relations within this process. In particular, emphasis is placed upon the interrelationship between the historical foundation of modern science, the birth of the modern state, the capitalist world economy, and the separation of gender roles and the reliance upon the 'nonproductive' labour of women, which it has been argued, kick-started the process of global capital accumulation, and resulted in the delegitimisation of the feminine in public space (Tickner, 1992: 135). For True (2012) it is this gendered public–private division of labour, along with gender ideologies that allocate women as primarily responsible for unpaid work within the private sphere, which generated a disparity in bargaining power between men and women, inhibiting public participation and access to educational and employment opportunities. For both authors, women currently face an enormous disadvantage in terms of power and wealth with considerable implications for mobility (geographic and economic), opportunity and security. Women, we are reminded, do not share equal social and economic rights with men, and do not have the same access to productive resources. In particular, women earn less than men on average, even when performing similar tasks, remaining disproportionately represented within low-paid, less prestigious jobs, facing wage discrimination, harassment and intimidation, with childcare issues impacting upon job security, retention and opportunities for progression (Tickner, 1992: 86; True, 2012: 5).

This body of work consequently reframes the recognised association between imperialism, colonialism, the development of early capitalism and the state system with the consolidation of gendered and racial hierarchies permitting the exploitation and domination of the natural world, other nations and subordinated groups of (racial, gendered and cultural) Others. For Broadhead (2000: 39) economic liberalism and the deepening of free-market principles are unlikely to result in the eradication of economic deprivation, arguing that 'as states rush to lower environmental and labour standards in order to attract capital investment, human rights abuses are likely to increase'. Indeed, as already noted, a growing body of evidence points to the realisation that liberal strategies have a differential impact on men and women (Tickner 1992: 78). International approaches which fail to recognise the connection between financial crises, macroeconomic policies, trade liberalisation and violence against women are therefore viewed as inadequate. Scholars therefore emphasise the need to contextualise violence within the gendered structures of economic impoverishment and lack of opportunity which reinforce gender inequalities and make women vulnerable to violence, by curtailing the economic, political, and social options available to women (Tickner, 1992: 105; True, 2012: 5–8; Arnold and Bertone, 2002). This work also suggests that the reduction in protective mechanisms, associated with structural adjustment, austerity and neo-liberal economic policy make women easier targets for abuse and make women more vulnerable to the abuse of disempowered men who may be responding to material and identity-based losses as a consequence of global economic transformations (Jacobs, 2000: 219; True, 2012: 15).

It is evident then that while the human trafficking strategies discussed within this chapter claim to employ gender sensitivity and purport to address the root causes of trafficking, each approach fails to question the economic structures and power relations underpinning the current world system and relations between states (Broadhead, 2000: 37). For Broadhead (2000: 32–42) as for True (2012: 6–7) this refusal to address the underlying causes of poverty and the political-economic causes of violence and exploitation is a consequence of the liberal assumptions underpinning international society which inhibits radical thinking and serves to perpetuate the conditions of insecurity of which trafficking and migration for work are a part. For Broadhead, it is the international system, with its economic inequality, its lack of ecological concern and its militarised structures which remains the cause of insecurity and this in turn is related to the power relations embedded in the system. True (2012: 61–2) similarly challenges current state policies which treat trafficked women as criminals, or as victims in need of rescue and rehabilitation. Current approaches are therefore regarded as less resource intensive and politically challenging, ignoring the social and economic root causes of trafficking and failing to address the labour migration aspects of the problem, which would require a prioritisation of economic agency, the protection of human rights (including social and economic entitlements) to facilitate empowerment. As it stands, critical scholars argue that 'rarely do counter trafficking strategies expand employment choices or bolster an individual's ability to protect themselves against migration and employment-related violence' (True, 2012: 54–55), while restrictive immigration policies result in greater economic exploitation, physical abuse and violence against migrant women workers (True, 2012: 61–2). For True (2012: 75), one potential avenue would be to formalise informal sector employment, extending the same working conditions, rights, benefits, and protections to non-citizens as are available to citizens while simultaneously tackling the social norms that make it acceptable to exploit the vulnerable labour of other human beings (True, 2012: 75).

The dominant liberal law-and-order framework, generating a normative consensus prohibiting trafficking as a violation of human rights, promoting the strengthening of legislative and institutional frameworks, law enforcement and judicial cooperation, detailed previously within the chapter, is therefore seen to fall short of the feminist emancipatory project, which is interpreted as serving to reinforce the liberal vision and existing institutional, political and economic framework (Broadhead, 2000: 42). For Tickner (1992, 2014) as for others, without addressing the economic, cultural, and social structures of society, normative, legislative and institutional responses are likely to perpetuate existing relations of domination and subordination. The liberal framework, interwoven with the history of imperialism, colonialism, capitalism, the society of states and with gender and racial hierarchies, is therefore regarded as an ideology serving to legitimise and sustain the status quo. Radical scholars consequently view this framework as limiting, serving to divert attention away from the dual application of patriarchy and capitalism as potential lenses through which to appreciate the continuum and interconnected nature of contemporary conflict, violence and exploitation. As such the existing framework is thought to lead to further insecurity and injustice. The elimination of structural violence therefore requires a restructuring of the global economy, reprioritising the individual's basic material needs over the market-driven desire for profit (Tickner, 1992: 138).

For Tickner, not only is it important to address socio-economic and political structures, it is also imperative that attention is directed towards gender hierarchies that privilege men's characteristics, knowledge and experience and perpetuate global insecurities. Hierarchical binary oppositions, gendered metaphors, gendered stereotypes and linguistic constructs are viewed by Tickner, Jacobs, Jacobson and Marchbank and True as fundamental to developing misogynistic and racist attitudes, underpinning justificatory narratives for protection and exclusion, and remaining consistent with the exploitative tendencies of the international system in its relationship to the environment, women and non-Western people. Tickner (1992: 15) therefore reminds us that 'women are oppressed by the system of patriarchy that has existed under all modes of production – institutionalised through legal and economic, as well as social and cultural institutions'.

Notes

1 Replacing Council Framework Decision 2002/629/JHA.

2 Further EU instruments within a range of policy areas are also cited within the directive as having contributed to addressing trafficking in human beings, including: the Proposal for the Directive on the Rights of Victims (COM (2011) 275 final); action on violence against women; an EU Agenda for the Rights of the Child (COM (2011) 0060 final); the Action Plan on Unaccompanied Minors (COM(2010) 213 final); Directive 2009/52/EC on sanctions against employers who knowingly employ illegally staying third country workers; and the proposal for a Directive on seasonal employment of third-country nationals (COM (2010) 379 final). The EU Internal Security Strategy in Action: Five steps towards a more secure Europe, (COM (2010) 673 final) and the EU External Migration Policy, the Global Approach to Migration and Mobility, also examine trafficking in human beings, seeking to extend the legislative framework beyond the internal boundaries of the EU to encompass third countries of origin, with a view to closing legislative deficits within countries of origin, transit and destination. EU Directive 2011/36 of the European Parliament and Council of 5 April 2011 (OJ L 101/1) 'on preventing and combating trafficking in human beings and protecting its victims', which replaced the earlier Council Framework Decision 2002/629/JHA, advocate action in third countries of origin, including, again, the development of anti-trafficking legislation, following recommendations made within the 2009 Action Oriented Paper on strengthening the EU external dimension against trafficking in human beings (COM (2012) 286 final: 3–4).

3 Within the EU, this work is granted particular salience due to the recent reduction in convictions secured, from 1534 in 2008 to 1445 in 2009 and 1144 in 2010 (EU Strategy COM (2012) 286 final: 9–11).

4 Such as the United Nations Convention against Transnational Organised Crime and the Protocols thereto, the 1990 Council of Europe Convention on Laundering, Search, Seizure and Confiscation of the Proceeds from Crime, Council Framework Decision 2001/500/JHA of 26 June 2001 on money laundering, the identification, tracing, freezing, seizing and confiscation of instrumentalities and the proceeds of crime (2), and Council Framework Decision 2005/212/JHA of 24 February 2005

on Confiscation of Crime-Related Proceeds, Instrumentalities and Property; UK Proceeds of Crime Act 2002.

5 For example, the UK Policing and Crime Act 2009 amended the Sexual Offences Act 2003 to introduce an offence of paying for the sexual services of a prostitute subjected to force, deception, threats or any other form of coercion. This means that someone who pays for the sexual services of a trafficked woman (whether or not they know the woman has been trafficked) can be arrested and prosecuted (HM Government, 2011: 23). Also Article 18(4) EU Directive 2011/36 recommends that Member States shall consider taking measures to establish as a criminal offence the use of services which are the objects of exploitation to 'discourage demand'.

6 On residence permits issued to third-country nationals who are victims of trafficking or who have been the subject of an action to facilitate illegal immigration.

7 Providing for minimum standards on sanctions and measures against employers of illegally staying third-country nationals.

8 UN Convention on the Elimination of All Forms of Discrimination Against Women, New York, 18 December 1979, Treaty Series, vol. 1249, p. 13, United Nations, Treaty Series, vol. 1577, p. 3, ILO Forced Labour Convention, 1930 (No. 29), ILO Abolition of Forced Labour Convention, 1957 (No. 105), ILO Worst Forms of Child Labour Convention, 1999 (No. 182) and ILO Domestic Workers Convention, 2011 (No. 189).

9 '"Trafficking in persons" shall mean the recruitment, transportation, transfer, harbouring or receipt of persons, by means of the threat or use of force or other forms of coercion, of abduction, of fraud, of deception, of the abuse of power or of a position of vulnerability or of the giving or receiving of payments or benefits to achieve the consent of a person having control over another person, for the purpose of exploitation. Exploitation shall include, at a minimum, the exploitation of the prostitution of others or other forms of sexual exploitation, forced labour or services, slavery or practices similar to slavery, servitude or the removal of organs.'

10 '"Smuggling of migrants" shall mean the procurement, in order to obtain, directly or indirectly, a financial or other material benefit, of the illegal entry of a person into a State Party of which the person is not a national or a permanent resident.'

References

Aas, K. (2007). *Globalisation and Crime*. London: Sage.

Andreas, P. and Nadelmann, E. (2006). *Policing the Globe*. Oxford: Oxford University Press.

Anthias, F. (2014). 'The Intersections of Class, Gender, Sexuality and "Race": The Political Economy of Gendered Violence', *International Journal of Politics, Culture and Society*, 27: 153–171.

Arnold, C. and Bertone, A. (2002). 'Addressing the Sex Trade in Thailand: Some Lessons Learned from NGOs, Part 1', *Gender Issues*, 20(Winter)(1): 26–52.

Bernstein, E. (2012). 'Carceral Politics as Gender Justice? The "Traffic in Women" and Neoliberal Circuits of Crime, Sex, and Rights', *Theory and Society*. 41: 233–259.

Bigo, D. (2000). 'Liaison Officers in Europe: New Officers in the European Security Field', in Sheptycki, J.W.E. (ed.), *Issues in Transnational Policing*. London: Routledge.

Bowling, B. and Sheptycki, J.W.E. (2012). *Global Policing*. London: Sage.

Brennan, D. (2003). 'Selling Sex for Visas: Sex Tourism as a Stepping-stone to International Migration', in Ehrenreich, B. and Hochschild, A.R. (eds), *Global Woman: Nannies, Maids and Sex Workers in the New Economy*. London: Granta Books.

Broadhead, A. (2000). 'Re-packaging Notions of Security: A Sceptical Feminist Response to Recent Efforts', in Jacobs, S., Jacobson, R., and Marchbank, J. (eds), *States of Conflict: Gender, Violence and Resistance*. London: Zed Books.

Clarke, R. (1997). *Situational Crime Prevention: Successful Case Studies*. New York: Harrow and Heston.

Crawley, H. (2000). 'Engendering the State in Refugee Women's Claims for Asylum', in Jacobs, S., Jacobson, R., and Marchbank, J. (eds), *States of Conflict: Gender, Violence and Resistance*. London: Zed Books.

Deudney, D. and Ikenberry, J. (2009). 'The Myth of the Autocratic Revival: Why Liberal Democracy Will Prevail', *Foreign Affairs*, 88(1): 77–93.

Doezema, J. (2000). 'Loose Women or Lost Women? The Re-emergence of the Myth of White Slavery in Contemporary Discourses of Trafficking in Women', *Gender Issues*, 18(1): 23–50.

Enloe, C. (1990). *Bananas, Beaches and Bases: Making Feminist Sense of International Politics*. London: Pandora.

European Commission. (2012). Communication from the Commission to the European Parliament, the Council, the European Economic and Social Committee and the Committee of the Regions. The EU Strategy towards the Eradication of Trafficking in Human Beings 2012–2016 COM (2012) 286 final.

HM Government. (2011). *Human Trafficking: The Government's Strategy*. London: The Stationery Office.

Home Office. (2015). *The Modern Slavery Act 2015*. London: The Stationery Office.

Hughes, D. and Denisova, T. (2001). 'The Transnational Political Criminal Nexus of Trafficking in Women from Ukraine', *Trends in Organized Crime*, 6(3 and 4) Spring/Summer: 43–67.

Human Rights Watch. (2002). 'Hopes Betrayed: Trafficking of Women and Girls to Post-Conflict Bosnia and Herzegovina for Forced Prostitution'. Available online at: http://lastradainternational.org/doc-center/1905/hopes-betrayed-trafficking-of-women-and-girls-to-post-conflict-bosnia-and-herzegovina-for-forced-prostitution (accessed August 28, 2015).

Ikenberry, J. (2009). 'Liberal Internationalism 3.0: America and the Dilemmas of Liberal World Order', *Perspectives in Politics*, 71(1): 71–87.

Ikenberry, J. (2011). 'The Future of the Liberal World Order: Internationalism After America', *Foreign Affairs*, 90(3): 56–68.

Iñiguez de Heredia, M. (2008). 'People Trafficking: Conceptual Issues with the United Nations Trafficking Protocol 2000', *Human Rights Review*, 9: 299–316.

Jacobs, S. (2000). 'Globalisation, States and Women's Agency: Possibilities and Pitfalls', in Jacobs, S., Jacobson, R., and Marchbank, J. (eds), *States of Conflict: Gender, Violence and Resistance*. London: Zed Books.

Jacobs, S., Jacobson, R., and Marchbank, J. (2000). *States of Conflict: Gender, Violence and Resistance*. London: Zed Books.

Jahic, G. and Finckenauer, J. (2005). 'Representations and Misrepresentations of Human Trafficking', *Trends in Organized Crime*, 8(3): 24–40.

Johnston, L. (2000). 'Transnational Private Policing: The Impact of Global Commercial Security', in Sheptycki, J.W.E. (ed.), *Issues in Transnational Policing*. London: Routledge.

Kelly, L. (2000). 'Wars Against Women: Sexual Violence, Sexual Politics and the Militarised State', in Jacobs, S., Jacobson, R., and Marchbank, J. (eds), *States of Conflict: Gender, Violence and Resistance*. London: Zed Books.

Loader, I. and Walker, N. (2007). 'Locating the Public Interest in Transnational Policing', in Goldsmith, A. and Sheptycki, J.W.E. (eds), *Crafting Transnational Policing: Police Capacity-Building and Global Policing Reform*. Oxford: Hart Publishing.

Marshall, E. (2001). 'Globalization, Migration, and Trafficking: Some Thoughts from the South-East Asian Region.' Occasional Paper No. 1. UN Inter-Agency Project on Trafficking in Women and Children in the Mekong Sub-region.

Michalowski, R. (2010). 'In Search of "State and Crime" in State Crime Studies', in Chambliss, W., Michalowski, R., and Kramer, R. (eds), *State Crime in the Global Age*. Cullompton: Willan Publishing.

Official Journal of the European Union. (2011). Directive 2011/36/EU of the European Parliament and of the Council of 5 April 2011 [on preventing and combating trafficking in human beings and protecting its victims, and replacing Council Framework Decision 2002/629/JHA]. L 101/1.

Papanicolaou, G. (2008). 'The Sex Industry, Human Trafficking and the Global Prohibition Regime: A Cautionary Tale from Greece', *Trends in Organized Crime*, 11: 379–409.

Shannon, S. (1999). 'Prostitution and the Mafia: The involvement of organised crime in the global sex trade', in William, P. (ed.), *Illegal Immigration and Commercial Sex*. 119–144. Portland, OR: Frank Cass Publishers.

Sheptycki, J.W.E. (1995). 'Transnational Policing and the Makings of a Postmodern State', *British Journal of Criminology*, 35(4): 613–635.

Snajdr, E. (2013). 'Beneath the Master Narrative: Human Trafficking, Myths of Sexual Slavery and Ethnographic Realities', *Dialectical Anthropology*, 37: 229–256.

Tickner, J.A. (1992). *Gender in International Relations*. New York: Columbia University Press.

Tickner, J.A. (2014). *A Feminist Voyage Through International Relations*. Oxford: Oxford University Press.

True, J. (2012). *The Political Economy of Violence Against Women*. Oxford: Oxford University Press.

United Nations General Assembly. (2006). *Report of the Secretary General 'Uniting against terrorism: recommendations for a global counter-terrorism strategy'*, April 27. A/60/825.

UNODC. (2004). *United Nations Convention against Transnational Organized Crime and the Protocols Thereto*. New York: United Nations.

UNODC. (2012). *A Comprehensive Strategy to Combat Trafficking in Persons and Smuggling of Migrants*. United Nations Office on Drugs and Crime. New York: United Nations.

Vold, G., Bernard, T., and Snipes, J. (1998). *Theoretical Criminology*. Oxford: Oxford University Press.

Wallerstein, I. (2005). *World-Systems Analysis: An Introduction*. London: Duke University Press.

9 Conclusion

Global injustice and crime control

Policing has been defined as a 'crucial building block' and 'defining feature' of global governance (Sheptycki, 2000: 201; Bowling and Sheptycki, 2012: 132), the study of which, while frequently neglected, has been regarded as potentially offering 'a window onto the emerging governmental practices of the transnational state system' (Sheptycki, 2000: 201). As noted by an increasing body of scholars working both within and across the disciplines of criminology and international relations, and as observed in Chapter 4, we are currently witnessing the recent proliferation and expansion of international and regional instruments, organisations, agencies and networks dedicated to combating crime and terrorism. Indeed, surveillance and policing capacity continues to be shaped by advances in technology, communication and transportation systems, developments reflected within the apparent growth in remit, capacity and ambition of the various actors involved within a newly emerging 'pluralised' and interconnected infrastructure (Brown, 2008; Bowling and Sheptycki, 2012; Sheptycki, 2000; Aas, 2007; Andreas and Nadelmann, 2006). Crime control within such a globalised environment is evidently rather complex and even bewildering, evading simple explanation and generalisation. While for some, such trends and developments are interpreted as fundamentally new and different, marking the emergence of a new period of societal organisation and global politics, others observe continuities with the past, rejecting assertions that the recent fusion between criminal justice and security concerns, politicisation and militarisation (blurring the boundaries between law enforcement, security, border control and military action), and the pluralisation of actors, are anything new or unique (Nadelmann, 1993; Andreas and Nadelmann, 2006; Aas, 2007; Bowling and Sheptycki, 2012).

This text has been concerned to introduce students to such ongoing debates within globalisation scholarship, which, it is argued, have relevance for those concerned with the broad topics of 'transnational crime', 'transnational organised crime', 'international crime' and 'terrorism'. *Global Injustice and Crime Control* has sought to identify divergent positions, in relation to the utility of the concept of 'globalisation' as a heuristic device through which to interpret and understand the present and concerning assumptions regarding the consequences of globalising trends, for crime and terrorism, law enforcement and governance arrangements. In doing so, this work has sought to flesh out the implications of contemporary global transformations for the salience of key theoretical insights and perspectives from within international relations, criminological and sociological scholarship. In this endeavour, this text has presented a number of perspectives for deliberation. However, returning to Bauman's quote in the Preamble to Chapter 1, the objective from the outset has been to provoke dialogue and reflection. The conclusion to be drawn will ultimately therefore be the reader's own and for that, I am unapologetic.

For over ten years, I have taught within the area of 'Transnational Crime', 'Global Justice and Crime Control' and 'Policing', focusing both domestically within the UK and within a global context. This text was originally motivated by a perceived gap in undergraduate and postgraduate student awareness of key sociological debates about the conceptualisation of contemporary society, awareness regarding key historical events and transformations, and an awareness regarding the structure (and history) of the international society of states. There was, it seemed, a general lack of awareness regarding the relationship between criminology and sociology and the relevance (and value) of interdisciplinary analysis for the study of crime and crime control.

In addressing this need, Chapter 1 provided evidence to suggest that globalisation discourse has currently gained currency within the national, regional and international security strategies of the United Kingdom, the European Union and within the United Nations and its affiliated agencies. Through a comparison of security strategies, it is argued that there has been a convergence in narratives depicting globalisation processes as facilitators of social progress, generating opportunities, with the potential to achieve democratisation, peace and prosperity worldwide. This narrative, emphasising the benefits of globalisation, is, however, also simultaneously accompanied by a recognition of associated threats and of an intensification of risks, which are presented as having the potential to undermine development and security. Taken together, this position has been described as 'the standard view of globalisation' (Andreas and Nadelmann, 2006), or as the 'functionalist argument' (Deflem, 2002: 224). For Andreas and Nadelmann (2006: 224), this conventional wisdom regarding the consequences of globalising processes has been used by academics, policy-makers and practitioners, to account for the recent expansion and intensification of the internationalisation of crime control, which has been explained as a natural, functional response to a growing global crime challenge associated with aspects of globalisation. Associated with this view is the notion that global policing and international policing cooperation have spontaneously responded to alterations within the external security environment and the internationalisation of crime and terrorism (Bowling and Sheptycki, 2012: 132; Deflem, 2002: 224; Naim, 2002). Thus, Chapter 1 further revealed how the conceptualisation of security has recently expanded from a concern with interstate conflict to a broad range of security threats, resulting in the emergence of a new security landscape and fundamental shifts within the security agendas of individual states, regions and globally. Motivated by an explicit objective to secure states as the basic unit of the international system, this reconceptualisation has resulted in the inclusion of non-state actors, recognition regarding the perceived interconnection between varieties of threats, and has served to blur the boundaries between conventional categorisations, destabilising traditional distinctions leading to a convergence of militaristic, law enforcement and security contexts. Chapter 1 consequently engaged with the wider debate regarding the role and capacity of the state to fulfil their fundamental responsibilities within this altered security environment.

Linked to this 'standard view of globalisation' is a further argument that claims that, 'as the processes of transnationalisation unfold, the very bases for the emergence and sustenance of the nation-state-system alter', a situation resulting in disempowerment and an erosion of the nation-state from 'above' and 'below', as states become subordinated to the power of transnational capital, supranational bodies and sub-state actors (Sheptycki, 2000: 3–6). Described by Sheptycki as the 'radical globalisation thesis', this position, which addresses issues of governance, conceives states 'as the neutered instruments of an outmoded type of social power' (Sheptycki, 2000: 7), a position also commonly described as 'the hollowing out of the state thesis'. Examined historically, this position recognises that the existing nation-state system has been socially constructed and is temporally bounded, a recognition that acknowledges that the basis of the political organisation of humanity is subject to change over time.

This theme was again picked up in Chapter 2, which retained the emphasis upon the role of the state and the key actors involved within regulatory systems also drawing upon the theme of continuity and change. In particular, Chapter 2 examined early control efforts directed towards the eradication of slavery and piracy, emphasising the significance of perspective upon the interpretation of such developments and, drawing upon the work of Nadelmann (1993), Andreas and Nadelmann (2006), Pogge (2008), Hardt and Negri (2001, 2011), and Felson and Kalaitzidis (2005), to challenge the dominant interpretation regarding the emergence of anti-slavery and anti-piracy regimes, namely, as an inevitable consequence of modernity, and as markers of social progress and humanitarianism. This valuable theoretical work sensitises readers to the significance of geo-politics for crime control efforts, both within the past and today, problematising overly deterministic accounts and raising questions regarding the adequacy of state-centric accounts, which, it is argued, fail to account for the emergence of new players within the arena of international crime control. Chapter 2 consequently engages with scholarship which transcends legalistic and functionalist accounts of crime and crime control, reconceptualising the use of law, and specifically, anti-slavery and anti-piracy regimes (along with the criminal behaviours themselves), as a tool of statecraft, used to weaken competitors and to strengthen and maintain national state-building efforts. Employing a historical lens, Chapter 2 therefore engages with critical theorists who examine criminal law enforcement, international policing strategies and international criminal justice as tools of global governance (Findlay, 2008: 217), as methods of social control (Sheptycki, 2000), and as instruments of geo-political strategy and state-crafting (Goldsmith and Sheptycki, 2007: 1). Thus, returning to the political origins of international policing strategies and law enforcement activities, Andreas and Nadelmann (2006: 227), Deflem (2002: 215) and Findlay (2008: 218) remind readers that both international criminal justice and international criminal law have frequently been utilised by states to suppress political opposition to established regimes and challenges to state integrity, with such activity remaining 'a relatively minor option on the menu of control responses in Great Britain until the period of 1960s' (Sheptycki, 2000). Findlay (2008: 217) further suggests that such practices have become 'a central model of global regulation' and a 'key element of post military global governance within the current phase of globalisation', an argument extended to study of gender dynamics within Chapter 8 relating to trafficking in human beings (Papanicolaou, 2008; Snajdr, 2013; Hughes and Denisova, 2001). These contributions, along with that of Goldsmith and Sheptycki (2010), therefore emphasise the normative dimension of such diverse instruments and activities, directed towards order maintenance. For Findlay, the new globalisation is committed to endorsing the dominant political alliance against cultural challenge and violent resistance, a position which rejects normative and value pluralism and which works in the interests of a global citizen community criminalising resistant communities and contrary cultures (Findlay, 2008: 219). Chapter 2 consequently highlights the changing priorities and agendas of states, the altered means to achieve their objectives, and the salience of state complicity and corruption in the furtherance of criminal acts and their prohibition. The chapter also points to the hypocrisy of great powers in asking states to prohibit practices that they themselves once engaged in and benefited from (Andreas and Nadelmann, 2006: 25, 227). It further serves to emphasise the significance of wider social structures, social inequalities and the legacy of slavery, colonialism, imperialism, industrialisation, interstate conflict and international relations for the contemporary world political order, issues omitted within international regional security policy and by mainstream criminological theory.

Retaining the notion that criminal law enforcement has been historically applied in the service of maintaining social order, Chapter 3 is concerned with charting the liberal institutional framework of the contemporary world order. Specifically, the chapter details the emergence and eventual embedding of liberal ideas within classical thought, the academic disciplines of international relations, sociology and criminology, and within the institutional and ideological framework of the contemporary structure of the society of states. The objective of Chapter 3 was therefore to contextualise the dominant normative framework of the international society of states, and to theoretically frame Andreas and Nadelmann's 'standard view of globalisation'. In exposing the theoretical roots and assumptions of the existing order, and by examining processes of modernisation, Chapter 3 sensitises readers to the legacy of imperialism and colonialism and the interrelationship between the development of the capitalist world economy, the birth of the modern state, Western structures of knowledge, hierarchies of race and gender and global inequalities. Chapter 3 thereby sheds light upon the normative and political underpinnings of contemporary security and crime control strategy, introducing a range of perspectives through which to assess the adequacy of current approaches to counter international crime, transnational crime and terrorism.

Chapter 4 provided an overview of key international and regional organisations and agencies tasked with combating crime and terrorism, providing information regarding their respective roles, mandates and structures. Engaging with the earlier theme, regarding the role of states and non-state actors within the current regularity system, and supporting the observations of Brown (2008), Bowling and Sheptycki (2012), and Deflem (2002), it was revealed that while the existing framework continues to fall short of a supranational, international or global police force, efforts towards international policing, judicial, security and border cooperation have recently expanded, with the chapter detailing a bewildering array of organisations, agencies and bodies. Agencies derived from military, intelligence and security services, national police services, border and immigration, customs and financial services, are evidently currently cooperating with both private sector and civil society providers reflecting overlapping remits and a convergence in agendas. This homogenisation and cross-fertilisation of issues remains consistent with the expanded conceptualisation of security detailed in Chapter 1 and must be understood as embedded within the changing geopolitical transformations and liberal institutional framework detailed in Chapter 3. Chapter 4 consequently lends support for commentators who have articulated the need to transcend state-centric approaches.

This work therefore recognises that, while the state is no longer centre stage (indeed, if ever it was), states still remain important within the evolving cooperative globalised environment. This environment entails increasing diversity in provision, incorporating public, private and civil society actors within an increasingly multilateralised, pluralised or polycentric governance framework, within an increasingly global networked society, involving a wide range of transnational practices, both formal and informal and involving both hard and soft power (Johnston and Stenning, 2010: Brown, 2008; Bowling and Sheptycki, 2012; Sheptycki, 2000; Aas, 2007; Andreas and Nadelmann, 2006; Goldsmith and Sheptycki, 2010). Within this internationalised and increasingly privatised context, the institutions detailed in Chapter 4 direct attention to scholarship which has raised concerns regarding issues of accountability, transparency and legitimacy. Bowling and Sheptycki (2012: 133) therefore remind us that transnational policing is no longer anchored by national sovereignty, with other authors questioning that police institutions ever were, conceiving them instead as relatively independent, only appealing to national and international bodies retrospectively to sanction action that had already taken place (Deflem, 2002: 228). The dispersal and pluralisation of governance, whether occurring recently, or alternatively having roots within past practice, is for Bowling and Sheptycki (2012: 132) an unsettling development, which has failed to attract the world's media or public scrutiny. Commentators have consequently observed that within the current polycentric power system, a universally recognised source of authority is absent, generating a widening democratic deficit as democratic accountability mechanisms have failed to keep up with the pace of change and in the absence of a global social contract legitimising the authority of contemporary structures. For Johnston and Stenning (2010), trends toward the diversity in police provision, the marketisation of policing and security, globalisation processes, and the apparent emergence of a polycentric governance complex, have cumulatively served to undermine traditional distinctions between 'public and private', 'internal and external security', 'military and police' resulting in legal plurality and jurisdictional contestation raising considerable challenges for accountability. Such concerns are ongoing, and while the mechanisms of accountability, oversight and transparency continue to evolve within the supranational and intergovernmental frameworks (as detailed in Chapter 4), reservations remain, an issue which becomes particularly salient in the light of the normative, political and social control functions of law enforcement detailed by Goldsmith and Sheptycki (2010), Findlay (2008), Andreas and Nadelmann (2006), Deflem (2002), and Sheptycki (2000). While it is evident that the current institutional framework continues to expand and evolve, Chapter 4 also cautions against exaggerating the degree of convergence, reflecting upon scholarship that acknowledges limits upon such cooperative endeavours, including the continuing salience of jurisdictional conflict, inter-agency competition, rivalry, limited resources, issues of trust, national self-interest, national variation, and a range of pragmatic barriers (Lemieux, 2010; Sheptycki, 1995; Anderson, 1989; Brown 2008; Andreas and Nadelmann, 2006).

As a precursor for Chapters 6, 7 and 8, Chapter 5 engages with critical scholarship from within criminology, which has explicitly addressed the normative and political basis of criminalisation and law enforcement. This significant contribution, with its roots within symbolic interactionism, focuses upon the importance of the meaning people give to themselves and to others, with consequences for the processes of criminalisation, societal responses to behaviour and the impact of mechanisms of societal control. Rejecting the legalistic approach, which views crime and law enforcement efforts narrowly, in terms of the enforcement of legal norms, the scholarly work detailed in Chapter 5 reminds us that crimes, crime control regimes and even the current structure of international politics are socially constructed. The chapter consequently provides an introduction to constructivist theory within international relations and criminology, an approach which places a premium on 'ideas', 'discourse' 'meaning' and 'interpretation'. This contribution, which transcends what Andreas and Nadelmann describe as 'the conventional wisdom' regarding the internationalisation of crime control, permits the inclusion and contextualisation of previously excluded phenomena, provoking attention to the role of knowledge systems and normative frameworks in constructing and maintaining inequalities and relations of production.

Chapters 6, 7 and 8 examine contemporary international, regional and national strategies for countering international crime, terrorism and transnational crime, addressing specifically efforts to prevent genocide, Al Qaeda-related terrorism and human trafficking. Each example reflects the existence of the 'standard view' narrative implicating aspects of globalisation in enhancing opportunities to engage in such action, underpinned by modernisation beliefs. In examining these topics and through an analysis of strategy, it is argued that the forging of normative consensus, political, legislative and institutional reform, alongside enhanced cooperation and harmonisation remain the preferred method of closing the gap between criminal opportunities and criminal justice responses within the current period of social transformation. Drawing upon situational crime prevention methods and uncoupled from its normative and political roots, critical scholarship suggests that this liberal institutional framework is unlikely to achieve its stated objectives. Devoid of historical contextualisation, and insensitive to the role of geo-politics, social crime prevention efforts are further challenged for being narrowly conceived and thereby unable to grapple with the legacy of injustice, inequality and the continuing relevance of power politics which continues to undermine contemporary collective security responses and cooperative endeavours. Within each example, critical scholars direct attention to the need to employ a more complete analysis and strategic framework, remaining sensitive to the structural issues and power relations within the current international society of states and the international political economic system. Aas (2007: 180–184) for example, suggests that the contemporary administrative focus functions to block insight and prevents alternative framing and solutions to the problems of crime and punishment, along with the wider spectrum of acts and harms which transcend state defined concepts of crime, losing sight of enormous global injustices and inequalities. Andreas and Nadelmann (2006: 251) further lament that criminalisation and international crime control have too often substituted for and distracted attention away from the need for more fundamental political, social and economic reforms.

Reflecting upon such limitations, Chapters 6, 7 and 8 also engage with the themes of resistance, challenge and change, raising questions regarding the future direction of 'global policing', 'international criminal law enforcement', 'policing and judicial cooperation' within the emerging global social order. In making any projection regarding the future, it is useful to return to the notion of security, the interpretation of which has a profound bearing upon the proposed solution and direction of change. Williams (2013: 6–7), for example, distinguishes between two prevalent philosophies of security. The first views security as a commodity, understanding security as virtually synonymous with the accumulation of power. Thus, power is conceived within this position, as the route to security: the more power actors can accumulate, the more secure they will be. The second philosophy detailed by Williams conceives security as a relationship. This position therefore rejects the notion that security is the ability to exercise power over others and rather presents security as emerging from sharing commitments and from cooperation.

These diverging positions are evident within the realist and liberal perspectives within Andreas and Nadelmann's analytically eclectic approach, and are also evident within the World Systems and modernisation approaches detailed within Chapter 3. Thus, both the realist and World Systems positions acknowledge the persistence of tension and conflict, conceiving interstate relations as continuing to be characterised by the ongoing struggle for power, as states seek to take advantage of one another. While both realists and liberals identify the root of the problem within the anarchic structure of international relations, where there remains an absence of central authority capable of controlling state behaviour, for liberal institutionalists and modernisation theorists, cooperation between states is essential. Viewed as a cooperative endeavour, liberals are consequently far more optimistic regarding the prospects for security, promoting the construction of international institutions to facilitate dialogue, build trust and achieve cooperation and stability (and normative consensus).

Reflecting Mittelman's observations (detailed in Chapter 3) regarding the shift (post 9/11) from 'consent-based' globalisation to 'coercion based' globalisation, and taking into account Wallerstein's assertion that the current capitalist world economic system has reached 'systemic crisis', which for Ikenberry amounts to a 'liberal crisis', it is perhaps plausible to suggest that there has been a fusing of Williams's security philosophies, entailing the realist exercise of power under the guise of liberal collective security and cooperation. As detailed within Chapters 6, 7 and 8 however, the continuing salience of state self-interest, power-politics and the failure to tackle wider structural issues underpinning inequalities, injustices and exploitation have undermined crime control efforts and raised questions regarding the legitimacy of the existing liberal institutionalist framework. Addressing the future, and seeking to theorise a constructive role for policing within the emerging order, Sheptycki (2010) argues that those involved in policing, transnational and otherwise, must be positively involved in the project of global governance, further suggesting, 'either they are part of the solution or they are part of the problem, there is no middle way' (Sheptycki, 2010: 299). Explicitly recognising the normative and political dimension of policing, Goldsmith and Sheptycki (2010: 7) acknowledge that 'historically speaking, the global police mission was undertaken because it was good for the policeman', a view recognised within Chapter 2 in relation to efforts to eradicate slavery and piracy. This work, therefore, joins an increasing body of scholarship which recognises the culturally elitist, discriminatory and exclusionary logic of the modernisation project attached to free market economics and liberal democratic governance structures, a position which exacerbates cultural divisions and criminalises resistant or opposed communities and results in discriminatory law enforcement and criminal justice delivery (Findlay, 2008: 222). Andreas and Nadelmann (2006: 244), Wallerstein (2005) and Ikenberry (2009, 2011) each question how long US hegemony will last, deliberating alternative solutions within the contemporary period of crisis. For Findlay (2008: 239), a commitment is required to a vision of world order which is tolerant of cultural diversity, directing attention to the 'resilience of cultural difference in the face of impressive and intrusive political domination internationally and challenges to traditional identity' (Findlay 2008: 221). Political and religious fundamentalist challenges to the existing international liberal institutional framework, such as those detailed in Chapter 7 regarding terrorism, are consequently located by Findlay as resulting from the incompatibility of the Western democratic aspirations and those of single party states or nations and jurisdictions where religion and the state are one. International criminal justice within this position is therefore conceived as part of a global strategy of distant, indirect rule and intrusive economic manipulation, a project initiated with the signing of the Treaty of Westphalia, which, it is argued, marked the defeat of religion as the legitimate basis for social organisation (Tickner, 2014), and continues to the present day.

While the strategies detailed within Chapters 6, 7 and 8 clearly present the law enforcement development assistance offered to less affluent parts of the world, as a crucial driver for improving both local and upstream disruption against international crime networks (Brown, 2008), such measures (which remain a key aspect of genocide prevention, counter-terrorism and human trafficking prevention), are viewed by Goldsmith and Sheptycki (2010: 1) as instruments of geo-political strategy, involving international organisations, donor states and agencies building and strengthening states, particularly within weak, fragile, failing or failed states within the Western neo-liberal democratic image. For Findlay (2008: 224, 226), '[w]hether states and cultures outside these governance traditions like it or not, global governance will require their acquiescence or will treat their resistance as a threat … worthy of harsh and immediate security intervention'. For Findlay then, international criminal justice and the law are regarded as 'uncertain weapon[s] for resolving the fundamental clashes endangering world order'. Despite the currency of the dominant rhetoric which promotes the liberal solution as a means of generating opportunity, development, prosperity and peace, Sheptycki argues that current modes of transnational policing are not primarily intended as a means for ensuring a just and equitable world order. Sheptycki consequently identifies a paradox within the current liberal democratic policing framework, one which curtails freedom through its activities as a means to promote conditions in which freedom can flourish (Sheptycki, 2010: 302–3). Findlay (2008: 224–5) goes further, implicating the monocultural imperative of the current world order in the facilitation of crimes against humanity, ethnic cleansing, genocide, war crimes and terrorism. Thus for Findlay international criminal justice provides the contemporary global governance framework with 'a mantle of legitimacy' in resolving conflicts. However, such conflicts are further explained as arising 'as a direct result of globalising the preferred global economic and cultural model' (Findlay 2008: 225), a view similarly espoused within the work of Pogge (2008).

This position, reminiscent of Michalowski's (2010) typology of state crime, presented in Chapter 5, consequently asks scholars to redirect attention to the 'layered dynamics' that 'lay beneath more obvious varieties of crime', examining the structural violence associated with neo-liberal globalisation and transcending legalistic approaches. This alternative perspective permits attention to a wider range of societal harms alongside state-facilitated forms of poverty and inequality, a position reflected within the World Systems approach of Wallerstein, alongside feminist international political economy and international relations scholars, like True (2012) and Tickner (1992, 2014). This work therefore directs attention to the need to attend to the current crisis of legitimacy and authority within the current liberal international order, attending to historically inherited vulnerabilities and grievances, alongside social and economic injustices. For Findlay (2008: 221), this means confronting globalisation and its universal ideals for governance and economic advancement. The solution, for Goldsmith and Sheptycki (2010: 3) entails 'the commission of police practice to be carried out according to clearly defined and publicised standards, with, and on behalf of, a broadly inclusive community which understands, endorses and cooperates in policing', namely the creation of 'a global social contract that could hold global policing to account or provide it with legitimating authority' (Bowling and Sheptycki, 2012: 131). The existing framework, characterised by social exclusion, impoverishment, the language of elimination of enemies, commodification of security and a 'reckless disregard for disempowered communities', is consequently viewed by these authors as undermining a just and equitable social order, and as such, remains a spoiler for global peace and prosperity, generating resentment and resistance with implications for the fulfilment of human rights and security. In order to secure a lasting peace, Sheptycki (2010: 317), Aas (2007: 185) and Tickner (1992) advocate the replacement of the current focus upon national security, securitisation and militarisation (associated with global insecurity) with the notion of human security.

The 'high policing' function associated with political policing and the maintenance of social order, directed towards the preservation of individual nation-states and their interests, and more recently towards the preservation of the existing international order of society of states and its attendant liberal framework, is therefore rendered problematic. For critical scholarship, this ideological and normative function is regarded as underpinning contemporary counter-piracy, genocide, corruption, terrorism and human trafficking strategy. Commentators therefore argue that international, regional and national efforts must be redirected to the preservation of universal human security, in order to secure both the integrity and legitimacy of the existing international political system, and to become truly accountable to the international community, in whose name it serves. However, as detailed within the preceding pages of this book, the extent to which this is viewed as possible, desirable and/or even imaginable, remains influenced in large part by the lens through which we look. In the meantime, universal justice remains aspirational.

Bibliography

Aas, K.F. (2007). *Globalisation and Crime*. London: Sage.

Anderson, M. (1989). *Policing the World*. Oxford: Clarendon Press.

Andreas, P. and Nadelmann, E. (2006). *Policing the Globe: Criminalization and Crime Control in International Relations*. Oxford: Oxford University Press.

Bowling, B. and Sheptycki, J.W.E. (2012). *Global Policing*. London: Sage.

Brown, S. (ed.). (2008). *Combating International Crime*. Abingdon: Routledge.

Deflem, M. (2002). *Policing World Society: Historical Foundations of International Police Cooperation*. Oxford: Oxford University Press.

Felson, D. and Kalaitzidis, A. (2005). 'A Historical Overview of Transnational Crime', in Reichel, P. (ed.), *Handbook of Transnational Crime and Justice*. London: Sage. Pp. 3–19.

Findlay, M. (1999). *The Globalisation of Crime: Understanding Transitional Relationships in Context*. Cambridge: Cambridge University Press.

Findlay, M. (2008). *Governing through Globalised Crime*. Cullompton: Willan Publishing.

Goldsmith, A. and Sheptycki, J.W.E. (2007). *Crafting Transnational Policing: Police Capacity-Building and Global Policing Reform*. Oxford: Hart Publishing.

Hardt, M. and Negri, A. (2001). *Empire*. London: Harvard University Press.

Hardt, M. and Negri, A. (2011). *Commonwealth*. London: Harvard University Press.

Hughes, D. and Denisova, T. (2001). 'The Transnational Political Criminal Nexus of Trafficking in Women from Ukraine', *Trends in Organized Crime*, 6(3 and 4) Spring/Summer: 43–67.

Ikenberry, J. (2009). 'Liberal Internationalism 3.0: America and the Dilemmas of Liberal World Order', *Perspectives in Politics*, 71(1): 71–87.

Ikenberry, J. (2011). 'The Future of the Liberal World Order: Internationalism After America', *Foreign Affairs*, 90(3): 56–68.

Johnston, L. and Stenning, P. (2010). 'Challenges of Governance and Accountability for Transnational Private Policing', in Lemieux, F. (ed.), *International Police Cooperation*. Abingdon: Routledge.

Lemieux, F. (ed.). (2010). *International Police Cooperation*. Abingdon: Routledge.

Michalowski, R. (2010). 'In Search of "State and Crime" in State Crime Studies', in Chambliss, W., Michalowski, R., and Kramer, R. (eds), *State Crime in the Global Age*. Cullompton: Willan Publishing.

Nadelmann, E. (1993). *Cops Across Borders: The Internationalization of U.S. Criminal Law Enforcement*. University Park, PA: Pennsylvania State University Press.

Naim, M. (2002). *Five Wars of Globalization*. The Grotius Lecture Series. Lecture presented at the American Society of International Law's ('ASIL') 96th Annual Meeting on March 13–16. American University Washington College of Law, the ASIL, and the International Legal Studies Program.

Papanicolaou, G. (2008). 'The Sex Industry, Human Trafficking and the Global Prohibition Regime: A Cautionary Tale from Greece', *Trends in Organized Crime*, 11: 379–409.

Pogge, T. (2008). *World Poverty and Human Rights*, second edition. Cambridge: Polity Press.

Sheptycki, J.W.E. (1995). 'Transnational Policing and the Makings of a Postmodern State', *British Journal of Criminology*, 35(4): 613–635.

Sheptycki, J.W.E. (2010). 'The Constabulary Ethic Reconsidered', in Lemieux, F. (ed.), *International Police Cooperation*. Abingdon: Routledge.

Sheptycki, J.W.E. (ed.). (2000). *Issues in Transnational Policing*. London: Routledge.

Snajdr, E. (2013). 'Beneath the Master Narrative: Human Trafficking, Myths of Sexual Slavery and Ethnographic Realities', *Dialectical Anthropology*, 37: 229–256.

Tickner, J.A. (1992). *Gender in International Relations.* New York: Columbia University Press.

Tickner, J.A. (2014). *A Feminist Voyage Through International Relations.* Oxford: Oxford University Press.

True, J. (2012). *The Political Economy of Violence Against Women*. Oxford: Oxford University Press.

Wallerstein, I. (2005). *World-Systems Analysis: An Introduction*. London: Duke University Press.

Williams, P. (ed.). (2013). *Security Studies: An Introduction*. London: Routledge.

Index